£4·99

31

Welfare and Culture in Europe

of related interest

Lone Mothers in European Welfare Regimes
Shifting Policy Logics
Edited by Jane Lewis
ISBN 1 85302 448 1 hb
ISBN 1 85302 461 9 pb

Child Welfare Services Developments in Law, Policy, Practice and Research
Edited by Malcolm Hill and Jane Aldgate
ISBN 1 85302 316 7

Literacy, Socialization and Employment
Catherine Stercq
ISBN 1 85302 209 8

Disability Politics and Community Care
Mark Priestley
ISBN 1 85302 652 2

Social Workers, the Community and Social Interaction
John Offer
ISBN 1 85302 731 6

Welfare and Culture in Europe

Towards a New Paradigm in Social Policy

*Edited by Prue Chamberlayne, Andrew Cooper,
Richard Freeman and Michael Rustin*

Jessica Kingsley Publishers
London and Philadelphia

First published in the United Kingdom in 1999 by

Jessica Kingsley Publishers Ltd,
116 Pentonville Road,
London N1 9JB,
England

and

325 Chestnut Street,
Philadelphia
PA 19106, USA.

www.jkp.com

© Copyright 1999 Jessica Kingsley Publishers

Library of Congress Cataloging in Publication Data
A CIP catalog record for this book is available from the Library of Congress

British Library Cataloguing in Publication Data
Welfare and culture in Europe
1. Public welfare – Europe
2. Europe – Social policy
I. Chamberlayne, Prue II. Cooper, Andrew
III. Freeman, Richard IV. Rustin, Michael
361.9'4

ISBN 1 85302 700 6

Printed and Bound in Great Britain by
Athenaeum Press, Gateshead, Tyne and Wear

Contents

Part III: Theorizing welfare as culture

Preface

This book arose from a project whose origins are worth reflecting upon because they say something both about the territory which was subsequently traversed, and about the ideological and methodological departures involved. A group of British researchers came into contact because they recognized they had each been undertaking research into familiar aspects of European welfare policy and practice: Prue Chamberlayne was completing work on caring in England and Germany and was working with Michael Rustin on a comparative project on social exclusion, and on a book on contemporary Europe. Andrew Cooper was finishing research on child protection work in England and France; Richard Freeman had edited a book on social policy in Germany and was writing about health care in Europe. For each of them, 'culture' had re-emerged or been revealed as a significant dimension of analysis and, in conversation, they had begun to wonder why.

Part of the answer seemed to lie in an openness to interdisciplinary thinking and to methodologies not usually associated with cross-national policy research. In particular, a comparative focus on the biographical narratives of welfare recipients (King and Chamberlayne 1996) and on the guiding assumptions of practice behaviour in child protection workers (Cooper *et al.* 1995) had required contextual interpretation which seemed hard to describe as anything other than 'cultural'. Notwithstanding evidence of repetitive tensions and conflicts, the lived experience of welfare appeared to be embedded in a complex network of re-lationships and shared assumptions whose character was as much symbolic as material. Satisfactory accounts of relatively stable but contrasting patterns of micro-social behaviour and relationships entailed reference to a multiplicity of interacting macro variables – including the nature of citizenship within different state formations, different conceptualizations of the public/private dichotomy, different socio-legal assumptions and practices bearing on the constitution and reproduction of the family and different patterns of opportunity and risk in informal welfare provision.

Funding for a series of seminars meant that this conversation could be pursued in a more elaborate, more productive way. Its purpose came to be to show how and why welfare research in and on Europe might 'take culture seriously'. Participants included nationals of nine different European countries, and welfare practitioners as well as academic researchers. In retrospect, this diversity of national, prof-essional, disciplinary identities was a key condition of our explorations. The significance of culture becomes apparent (is made visible and audible) through diversity in academic and expert communities as much as in any other. At the same time, however, what we have learned is that understandings of culture (as of welfare) are themselves culturally specific: how we think of culture (and welfare) depends on the culture – national, professional, disciplinary – we come from.

Research papers presented in this series of seminars have been revised and collected in this book. The first part illustrates the creation or emergence of culture as a topic in the comparative study of welfare; the second emphasizes a distinct set of research strategies; while the third points to key theoretical resources both of current and future work. Other papers, principally presentations by practitioners, were published in issue 8 (Spring 1998) of *Soundings*, under the title *Active Welfare*.

The editors are indebted to all participants in the seminar series *Welfare and Culture in Europe*, and to the ESRC for its financial support. Zoë Fearnley, Administrator of the Centre for Biography in Social Policy at the University of East London helped to organize a number of seminars and meetings and Lesley Maroni undertook what was a particularly daunting copy-editing task. We are enormously grateful to them both.

References

Cooper, A., Pitts, J., Hetherington, R., Baistow, K. and Spriggs, A. (1995) *Positive Child Protection: A View from Abroad.* Lyme Regis: Russell House Publishing.

King, A. and Chamberlayne, P. (1996) Comparing the informal sphere: Public and private relations of welfare in East and West Germany. *Sociology, 30*, 4, 741–761.

Prue Chamberlayne, Andrew Cooper,
Richard Freeman, Michael Rustin
December 1998

Introduction

Welfare, Culture and Europe

Richard Freeman and Michael Rustin

Introduction

Every aspect of a way of life has its constituting, and often contested, culture. But this 'culture' just as often seems to be as invisible as the air we breathe. Ways of acting, thinking and feeling and their complex social meanings may not always be evident, or available as a topic for reflection or discussion.

For several decades, this has been the case for the cultures underlying our systems of welfare. There was, in Britain in particular, a broad consensus around ideas of extended citizenship, basic minimum standards and norms of equality of opportunity which were honoured in the rhetoric if not always made real in fact. There were important disagreements, too, between the contrasting values of 'freedom' and 'equality', and over what was best done by means of the market and what through the agency of the state in its national or local form. In Britain, characteristically, both systems and ideologies had their allotted place: private and state education; home ownership and a large public housing sector; even, alongside the NHS, a small sphere of private health provision. The frontiers between these competing systems moved somewhat but, between 1945 and 1979, not all that far. Even opponents on these issues seemed to inhabit largely the same conceptual universe. Those holding different ideological positions had no difficulty in understanding and accounting for the position of their opponents.

Despite their submergence, however, cultural norms have always remained implicit in ways of thinking about welfare within the tradition of mainstream social policy. Functionalism, the orthodoxy of early post-war sociology and social policy in Britain and the United States presupposed that societies were a normative order. The social policies of this era were constructed around norms and ideals of enhanced equalities of opportunity. Instead of individual destinies being determined by birth or inheritance, the ideal was that individuals would be enabled to take the place in society which their desires and talents justified. The civil, political and socio-economic entitlements of citizenship envisaged by T.H. Marshall were a way of theorizing a benign compromise between universalistic provisions made by the democratic state, and the competitive allocations of life-chances secured by markets. But this theoretical system allowed little scope for disagreement or conflict about values, and once serious conflicts, of class, race, generation and gender emerged in the 1960s, functionalist approaches lost their hegemony.

Where, rarely, questions of culture were made explicit was in the debate on 'cultures of poverty' and 'dependency culture', as they were called. This was an attempt by neo-Conservatives, initially in the United States, to deploy ideas of culture taken out of their original universalistic functionalist context, apply them to the poor and disadvantaged, and use the resulting theory to attack 'liberal' or, as the Europeans would say, social democratic conceptions of welfare. Poverty engendered habits ('cultures') of incapacity, demoralization and dependency, and these were transmitted through the generations. Efforts to support the poor by material means merely reinforced this culture of helplessness and passivity. The disadvantages of the poor were redefined, by this means, as failings of motivation, or even morality. This argument falls within the category of what Albert Hirschman has described as the 'perversity' thesis of reactionary thought, by which progressive ideas are deemed to have an effect diametrically opposite of what was intended: there is no point in providing welfare programmes for the poor, since to do so will sink them deeper, by force of morality and character, into poverty. This view of the world has had a significant effect on Western policy-makers, serving to undermine and discredit programmes which aim to remedy poverty by raising the income-levels of the poor. From our point of view here, its effect has been to discredit also the association of culture with welfare. It has made a cultural approach seem inherently biased against those in need who have been among the primary objects of reformist social policy.

But the cultural foundations of welfare states have been made newly visible, for two principal reasons. First, the intensity of change in social policy since the 1970s has made its cultural grounding or embeddedness seem less secure, more arbitrary, less organic. Across Europe, changes to welfare arrangements made in a climate of retrenchment have been surrounded by conflict and uncertainty. Second, a new interest in the cross-national, comparative study of social policy has made established conceptions of culture and its relationship to welfare problematic. In part, comparison was prompted by crisis – a standard response to failure is to look for lessons or examples elsewhere. And, in trying to understand other ways of thinking and acting, researchers have begun to understand their own systems as culturally determined.

There has ceased to be, in Britain, a common ideal of citizenship to which almost all mainstream politicians and opinion-formers pay at least lip-service. Major foundational categories of social life – nationality, ethnicity, sexual identity and its appropriate norms and boundaries, the normal character of family life – have been brought into question. The structures and cultures of class, constraining as they were, have begun to dissolve. In all these fields, individuals are more often called upon to choose, to define meanings for themselves that once would have been more strongly defined for them. The effect of this exposure to what some have called 'risk', others 'reflexivity', has been to make explicit and problematic issues of meaning and value which once might have been invisible and therefore unthinkable. People may find that the assumptions on which they built their lives no longer match the realities around them, so their assumptions, and the realities, have to be looked at anew. Or they find that the goals and values to which they dedicated their careers seem to have fallen out of fashion, and to make headway they need to find some other guiding stars.

New social movements have brought new subjects and perspectives to the study of social policy. At the same time, the field has been exposed to the different ways in which other nations construct their welfare systems. If one works largely from the perspective of one's own country, or even assumes that one's own country has some tradition of moral leadership in these matters (as after the Second World War the British did think), it is easy to be unaware of all the other possible ways there might be of constructing problems of family, national membership, or economic entitlement or obligation. But once the study of welfare and social policy becomes genuinely comparative, this complacent luxury of considering one's own ways as the normal, or as at least the ideals to be aimed at, disappears. This has been the experience of the contributors to this book, as they have learned about each other's experiences and understandings of welfare systems and practices.

In more specific ways, too, this developing comparative awareness among social policy researchers has made for a new (if largely ignored) problematization of the relationship between welfare and culture. The primary foci of comparative research have been on one hand the origin and subsequent development of welfare states, and on the other the measurement of performance, either in general or at the level of specific programmes. Culture, itself sometimes labelled merely 'tradition', has either been consigned to a category of residual variables, or ignored. Yet, as a recent review acknowledges, 'The fluidity of the boundary between private and social provision constantly bedevils international comparisons' (Parry 1995, p.378). Much of the difficulty here is that these boundaries are cultural: state, market, community and household represent different patterns of assumption about right, responsibility and consequent behaviour, and they are drawn differently in different cultural contexts. In turn, problems of definition make for problems of explanation. For the moment, though, comparativists are stuck with formulations which conceal as much as they reveal: 'The structures and governance of European welfare states express the philosophy behind them' (Parry 1995, p.383). What is this philosophy? Where does it come from? Is 'philosophy' really the right word? The irony is that it is comparative social policy research that seems to require a concept of culture but which has hesitated to develop it.

An appreciation of culture is fundamental to thoroughgoing understanding, or Weberian *verstehen*. Yet, for all its industry, there remains a sense that existing research has done little to develop any real appreciation of what goes on and how things are done elsewhere. We have little comparative knowledge of welfare provision as such, that is of the interaction between providers and users of formally established services, let alone of the assumptions they bring to that interaction or of the myriad informal alternatives which may or may not be available to them.

So two kinds of displacement of the taken-for-granted bring 'cultural' issues – that is questions of meaning and moral value – to the fore in the welfare field. One is the displacement brought about by changes taking place over time as the post-war settlement and its ensuing near-consensus has been swept away, leaving deep uncertainties about what should be done, or what is possible. The second is the displacement which takes place in space, in geographical terms, as countries find themselves obliged to compare their practices with those of other countries, and are forced to think about the desirability or necessity of 'harmonization' or convergence within a more unified Europe. Sharp disjunctions between past, present and immediate future, and between the practices of one country and those of others that impinge on it, make it clear that the provision of welfare is culturally defined.

To say this much, however, is merely to beg a series of questions. Some of these are generic, in that a particular set of problems of theory and method inhere in the topic (culture) itself. In the rest of this chapter, our purpose is to acknowledge what seem to be some of the most salient of these problems and questions by relating them to the specific concerns of comparative research, and to the work collected in this book. Our perception is not only that culture is an intrinsic aspect of welfare, but also that it is contingent in time and space and that this contingent status has fundamental methodological implications. The tensions to which we point are not ones which can be easily resolved; indeed, much of the work presented here shows them to be a source of creativity. They are prompted by questions which can be simply expressed: what is culture, where is it to be discovered, and when and why does it appear problematic? What are the cultural aspects of welfare – or the welfare aspects of culture – and how might they be 'captured' in research?

What is culture?

There are many definitions of culture: so many, that the issue is not merely to distinguish between different definitions, but between different kinds of definition (cf. Williams 1981). Zygmunt Bauman distinguishes between hierarchical, generic and differential concepts of culture (Bauman 1973). The hierarchical notion is essentially the lay concept of 'high' culture, of culture as arts and media even if they take popular forms (Williams refers to 'the active cultivation of the mind' (Williams 1981, p.11)). The generic notion is concerned with a fundamental problem of the scope of social scientific inquiry and the ways in which its concerns differ from those of, for example, biology: culture is an attribute of human societies. The differential notion, meanwhile, identifies culture as the 'otherness' of alien groups and societies, and may be the one closest to social scientists' (and certainly comparativists') interests.

That said, different social scientists use the term in different ways. Among recent work in politics and sociology, for example, Ellis and Coyle use culture 'in a broad sense to encompass social relations as well as values and beliefs' (Ellis and Coyle 1994, p.1). Zetterholm and colleagues, similarly, 'use "culture" ... as a term summing up beliefs, norms, institutions and traditional ways of "doing things" in a society' (Zetterholm 1994, p.2). Wildavsky conceives of 'shared values legitimating different patterns of social practices' (Wildavsky, cited in Keraudren 1996, p.84), while Garland emphasizes both cognitive and affective aspects of culture: 'The fact that thought and feeling are closely intertwined ... means that when we talk of "culture" we refer not just to intellectual systems and forms of consciousness but also to structures of affect and what might be called emotional configurations or "sensibilities"' (Garland 1990, p.195). And, in something of a textbook definition, for Giddens: 'Culture consists of the values the members of a given group hold, the norms they follow, and the material goods they create' (Giddens 1989, p.31).

Culture, then, seems to refer to values, practices, emotions and artefacts, as well as institutions and 'ways of doing things'. But what does this really mean? What might we mean by culture in relation to welfare? Take education, for example. The values of an educational system might include equality of opportunity and the self-realization of the child. Its practices will include examinations and PTA meetings, but also waiting in line, the time and place of children's eating and the timing of the school day. The emotions it generates will include those of belonging, success and, inevitably related to each, a sense of anxiety. Its artefacts are the register, the written curriculum, the newsletter, the desk, the uniform and the school bag. All of these, values, practices, emotions and artefacts are invested with meaning; the experience of teachers, pupils and parents is expressed primarily in their terms rather than those of ministerial policy statements.

Each of them, too, is intimately connected with the others, and the wider range of phenomena to which they relate seems almost limitless. There is nothing which is not 'culture'. Raymond Williams (1981) takes anthropological usage of the concept of culture to indicate the 'whole way of life' of a people or group. The problem, however, is that, if culture is everything, there may be nothing to say. Culture understood as a 'whole way of life' leaves few relational terms, perhaps only nature, beyond it; to be useful, it must be formulated as a more specific and limited concept. While it should not be seen as a separable or independent entity – cultural practices are themselves constitutive of any given social order – it is vital to retain a sense of culture as an aspect of social order, not as social order itself. Contemporary sociology, partly for this reason, 'sees culture as the signifying system through which necessarily (though among other means) a social order is communicated, reproduced, experienced and explored' (Williams 1981, p.13). (Cultural studies, similarly, is concerned with 'documenting and explaining the processes of producing and circulating meaning through the channels of the artefacts and practices of culture' (Lupton 1994, p.16).)

Even then, there is a danger in seeking coherent wholes. As Garland warns, '… a culture is not a monolithic kind of thing which can feature as a simple variable in an explanatory formula. It is, instead, a rich composite of densely interwoven meanings which loses all its content wherever it is discussed in generic terms. Cultures are bric-a-brac ensembles of specifics, local details and peculiarities' (Garland 1990, p.200). Garland echoes Levi-Strauss's concept of culture as 'bricolage'. In Bauman's words, '[Culture] construes ever new signs out of anything that happens to be handy, and it pours ever new meanings into everything that happens to be within reach, waiting to become a sign …' (Bauman 1997, p.139). In a similar vein, but changing the metaphor, Margaret Archer (1990) posits a need for a 'cultural cartography' as an antidote to 'cultural monism'. What is useful here is the reference to territory, space and situation. In practice, the papers in this volume uncover and explore 'welfare culture' in particular contexts and locations; culture is an aspect of situated action. As often as not, the question being addressed has not been 'What is culture?', but 'Where is culture?'.

Where is culture?

Cross-national research in social policy tends to deal in large units, such as whole states. Following this lead, we might take different countries to constitute discrete cultural units, expecting that different welfare states might express different welfare cultures. There are good reasons for doing so, recognizing what have been described as the 'homogenizing effects' of the nation state (Zetterholm 1994): states shape national identity and cultivate legitimacy by establishing norms, values and behaviours in their own image. What is more, this is a process in which welfare (and especially education) plays a prominent part. At the same time, conversely, 'culture … is expressed in social practices that are politically and legally guaranteed by the state' (Zetterholm 1994, p.3). Culture, perhaps even more so 'welfare culture', and the state stand in a reciprocal relationship to each other. Walter Lorenz's chapter makes this point, showing that if welfare is a critical aspect of nation-state formation, as it was in Germany at the end of the nineteenth century, we should expect it also to be deeply implicated in the crisis of the nation-state at the end of the twentieth. The argument is that the solidarity expressed in welfare requires some cultural logic, which is regularly found in nationhood. And when the legitimacy of the nation as an organizing principle of social life breaks down, welfare must be re-thought, too.

If, in countries like Germany, culture is an explicit goal or welfare project, in others it seems almost to be denied (though the denial of culture itself is to be read as a distinctive cultural formation). In some respects, the welfare state, in its universalism, its bureaucracy and its rationality, appears as an elaborate, sustained attempt to do without culture. What is interesting about the case studies which follow here is that it seems to be the most universal and state-led systems which have been most deeply riven by cultural change. As Martin Peterson explains, the success and stability of the Swedish model has been predicated on a particular and long-established social formation, which he traces from the *bruk* through to modern corporatism (the passing implication is that, while being widely taken as a model worthy of emulation, for most other countries it is more or less unrepeatable). More pertinent here, it seems peculiarly and increasingly vulnerable to the kinds of social and economic change attendant on globalization. The irony is that it is precisely that model of welfare which has seemed best able to compromise between capital and labour which may be the least able to cope in conditions of racial diversity. In a different way, as Prue Chamberlayne and John Baldock and Clare Ungerson show in their chapters, it seems that it is the traditional neglect of the personal and informal in social policy in Britain which has left the users of services there so disoriented by change.

In comparative terms, this collection points to homogeneity at a level much greater or higher than that of the state, and diversity in specific experience at a level much lower, among the poor, and among carers of the chronically sick. Michael Hornsby-Smith, for example, begins by modelling types or families of nations, assembling an array of quantitative data, and uses structural (cultural) differences to explain differences between countries in policy outcomes. His categorization begins with Esping-Andersen's construct of decommodification, which is expressed as a set of political (conservative, liberal and social democratic) configurations and to which he adds legal, linguistic and liturgical dimensions. In other papers, the idea of culture is introduced where national regimes are seen to be experienced in different ways, as is the case for carers in both Britain and Germany (Baldock and Ungerson; Chamberlayne) and for the poor in Italy (Spanò). At the same time, Chamberlayne points to marked similarities in the experience of carers in markedly different systems. In Steven Trevillion's study of social work in England and Sweden, what appears to be a common organizational technology (networking) operates in very different ways.

There is a lesson in this, which is that the social and organizational bases of culture may not necessarily be national or public but organizational, ethnic, linguistic, religious, gendered, local and personal. In the end, the idea of different countries' 'welfare cultures' makes no more or less sense than that of their 'welfare states'. (The methodological corollary is that welfare, like culture, is no single thing. If 'welfare' refers 'to the whole complex of social arrangements for meeting needs' (Carrier and Kendall 1977), then it will prove as chimerical as culture if pursued in that way.) To take our earlier example, 'educational culture' may be more clearly expressed in the local state, the sector, the community, the school and the classroom than at the level of national government. Studying welfare culture demands that the welfare state be disaggregated, if only to be recomposed. For culture is made visible at the micro level: in organizations, in meetings, conferences and consultations, in interactions between people. In their work on Spain, for example, Eli Tejero and Laura Torrabadella link biographical material to regime change. Cross-national understandings of culture are predicated upon an unusually testing synthesis of macro and micro level research.

When (and why) is culture?

For a long time, and significantly in a period of notable stability, social scientists interested in social policy dealt with a conception of culture as unchanging, resistant, and ultimately conservative. But culture is deeply implicated in changes in welfare, and not only because the cultural bases of welfare are made apparent through crisis and change. There is a methodological point here, which is that culture only becomes visible as something challenged or changed, when 'common sense' seems no longer either common or sensible. In almost every instance, both the general (national) and specific (individual) experiences reported here are experiences of change. Yet just as it is change in social policy which has brought attention to culture, so it is conflicts and contradictions within cultures which may be important in precipitating change itself. Culture has dynamic properties, for it is constituted and recreated through interaction between people and groups. We should expect it to be contradictory, and expect, too, that these contradictions will be sometimes debilitating and sometimes regenerative:

> A cultural system should be considered both as a dynamic and a contradictory system with tendencies and counter-acting tendencies giving rise to tensions and change over time. Old and new elements may co-exist within a given system, but seemingly 'old' cultural traits inserted into a 'modern' context are not necessarily 'left-overs' from the past. They can also 'reappear' as a response to other 'modern' developments. Any system is obviously a result of historical developments and thus of the past, but the form of the insertion of 'the old' into 'the new' will depend on concrete configurations of political forces and processes. Major changes in a cultural system are likely to occur as a result of social crisis or upheaval, such as major wars, revolutions or the formations of states. (Plaschke 1994, pp.120–121)

As Margaret Archer points out, 'cultural contradictions within and between belief systems make just as important a contribution to social change as anything going on in the structural domain' (Archer 1990, p.117). By the same token, it is the points at which culture and policy diverge which are likely to produce new insights into the relationship between the two (Garland 1990; Baldock and Ungerson, this volume).

The mutability of culture, and the relationship between changing societies and social policies, raise fundamental theoretical questions. The 'when' question is really a 'why' question. (This 'why' question is also one common to almost every school in social and political theory. What follows here is not meant as an introduction to such debates, merely an acknowledgement of their significance. For introductions to cultural theory, see Alexander and Seidman (1990) and Swingewood (1998).) It is important to remember that the study of culture is theoretically driven: 'If the processing of experiences into actions were uniform ... then mediating mind-stuff could simply be left out of theory' (Eckstein, cited in Keraudren 1996, p.74). At the same time, culture is not itself a theory. As Gabriel Almond described political culture: '[It] is not a theory; it refers to a set of variables which may be used in the construction of theories. But insofar as it designates a set of variables and encourages their investigation, it imputes some explanatory power to the psychological or subjective dimension of politics, just as it implies that there are contextual and internal variables which may explain it' (Almond 1989, p.26).

The analytic problem can be reduced to that of the relationship between culture, structure and agency. What matters is whether culture is treated as subject or object, as an independent or a dependent variable, as organic or fabricated, whether it is willing or caused. The tension here is between understandings of culture which allow it some independent status and those which see it as a mechanistic or functional expression of social and economic relations. The dichotomy can be derived from that between Marx and Hegel, though there is some convergence in contemporary social theory on the relative autonomy of culture from social structure (Alexander 1990). 'We cannot understand culture without reference to subjective meaning, and we cannot understand it without reference to social structural constraints. We cannot interpret social behaviour without acknowledging that it follows codes that it does not invent; at the same time, human invention creates a changing environment for every cultural code. Inherited metaphysical ideas form an inextricable web for modern social structures, yet powerful groups often succeed in transforming cultural structures into legitimating means' (Alexander 1990, p.26). It is for this reason that we do not pretend that the discrete accounts of welfare and culture presented here develop a coherent theory of 'welfare culture'. What has seemed important has been to provoke a range of insights on a range of topics from a range of perspectives. Walter Lorenz's account of culture as an ideological project, for example, differs radically from that of Caroline Knowles, for whom culture inheres in the social regulation of place.

Culture has structural properties, though it is not itself structure. Using the term culture seems to change something: it seems less rigid, more permeable, readier to allow for agency, to introduce the possibility of change. This may be why the concept seems newly salient now. Where social structures come to be strained, if not stressed beyond repair, culture is one of the principal ways of understanding patterns of behaviour. We may begin to think of culture as the local rules of the relationship between structure and agency. And at the same time, the most useful questions may not be about the structure–agency dichotomy, but about what kinds of agency are possible or assumed in any given context. What Elkins and Simeon observe in relation to policy might hold for individual or social action of any kind: '(C)ulture remains primarily permissive: it does not determine precisely what will be done; it conditions the range of issues to which attention will be devoted; it influences the way those issues will be defined; and it limits the range of options considered within a given issue domain' (Elkins and Simeon 1979, p.143).

There is an important caveat here, however. The lesson of the Anglo-American tradition is that talking about culture will raise as many normative problems as it might solve analytic ones. If culture is to be 'brought back in', it will matter very much just how it is done. Different constructions of culture and its significance are innately ideological. Identifying a need to talk about poverty and culture without talking about a 'culture of poverty' (above, and Spanò) does not mean that it can be quickly or easily overcome.

Welfare has always been concerned with fundamental issues of social inclusion and exclusion, the means of survival and subsistence, opportunities to live fulfilling lives, or their absence. The moral centrality of 'welfare' to a society has tended to be occluded by the practical and technical quality of policy debates. Welfare has been made to seem less like a set of constituting social principles than a field of specialized administrative practice. One consequence of the need to recognize and rethink these principles, since they can no longer be taken for granted as the invisible underpinnings of policy, is the possibility of generating new debates about the moral and behavioural foundations of citizenship, in which different alternatives, each grounded in different traditions and practices, can be elaborated and considered. How such debates might be constituted is the subject of Samantha Ashenden's chapter.

Of course, there are many precedents for the project represented in this book. Social policy has remained insulated longer than most subject-areas from the profound effects of the 'cultural turn' in the social sciences. Criminology, the sociologies of education, organizations and science, socio-legal studies and geography are all examples of fields of study which have been turned upside down in the last thirty years by the recognition that to attempt explanations without reference to the meanings and values held by actors, and without regard to their underpinning symbolic codes, is to provide a very thin account of reality. Even the study of the mass media had to undergo this paradigm-shift, with the development of 'cultural studies', from a model which mainly described empirical outputs and effects, to one which investigated what different forms and codes of communications actually meant to those who produced and received them (Morley and Chen 1996).

The 'precultural' empiricist sociologies of these fields were not only descriptively thin, but were also inclined uncritically to reproduce the dominant ways of thinking of the institutional fields which formed their subject-matter. Culture was not absent, but was rather reproduced as an implicit set of assumptions about goals and values, success and failure, conformity and deviance, as these were perceived by those who controlled the practical agendas of the relevant institutions.

Earlier examples of a culturally sensitive sociology had identified and given expression to the experience of different social subjects, usually in opposition to the world-view of the system-managers. These included those forming and being formed by the new youth cultures, low-stream secondary school pupils and drop-outs, drug-users, and shop-floor workers, among many others. This 'sociology from below' was initially influenced mainly by American symbolic interactionists, but ways were soon found of giving due weight to class and other structures without losing sight of their symbolic and subjective processes. A 'culturalist' Marxism was one development, culturally-sensitive studies of gender and ethnicity were others.

It is not our purpose at this stage to insist on the recognition of the experience of any particular group of social actors, oppressed or otherwise. It is too late in the debate about 'bringing culture back in' for this to be generally necessary, though some chapters in this book (for example Caroline Knowles' descriptions of psychiatric outpatients) may have this effect. Our comparative European perspective gives us another pressing task, of understanding the different subjectivities and cultures to be found across the continent.

What seems striking (yet also in some way ordinary and self-evident) about almost all of the research presented here is that the dominant emotion described is one of anxiety. It is borne by workers, clients and others; it is perhaps the logical corollary of Beck's 'risk society'. It is striking, too, to what extent these anxieties must be managed privately. Michael Rustin explores the roots and implications of the disjuncture between the rational and the emotional in the experience of welfare, showing how psychoanalytic understandings can be used to restore what might be described as its 'affective coherence'.

The study of culture, in a simple sense, is concerned with what people think and do. One of our aims in initiating a cross-national discussion of welfare and culture was to restore human agency, identity and values at conscious, emotional and unconscious levels, to comparative social policy. Conversely, it may be that we know little about culture in part because we know very little, in comparative terms, about people – users, providers and policy makers – and their relationship to welfare. One of the effects of a new attention to culture may be to make comparative social research – seemingly more interested in institutions, policy and numbers – more human.

References

Alexander, J.C. (1990) Analytic debates: understanding the relative autonomy of culture. In J.C. Alexander and S. Seidman (eds) *Culture and Society. Contemporary Debates.* Cambridge: Cambridge UP.

Alexander, J.C. and Seidman, S. (eds) (1990) *Culture and Society. Contemporary Debates.* Cambridge: Cambridge UP.

Almond, G. (1989) The intellectual history of the civic culture concept. In G. Almond and S. Verba (eds) *The Civic Culture Revisited.* Boston: Little, Brown.

Archer, M.S. (1990) Theory, culture and post-industrial society. In M. Featherstone (ed) *Global Culture. Nationalism, Globalization and Modernity.* London: Sage; *Theory, Culture and Society, 7,* 97–119.

Bauman, Z. (1973) *Culture as Praxis.* London: Routledge and Kegan Paul.

Bauman, Z. (1997) Culture as consumer co-operative. In Z. Bauman. *Postmodernity and its Discontents.* Cambridge: Polity.

Carrier, J. and Kendall, I. (1977) The development of welfare states: the production of plausible accounts. *Journal of Social Policy, 6,* 3, 271–290.

Elkins, D.J. and Simeon, R. (1979) A cause in search of its effect; or What does political culture explain? *Comparative Politics,* 127–143.

Ellis, R.J. and Coyle, D.J. (1994) Introduction to Coyle, D.J. and Ellis, R.J. (eds) *Politics, Policy and Culture.* Boulder: Westview Press.

Garland, D. (1990) *Punishment and Modern Society. A Study in Social Theory,* Pbk edition 1991, Oxford: Oxford UP.

Giddens, A. (1989) *Sociology.* Cambridge: Polity.

Keraudren, P. (1996) In search of culture: lessons from the past to find a role for the study of administrative culture. *Governance, 9,* 1, 71–98.

Lupton, D. (1994) *Medicine as Culture. Illness, Disease and the Body in Western Societies.* London: Sage.

Morley, D. and Chen, K.-H. (eds) (1996) *Stuart Hall: Critical Dialogue in Cultural Studies.* London: Routledge.

Parry, R. (1995) Redefining the welfare state. In E. Page and J. Hayward (eds) *Governing the New Europe.* Cambridge: Polity.

Plaschke, H. (1994) National economic cultures and economic integration. In S. Zetterholm (ed) *National Cultures and European Integration: Exploratory Essays on Cultural Diversity and Common Policies.* Oxford: Berg.

Swingewood, A. (1998) *Cultural Theory and the Problem of Modernity.* Basingstoke: Macmillan.

Williams, R. (1981) *Culture.* London: Fontana.

Zetterholm, S. (1994) Introduction: cultural diversity and common policies. In S. Zetterholm (ed) *National Cultures and European Integration: Exploratory Essays on Cultural Diversity and Common Policies.* Oxford: Berg.

PART I

From Welfare to Culture

Introduction to Part I

Prue Chamberlayne

All of the chapters in this section, despite their different national contexts, pivot on a central point of crisis or breakdown not only in the management and functioning of social work services, but also in understandings and methods of analysis in social policy, and in political thinking. In this way, they corroborate the argument of the opening chapter (Freeman and Rustin), that questions of culture are emblematic of social crisis, of the questioning of fundamental values and procedures, and 'ways of seeing'. The section takes a broad historical and theoretical view of the cultural shaping of welfare systems. From global and national heights of analysis, different chapters swoop down to the everyday practices of professional life (Trevillion), or forward across two centuries of welfare as a component of nation building (Lorenz), or, starting from current social turmoil, sweep backwards to review from a new vantage point the hundred-year history of a model welfare system (Peterson). Taking a narrower time span, Baldock and Ungerson plunge from national level discourse on community care to reveal its frightening degree of disconnection from the everyday concerns and life worlds of vulnerable user groups.

'Culture' in these chapters is treated in richly different ways. In Walter Lorenz's 'life history' of social pedagogy in German social thinking and practice, culture is an explicit and central concept, subject to different ideological permutations. What is new here is not so much the discovery of culture, but its careful and intriguing exposition in the context of Europeanization. New also, and just as much part of the Europeanization process, is the political and social re-evaluation of social pedagogy, from the vantage point of more liberal preoccupations with equality and difference. For Lorenz's chapter is framed by a probing of the tensions between national unity and respect for difference, between redistribution and recognition. He makes a passionate plea for a continuing negotiation or balancing in social work practice between cultural recognition and universal rights.

In Lorenz's chapter, culture is treated as an ongoing instrument and object of policy. In Martin Peterson's account of Swedish welfare, by contrast, culture bursts much more immediately and explosively onto the scene, under the twin impacts of globalization and immigration. Arriving as a potent agent of change, multiculturalism has a transforming effect on social policy, shaking it out of its positivism into more qualitative and action-based approaches. The highlighting of cultural issues in the present, however, leads to culture being newly revealed, emerging out of the mists of the past, challenging the very fundamentals of the Social Democratic welfare settlement, as Peterson poignantly depicts.

In Steven Trevillion's case, culture is deployed in a new approach to the analysis of social work, one which treats subjectivity as an essential element in tracing both how social work operates and how it is changing. The approach starts from the Foucauldian and post-modern premise that subjectivity is socially and historically contingent, and, drawing on Simmel and Elias, adds in the notion that culture derives from patterns of interaction in everyday life. Thus, rather than being – as in conventional social work theory – something 'outside' to which social workers are sensitive, or some professionally designated core of values to which they subscribe, this analysis suggests that social work is itself generative of culture; social workers are making, or actively constituting, culture in their daily activities and interactions. Building on an incisive review of the often paradoxical conceptualizations of globalization, Trevillion points to those aspects which highlight the global diffusion of both key ideas in social work and of common patterns in the reconfiguring of working relationships as networks. The 'figurational flow' within which global pressures are internalized may differ greatly in different societies, however, as is illustrated by a comparison of 'relationship' and 'entrepreneurial' networking cultures in Sweden and London. Such differences in culture, construed here as organizational technologies, affect working relationships between colleagues, with service users, and with employers.

The chapter by John Baldock points to the clash between public policy and users' lives. Here culture is treated on the one hand as ideology, on the other as a missing resource. Policy, they argue, needs to be 'in tune with the deeply-rooted values and norms that govern the private order of people's lives': if it is to be effective, it has to gauge users' knowledge of services as well as their ability to incorporate new developments into their own experience. Ordinarily, elderly stroke sufferers have restricted opportunities for social learning and few cultural norms to guide them through uncharted territory. Their 'unscripted' roles, meanwhile, are busily rewritten by extraneous discourses, each with its own, far too simple assumptions. These range from government ideologues to disability lobbyists to reminiscence enthusiasts, none of them acknowledging stroke victims' and their carers' struggles to make sense of their new situation in the light of understandings of their previous lives, and of their accumulated experience and skills. Discourses of autonomy and 'dependency' conflict with a concern for the quality of dependent relations.

Yet these chapters are by no means bleak. While depicting the awful contradictions between multiculturalism and tolerance of nationalist extremism, Lorenz suggests that social workers will continue to struggle for democratic solutions. The tightrope of national integration and respect for cultural difference, which can so easily turn into assimilationism and social exclusion, is also underpinned by rich philosophical and political resources. In Sweden, while creating immense problems, globalization and immigration bring new resources and opportunities for critical rethinking, for lifting the carpet of established values and beliefs. Trevillion, likewise, is purposively looking ahead. To call for the analysis of social work to include professional subjectivity is to propose that it do now what it should long ago have done. Likewise Baldock points to the potential for social policy research and analysis to listen and adapt to user experience. It seems hard, from the British perspective, to recall the social optimism and sense of progress which has been celebrated at many turning points in the development of welfare: Blair pales beside Beveridge or Bevan. Yet, though there may be an appalling material and intellectual deficit to be made up, there are also multiple historical and comparative resources intimated here with which to do so.

Despite the variety of ways in which the concept of culture is deployed, there are rich cross-overs between these chapters, and with chapters in other sections. The dilemmas posed by multiculturalism within Sweden's integrated and egalitarian model (Peterson) are precisely those which Lorenz traces through in the different case of Germany. The mismatch of service and user cultures in Baldock's chapter can be usefully read as an extension of Trevillion's argument for greater attention to the production of culture in social work interactions. Meanwhile, Lorenz's exposition of the concept of the social in nineteenth-century Germany and its development in the concept of social pedagogy may be enhanced by Hornsby-Smith's elucidation of Christian Democracy's notion of social solidarity, and by Chamberlayne's discussion of the difficulty of grasping the social at the informal level of caring (Part II). Baldock's and Chamberlayne's chapters both explore the cultural realities of everyday caring. Trevillion's discussion of Foucauldian perspectives reads well in conjunction with Knowles (Part III).

CHAPTER I

Social Work and Cultural Politics
The Paradox of German Social Pedagogy
Walter Lorenz

Social work impinges on people's identity. While a classical view of social work presumed that the various fields of social work, mental health, family work, probation etc. met social service users 'as they were' before coming into contact with social workers, the more recent post-structural perspective began to focus much more on how social work in turn defines and constructs their clients' identity (Rojek, Peacock and Collins 1988). This in turn highlights the danger which the profession has long been anxious to avert, that through its interventions people might become labelled, confirmed as being merely a category of people with deficiencies, excluded from the 'normal' part of society. Social work's declared project was instead to make a contribution to the integration of society. And yet, 'differences' are today being affirmed by minority groups in society ever more confidently and vociferously, where labels become tools for emancipation, and separate identities are being reclaimed as a defence against levelling, stifling homogeneity:

> In the very moment when modern liberal states fully realize their secularism (as Marx put it in 'The Jewish Question'), just as the mantle of abstract personhood is formally tendered to a whole panoply of those historically excluded from it by humanism's privileging of a single race, gender and organization of sexuality, the marginalized reject the rubric of humanist inclusion and turn, at least in part, against its very premises. Refusing to be neutralized, to render the differences inconsequential, to be depoliticized as 'life-styles', 'diversity' or 'persons like any other', we have lately reformulated our historical exclusion as a matter of historically produced and politically rich *alterity*. (Brown 1995, p.200)

Identity, and with it cultural identity as the key to diversity, matters within and not just between societies. At the same time, such cultural differences serve as justifications for inequality, as arguments against the socialist aspiration of equality, and as a means of unhinging the network of obligations which had undergirded the nation state.

To raise the question of culture and social work means therefore identifying a paradox and calls for an investigation of the history of that paradox, which will be attempted in the next chapter. The paradox lies in the observation that for most of its history, social work strove to rise above the level of the culturally particular and reach a level of universalism as the hallmark of its professional autonomy. However, it was precisely this universalism that played into the hands of particularism, in the form of nationalism (and indeed at times fascism and racism). Investigating the history of that paradox might indicate ways of avoiding new unintended outcomes of today's greater attention to cultural differences, namely that they would serve to justify and solidify exclusion and inequality. Culture and difference cannot be dealt with responsibly by either embracing these concepts uncritically or by rejecting them as irrelevant.

The renewed focus on culture and difference occurs at a time of economic globalization. This amounts to a fundamental restructuring of time and space in as much as the mobility which allows for the exploitation of market opportunities has become the prerogative of a dominant élite who can conduct their business in electronically aided virtual ubiquity. They then claim this global space and the resources it provides through their ever accumulating wealth. At the same time, this very mobility is being denied to those whose livelihood derives from labour rather than capital. They are being held to ransom by a combination of material factors, such as their poverty, their family obligations, their rootedness in particular geographic areas, restrictions on immigration and, not least, their identification with distinct cultural boundaries. Being tied to a given cultural identity means being written off as yesterday's person; being able to choose from the global supermarket of identities means being in control.

Globalization also threatens the broad welfare consensus that had developed in Western European nation states in the era immediately after the Second World War. This had ensured the constant 'recommodification of labour' (Bauman 1998, p.52) and at the same time the support of organized labour for the task of economic reconstruction and expansion for those nations. 'By providing good quality education, an adequate health service, decent housing and healthy nourishment for the children of poor families, it assured a steady supply of the capitalist industry with employable labour – an effect no individual company or group of companies would be able to secure on their own' (Bauman 1998, p.52). This had a levelling, liberating effect on identities – at least until the costs of this redistribution became clearer.

'The welfare state may be seen as a "completion" of the nation state, to the extent that individual social rights become an essential element of citizenship as the main basis of political legitimacy' (Flora 1986, p.xv). It substantiated the idea of belonging to a nation decisively by giving individuals a material stake in the state. The crisis of the welfare state therefore also spells the crisis of the nation state and vice versa. While the welfare state secured a high degree of integration (at the price of conformity and uniformity with assumed national standards, which will be discussed below), it depended also on a high degree of differentiation between nation states externally. This (and their military power) constituted their political sovereignty and autonomy, not least in the area of social policy. With the erosion of this sovereignty the seat of governance is moving away from the nation state, making room for identities and identity coalitions to form without reference to the nation, but also for new centres of power outside the national systems of democratic control. In a weakened nation state 'modern' forms of social integration via welfare may become less effective and legitimacy may become based more on differentiation and 'the politics of recognition' (Taylor 1992).

Social work is deeply bound up in these processes. The examination of the role of culture in social work requires therefore a critical examination of its relationship with the nation state project. This chapter seeks to illustrate this with the development of social pedagogy as the decisive paradigm in the German context by contrasting its origins with the social science paradigm prevalent in nineteenth century Britain. It considers the historical contexts in which both the distancing from cultural issues, as exemplified by the latter, and the explicit attention to culture in the former prevented social work from developing constructively the dialectics of particularism and universalism.

Early forms of social work in the nineteenth century were characterized by a fundamental ambivalence in relation to political issues and the treatment of culture and cultural identity. Charity workers in Britain, both as representatives of the middle classes and as women, regarded their work as being above state politics in their commitment to Christian or humanist values which they also considered to be above class politics. But their activities took place in the context of social and historical processes which had the potential of totally dissolving existing social bonds. Their efforts at re-establishing bonds run parallel to the nation state project, the unification of different geographic and cultural regions, which had set itself the task of creating a coherent and unifying national culture, not least in the interest of establishing a powerful base for an industrialized national economy. But it did this with reference to pre-modern cultural reminiscences and reconstructions. As Rattansi comments with reference to Bhabha's analysis of national narratives: 'The "people" thus must be thought of as existing in "double time", for the project of producing the nation as a community involves a tension between a "pedagogic" authority of continuity and a "performative" strategy in which the ragged, potentially transgressive cultures of everyday life are constantly brought under the sway of a narrative of what one might call a national "community"' (Rattansi 1994, pp.40–41).

Bearing in mind that the boundaries of most continental European countries were redrawn in the wake of the Napoleonic wars with the ensuing politics of national liberation and unification, this constitutes the paradox of the modern nation state. It had to interpret the romantic, modern dream of liberation and democratic self-determination with the traditional imagery of a community, in analogy to the family. Ideologically, nations like Germany and Italy constructed their identity and cohesion increasingly with reference to alleged pre-existing common ethnic and cultural bonds, instead of the mere social contract between free and therefore 'fundamentally different' individuals, which the push for democratic rights and civil liberties in the republican tradition had demanded (Lorenz 1996). But these cultural claims were far too weak to bring aboard the masses of rootless and disaffected people created by the industrial revolution. The state had to attend to social issues, concern itself with the affairs of people as private individuals and families, transform the vertical cleavages into a horizontal community of equals and distinguish itself from 'outsiders' (Balibar and Wallerstein 1991). This task required its own missionaries, provided first and foremost by the teaching profession, but with social work coming to fit equally into this project. It was largely an education project, carried initially by the 'lower and middle professional, administrative and intellectual strata, in other words the educated classes' (Hobsbawm 1977, p.167). It was a project that operated as the patchy, anticipatory construction of social citizenship in Marshall's sense, grafted on top of the emerging democratic political citizenship.

While the task was the same in all countries, different political and historical contexts affected the meaning and role given to the concept of culture. In the British tradition of liberalism the state was reluctant to go beyond the introduction of compulsory schooling and some public health measures as positive means of integration. It left the initiative to private organizations whose aims converged by the end of the nineteenth century on a version of national identity that was closely bound up with the political and economic successes of the empire. This emerging national culture was, as in France (where it was however a legacy of the revolution and the equalizing effects of a national culture) a sign of civilization. 'Both [terms] were used increasingly to describe a general process of human development, of becoming "cultivated" or "civilized"' (Thompson 1990, p.124). The role of the charity workers, in contrast to the staff of the expressly punitive and exclusionary institutions, was to further the progress of civilization and to spread its benefits. They patrolled the margins of the nation, saw to it that 'the right kind of people' were included, that the harsher social control measures of the state only excluded those who were not 'deserving' of the membership of the body of the national people. Reference points such as sobriety, industry and thrift, once cultural markers of distinct religious traditions, became universalized and served a very particular instrumental purpose for the national economy. 'In England between 1780 and 1830 the "average" English working man became more disciplined, more subject to the productive tempo of "the clock", more reserved and methodical, less violent and less spontaneous' (Thompson 1968, p.451). The actual educational scope of this project was poorly conceptualized and ultimately quite ineffective. 'Any such classification by merit was found to have no relation to the necessary classification according to needs ... Eventually the Charity Organisation Society was driven to drop the criterion of desert; "the test is not whether the applicant be deserving but whether he is helpable", we were told' (Beatrice Webb 1926, p.174). The 'one nation ideal' eventually inspired both religious and secular organizations, exemplified by the Settlement Movement which sought to express the need for both classes to meet and mould a new sense of belonging through 'colonies' in the inner cities.

The border patrol, rescue of the deserving from exclusion, and personal attention to the poor and destitute was the specific patriotic duty of women (and not just in their capacity as charity workers, but also in their educational role as mothers) in the same way as serving the country in war, in the defence of its external borders, or as administrators of the colonies was the patriotic duty of men. They helped to build the nation; they claimed to be the heart of the nation. Octavia Hill, in commenting in the preface to her book of 1875 on the Artisans' Dwellings Bill going through the British parliament at that time, strongly supports the intended provision of affordable housing for the poor but adds: 'There needs, and will need for some time, a reformatory work which will demand that loving zeal of individuals which cannot be had for money, and cannot be legislated for by Parliament. The heart of the English nation will supply it – individual, reverent, firm, and wise. It may and should be organised, but cannot be created' (Hill 1883, p.10).

The pronounced individualism of British charitable activities endorsed the basic tenets of the liberal state. Concerns over specific cultural norms and practices were regarded as a matter for private individuals and this restricted the relevance and impact of an independent working class culture politically (Jones 1983). Working class consciousness and identity, mirroring the globalizing rationality of capital but being denied a symmetrical role, typically extended across country borders. The labour movement was constantly accused of its unpatriotic internationalism through which it refused to be incorporated into the nation state project, at least until the surrender of large sections to the nationalist fervour which fuelled the First World War. Philanthropy and the state concessions in terms of early social policy measures served to de-politicize this consciousness of a separate identity and to establish a regime of power into which it could be incorporated (Donzelot 1979). If the nation state were to succeed in reinterpreting the political conflicts, created by glaring inequalities, into issues of a shared national culture, to which both the poor and the well-to-do could be committed and within which differences amounted to individual differences, then the political relevance of the class argument could be refuted. Cultural arguments can, especially in the form of the ideology of nationalism, have the function of legitimating the hegemonic role of the state as promoter of a shared sense of belonging, neutralizing the disruptive power of persistent inequality. Equally, the argument of cultural difference can have the function of legitimating the minimalist role of the state and its indifference towards the accentuation of inequality.

Historically, social work fitted into the former agenda even though individual workers would probably have denied playing this role. In the British tradition their search for universal reference points to underpin their work found social science paradigms, the diagnosis of social deficits which prevented an adequate social functioning of individuals within the wider society. Thereby they engaged in the creation of 'subjects', both for their emerging discipline and for the new organization of the modern state (Philp 1979). From this perspective cultural norms were brought in line with the principles of civilization as a set of rational behaviours, for which in turn the state was the ultimate custodian.

For the German nation, created from an array of independent kingdoms by the uniting force of war against France in 1871, culture had a much stronger and more substantial function. The programme of national unification could not be grounded in religion or in unambiguous claims of ethnic unity, nor indeed did geography provide clear assistance. Instead, the dominant élite utilized the cultural arguments developed by artists and intellectuals of the romantic period which had in turn fired the call for freedom and national unity in the revolutions of 1848. This meant that the new, 'belated' nation state of the second German empire had to tread a careful balance between concessions to the 'progressive' national forces which had regarded national aspirations as the vehicle for democracy and freedom and the conservative definitions of a shared national culture. This shared cultural heritage placed the German nation in a sharp contrast to the 'mere', superficial 'civilizations' of neighbouring countries (Zimmer 1996). From both political sides, however, the concern for a cultural renewal and consolidation as the basis for national identity was not separate from but coincided with the concern for 'the social', that is, for social solidarity expressed in social policies (a term which was already a central reference point in the decades before unification (Wendt 1985)). This gave the state a very different role from the liberalism of Britain: it had to become the embodiment of an idea, it had to create its own heritage and it had to see that the organization of a civil society and the potentially explosive diversity of its polarized cultural positions fitted into this superstructure and supported it. Corporatism and subsidiarity provided the solution and allowed Bismarck to launch almost immediately decisive social policy provisions while at the same time enlisting the 'voluntary sector' into the delivery of those services, under the close and constant inspection of the state. With the simultaneous outlawing of the social democratic party he also eliminated what he considered to be the unpatriotic source of instability (Briggs 1961).

The pioneers of social work and the intellectuals responsible for the development of a distinct German discourse tuned into this political context in a unique way. They found in the concept of 'pedagogy' the means of treating the cultural agenda as a social agenda and thereby as a political agenda, while retaining, on the whole, a critical distance to any particular governmental pro-gramme. In this tradition, going back to Rousseau and Pestalozzi, culture and civilization were not exchangeable concepts but contrasts. Where civilization emphasized the appearance, the polite manners, the outward conformity, culture was an inherent value. People's artistic products can only be measured against the authenticity with which those values are expressed. The actualization of the innermost core of one's humanity is never an individual act, but takes place in the context of a social community, since human beings are social beings. This, rather than the need by a state system to create a uniform culture, constitutes the ped-agogical mandate, although as a social programme it cannot be fulfilled without the full participation of the state, which ensures its extension to society in its entirety.

Social pedagogy as the constitutive paradigm of German social work is, in this fundamental sense, a cultural project and one that extends far beyond school pedagogy and hence the notion of 'education' in the English language. The term is normally attributed to an 1844 pamphlet by Karl Mager for whom 'Pedagogy [was] the theory of the acquisition of culture' (quoted in Kronen 1978, p.223) and therefore not directed primarily at individuals but at society as a whole. The concept received its first full academic exposition in the work of Paul Natorp, who used the term in 1894 in the subtitle to a book entitled *Religion Within the Boundaries of Humanity*. Natorp's intention was to develop an alternative to both the individualized charitable projects which aimed at the rescue of individual 'cases', and the emerging procedural and instrumental formality of the 'social state' in which he recognized the assimilatory pragmatism of 'civilization' (Niemeyer 1998). Ultimately his concept could only be realized by the transformation of society (*Gesellschaft*) into community (*Gemeinschaft*, with explicit reference to Tönnies), a community which determines its own cultural and thereby social parameters. The formation of culture can only occur 'in a community, through community and as community' (Natorp 1894, p.85).

This approach was endorsed, quite spontaneously, by the movement which influenced German pedagogy permanently, the youth movement at the turn of the century. It started typically as a bourgeois movement, channelling all the disaffection which this class felt with the industrial landscape of growing urban prosperity. This *Wandervogel* movement (literally 'the wandering birds', as some of the school groups called themselves) set its sights on a cultural renewal through the suspension of the effects of civilization. They hiked through the countryside, lived communally in tents, connected with the music and poetry of folk traditions; and these became signals which heralded a new sense of community and a cultural renewal in which young people set their own parameters. Youth work organized by every sector of civil society – church, humanist and political – sprang up in the wake of this spontaneous movement in an attempt to capture (and contain) the spirit it had set free (Wendt 1985).

This 'social experiment' illustrates, however, the central dilemma of the social pedagogy approach. Can social pedagogy, by placing culture in such a central position, make a contribution to what was termed 'the social question', i.e. to overcoming the social divisions on account of poverty and inequality, and above all a contribution that is different from both the charitable attention to individuals and the social engineering and social control programme of the state with its 'civilizing' educational and social policies? Or, to ask it the other way round, what guarantees that the process of emancipation, the authentic articulation of needs, interests and desires which the pedagogical process wants to foster, will actually lead to a viable society not driven apart by sectional (cultural and class) agendas and by the weight of its own diversity? For academic German social pedagogy in the 1920s this became a real challenge as the Weimar Republic took decisive measures to develop a coherent social policy and to ground its legitimacy in a comprehensive programme of social reforms. The cornerstone of that reform is the *Reichsjugendwohlfahrtsgesetz* (Child and Youth Care Act) of 1922/24. Its opening article states 'the right of every child to education (*Erziehung*)'. This is not an affirmation of compulsory schooling but affirms the principles of social pedagogy: all children have the right to the pedagogical attention which enable them to become full and competent members of a society. This is very much a cultural programme to which academic social pedagogy had to provide the appropriate concepts and tools. Its cultural mission, which amounted indirectly to a political programme, was the identification and formulation of culture as the basis of community; an all-embracing community, which would supersede and obviate actual cultural differences and their divisive power within the nation state. It expresses a compromise between the demands of the youth movement (and numerous other movements and organizations) which insisted on giving their programmes their own distinctive cultural flavour ('youth can only be educated by youth' was one of the slogans of the youth movement) and the institutional interests for integration enshrined in the state, which could not allow for these differences to 'matter'. Above all, it meant to secure a professional (and existential) foothold for social workers and pedagogues in the nascent welfare state institutions without alienating the spontaneous initiatives (Niemeyer 1998).

Conceptualizing culture as a universal entity while holding on to the notion of an educational process towards 'higher' forms of culture meant grounding it in universal principles. In the intellectual climate of German academia two options were lined up to oppose each other vigorously. The positivist camp of the human sciences ventured to emulate the objectivity of the natural sciences to arrive at 'hard data' as the basis for their concepts of human behaviour and society. A key representative of this approach in the history of German (and indeed international) social work is Alice Salomon who pioneered professional training for women in the 1920s. Taking up the title of Mary Richmond's textbook of 1917, *Social Diagnosis*, she seeks to combine in her own version the social science based positivism, consisting in the accumulation of a comprehensive 'factual' picture of people facing social problems, with a pedagogical concept of learning how to overcome these problems. Diagnosis, as in the natural sciences or in medicine, 'means a short, precise and absolutely fitting explanation' (Salomon 1926, p.7). But diagnosis is not an end in itself, rather it enables a process of using the material jointly with clients to work towards solutions. Anticipating the principle of 'client self-determination' she cautions that this learning must be a shared process between worker and client. For Salomon this amounts to nothing less than 'the art of living', and since insight and resources are always limited, this means 'coming to terms with one's circumstances' (Salomon 1926, p.52). This comprehensive design of the helping process is for her grounded in the specific 'nature' of women outlined in a key text of an earlier date:

> (As women) we want to express *our* nature. We must help to create something new for which men do not have the necessary experience and for which aim they also have to search for new energies and ideas. Women especially are equipped for this new task with one quality. It is the sense of the totality of the people as an organism (*Volksorganismus*), the social idea, which grows out of the destiny of woman to be a mother and which gives her the special ability to go beyond her own interests and those of her immediate vicinity in her feelings and actions. It is this thought which has to become the foundation of the people's state (*Volksstaat*) ... There is no true democracy as long as the life of a people is split by class interests and troubled and torn apart by class movements and class war. The people's state requires citizens who place the interests of the totality above their own interests. In its true manifestation, in its ideal form it would not contain parties any longer, only vocational groups and guilds (*Stände*). (Salomon 1919, p.10)

Salomon struggles with the dilemma of unity and division at all levels. For contemporary ears these jarring sentiments have to be taken as an attempt at formulating a programme that could be described as 'universalist identity politics of social work'. They take their departure from an essentialist view of women and particularly of motherhood which they elevate to the status of a universal criterion of welfare and national politics. Different starting points no longer matter once they all become subsumed under a joint goal.

The alternative model was provided in the anti-positivist tradition, represented most comprehensively by Herman Nohl, the figure that was to shape the German social pedagogy discourse lastingly. For him, life as a spiritual process cannot be captured by objectifying psychological methods but only through the hermeneutics of understanding (in the sense of Dilthey). It is this life and its ultimately unifying force which Nohl identifies at the heart of the various social movements, labour, women, youth, as the autonomous pedagogical energy which social policy and pedagogical methods have to harness. The great movements of the nineteenth century have a converging meaning: 'an awareness of the crisis of our culture which lacks an inner bond with an ideal, and the will to resolve this crisis from within a new form of being human, of which the most central characteristic is a new sense of community' (Nohl, reproduced in Thole, Galuske and Gängler 1998, p.126). For Nohl, social policy and particularly the new youth legislation of the Weimar Republic incorporate all these aspirations, although not without tensions. They unite ultimately in the concern for bringing about 'the humanity in human beings' as the basis for solidarity, grounded in 'knowing oneself contained within a unity of meaning which goes beyond all understanding and embraces all communities' (Nohl, reproduced in Thole *et al.* 1998, p.128).

Cultural differences are recognized as important in both approaches to social pedagogy. But each method aims at transforming the inherent divisiveness of culture into an integrated whole. For this project the state suggests itself then as the embodiment of an idealized, purified form of culture that corresponds to the 'highest' qualities of human nature. It had been the dilemma of pedagogy all along, how to reconcile the individualized or at least particularized concerns which inevitably manifest themselves when 'freedom from imposed norms' is promised, with the need to represent those particular aspirations in an organizational form corresponding to all of them collectively and legitimately. If this 'coming together' of diversity into a whole is not to be brought about by force, it requires a construct of Hegelian dialectics, that the historical unfolding of culture at the level of society, its 'coming into its own', corresponds to the innate educational growth, differentiation and social development of individuals over the life cycle. Only then can it make sense to postulate as the essence of modern social pedagogical thinking 'that all social adjustment presupposes the development of special individual capacities, that the true service for the community is only possible when human beings experience in it a certain fulfilment of their personal essence' (Mennicke 1930, quoted in Thole *et al.* 1998, p.184). This is how it was put by the social democratic pedagogue Mennicke whose convictions later earned him a long spell of incarceration in a Nazi concentration camp.

The irony, if not the tragedy, was that while these pedagogues sought to overcome the antagonism between 'person-oriented' and social policy perspectives and programmes, between individuals and society, between difference and unity in a conceptual way and by consensus, the regime that came to power in Germany in 1933 achieved it in practice by decree – at a terrible cost. In a way the entire Nazi programme was a continuation of a specific German education programme, highly selectively applied but nevertheless within a strong line of continuity, through a devious combination of scientific and political means. Hitler's government did not on the whole abolish the institutions of civil society, the diversity of humanitarian and religious associations (not even the Jewish welfare association), it got them committed to a common national goal (*gleichschalten*). Nor did it rescind the pedagogical measures, even the 'progressive' ones, that were developed throughout the Weimar period and aimed at reform rather than punishment. But it operated the pedagogical process with a racist criterion of 'difference' as the crucial, absolute yardstick (with absolute consequences). Racism recasts cultural differences as factual differences on a scale stretching from the superiority of the 'healthy' to the inferiority of the 'life-unworthy' (Bock 1983). The device of racism, combined with a distinct anti-individual and anti-intellectual brand of pedagogy, sought to create unity and uniformity by absolute measures of exclusion (Sünker and Otto 1997). If pedagogical institutions, if indeed the whole country, could 'rid itself ' of ineducable cases then the pedagogical project stood a chance of succeeding. It would thus be possible to keep 'diversity' within such bounds that ensured the stability of society. A report on the improvement of success rates of residential pedagogical reform measures states triumphantly in 1937, 'As pedagogical care measures have changed fundamentally since the year 1933, not only by coming in line with the pedagogical principles of the national socialist state, but also through an earlier referral of children and youth to such agencies and through being relieved from responsibility for the so-called 'ineducables', we can expect that this change will continue to show positive results for the entire field of child care' (Ohland 1937, p.12; Sünker and Otto 1997). This 'unsentimental', seemingly scientific, rebuilding of an organic people's community (*Volksgemeinschaft*) appeared to represent all the ideals of a correspondence between pedagogy and social policy. In the process all the principles of both pedagogy and culture were destroyed and its true barbarity was revealed in the systematic killing of people who did not fit into the ideological construct of a master culture for a master race (Lorenz 1994). Social workers did not necessarily have to apply racist, culture-specific and fascist criteria consciously in their work; it was enough that what appeared to be value-free, scientifically based diagnostic classifications served the state apparatus to perfect its system of exclusion and elimination.

The training programme of democratic reconstruction devised by the Western allies and the UN, notably also for social personnel, failed to recognize the specific dilemma of the social professions in Germany. The measures were based on the assumption that under fascism social service personnel had come under the spell of collectivism, had blindly followed instructions, had sought to promote authoritarian obedience to a leader figure and had compromised their professional and scientific standards with ideological elements which actively promoted a master culture. Hence the emphasis of those USA and UN sponsored (re)training programmes in social, group and community work was on value neutrality, individualism and client self-determination. The case work model (and the equivalent models of group and community work) studied in the USA were regarded as exportable to every country in the world. This model espoused a liberal notion of formal equality and democracy in the public realm which relegated all questions of cultural differences to the sphere of the private. What was not recognized by re-education programmes was the profession's blindness to the misuses of their idealism under Nazism. This had been constituted by the assumed value neutrality of the universalism, on which the pedagogical concepts as much as the social science derivatives of early case work had been based. What gained prominence instead was the notion of self-determination as a guarantee of democracy. This led to a disregard for the importance of any kind of collective identity, be that based on national, ethnic, regional, denominational or gender criteria, at least as far as the actual methods of intervention were concerned. Case work and group work methods alike developed under this 'democratic' precept. The famous training centre '*Haus Schwalbach*' (a training and conference centre in Hesse established by the American military government) aimed at bringing about freely chosen identities, irrespective of any 'given' identity elements among participants in group or case work sessions (Müller 1988). The model represented a pure form of 'the liberal conception of the public sphere' in Fraser's terms (Fraser 1995). 'This conception assumes that a public sphere is or can be a space of zero degree culture, so utterly bereft of any specific ethos as to accommodate with perfect neutrality and equal ease interventions expressive of any and every cultural ethos' (Fraser 1995, p.290). Even the churches and the big secular welfare organizations, which retained their crucial role in the delivery of welfare services in Germany after the Second World War, did not articulate their differences in the form of distinct methods. On the contrary, they were keen to 'treat people as people' and leave their clients to seek out cultural reference points in the nature of the service as their private preferences but not as a condition for receiving a service. In fact the social professions generally were only able to re-establish themselves slowly in Germany against the widespread suspicion that the 'social' in their title was associated with 'socialism', either of the Nazi or, in the even more threatening Cold War climate, of the Communist type (Müller 1988). It took quite some time in post-war Germany for the re-establishment of the socio-pedagogical tradition and it was only possible under the protection of a 'universal' social work paradigm – even where this, as in the case of Gisela Konopka, Hertha Kraus and other consultants of German origin operating from their US exile, had many roots in social pedagogy.

In an effort to avoid all references to the divisive power of cultural differences social work practice and training in Germany (as in most other western countries) became committed to a scientific programme of individual need definition and fulfilment. This, in fact, amounted to a programme of assimilation to a prevailing cultural and political orthodoxy. The underlying assumption was that processes and forms of communal life at individual and small group level corresponded to those at the societal level, that micro- and macrocosms of social life were coherently structured. There was indeed an intriguing correspondence at the macro-political level where the bloc-mentality of the Cold War era relativized cultural differences between nations and gave rise to a widely shared enthusiasm for internationalism as a means of overcoming old fashioned nationalisms.

This ideological construct generated a considerable integrative force in Germany, not least with the relatively successful integration of millions of refugees from beyond the Iron Curtain (being a victim of communism meant being 'one of us'). However, it started crumbling in the wake of a wave of new social movements in the late 1960s and 1970s and came crashing down with the fall of the Berlin Wall and the revolutions in former socialist regimes. Those new social movements produced, among other things, new discourses of identity. Inequality, it was 'discovered', had not been eliminated but had been bracketed out, the seemingly neutral public sphere was exposed as a gendered, class-biased arena. Social and protest movements eventually also exposed the vacuousness of the case work approach and its democratic promise, and challenged the social professions to examine their implicit political mandate.

At the level of academic discourse, pedagogy made itself gradually more receptive to questions of identity and culture by shifting its field of practice decisively from the 'system' (of welfare organizations, laws and structures) to the 'life world', in Habermas' (1987) distinction. Pedagogy matters in 'everyday contexts' (*Alltag*, Thiersch 1986), not in carefully controlled and abstract clinical, therapeutic or bureaucratic spaces. Questions of identity are very much part of the life world, not in the pre-cast form in which the 'system' produces them, but as expressions of collective interests, dynamic yet fuzzy. Young people, women, parents of children with disabilities, and neighbourhood groups began to claim forms of self-representation which challenged the 'universalism' of received social work definitions. This triggered a new kind of 'learning process' that pitted itself against the weight of expert professional cultures in the same way as the youth movement had done at the start of the twentieth century.

And yet, these assertions of identity by social and user movements still did not amount to a fundamental challenge of the traditional ambiguity towards the notion of culture contained in the socio-pedagogical paradigm. This challenge came from two other fronts, the presence of 'foreign populations' in Germany in the form of migrant workers, refugees and asylum seekers, and the rise in violent nationalism and fascism among young people in the wake of German unification. In relation to the former, German social pedagogy, like social work and education in other European countries that encountered immigrant populations, made efforts to accommodate 'the phenomenon' within its conceptual boundaries. It concentrated its efforts initially on giving assistance towards assimilation and integration, developing a special field of 'pedagogy for foreigners' (*Ausländer-pädagogik*), and later, realizing the absurdity of wanting to level all differences by pedagogical means, on forms of multicultural and intercultural pedagogy designed to preserve diversity (Hamburger 1993). The sudden open acknowledgement of a multiplicity of cultural positions brought the full weight of the pedagogical tradition to bear; that is, the humanistic aspirations both for the full development of the inherent potential of each individual and for the procedural respect for the equal value of 'the other'. But these aspirations also revealed their limitations. How could imparting better knowledge about foreign cultures and the practice of tolerance in the classroom or youth club change the nature of racism and exclusion which the minority 'foreign' populations experienced in their daily lives, in the streets, in offices, in dealing with the law. Undoubtedly, the shift from integrationist to multicultural concepts was significant as it brought the notion of cultural difference and of the right to an autonomously defined identity into play. Yet it also highlights the ambivalent political role of culture and the limitations of the traditional pedagogical project: once a plurality of cultural universes has become theoretically accepted, often to the point of an uncritical fascination with the exotic 'otherness', it renders itself powerless to fight the inequalities that can be masked as cultural differences and which a multicultural approach appears to even sanction. This paralysis seems to have beset the whole of German social work and social pedagogy in the context of the realization of the impact of cultural diversity (Müller 1995). Exciting and imaginative projects have developed for and with ethnic minority groups, but the issue of racism remains hidden.

This also shows in relation to the second, related challenge, the rise in violence directed at non-Germans. The moral panic generated in the wake of attacks on hostels for asylum seekers focused on young people and particularly on those in former East Germany. While there is undoubtedly a serious issue to be addressed and the behaviour of these young neo-Nazis is by no means inconsequential, it has to be asked whether the framing of the problem betrays the historical and conceptual limitations set by the 'match' between the pedagogical and the nation state project in Germany. Firstly, it is interesting that the focus is so explicitly on the behaviour of young people, precisely the group that is always the primary subject of pedagogy. Giving pedagogical attention to their behaviour diverts attention away from more widespread racism in German society, especially as the most favoured approaches are termed *akzeptierende Jugendarbeit*, 'accepting youth work' (Scherr 1994). This implies that their lack of tolerance for ethnic minorities and foreign cultures should be countered by giving them, in the face of the 'mere diversity' of their obnoxious behaviour, a minimum of recognition as the precondition for any pedagogical progress towards greater tolerance (Krafeld, Müller and Müller 1993). Secondly, their behaviour is usually framed as 'violence against foreigners' (*Fremdenfeindlichkeit*), a term which sanctions the presumption that the defining characteristic of the victims is their status as foreigners. True as this may be in the majority of cases in the legal sense (although violence against people with disabilities occurs also), their lack of German citizenship is in itself a product of the German citizenship laws which make the acquisition of a German passport very difficult even for second generation immigrants. The 'diagnosis' therefore endorses an underlying assumption of essentialism in cultural differences. It does not allow the social and political construction of these differences to be raised in the process. Thirdly, the panic concentrates on the *Länder* of former East Germany and implies that they are culturally lagging behind West Germany where a multicultural society has gained greater acceptance. The approaches therefore reveal the old zeal of a combination of the pedagogical and the national project in Germany. This also manifested itself in the wholesale export of the entire welfare system, including the training courses for social workers and social pedagogues and most of the teaching staff from the West to the East.

At this moment a critical historical reflection on the place and function of culture in social work would have been of great usefulness. Contrary to the main thrust of pedagogical efforts in Germany around the issues of migration, cultural minorities and fascist violence the problems are neither of recent origin, created by the influx of foreigners and by German unification, nor are they specific to the relation between self and 'others'. Rather, the core problem is the inherent commitment of the pedagogical project to the national cause which ultimately seeks to suspend, sublimate and merge (to spell out Hegel's untranslatable term of *aufheben* in some of its components) diversity in one authoritative public norm.

This is indeed not just a German problem and social work everywhere has to confront the complex dilemmas posed by cultural diversity even in seemingly homogeneous societies (as for instance Ireland). Neither the withdrawal to the ostensible safety of positions of universalism and neutrality nor the uncritical acceptance of positions of cultural relativity and subjectivity will save the profession from being in danger of becoming a collaborator in power politics carried out either in the name of cultural pluralism or of downright nationalism and fascism. The issues posed by the 'struggle for recognition' which 'is fast becoming the paradigmatic form of political conflict in the late twentieth century' (Fraser 1998, p.19) should be very familiar to social work which is constantly negotiating difference, the right to be different, and equality, the right to be treated the same, in daily practice. It is in this daily practice that cultural norms and reference points have their role as part of people's historical continuity. But it is here also where they are being transformed at the same time, where people claim the right to break out from imposed identities and take their own position towards given 'realities'. It is therefore here that the clash between the politics of recognition and the politics of redistribution yields to the practice of democracy. Laclau has argued convincingly that while 'universality is incommensurable with particularity', it is utterly dependent on the particular for its actualization (Laclau 1994, p.107). This paradox is the precondition for democracy: a modern, fair and civilized society can only emerge from the constant attempts to reach a temporary consensus over the significance of personal identity and cultural differences. There are no permanent solutions to the dilemmas and clashes of interest of a multicultural, diverse society, but there are forms of social practice which promote a constructive transformation of those clashes, a transformation into social policies. By refusing to sides in the controversy between a neo-liberal and a communitarian conception of society, between the 'new binary' of modern and postmodern models of social policy (Taylor 1998), between the dilution of traditional collective identities and the stubborn, aggressive affirmation of nationalism, social work can indeed make a contribution to the realization of cultural recognition and simultaneously of universal human rights as the preconditions for a democratically constituted social public sphere.

References

Balibar, E. and I. Wallerstein (1991) *Race, Nation, Class: Ambiguous Identities*. London: Verso.

Bauman, Z. (1998) *Work, Consumerism and the New Poor*. Buckingham: Open University Press.

Bock, G. (1983) 'Racism and sexism in Nazi Germany: Motherhood, compulsory sterilization and the state.' *Signs: Journal of Women in Culture and Society*, 8, 3, 400–421.

Briggs, A. (1961) 'The welfare state in historical perspective.' *European Journal of Sociology*, 2, 2, 221–258.

Brown, W. (1995) 'Wounded attachments: Late modern oppositional political formations.' In J. Rajchman (ed) *The Identity in Question*. London: Routledge.

Donzelot, J. (1979) *The Policing of Families – Welfare Versus the State*. London: Hutchinson.

Flora, P. (1986) *Growth to Limits: The Western European Welfare States Since World War II*. Berlin/New York: de Gruyter.

Fraser, N. (1995) 'Politics, culture, and the public sphere: Toward a postmodern conception.' In L. Nicholson and S. Seidman (eds) *Social Postmodernism – Beyond Identity Politics*. Cambridge: Cambridge University Press.

Fraser, N. (1998) 'From redistribution to recognition? Dilemmas of justice in a 'post-socialist' age.' In C. Willett (ed) *Theorizing Multiculturalism*. Oxford: Blackwell.

Habermas, J. (1987) *The Theory of Communicative Action, vol. 2: Life-world and System*. Cambridge: Polity Press.

Hamburger, F. (1993) 'Erziehung und Sozialarbeit im Migrationsprozess.' In M.J. Gorzini and H. Müller (eds) *Handbuch zur Interkulturellen Arbeit*. Wiesbaden: World University Service.

Hill, O. (1883) *Homes of the London Poor*, second edition. London: Macmillan.

Hobsbawm, E.J. (1977) *The Age of Revolution*. London: Abacus.

Jones, C. (1983) *State Social Work and the Working Class*. London: Macmillan.

Krafeld, F.J., Müller, K. and Müller, A. (1993) *Jugendarbeit in Rechten Szenen – Ansätze, Erfahrungen, Perspektiven*. Bremen: Ed. Temmen.

Kronen, K. (1978) 'Sozialpädagogik: Zu Entstehung und Wandel des Begriffs.' *Sociologia Internationalis, 16*, 219–34.

Laclau, E. (1994) *The Making of Political Identities*. London: Verso.

Lorenz, W. (1994) *Social Work in a Changing Europe*. London: Routledge.

Lorenz, W. (1996) 'The education of the nation: Racism and the nation state.' In A. Aluffi-Pentini and W. Lorenz (eds) *Anti-Racist Work with Young People – European Experiences and Approaches*. Lyme Regis: Russell House.

Mennicke, C. (1930) 'Sozialpädagogik und Volksbildung.' In Hauptausschuss der Arbeiterwohlfahrt (ed) *Lehrbuch der Wohlfahrtspflege*. Nuremberg.

Müller, B. (1995) 'Sozialer Friede und Multikultur.' In S. Müller, H.-U. Otto and U. Otto (eds) *Fremde und Andere in Deutschland, Nachdenken über das Einverleiben, Einebnen, Ausgrenzen*. Opladen: Leske & Budrich.

Müller, C.W. (1988) *Wie Helfen zum Beruf wurde. Eine Methodengeschichte der Sozialarbeit 1945–1985, vol. 2*. Weinheim/Basle: Beltz.

Natorp, P. (1894) *Religion innerhalb der Grenzen der Humanität. Ein Kapitel zur Grundlegung der Sozialpädagogik*. Freiburg/Leipzig: Mohr.

Niemeyer, C. (1998) *Klassiker der Sozialpädagogik, Einführung in die Theoriegeschichte einer Wissenschaft.* Weinheim / Munich: Juventa.

Ohland, A. (1937) 'Der erfolgderdeutschen Fürsorgeerziehung.' *Deutche Jugendhilfe 29, 6–16.*

Philp, M. (1979) 'Notes on the form of knowledge in social work.' *Sociological Review*, 27, 1, 83–111.

Rattansi, A. (1994) ' "Western" racisms, ethnicities and identities in a "postmodern" frame.' In A. Rattansi and S. Westwood (eds) *Racism, Modernity and Identity – On the Western Front.* Cambridge: Polity Press.

Rojek, C., Peacock, G. and Collins, S. (1988) *Social Work and Received Ideas.* London: Routledge.

Salomon, A. (1919) *Die Deutsche Frau und ihre Aufgaben im Neuen Volksstaat.* Leipzig / Berlin: Teubner.

Salomon, A. (1926) *Soziale Diagnose.* Berlin: Heymanns.

Scherr, A. (1994) 'Kulturelle Jugendbildung – ein Instrument der Gewaltprävention?' *Neue Praxis,* 24, 5, 427–434.

Sünker, H. and Otto, H.-U. (eds) (1997) *Education and Fascism.* Bristol: Falmer Press.

Taylor, C. (1992) *Multiculturalism – Examining the Politics of Recognition.* Princeton, Princeton University Press.

Taylor, D. (1998) 'Social identity and social policy: Engagements with postmodern theory.' *Journal of Social Policy,* 27, 3, 329–350.

Thiersch, H. (1986) *Die Erfahrung der Wirklichkeit. Perspektiven einer Alltagsorientierten Sozialpädagogik.* Weinheim: Beltz.

Thole, W., Galuske, M. and Gängler, H. (eds) (1998) *KlassikerInnen der Sozialen Arbeit.* Neuwied: Luchterhand.

Thompson, E.P. (1968) *The Making of the English Working Class.* Harmondsworth: Penguin.

Thompson, J.B. (1990) *Ideology and Modern Culture.* Cambridge: Polity Press.

Webb, B. (1926) *My Apprenticeship.* London: Longmans.

Wendt, W.R. (1985) *Geschichte der sozialen Arbeit,* second edition. Stuttgart: Enke.

Zimmer, H. (1996) Pädagogik, Kultur und nationale Identität. Das Projekt einer 'deutschen Bildung' bei Rudolf Hildebrand und Hermann Nohl, *Jahrbuch für Pädagogik* 1996, 159–177.

CHAPTER 2

The Traumatic Dismantling of a Model Welfare State

The Swedish Model in Global Culture

Martin Peterson

The somewhat dramatic title of this paper is an indication of a much harder reality in Sweden in recent years, and speculations as to why this is so have intensified during the 1990s. The statistics for the erosion of European welfare systems do not look very alarming; however, it is the gap between what social services are available on paper and what is accessible in reality that has eroded the faith of many people in the good will of the representatives of society. When statistics say that people have little to complain about and their everyday life experiences tell them that in reality they are not entitled to anything because in actual fact hardly any adequate service exists, then people tend to perceive of themselves as the wrong people demanding unavailable services at the wrong time for all the wrong reasons.

In fact, an unprecedented soulsearching began twelve years ago in the wake of the murder of Olof Palme. This traumatic event suddenly removed trust in societal institutions. Anybody involved in the handling of this particular murder case would invariably be viewed as either unbelievably incompetent or as someone covering up the real facts. Prior to these developments Swedish society had had as a role model the good intentions of chronic innocence.

In one stroke, the faith people had vested in public agencies and authorities was badly dented. The confidence in Swedish civil society, separate organizations as well as other institutional actors, which had previously been unbroken, was also shattered. Under these circumstances capital deregulations of the most radical and sweeping sort plus a comprehensive and liberalizing tax reform were introduced. Clearly, for the credibility of both civil society and the authorities, a platform for a reorientation of policy was very much needed.

Any major change of policy programme had to be both well rooted among all relevant parties making up the foundation of the Swedish model and be competently handled by experienced professionals. On both accounts there were overestimations. Most participants were only superficially informed of what was at stake and, in most cases, had to be satisfied with that. Overestimation of feasibilities in the global market, in particular in relation to real estate, led to an amazing series of incompetent decisions and investments by both public and private interests. The major reorientation of policy coincided with an unsolvable murder case that led to protracted soulsearching.

Social Democratic governments have been in power since the early 1930s. The few interludes (1976–82 and 1991–94) that the conservative opposition enjoyed in power during the post-war period seemingly prepared the Swedish public for different values. In reality there always existed a strong continuity of dualist values in respect to two essential features: both centralized and decentralized role models which are well reflected in, for instance, the strong local representation and the strong central organization of the trade union movement; and a pronounced preference for both reticent socialist/collectivist and competitively profiled capitalist/individualist value patterns, which seem to presuppose each other.

To this dualist profile, which has represented a formidable asset to Sweden the nation state, three developments have created new preconditions: globalization, regionalism and multicultural society. The first two have effectively reduced the role of the nation state in a structural sense, while the third has provided a new content to everyday life. Together they have made the dualist profile, which required both structural and cultural homogeneity, somewhat dated as sole factors for a viable and self-ascertaining society.

Homogenous cultural norms and the identification with a language represent hard currency in national strategies. Hard core Swedish norms emanated from the so-called 'bruk' society (pre-eminently Lövsta bruk in the province of Uppland north of Stockholm, see further on), an eighteenth century social structure predating the value patterns of the authoritarian/egalitarian postwar welfare state. The Swedish language was famously cultivated in an analogous fashion to the French one through a Swedish Academy (with eighteen members rather than forty). The model to the rest of the world is in this respect manifested in the annual Nobel prizes for literature. The eighteen members of the Swedish Academy with their rich language-cum-literature background have a natural prerogative to select the most deserving writers in a global context. This is aligned with the institutionalization of a more or less permanent social democratic regime. When these cultural institutions were challenged by globalization and multiculturalism an agonized, confused and neurotic response was to be expected. It must be stated that reactions to these developments in Sweden could have been much worse and have in an overall perspective been less disturbing than in many other parts of the EU.

What has made the Swedish crisis more emphatically illustrative is the coincident economic collapse of the early 1990s, when industrial production dropped almost ten per cent, unemployment figures grew by one to two per cent to, in real terms, almost twenty per cent, and an across-the-board cut in welfare entitlements created demoralization and a profound sense of existential insecurity among large sections of a population that had grown accustomed to a feeling of self-righteous security. One school of self-pronounced Keynesian economists persistently claimed that every cut has been an unnecessary caving in to monetarism and that the crisis could easily have been avoided. The overall consensus, however, is that the global image of a nation in debt has eroded Sweden's credit-worthiness, which in turn has worsened economic conditions.

There have been cuts in allocations to social security, health and hospital care, education and cultural events. There is a notable inertia in assessing the direct effects of social cuts. From a state financial angle cuts have been very successful with regard to social security and health but much more problematic when it comes to care of the elderly. Total reduction of costs has been more limited than expected but redistribution between various sectors has been significant, to the detriment of most of those affected. The number of beds in hospitals has been halved in fifteen years (1980–95). Medicare expenditure was reduced by 20 per cent during the same period at the same time as the pressure for healthcare increased markedly. According to hospital authorities a danger level has been reached, where patients cannot expect to get the care they are entitled to through the tax system, which is already overly burdensome for the lower and middle income groups.

Income inequalities have increased sharply during the 1990s. However, Sweden still belongs to the group of nations where inequality in terms of disposable income is lowest. Only Finland and Norway have substantially better equality rates, while Denmark, Belgium and Ireland are on the same level as Sweden. More alarming is that the income gap between generations has risen very sharply. The young and the younger middle-aged have had palpably the worst income development. Prospects are even less encouraging since, due to a high rate of unemployment, young people are taking a longer time to complete their education and, as a consequence, their income begins much later and is less secure. The poverty gap (how poor the poor are in relation to the rest of the population) in Sweden had been on the decrease from the mid-1970s up to 1990. After that it increased again during the 1990s. Then the salient risk groups were the younger generation and immigrants, and in both cases unemployment figured as the main factor. Among other risk groups the more obvious losers are the less qualified working class, people of under 25, and single parents.

In the municipality of Gothenburg, for example, the number of those living entirely on social security allowances in 1993 had more than doubled compared with the number in 1983. In a population of half a million people up to 125,000 or 25 per cent were classified as living in poverty in 1995. These figures are certainly conservative. This is a consequence of unemployment, a fall through the safety net and then exclusion. These negative developments have come quickly. The annual amount spent per person on drug abusers, the total number of whom has increased considerably during the 1990s, is equivalent to the very high annual salary of a headhunted executive. One influential scholar on poverty economics, B. Gustafsson, blames it all on Swedish membership of the EU. Conditions concerning poverty have become worse since Sweden joined the EU in 1995, according to him, as Sweden tries to adjust to the social norms of the rest of Europe.

Concerning other diverse indicators such as housing, exposure to violence and political resources the picture is varied. Housing conditions improved markedly up to the beginning of the 1980s. During the 1990s conditions have polarized among classes so that the better-off have acquired more expansive housing facilities and the less privileged are living in much less space. A more marked increase in exposure to violence appeared only in 1995, when figures doubled. The figures for violence against immigrants were larger but not dramatically so. Much more alarming is the growing expression of worry about violence among large sections of the population, which has risen by around 10 per cent since 1980.

Regarding political resources the picture is very mixed. Membership of political parties declined drastically between the 1970s and the 1990s, when less than 10 per cent of the eligible population carried a membership card of some party. The same decline concerns active participation in the political process, which has decreased from 5 per cent to 3 per cent. The frequency of attendance at political meetings has gone down from 10 per cent in 1976 to 6 per cent twenty years later. Active participation in societies and associations describes a different reality: 3.5 million, well over half the adult population, are members of one or several associations. Almost 2 million, close to one-third of the population, have some kind of responsible task and only 8 per cent are completely outside any association in Swedish life. In 1995 more than 83 per cent of employees were members of a union, which represented a (mostly female) increase of 8 per cent since 1976. Membership was, however, much lower at times during the 1980s and in the early 1990s. The number of active union members has, on the other hand, declined by one-third at the same time as general interest in discussing political questions has grown in parallel with an increased sense of civic competence, which is expressed in an increasing number of appeals against decisions by authorities.

In 1997 a so-called democratic audit was carried out by an independent but highly regarded research institute. Swedish democracy was summed up as showing certain definite bright spots due to the vital participation in associations but public opinion of the popular Swedish government was low because of perceived weaknesses in terms of control over the agenda, the inadequate quality of public debate and intolerance among parts of the population. Similarly, a high decision-making capability was compromised by insufficient control over the financial resources of the states. The overall verdict on democracy in Sweden was, at best, acceptable.

In the following, the perspective given is very much an attempt to reflect the experience of the population at large, which tends to be more extreme than the one made evident in official versions. It reflects, sometimes in more reinforced terms, a general sense of fear, confusion and insecurity among people in Europe. Hopefully, it provides some of those premises from which individuals from various exposed groups and collectives handle issues of survival in a strategic way. Such ways of handling things are now becoming known for the first time in a comparative perspective through the results of the SOSTRIS[1] project. There is no question that the Swedish cases researched for this project have revealed profound changes and new features in Swedish cultural and social life during this past century. This has helped to show political and social developments in a very new light.

Dangers in deteriorating ethnic relations

With regard to a multicultural society no opinion survey data exists to provide information about the climate of tolerance in each municipality. Hence the indicators used are indirect ones. One periodical has taken it upon itself to chart the prevalence of racism in Sweden. The data collected has been used to make up a composite report, municipality by municipality, in the presence of the more obvious criterion of racism. Only 112 of the nation's 288 municipalities do not appear, which means that in almost two-thirds of the municipalities expressions of racism occur. In 23 municipalities there are four or more instances of racist opinion formulated. After the elections of 1994, right-wing racist and populist parties were represented on the councils of 50 municipalities.

The picture of Sweden towards the end of the century appears to be a far cry from the prosperous, racially unprejudiced welfare model of the late 1980s. During the first half of the 1990s it was common rhetoric among Social Democratic members of parliament to stress that at the time Sweden led the league of racist murders in Europe. Simultaneously anti-racism spread in a more profound way through layers of the population. The puzzling thing was that the authorities did very little to counter blatant racism in spite of the fact that many of the racist acts were unacceptably odious in character. Equally disturbing is the tendency of the courts and the legal apparatus to trivialize some of these crimes to the extent that for some time they seem to have been able to be committed with impunity.

Within legal circles the opinion is that prosecutors and the courts are reluctant to handle racist cases because of the risk of reprisals. Politicians and public

---

[1]   The author lead the Swedish team in the seven-country EC-funded *SOSTRIS* project (Social Strategies in Risk Society, 1996–99), which was based on biographical methods.

opinion makers are routinely threatened in the grossest of ways by activists of the radical right, who constitute small groups spread fairly evenly across the nation. The radical right movements are badly anchored and lack a basic infrastructure. In spite of these circumstances the police have forbidden their own representatives from going public or making statements on racism and neo-fascist tendencies. The end result is a dwindling faith on the part of the public in the legal system.

Instead of massive measures to root out neo-fascism once and for all, rather defensive postures were taken up to the beginning of 1998. The turning point was the passive police attitude to an illegal neo-Nazi demonstration in the heart of Stockholm on 7 November 1997, the day before the anniversary of the Kristall-nacht, where openly anti-semitic slogans were heard for the first time since the war. The police at the time concentrated on clamping down on anti-racist opposition at the illegal demonstration. The criticism was scathing afterwards. Since then more of a proactive approach has been taken by the police against neo-fascist activities on Swedish territory.

There are by definition deficiencies in the markedly positivist Swedish legal system in relation to multicultural matters. Legal positivism has never been easily adaptable to changing conditions. There is a growing realization in legal circles today of acute shortcomings when it comes to adequate protection of immigrant rights. Here British legislation against racism is held up as a model. Flexibility is the new catchword among jurists, which, for them, has an odd but nevertheless innovative ring to it.

The month of January in 1996 was dominated by another incident, which illustrated the growing credibility gap in the relations between the public and the polity. A Kurdish family from Turkey, who had lived in Sweden for some years and whose children had assimilated extremely well into Swedish society, were ordered back to eastern Turkey where certain death awaited them.

Significantly and symptomatically public opinion was outraged and a substantial number of people, adults as well as schoolchildren, from the northern Swedish town where the Kurdish family had been living, took action in order to obstruct the implementation of the government's extradition order. In short, a notably united Swedish civil society rose furiously against what was perceived as the callous and incompetent government machinery. The government responded by threatening more similar extraditions in order to make it clear who was in authority.

If anything, this case proved that in spite of the crises during the 1990s, which would have been expected to increase ethnic tension in the nation, a growing public opinion defended the presence of a multicultural society. It is rather the puzzling behaviour of the authorities that creates confusion. Irrespective of political regime the state has on a number of occasions acted as if it were trying to placate a racist public opinion. In recent months it has tried to improve its image in this respect. Overall, although it was feared that instances of racism would grow in the wake of the sharp rise in the mass unemployment of the 1990s, this situation has been less severe than anticipated. There have been worse cases elsewhere in Europe. Moreover, it was immigrant groups who were most badly hit by unemployment. From having had an employment rate that was higher than that of Swedish nationals, recently immigrant employment has plummeted to between 30 and 90 per cent. The statistics on living standards give a united picture of immigrants from outside the Nordic countries as having about half of that of the average Swede with regard to facilities such as houses, cars, household appliances, etc., whereas Nordic immigrants have access to about 90 per cent of the facilities available to Swedes.

At present the Swedish government is spending the equivalent of almost 100 million pounds, taken directly from the development assistance budget, on repatriation schemes. Among the Somalians (who incidentally are, in most cases, equipped with Swedish citizenship documents because Sweden does not recognize the Somalian government), unemployment has become virtually 100 per cent during the economic crisis of the 1990s. The Swedish authorities are organizing courses in development aid consultancy for a number of those Somalians, whom they want to repatriate, so far with scant success. The Chilean and Argentinian refugees of the 1970s have been more willing to let themselves be repatriated although this has often led to disappointments and a frustrated return to Sweden where they have to start again at the bottom of the ladder.

It is far from an exaggeration to suggest that Swedish immigration policy has reached an impasse. In 1975 Swedish immigration policy stood out as a model (see below). It was largely the work of one dedicated man, an earlier ambassador to China, who, during the late 1960s, took it upon himself to investigate how immigrants looked upon Swedes after many years of living in Sweden. He met with despondency in many cases. The host population appeared as total strangers to most immigrants.

Those who had been handpicked in Italy during the 1950s for work in two particular industries, ASEA (today part of the Swiss-Swedish multinational ABB) and SKF (the ball-bearing factory), mostly stayed on in the respective municipalities, Västerås and Göteborg. The Yugoslav labour immigration that was recruited at approximately the same time tended to be spread more widely. Labour immigration was followed by political refugee immigration during the 1960s and 1970s. It clearly became time for a coherent and systematic immigration policy. In 1972 a new state agency for immigration was established with the original pioneer at its head. In 1975 a multicultural immigration policy was drawn up. In 1984 a state committee on discrimination noted that public opinion was becoming increasingly less prejudiced. Hence the racist excesses of the 1990s and the passive, almost condoning, reaction on the part of the government authorities were met with alarm and as a gross betrayal by those who had pioneered the enlightened immigration policy.

Even though in Swedish society more people than ever before are accommodating themselves to a future multicultural society, in the larger municipalities there has been an escalation of paranoid racial confrontation, caused in part by the unplanned immigration of, for example, Bosnian and Somalian refugees and their consequent built-in segregation. Militant groups of immigrant youth are regularly confronting racist local groups. This gives suburban immigrants the strength to stand united, with a cementing of solidarity that crosses ethnic boundaries. At the same time the police, reinforced by bored security officers from the post cold war period, have stepped up their close watch of immigrant quarters with zoom lenses and other 'spy catching' devices.

The economic plunge: from third to eighteenth position

In the early 1990s the Swedish economy became a shambles. A steady inflationary economy, where for a long time it had paid to borrow, and borrow heavily, was drained of its energy and transformed into a deflationary economy where it did not pay to borrow. All the capital placed by Swedish credit institutions in 'safe' investments abroad, such as in speculative real estate, was blown away. Members of the Swedish polity had to a surprising extent assumed leading positions in these credit institutions. Once again the limited competence thus demonstrated in handling another sensitive matter put the nation at great risk. What people could see this time was an international speculative economy co-existing with ridiculously high sums of money paid as retirement compensation to those executive mediocrities who had caused the disaster, while, at the same time, the wage earners' social security allowances, on which many households depended, were substantially reduced.

Ever-growing numbers of people now have great difficulties making ends meet. This affects the lives of children, who are growing up in deprivation and see no way out. The stark class differences, which have emerged as a result of these conditions, have reduced buying power and the rate of consumption that is essential to economic growth. The downward spiral in the economy was due to a loss of market shares in the export sector and a worsening situation for the small to middle-sized firms making up the sector of subcontractors. Both these developments were the effects of a long-term neglect. Hence Sweden has dropped in the last few years from her habitual second or third place to eighteenth place in the economic league table, ahead of only Portugal, Greece and Spain.

The political effects

The custom of rewarding people with top positions after they had been sacked for their incompetence was not confined to the private sector. Golden handshakes encompassed the public sector as well as the scrutinizers themselves, the media.

This recent pattern of establishment behaviour indicates a loss of control, perhaps deliberate, of the belief patterns of the welfare state model. This was mirrored in two surprising events at the poll in 1996. One was that the Conservative party came out ahead of the Social Democrats when they were not even equal with the Social Democrats in the monthly opinion polls. The other was that for almost a year the numbers supporting the Greens and the Leftist party together were as great as those supporting the Social Democrats. In real terms this surpassed even the political polarization of the first faltering years of parliamentary democracy in the 1920s.

Civil society reacted strongly. A number of nation-wide unemployment organizations and movements were set up in various locations. The rage on the part of a whole generation of middle-aged people on the one hand and the young on the other, both of whom felt equally cheated but from different points of departure, was manifested in actions directed at the state. The former group had lived according to their beliefs and could never regain the life they had been groomed for. The younger generation on the other hand got the message that they faced a bleak future unless they fended for themselves with socially disloyal acts. This break with the social learning process was manifested in the new redundancy movements. A newly unemployed single mother in her early thirties and with four children became the figurehead of the most headline catching of these movements during the latter half of 1996. The First of May demonstrations in 1997 became demonstrations against the mainstream of the Social Democratic party. However, none of the new movements brought about any ideological debate nor any alternative strategies to speak of. In the end they turned out to be loyal to the main monolithic body of the labour movement and had just hoped to exert some influence upon it. A peculiar feature in Swedish political culture was again illustrated: Sweden has perhaps the world's most transparent state system, where every piece of information is not only wide open for the sake of openness but also, accordingly, susceptible to harsh and damaging criticism; however, little of this is of consequence in practice since as a body politic the state system remains unchanged.

By early 1998 the Social Democrats had recovered some of the lost ground at the expense of the Conservatives. The Greens and the Leftists had lost ground, though more marginally. Both have declared themselves eager to enter a coalition government with the Social Democrats, a prospect that was unthinkable only a couple of years ago. The economy is again more balanced but still at the expense of living standards for very large sections of the population, who experience a steadily worsening quality of life. The obvious desire on the part of the current Social Democratic government to keep as much control of the economy as possible, while at the same time recognizing the overriding importance of being cleared by the global market forecasters, has guided its decision to wait and see when it comes to joining the EMU. This attempt to balance two opposites is symptomatic of the ambiguity of the economic situation, which is one of the people's main preoccupations.

Energy double-speak

In 1980 a referendum took place on the future energy policy. The crucial question was: nuclear power or not? As those canvassing for a no vote acquired a clear majority in the polls those political parties – the Social Democrats and the Liberals – which were dependent on a growth economy with nuclear power as a chief ingredient devised a compromise. It said that the nuclear power already in use should be kept until 2010 when alternative sources of energy would replace it.

Fifteen years after the referendum and before the abolition of nuclear power it appeared obvious that the commitment to the compromise line could not be honoured. The accumulation of structural crises made it impossible for those political parties constituting the Swedish polity to abolish the prevailing production system without at the same time abolishing themselves. The risks involved in retaining a dependency on nuclear power stood against the risks of abandoning adjustment to a global economic system.

How has this state ever been allowed to arise? Can it be remedied quickly enough or at least within the foreseeable future? At present there is no doubt that the infrastructure is firmly in place. The adjustment to the IT world is more established than in most nations. In a formal sense no obvious shortcomings or shortages of essential needs exist. However, the great vulnerability inherent in the ambitious original design of the Swedish model was incrementally exposed as the economy was strained, the welfare system provided less and those public service employees who tried to preserve standards became so overburdened that their perspectives began to become illusory.

The impact of la longue durée

Obviously for an adequate grasp of the turbulent and sometimes traumatic events of the mid-1990s we have to go back some time in history. Moreover the new situation of crisis in the present precipitates a re-evaluation of the past, and in particular of the forms and nature of 'solidarity' which have been so central to national identity.

Modern Sweden with its common language and the perception of a unique culture developed during the course of the eighteenth century. A semi-feudal institution of exceptional importance was established during this period. This was the 'bruk' community which grew up around a foundry or a paper mill. It had a strict patriarchal hierarchy, where the social well-being of all the layers of the community depended on working together for commercial results.

In short, it was an embryonic welfare state in a *gemeinschaft* frame. With the launch of modern capitalist society towards the end of the nineteenth century, the 'bruk' community was at once in trouble. The patriarch–owner, whose Swedish title actually was '*patron*', typically did not sell off his assets in order to transfer business to more lucrative domains. Like a model *gemeinschaft* patron he looked to the well-being of the community members first and sank with them rather than abandon them.

Although the relative closeness between production managers and workers in the '*bruk*' environment eased up, it did not disappear, whatever social barriers there were between professions. The combination of a highly centralized state apparatus with a fairly harmonious balance between the major regions, where no one part colonized the other, created ideal conditions for the founding of a modern corporate society. In 1908 the first ever corporate social security system was instituted on a national level.

Another well known institution, the Academy of Engineering Sciences, was established some few years later to guarantee close ties between the state and industry. In the mid-1920s a treaty was signed between the employers' federation and the trade union federation, where common goals on rationalizations for growth and profits were agreed upon. Wages would be duly affected. It meant the beginnings of a subsumed collaboration, a hidden contract on the shop floor, which in 1938 was crowned by the agreement between employers and labour to settle wage and other labour-related issues without any intervention by the state.

In reality it meant that any working class lad could cross the so-called class divide to become first engineer and then enter management without much ado. Class difference and class antagonism certainly existed in vigorous forms but were greatly alleviated by the close contacts on the shop floor. There was no sign of any preparedness to institutionalize industrial democracy since the hidden contract was ultimately ruled and mutually controlled by representatives at the top of each federation. In the wake of the Second World War, however, proposals for increased industrial democracy, i.e. control of production from below, were indeed presented. But they shared the fate of similar proposals in other nations as they were shelved and replaced by a centralized welfare state that relied on redistributive fiscal policy.

The whole welfare state conception is in line with the *raison d'être* of social science inherent in the project for modernity. In the pluralist division of pedagogy the task of natural science was to establish facts and create laws, the mission of social science was to promote ethical norms and social justice, and the humanities were to sensitize and predict. However, in the developments of social engineering during the 1930s, the aim of which was to hasten the emancipation process of the Swedish working class, the social policy concept of modernity was distorted.

'Social engineering' was borrowed from Saint Simon. He did, however, develop his ideas around social engineering in a completely different environment. Only this circumstance would be enough to distort its original intentions in the strained environment of the 1930s. Nevertheless, social engineering was launched as a short cut to the good society. The results were ambiguous. If ever the notion of 'de-commodification' (Esping-Andersen) was realized it was here and much more so than at any time during the post-war period.

For instance the 'collective house' was seen as the solution to the household problems of professional women, who were to be relieved of those tasks which a collective could handle in a much cheaper and more rational way. What was more, the collective house was rational in an urban environment with forbiddingly high prices on land and construction sites. Child minding was obviously included among its main tasks. But children were not to be emotionally engaged – that would only hamper their choice in life. Nor should physical contact between parents and children be encouraged.

The important aspect concerned the negative influence of the nuclear family upon not only children and child rearing but upon society as a whole. The nuclear family was seen as inherently pathological in that it generated a neurotic individualism. Children had to be saved from this socially debilitating institution, which also bred a negative political culture. Public space for socialization of children was crucial for an improved political culture (Myrdal and Myrdal 1935, p.189).

The most dubious part of social engineering was, crudely speaking, reserved for the cleansing of less wanted elements or the reinforcement of the working class stock, which could easily be translated into the national stock. If the less privileged classes could be rid of those elements, such as demented or physically handicapped people, who enfeebled them, they might emancipate themselves to become one day a dominating influence over society. Sterilization programmes of impressive dimensions were carried out so as to attract eager students from Nazi Germany (Broberg 1983, pp.178–220). Amazingly they lasted until 1976 – well into the humane welfare state. This fact had been publicly known for many years in Sweden although it was only revealed to the rest of the world at the end of August 1997.

In other words, social engineering effectively negated the ethical norm. The horrifying consequences of the Second World War produced a radical change in approach. This has recently been explained partly by the more than doubtful role played by Sweden during the war. This issue was not brought into public debate until the 1990s. Rather the advanced welfare state, which was strongly directed to alleviate the conditions of the weak, is now seen in a new light. It was one way of handling a bad conscience without admitting any guilt.

The model welfare state

If Sweden was able to present the most advanced welfare state where even the weak and the handicapped were fairly well off she could simply not have played any suspect part during the war. A social policy catering to the weak and a corporatist economic model based on eminently liberal principles constituted a subconscious but nonetheless progressive compensation for a bad war conscience. The overall system, however, testified to a genuine concern, which became a prominent part of both national and political culture. Indeed it assumed the role of a national ethos.

The new social security system, which became largely finalized after a plebiscite on the pension system in 1957, was meant to be paid for by the few to the many. This did in fact happen. It further aimed, through the specific wage earners' policy for solidarity, at levelling off income differentials between branches, professions and the sexes. By the early 1980s this policy had reached its maturation. From 1983 onwards solidarity lessened considerably. Like any well-entrenched system it did not give in immediately; however, it produced its own preference groups. This was a process that preyed on solidarity, which after all was the very element making both the social security system and the solidarity of the wage policy into the cornerstones of the Swedish model.

The disposable incomes of households in European nations at the beginning of the 1980s was least unequal in Sweden, Norway and Finland (Korpi 1995, pp.132–136). These three nations had the same relatively comprehensive social security system in common. It implied general programmes for all citizens and income-related remuneration. In nations with only a basic security system, such as the United Kingdom, the Netherlands, Switzerland and Canada, inequality in income distribution tended to be much greater. Inequality was also much more conspicuous in Australia, which has means-tested pensions, health compensations and unemployment benefits.

Means testing and the basic security system do indeed yield more actual redistribution than income-related remuneration systems. The snag is, however, that since the higher income earners do not get very much out of those systems, in spite of Lord Beveridge's aims and intentions, compared with the income-related model, they tend to become increasingly reluctant to pay for such systems. The more privileged groups prefer to opt for private insurance solutions. The public systems will then only concern those who are least well off. Hence the resources to redistribute will inevitably shrink in those systems.

Social mobility may be hypothesized to affect thinking on social security systems. Social mobility is also the most prominent indicator of the 'openness' of a society. Sweden has had a social fluidity that is second to none in Europe and comparable to that in North America. The causes are, however, different in the sense that, whereas the 'land of opportunity' notion has influenced the North American case, it is more the absence of feudalism in rural Sweden and the land of social emancipation and opportunities inherent in the political culture that distinguishes Sweden.

During much of the post-war period the welfare state appeared to have an unproblematic strategy towards equality. At the beginning of the 1980s, however, a British economist, Julian Le Grand, claimed that inequality was reinforced by welfare state interventions. Yet the Swedish welfare system tried explicitly from the start to steer clear of such effects by inventing a Robin-Hood-in-reverse system based on the Gospel-according-to-Matthew principle – 'to him who has shall be given'.

With a general model of income-related remuneration and corporatist status maintenance the more well off groups also have a vested interest in protecting and securing their own living standard. The inclination to pay tax for a public system will vary in relation to private solutions, hence there will be more to redistribute, and the more comprehensive the system the more there will be to redistribute. Thus the Swedish social security model, which nominally gives more to the rich than to the poor, does in the final analysis bring less inequality than other systems (Korpi 1995, pp.138–144). This Robin-Hood-in-reverse, which yields less inequality in the end, shows how wedded to Saint Simonian thinking (the one on the bottom rung improves his position substantially without reducing or jeopardizing the one on the top rung, who gains in a relative sense) Swedish social policy ethos remains. From this thinking there is a straight line to John Rawls' *A Theory of Justice* and in particular the seven chapters on the principles of justice, where he discusses the institutional aspects of formal justice, equality of opportunity, the basis of expectations and the principle of fairness.

Rawls has had a redoubtable effect upon much of the recent Swedish debate. Up to the latter part of the 1980s the better-off groups may often have contemplated violations of the general model rules but eventually refrained from such action. A non-compliant behaviour hardly risked sanctions but could be exposed, which was deemed to be much worse. The sensitivity to social opprobrium that accompanies violations of widely accepted behavioural prescriptions and rules has notably ensured adjustments to public virtues or what otherwise could be called the moral community (Rawls 1971, pp.54–114). Thus the general appearance of a tendency to decommodification was upheld, although the implication and meaning of this concept was not easy for a wider public to understand. There was no mobilization strategy emanating from it other than vague calls for moral instead of material incentives.

In the latter part of the 1980s, with the deregulation of currency and credit facilities, new rules of the game followed. A sudden abundance of accessible capital created a new climate where new market-adjusted expectations could find private solutions. Hence, contracts with built in 'parachutes' began to become increasingly standard. Anyone in even a moderately high position who was sacked for incompetence after six months would inevitably have negotiated a parachute contract worth several millions. That clearly secured a very comfortable future life-style.

Such parachute contracts became in varying forms the norm all over the western world. In *The State We Are In* Will Hutton (1996) mentions their existence in the UK (the golden handshakes) as another sign of the depreciation of public morale and indeed the political culture. This practice, not only in the private but also in the public sector and among trade union officials, was unknown to the Swedish public up to the current economic crisis.

The Swedish economy found itself in severe trouble in the early 1990s, due to a long series of incompetent decisions by business leaders and politicians alike (trusted leading personalities of both communities had been conned into investing the general public's money into bankrupt business enterprises, hollow industries and suspicious real estate abroad). A wave of sackings started, first in industry and then closely followed by dismissals in the public sector, too. Parachute contracts came out into the open and profoundly shocked the public at large. The concept of 'de-commodification' had no further relevance, if in reality it had ever had more than a metaphoric significance to a fairly closed group at social science seminars across Europe. The outrage against the abuse of a deregulated economy has, however, not changed anything in real terms other than increasing awareness and political sensibility. New associations of networks consisting of the victims of such abuse make up unprecedented elements in the political landscape. The new situation has, on the other hand, created a completely fresh and incomparable contempt for the political class and a general distrust of public institutions.

It is under these conditions that the overhaul of the entire social security system has been called for by an increasing number of political parties, including the Social Democrats. There is no question that the public deficit has to be reduced in order not to create further hardships to the less well off. At the same time there is no denying that the social policy system has had a tremendously humanizing effect upon Swedish society. Opportunities for individual improvement, in a Weberian as well as a Dahrendorfian sense, rose steadily. This meant that the modernization process offered new, rewarding opportunities of changed life-style without compromising social bonds too much, while normally it would be hard to let one expand without cutting back the other.

If mortality among infants and men aged between 20 and 64 years could be any indication of equality and opportunity then the Swedish system has been vastly superior to other social policy models. Norway, Finland and Sweden, which have the relatively lowest numbers of poor people, also have a much lower rate of infant mortality. In a comparison between Sweden and the UK on mortality, risks among professional men are lower relative to social class. In the UK, however, the starting point is much higher than in Sweden and it rises much more steeply as the curve reaches the more unqualified and poorer classes. The connection between social class and mortality is much less pronounced in Sweden than it is in the UK (Korpi 1995, pp.143–146).

Statistics of this sort may on one level very well validate the post-war Swedish welfare system. There is no question that humanity acquires a more elevated level when opportunities are more evenly distributed. On the other hand there are some problems with comparisons of this kind. It is not certain that the general model of social security practised in Sweden, Norway and Finland would result in the same equality pattern in other countries. It is even likely that these three nations are uniquely well suited for this model.

Contrary to expectation the State Agency for Technical Renewal (NUTEK) recently (1995) found that in terms of income levels and basic material resources only negligible differences existed between regions in Sweden (Wetterberg 1995, pp.226ff.). All indicators suggest that the same is even more true of Finland and Norway. It may well be that the general model, the Robin Hood in reverse, is only possible here and would be a disaster where inequality between regions is more blatant. The glaring injustice of the well off in the more prosperous regions of more densely populated nations deliberately getting the same public benefits as the worse off in poorer regions would defy any welfare logic.

It is also probable that both the general environment and the industrial work environment in northern Europe tend to be less dangerous than in the rest of Europe. What is more, the scope of the secondary sector, i.e. the rate of industrial production and employment in industrial work, was comparatively more substantial in Sweden than in most other nations, with the exception of West Germany, which has always had the most extensive industrial sector in post-war western Europe.

A larger industrial sector inevitably entails a high rate of equality. Industrial products have set prices with little fluctuation. They are in principle available to anyone irrespective of social background. By contrast, the price of products in the service sector are much less subject to control and their supply is more restricted and hence less evenly accessible. More relative quality and their services being more prone to manipulations, contribute to making this sector more unequal and insecure and dependent upon the political climate. So there may in fact be a correlation between favourable natural and historical preconditions, size of sectors, political culture and social security systems and their combined impact upon quality of life, opportunities and rates of inequality.

The welfare state in question: the debate

The Swedish debate on which social security system to adopt is presently raging back and forth. It is clear that the political uncertainty here and the frequent changes in policy play a part in making people less motivated to act in a socially loyal way. Arguments remain primarily and safely within the confines of what is economically realistic and less about how society may be socially improved. Many critics, including leading Social Democratic ideologues, fear for instance that the general model is stifling the economic climate and inhibiting the kind of initiatives and entrepreneurship that they consider necessary for any post-industrial nation to face the new global reality. They argue that the decline of national mass-producing industries and corporate collectives fundamentally changes the content of social policy.

One argument is that people want to take more responsibility for their own social security, which may be seen as a logical step since practically all insurance and pension funds own shares in those globally oriented companies which are running the market today. There is a general view that it will take some time and radically changed political strategies before politics can match the market again in terms of who is in control. Until then it has to be recognized that cuts will hit all sectors of society even if the activity is vulnerable, such as medicare, nurseries, schools and education in general. Only by cuts across the board can a semblance of the general model be retained.

However, that is clearly not enough to maintain the humane approach in society. The health sector is presently subject to what is conceived as a 'healthy amount of competition between functions'. Cities have suddenly been revealed to be much more segregated than was known. The famous fragmentation of the post-modern society that is supposedly directed by global forces is undoubtedly a contributing factor. But urban segregation in Sweden has much earlier roots.

The serious matter is that both the Swedish economic policy model and the social security model have turned out to be far more vulnerable to economic setbacks than was earlier anticipated. While the going was good the question of compatibility between equality, democracy and what is fair and just simply never arose. Today this question is as dominant as in the British debate. Those who separate fairness and equality are basically adherents of epistemic democracy. They are convinced that the democratic process will somehow come up with adequate and correct responses to social problems and questions. Equality is in their view merely a culturally embedded principle acting as a coercive force independently of either justice or freedom.

There has been a growth in idealist and voluntary activities (Amnå 1995). These are aimed at resolving the problem of shortages in the supply of regular services such as nursery places. The commodification of the nursery service for pre-school children has grown exponentially since the 1960s, when it was essentially free of charge but mostly catering to the needs of educated middle-class parents. As other less privileged social groups have begun to use their rights to this service, market principles have encroached upon the whole sector.

One crucial indicator is represented by the degree of employment among women. During the 1970s employment rose very rapidly among the female population. But this was only part-time employment. In the 1980s a dramatic increase in female full employment took place due to a major tax reform reducing basic taxes for the full-time employed. Then the economic crisis of the 1990s caused female full employment to fall equally steeply. There is a telling desperation, anger and apathy among qualified and semi-qualified women of 40 years of age who have become redundant for the first time in their lives and who have only dim prospects of finding any new employment. The authorities are creating so-called new life chance courses. These consist of analyses of the environment preceded by a 'positive breakfast', i.e. professional pep talk with popular versions of social trends and state affairs in order to keep up the mood of the participating women, but to little avail (Sundström 1993).

In Sweden new initiatives become rapidly co-opted, and idealist activities operate in fairly close contact with public authorities. They are far less disruptive than new social movements in other European political cultures. But their incidence is rising with the distrust of the political institutions: there are at least four new national organizations for the unemployed. A new political party is called The Justice Party – Socialists. It works hard against segregation and discrimination on the labour market and in housing.

The incumbent Social Democratic government has solemnly promised to reduce unemployment by half before the end of the century. Unemployment now stands at 9 per cent officially and 15 per cent in real terms. Some claim that the real rate is much higher still. Nobody believes the government's promise, which is not good for morale, since all other scenarios, in particular those outlined by regional authorities, speak of cost savings through the sharply rising use of automation and as a result growing numbers of redundancies.

Even though the redundancy situation stabilized in 1998 there is no obvious sign that it will improve in any sector. The government is intent on investing in raised competence in the public sector and has begun to recruit new pedagogic and health care personnel. But that is an investment that will take some time to take effect. Swedish economists at a smaller regional university college were asked by the European Commission to calculate how much unemployment costs in the Swedish context. The answer was 153 billion SEK, or more than the entire healthcare system. Between 10 and 20 per cent of those who have become redundant during the 1990s now need permanent medical care.

A particularly sensitive issue for the future maintenance of the welfare state system concerns the growing number of minority cultures. In the 1950s and 1960s immigrants from mainly Finland, Italy and Yugoslavia and somewhat later from Greece and Turkey constituted cheap manual labour for the expanding industrial sector. During the late 1960s and the 1970s waves of political refugees from Latin America, Asia and Africa followed. The 1980s and the early 1990s saw a less clear pattern of immigrants other than those pouring in from former Yugoslavia.

However, the general standards of education and the qualifications of immigrants, in particular those from Asia and Latin America, have on average been much higher than those of Swedes. Moreover, immigrants do generally constitute a fairly strong group when they arrive. To go into exile is a very hard experience for most people. To be able to settle in a new nation requires both strength and personal resources on the part of the immigrant.

Certainly there existed a very rooted *gemeinschaft*-type sense of responsibility for the weaker groups in the heritage of the *bruk* society. But given the orientation of primarily catering to weak groups by the Swedish social policy makers, and considering that immigrants were by definition classified as a weak group on arrival, Swedish social policy made weak and disabled cases out of strong and resourceful categories. This process is today known as the *clientelization* of the immigrant, which has grown very much worse due to the absence of ontological security in society at large. On the contrary, with the economic crisis and the sudden quantum-leap in unemployment figures the average immigrant began to feel instinctively that new employment was not for him or her.

In 1989 Sweden was still at the top of the list of advanced economies among members of the OECD. Some three to four years later Sweden had nose-dived to a rock-bottom position. And in 1989 the immigrant population had a 3 per cent higher rate of employment than the Swedish population. Three to four years later unemployment was approaching a catastrophic 95–100 per cent rate in the worse-off ethnic cases such as the Somalians. The redundancy figures for immigrants are at any rate far worse than those of any other group. It is not hard to tell which groups in society have borne the brunt of the economic crisis. This leaves the situation in multicultural but segregated Swedish suburbia extremely explosive, as described above.

It must be recognized that 15–20 per cent of the population come from, and still more are aligned with, a multicultural background. Of 1.6 million people classed as immigrants in the official statistics, about 60 per cent are first generation whereas the Swedish born second generation and their Swedish partners also belong to the overall category. The first well considered immigration policy was, as mentioned above, formulated in 1975. It was nicknamed 'Swedish vertical mosaic'. It took its point of departure in the ideology of cultural pluralism and the goals defined by the slogan 'equality, freedom of choice and cooperation'. This implied that the state gave the different ethnic groups possibilities to develop simultaneously a loyalty and affinity with the state and the majority population, while retaining and developing their own languages and ethnic characteristics. The state saw a value in cross-fertilizing the coexistence of several cultures. This was a decisive turn away from the assimilation policies and conformist ideologies prevailing in the 1960s and again in the 1990s (Ålund 1987).

Conclusion

In the 1990s the reality has become both challenging and demanding and social needs more urgent. It is quite evident that the welfare state as it was established during the 1950s was based exclusively on the idea of one homogenous Swedish nation state with one common language and one unique and coherent culture. The homogeneity was important for the cohesion of the welfare ideology. The principles of this welfare state remain those of the one nation, one language, one culture of the 1950s. These conditions are no longer viable nor are they in any sense adequate. The new welfare state will have to be built from scratch on the principles of a multicultural reality. To contribute to the realization of a multicultural welfare state, considering all the resources and assets of a multicultural society, remains one of our supremely difficult tasks of the next few years.

Only by recognizing the presence of a global context and a multicultural society can the new welfare state be re-created. The present one has turned out to be manifestly vulnerable. It has been built on principles which have ended up much less mechanical in terms of benefits, and far more demanding in terms of the need to cultivate people's qualitative social competence, than seemed to be the case in its original post-war 1950s setting. What is implicit in a welfare system – the need for a cognitive accumulation process in a demanding social context – becomes explicitly clear when it is deprived of its basic and essential foundations.

References

Ålund, A. (1987) Den svenska 'vertikala mosaiken', paper presented at the conference Social struktur, social mobilitet och social förändring. Umeå 23–25 April 1987.

Amnå, E. (ed) (1995) Medmänsklighet att Hyra? Åtta Forskare om Ideell Verksamhet. Libris Stockholm.

Broberg, G. (1983) 'Statens institut för rasbiologi – tillkomståren.' Idéhistoriska Perspektiv. Stockholm.

Hutton, W. (1996) The State We Are In. London: Vintage.

Korpi, W. (1995) 'År det svenska socialförsäkringssystemet långsiktigt hållbart?' In N. Karlsson (ed) Sveriges Framtida Socialförsäkringssystem. Stockholm: City University Press.

Myrdal, G. and Myrdal, A. (1935) Kris i Befolkningsfrågan. Stockholm: Bonniers.

Rawls, J. (1971) A Theory of Society. Cambridge, MA: Harvard University Press.

Sundström, M. (1993) 'The growth in full-time work among Swedish women in the 1980s.' Acta Sociologica, 36, 139–150.

Wetterberg, G. (1995) Det Nya Samhället. Om den Offentliga Sektorns Möjligheter. Tiden Stockholm.

CHAPTER 3

On Being a Social Worker
Globalization and the New Subjectivities
Steven Trevillion

Introduction

Some might argue that individuals no longer matter in organizations dominated by managerialism and that we should not waste our time on explorations of subjectivity when there are more important matters to be addressed. However, in many respects, individuals have never been more important. As welfare organizations, like other organizations, become increasingly complex, it is also becoming clear that if we are to understand how they operate and why they act in the ways they do, we need to consider the motivations and strategies of those that work in them (Hall 1995). It is impossible to do this if we do not also have some way of understanding what those concerned think about themselves and their work. This is a preliminary sketch for a new model of professional social work subjectivity. The distinctive feature of this model is that it draws on the concept of culture to resituate this topic within the interdependencies of practice and links the process of being a social worker with the new complexities of organizational life in an era of globalization.

While people have been asking, 'What is it like to be a social worker?', for almost as long as they have been asking, 'What is social work?', the attempt here is to inject a fresh note into what might otherwise seem a rather familiar debate, by making use of a number of key concepts such as 'culture', 'figuration', 'network' and 'technology', which owe more to the work of social scientists such as Simmel, Elias and Barnes than to the rather inward-looking traditions of mainstream social work theory but which can help to bridge the gap between the inner and outer worlds of social work.

Subjectivity

The conventional distinction between 'subject' and 'object' has been brought into question by a wide range of thinkers who have rejected 'Cartesian Dualism' (Sutcliffe 1968, p.21) in favour of alternative perspectives which stress the connections between these categories. But while most Freudians and Marxists have tended to retain a concept of the natural or essential self, however damaged by early childhood experiences or distorted by the effects of ideology, post-modern philosophers and psychologists have gone much further down the road of problematizing subjectivity. Some have even suggested that there is ultimately no difference between subject and object (Baudrillard 1981) and many would agree with Foucault that subjectivity is socially and historically contingent so that over time new forms of subjectivity have arisen as an integral part of the process of social change (Foucault 1982, p.216).

While rejecting the cultural determinism implicit in some of this recent work, a view of subjectivity as embedded in a particular time and place makes it possible to see the question of professional subjectivity in a new way. In particular, it opens up the possibility of thinking about the 'sense and sensibility' of contemporary social workers in terms of broader changes in the world of social welfare. Rather than seeking to establish essential truths about how social workers think, we might begin to enquire about the ways in which social and organizational change is influencing or reshaping the subjectivity of social workers.

Complexity and globalization

Of all the forces which might be considered to have contributed to the complexity of organizational life, the most discussed must be that of globalization. In recent years, the subject of globalization has attracted an enormous amount of interest from journalists and politicians as well as from academics. It has proved difficult to define in a satisfactory way, although there appears to be some agreement that while it can be described as a process of 'increased international economic inter-dependence' (Memedovic, Kuyvenhoven and Molle 1998, p.3), it also consists in part of political and managerial ideologies and trends. Perhaps one of the most succinct descriptions of globalization emphasizes its mixed or pluralistic charac-teristics by suggesting that it consists of a set of enabling factors (associated with economic and technological developments) combined with specific government policies and 'corporate strategies' (Van Liemt 1998, p.238).

But whatever the difficulties in coming up with a precise definition of globalization, there can be little doubt that the whole complex of economic/ technological, political and organizational changes which go by this name have had a major impact on organizational life and in particular working conditions and employment practices.

Within Europe, the public sector as well as the private sector has been increasingly exposed to the new emphasis on 'quality, productivity and flexibility' (Van Liemt 1998, p.241). Phrases like 'Total Quality Management' and trends toward the casualization and fragmentation of the workforce have become all too familiar to those employed by welfare organizations throughout the European Union, in spite of attempts to soften the blow of these changes through employment protection measures such as the 'Agreement on Social Policy' appended to the 1992 Maastricht Treaty (Van Liemt 1998, pp.242–246).

Any survey of recent developments in social policy throughout the European Union could hardly fail to note many of the distinctive characteristics of globalization (Trevillion 1997). These include deregulation in France, the increasing market orientation of services for older people in Germany (Lorenz 1994, p.164), the crisis in the Swedish model of welfare (Olsson 1987) which is leading to an upsurge of interest in the private sector as a provider of care service (Gould 1993, pp.197–198) and of course the continued growth of the 'mixed economy of care' in the UK (Griffiths 1988). To this might also be added the debates raging in Holland, Italy, Spain and elsewhere about the costs of health care (Trevillion 1996a).

At the same time, and again throughout the European Union, we have seen the rise of new forms of partnership and collaboration. These include the joint commissioning structures developed in the UK for linking health and social care agencies together in the strategic planning of community care (Lewis and Glennerster 1996) and the 'New Community Partnerships' designed to generate links between community groups, local government and local business and which can be found in almost all European countries (Macfarlane and Laville 1992). 'Private/public partnerships' of these kinds simultaneously face in two distinct directions.On the one hand, they can be seen as ways of opening up bureaucratic systems to market forces. On the other hand, they can also be seen as attempts to counteract the excesses of commercialization and marketization by re-emphasizing social and community values and promoting social inclusion. Therefore, in their own way, these partnerships are as much a feature of the complexities of globalization as deregulation and free trade.

While it is perfectly possible to describe all these developments separately and without reference to globalization, to do so would be to ignore the relationships they exhibit between the enabling forces of the market place, government policies designed to promote greater flexibility and the rise of new organizational forms and managerial strategies oriented towards the mantra of 'quality, productivity and flexibility'. As these are precisely the elements which most commentators associate with globalization, there is a very strong case for looking at their combined impact on individuals, teams and networks, even if they cannot all be reduced to the same cause.

How is the new complexity associated with globalization and its organizational implications affecting the ways in which social workers think about themselves and the world of social welfare? To ask this question means exploring the relationship between globalization and changes in the warp and weft of their everyday experience. To put this another way, is there a particular culture associated with globalization which all social workers could be said to share?

World system – world culture?

At the heart of the globalization concept is the idea of a 'world system' (Wallerstein 1974). It has now become commonplace to associate this with an increasing integration and convergence of social, political and economic systems and the creation of an international culture often described in terms of pop music, Coca-Cola and Nike trainers. While some have regretted the passing of distinctive national and regional identities, there has been a tendency to assume that this is just another chapter in the evolution of human society. Globalization has in this way been linked to the narrative of social progress, with the implication being that the development of a world culture opens up new opportunities and possibilities for individuals.

Those who have tried to justify linking globalization to social progress have usually focused on the cultural implications of the new communication systems associated with micro-technology. For example, Robertson argues that 'globalization as a concept refers both to the compression of the world and the intensification of consciousness of the world' (Robertson 1992, p.8). From this, we get the idea of the global village as the telecommunications revolution and the spread of capitalist markets together with the international division of labour which allegedly combine to create small, flexible and responsive organizations and networks which have a distinct evolutionary advantage over the large corporations. This is a persuasive image of ever-greater degrees of individual freedom and creativity in the workplace as well as outside it.

But the paradoxical nature of the global village concept has been noted even by its proponents. This 'global paradox' is usually described purely in economic terms – as the world economy grows so too does the tendency for organizations to get smaller (Naisbitt 1994). But this economic/organizational paradox contains a second cultural one, which is less amenable to the tenets of 'progress theory'. As organizations become smaller and potentially more diverse in terms of their orientation to particular specialist niches in the world market, they also come to resemble one another more and more in terms of their internal characteristics. So, tendencies towards both pluralism and self-expression can be matched by tendencies towards a degree of conformism which is usually associated with the allegedly defunct mass production culture of the Fordist age!

We also need to be cautious about accepting other features of global culture at face value. The much vaunted flexibility is frequently accompanied by fragmentation (Van Liemt 1998, p.245) which is not just a question of downsizing. For example, for many within the public sector in the UK, globalization is coming to mean the literal disappearance not only of large organizations but also the disappearance with them of job security, predictability and long-term strategic planning together with the marginalization of equal opportunities Whatever the advantages of the new markets and private/public partnerships, these personal losses are also inscribed in global culture.

All of this should make us question whether there is a single global culture associated with globalization. Economic convergence does not necessarily imply a convergence of meanings and experiences, even between closely related organizations. It may well be that different social workers in different organizations in different countries may be having very different experiences, all as a result of globalization. While globalization as a phenomenon clearly has cultural implications and therefore an impact on individual social workers and their view of themselves and the world, it is not at all clear that concepts such as 'compression' 'intensification', 'global villages', 'global paradoxes' or even 'convergence', on their own, really help us to understand very much about these implications. In relation to social work, it may therefore be better to use these ideas in a more limited way, as tools to further our understanding of the diffusion of some key ideas and the reconfiguration of working relationships. It is possible to illustrate this through the application of Robertson's concepts of 'intensification' and 'compression'.

Global values in social work?

Where studies of professional culture exist, they tend to support the idea that there has been a growth in universal social work values (Walls 1994, pp.218–224). These values are global in two distinct ways: first, because they are universalistic in nature; and second, because they have shown an ability to take hold amongst groups of professionals in many different countries. One example is the move away from institutional care towards various versions of community care in the UK, North America, Sweden, Germany and elsewhere. This has been accompanied by a considerable interest in a number of associated universalistic values such as choice, integrity, 'normalization' and user involvement and participation.

This global discourse of values may not translate readily into a common set of policies, structures or services, which is hardly surprising given the range of welfare regimes, political ideologies and levels of prosperity even within Europe. But, at the very least, Robertson's (1992) concept of 'intensification' provides a framework with which to begin thinking about the way in which some key professional ideas have been able to cross national borders. By itself, however, this is hardly sufficient to demonstrate the existence of a world-wide social work culture. For this, we would need to point to more than a few shared values.

Overcoming traditional barriers in social work?

In social welfare, the term 'compression' refers less to the reduction of geographical distance than to the opening up of new forms of contractual relationship and new patterns of linkage between traditionally separate sectors of welfare – voluntary, statutory and private. This process has undoubtedly gathered pace in recent years and effectively changed the nature of welfare as a social space by making it a more and more interdependent one. Computers and telecommunications have played their part in this and every new initiative seems to reinforce the trend.

These new kinds of welfare networks have not necessarily expanded choice but they have changed the nature of practice, not only in the UK but also in other parts of Europe, and as a result they have helped to change professional subjectivity, as well. For example, in the UK, the new Health Action Zones are likely to involve a wide-ranging process of what has been described as 'system re-design' (Peck and Poxton 1998, p.11) involving social workers and others in fashioning new kinds of links with different types of organizations. These kinds of processes must have an impact on culture and subjectivity as they entail major changes in roles and responsibilities. But beyond suggesting a greater awareness of interdependency, it is not clear what form this impact is taking.

To take this exploration of the relationship between the subjectivity of social workers and the globalization process any further, we plainly need to draw on other ways of thinking about social work culture/cultures in a global context. The most obvious place to look for such models is the longstanding debate about the meaning of social work professionalism. However, although this debate about professionalism and professional culture contains many interesting ideas, it is not at all clear that it contains much of value in relation to exploring any new forms of subjectivity associated with globalization, as we shall see.

Roles, tasks and 'professional' culture

One of the things that differentiates debates about the social work profession from that of other professions is the focus on heterogeneous concepts of task rather than homogeneous concepts of expertise. Many years ago, Martin Davies argued that 'there is no such thing as the social work task' (Davies 1981, p.3) and the dominant trend since then has been to define social work not in terms of one holistic identity but rather in terms of a number of complex and overlapping 'roles and tasks' (Barclay 1982). But this leaves a hole where the subject ought to be. Awareness of this problem explains the almost fetishistic attachment to statements about 'core values' in the contemporary social work literature, as it is these which are used to provide a foundation for what might otherwise be a rather shapeless aggregation of loosely associated activities.

Values

In focusing on 'values' as the key to understanding the way in which professional roles and tasks relate to professional identity, social work theorists have, in this context of epistemological insecurity, almost inevitably resorted to a Parsonian functionalism in which values serve to integrate a complex and diverse set of roles and activities. This almost inevitably produces highly conservative accounts of the relationship between subjectivity and social work practice – a discourse in which an unchanging core of integrative and defining values acts as a brake on change and pulls the practice system constantly back into homeostasis. It is simply not clear how such a theory can accommodate change, least of all the kind of fundamental change which is associated with globalization.

One other feature of the focus on values is that they have been regarded as something which is acquired through education and training, whereas in contrast, the process of working as a social worker is often seen in terms of a challenge to 'professional values'. In the UK, the introduction of care management and other social welfare practices which appear to have a new kind of value base has precipitated a spate of articles on the conflict between professionalism and the nature of day-to-day experiences (Simic 1995). Whatever the rights and wrongs associated with these issues, this focus on values generates a platonic image of professionalism as something timeless and essential, separate from or even opposed to the everyday and contingent world of practice. This is all very well. But if it is change in which we are interested, platonic definitions of professionalism provide little help.

Competences

When we move away from values and into debates about knowledge and skills, we seem to move even further away from any notion of what it means to be a contemporary social worker. Even in their own limited terms, statements linking any one profession to an exclusive body of knowledge and skill are problematic.

Although it might seem obvious that 'a person who is described as competent in an occupation or profession is considered to have a repertoire of skills, knowledge and understanding which he or she can apply in a range of contexts and organisations' (Jones and Joss 1995, p.15), we also know 'how difficult it is to find an agreed set of characteristics which distinguish the professions from other occupational areas' (Jones and Joss 1995, p.16). In the case of social work with its commitment to inclusive definitions and its orientation to task performance, the problems are particularly acute. For example, how do we distinguish between social work and other social care occupations and what is the difference between a social worker care manager and an occupational therapy care manager? These kinds of questions can easily turn into an obsessive type of academic pedantry which has little connection with the concerns of those engaged in day-to-day social work practice.

The response within social work has been largely to abandon holistic definitions in favour of lists of competencies. This tendency to *objectify* professionalism by examining the things that social workers do, has perhaps now been taken to its logical conclusion with the creation of a competency-based model of education and training by the Central Council for Education and Training of Social Workers (CCETSW 1989). Here the definition offered of professionalism is that of overall competence in all the defining areas of knowledge, skills and values. There is, however, a curious coda to this as one of the areas of competency is professional development itself ! This highlights the difficulty encountered in trying to comprehensively define professional subjectivity through outcome measures, and shows that even a competency-based model may be forced to recognize that there is more to professionalism than a bundle of specific competencies.

Models like this are designed to tell us what practitioners need to know to perform a specific range of tasks. They do not tell us anything about how individuals adapt to or make sense of change, nor do they locate the subject within a particular culture except in so far as the culture is represented by occupational standards derived from an analysis of the tasks which need to be performed.

Reflectivity

An alternative to the dominant behavioural model is that which is often described as the 'reflective' or 'hermeneutic' approach. Rather than trying to objectify the professional subject, this concerns itself with both social and intra-psychic processes and cognitions generated by the experience of doing and talking about social work. Drawing on the more general work of Schon and the communicative rationality model of Habermas, the emphasis is on reflective practice and constant dialogue with others as a way of making subjectivity more explicit and less divisive. Yelloly and Henkel argue that this answers the need for a practice model showing how 'the way the world without is inextricably intertwined with the world within' (Yelloly and Henkel 1995, p.9).

This turn towards the hermeneutic approach is helpful in once more focusing attention on the active role of the professional subject. But reflection by itself does not provide us with an altogether adequate concept of subjectivity. This is partly because it tends to exaggerate the role of individual agency and to reduce the role of structure to little more than a loose context within which professional identity can be constructed and reconstructed by individuals. Moreover, as the principal concern is with communication in a context of difference, the approach has relatively little to say about the way different subjectivities are constructed in the first place.

Without entering into a major philosophical debate about the nature of the social domain, I simply wish to point out that the questions we need to ask about social work subjectivity, at this moment, are at least as much to do with 'structure' as with 'agency'. The challenges to social work, as a profession, are being shaped by major social upheavals, which at their most obvious, take the form of new policy objectives, organizational structures and legal requirements.

The reflective approach can certainly help us to understand how specific social workers in specific situations go about making sense but it has little to say about general predispositions or cognitive maps, let alone questions about the relationship between professional belief systems, professional styles, images of others or types of intervention.

Beyond professionalism: social work and the new welfare organizations

There have been attempts to suggest that the 'new organizations' still need professionals who can be relied upon to operate according to agreed codes of conduct and to agreed standards, but even those holding this view have been forced to acknowledge the tensions between professionalism and the neo-liberalism associated with a market ethos (Broadbent, Dietrich and Roberts 1997). To this one might add that there are also tensions between traditional professionalism and the demands for increased accountability associated with at least some of the new organizations, especially those that involve collaborative partnerships of one kind or another (Finn 1996). If we put these problems alongside the more fundamental questions already raised about our understanding of professionalism and the culture of professional social work, it becomes clear that we simply do not have a vocabulary with which to explore the questions about culture raised by the globalization debate and which might enable us to grasp the elusive patterns of subjectivity emerging among contemporary European social workers as, day by day, they *internalize* (Best and Kellner 1991, pp.50–51) the 'social processes' of globalization. However we look at it, there is a need to explore the culture of social work in a different way.

Social work, subjectivity and culture

To attempt to make use of concepts of culture to answer questions about subjectivity may seem unremarkable to anthropologists or sociologists, but what is so striking about the literature on social workers is the way in which debates about culture have been marginalized. In general, culture is seen, not as something which social workers have, so much as something to which they need to be sensitive. So, for many years, we have had 'ethnically sensitive social work' and 'multicultural' social work. But as well as being of sometimes doubtful value in the anti-racist struggle (Dominelli 1988), these concepts tell us little about social work as a *culture*. This problem extends to the literature on professionalism itself. Part of the problem with the 'professional' models that we have analysed is that although they may present themselves as accounts of professional culture, they tend to make little or no use of the culture concept itself. This might go back to the essentialism characteristic of the professional project and the relativism associated with the idea of culture. Professionals of any kind, including social workers, may hesitate to embrace the culture concept because to do so could render problematic the attempt to anchor professional legitimacy in statements about the defining or essential features of their profession.

In so far as the concept of 'professional culture' does play a significant part in debates, it tends to do so only in as a way of explaining resistance to change, as in debates about interprofessionalism, collaboration and organizational change. In these debates, culture signifies a kind of defensive and ultimately irrational professional defensiveness (Trevillion 1996b). With few exceptions (Beresford and Trevillion 1995) the culture concept is rarely used in a positive way to describe new ways of thinking about practice, let alone new ways of thinking about social workers as subjects.

The concept of subjectivity has, in the past, either been explored on a case-by-case basis or has been assimilated to the concept of professional roles and tasks, neither of which have been seen in cultural terms. To some extent, the explanation for this resides in the way in which the problem of social work subjectivity has been articulated over the years, especially in the Anglo-American tradition. Instead, what will now be proposed is a cultural model of organizational subjectivity which focuses on the interplay between patterns of social interaction and those concepts of what it means to be a social worker, which are acted out in practice on a day-to-day basis.

The cultural construction of the social work subject

One major obstacle to the use of the culture concept is the number of different definitions of culture which have been coined, most of which are plainly unsuitable or unhelpful because they have been designed to explain traditional, relatively closed and unchanging social systems or because they tend to reify the concept, so that individual subjects become little more than representatives of 'The Culture'. One exception to this is the concept of 'culture' as an 'emergent' property of social interaction, which is associated with Simmel and Norbert Elias. This can help us to explore the way in which social workers as subjects are actively involved in the making of a culture which, in turn, defines their subjectivity.

Simmel was the first person to argue that society consisted of a web of social interactions. Building upon Simmel's work on interdependency, Elias began to relate individual subjects to a concept of 'figuration' which he defined loosely as a specific pattern of 'interdependent individuals' who are involved together in some kind of activity. In doing so, he self-consciously tried to create an image of culture which was actively constituted by individuals, rather than external to them and through which they developed their sense of identity (Elias 1978, p.15).

Elias pointed out that we are so deeply embedded in social process that we are literally carried along by our social networks. This provides us with a way of defining subjectivity which avoids both psychological reductionism and sociological determinism. The subject is located in 'the processes and structures of interweaving and the "figurations" formed by the actions of interdependent people' (Elias 1978, p.103). The benefit of this kind of thinking is that it provides a framework by which to relate changes in social work subjectivity to the increasing complexity of organizational life and the curious cultural paradoxes generated by globalization. More specifically, we can relate subjectivity to social welfare figurations consisting of characteristic patterns of interaction with service users, other professionals, employers, etc. without over-generalizing. For the first time we have a cultural paradigm which avoids focusing on the individual professional in isolation or standards of task performance or the specificities of particular casework relationships.

Another reason why the figuration concept is so helpful in the professional arena is that it can be used to explain professional subjectivity in a context of complex interdependency, without reifying the notion of culture or professionalism or implying that it is static or timeless. The idea that any one figuration exists within a 'figurational flow' (Elias 1978, p.164) is quite a powerful one. It enables us to locate particular contingent patterns of thinking/feeling within the context of equally contingent patterns of interaction and interdependency which can, nevertheless, be related to one another in time, and linked back to economic and political developments.

The figuration concept also contains an analysis of the relationship between culture and power. As interdependency increases, so complexity and power appears, to those involved, to pass from individuals to the pattern of interdependency or figuration, itself (Elias 1978, pp.71–103). Of course, for social workers, this is not a recent phenomenon. Social work has always involved complex figurations and social workers have probably always felt that power has in some way slipped away from them to legal and organizational systems of one kind or another. The relationship between social workers as subjects and their social worlds has therefore always been profoundly cultural. What may have changed, however, are the patterns of social interaction and therefore the figurations within which the social work subject is situated and which mould his or her sense of self and relationship to others. Intensification, compression, convergence, downsizing and the move towards complex partnership arrangements and inter-organizational networks can all be seen as major transformations of the social work figuration and globalization, which can also be seen as a dynamic factor influencing the direction of the figurational flow.

One consequence of thinking about subjectivity in this way is that it becomes impossible to limit the discussion to the idea of being a member of a profession or even being a member of a team or organization. Elias encourages us to link one pattern of interdependency with another. We are forced to think about subjectivity in the context of networks of social relations which flow across all conventional boundaries: '... a functional relationship which stretches right across the world' (Elias 1978, p.103).

This generates a new kind of approach which links the study of subjectivity to the sociology of knowledge in an integrated way. But it is not just a question of 'how do people [in this case social workers] perceive and conceptualise the changing and growing webs of interdependence in which they find themselves bound up' (Mennell 1974, p.84). It is also a question of how the figuration influences the way they see themselves.

Unfortunately, the concept of a 'web of interdependency' is so fluid and open that it is very difficult to define figurations in ways which are specific enough to be related to specific aspects of subjectivity. This might not matter much if we were concerned only with generalities but if we want to pursue particular lines of inquiry about the relationship between subjectivity, social work practice and social interaction we need some way of focusing on a particular zone of social interaction which can be related systematically to the experience of being a social worker. In particular, for our present purposes, we need a way of doing this which also captures some of the key issues around globalization at the level of social interaction as well as culture. The answer may be to link subjectivity, social interaction and figuration together through the concept of 'technology'.

New technology, new relationships and new subjectivities

We generally do not think of social work as a 'technology'. This is because we associate this word with complex mechanical devices which are not relevant to social work. However, even if we put to one side the way in which technological hardware has become incorporated into social work through computers, telecommunications and complex electronic accounting processes, this failure to consider the idea of technology as relevant is based on a fundamental misconception about the nature of both technology and social work.

In fact technology should be seen as a *pattern of social relations* associated with the need to operate a particular technical system. (This idea, for which I am indebted, was first proposed by Professor Stephen Woolgar during the course of his 1997 Brunel Innovation Lecture 'A New Theory of Innovation'.) If the study of technology is the sociological study of the way in which social relations are constructed and reconstructed through the innovation process, then thinking of the social work process as a technological process enables us to link practice innovation to changes in the social work subject as networks of social work relations are re-ordered, and reconceptualized.

So, a new technology of social care involves a cultural shift of potentially considerable magnitude which can, nevertheless, be mapped out in some detail, by exploring the innovation process in terms of the changing social fields, patterns of linkage, interdependency, etc. generated by those involved as they seek to achieve personal, professional and organizational goals within their new social world. They are, themselves, helping to create this world by their actions and interactions. It involves a movement from one type of figuration to another and both helps us to understand the dynamics lying behind this and provides us with a way of focusing on specific patterns of social interaction.

One implication of this is that we cannot separate the question of the subjectivity of social workers from the structural question of how the landscape of interpersonal and inter-organizational relationships is being actively constructed and reconstructed around the demands of the new systems of social care in which social work is embedded. The study of subjectivity becomes part of the study of the new technologies of social work/social care.

I want to focus on one example of innovation and to explore this in terms of the relationship between patterns of social interaction, culture and subjectivity.

Collaboration and re-figuration

We are most likely to find evidence of globalization where we can find new patterns of work, an exposure to market forces and policy objectives related to global shifts in the arena of values. In the UK the question of collaboration in community care enshrines policy objectives with a global resonance and a commissioning and care management process which has opened up social work practice to market pressures. It therefore corresponds quite neatly to the models of globalization put forward by various theorists such as Van Liemt in that it combines 'enabling' economic and technological shifts with 'government policies' and 'corporate strategies' (Van Liemt 1998, p.238).

The interest in promoting collaboration between different 'stakeholder' groups in the sphere of community care also provides us with a ready-made context within which to explore the organizational complexity which is a feature of globalization, especially as there are strong suggestions that collaboration itself is directly related to globalization. It is widely seen by management theorists as an 'antidote to [market generated] turbulence' and as a way for newly linked organizations to 'gain appreciation of their interdependence' (Gay 1996, p.58).

All of this adds up to a strong argument in favour of identifying collaborative arrangements as innovative figurations characteristic of the globalization process. To add weight to this, it has recently been recognized that collaboration produces new organizations. 'When groups and organisations begin to embrace collaborative processes to engage in intra or inter-organisational strategies management and change, they are in essence, inventing a new type of organisation' (Finn 1996, p.152). Can these new figurations be linked to a particular technology of social care?

Community care: a new technology of social care

Across Europe, and indeed beyond, there has been a shift from the older technology of institutional care to the new technology of community care. The old technology structured social work relationships in terms of highly organized and prescribed networks of care and control. It is now well established that the 'total institution' imposed a fixed structure of interaction on professionals, residents and their families alike (Goffman 1968). But this structure of institutionalized relations could be described in my terms as *an institutional technology of social care*. Over time, and especially during the period of post-war reconstruction, this *institutional technology* became linked to a broader range of *bureaucratic technologies* characteristic of social care all over Europe (Cannan, Berry and Lyons 1992, pp.47–70).

Institutional/bureaucratic technologies are related to Fordist welfare structures but community care technologies are related to the emergence of post-Fordist welfare structures. Therefore, some of the fundamental conditions under which welfare is constructed and delivered have changed, giving rise not only to a new managerialism and 'technocratization' (Dominelli and Hoogvelt 1996), but also to new organizational forms. With the decline of traditional Fordist welfare organizations, the conventional team is disappearing to be replaced by more complex and open-ended networks of cooperation and collaboration. These new figurations can be seen as networks of relationships organized around the technology of community care. In the UK this would involve such structured activities as hospital discharge arrangements, assessment, care planning, purchasing, the interweaving of formal and informal care, etc. We would therefore expect that these new networked organizations/technologies might be the crucible from which new identities would begin to emerge and there is some evidence of this.

A seminal experience for me has been the opportunity to study new social care networks in both London and Stockholm and the way in which individual social workers conceptualize their identity in the context of these new figurations.

From teams to networks

The team concept occupies a central place in the construction of social work subjectivity. Throughout Europe most social workers expect to work in teams, and teamwork is highly prized. However, the new collaborative organizations based on networks are beginning to shift professional subjectivity away from its location within the traditional team and into very different kinds of inter-organizational roles and relationships. However, the differences between the cultures of these new organizations may be as important as the similarities.

The tendency towards an increasingly networked model of service delivery was evident in both Stockholm and London. In London, the effect of the shift to community care has been to make social workers become more entrepreneurial and more instrumental as well as more networked in their practice. In Sweden, however, the effect has been to create a new notion of the 'co-operative social worker' exploring ways of overcoming bureaucratic boundaries in order to meet individual need and investing strongly in cross-sectoral relationships (Trevillion and Green 1998).

From a very detailed analysis of network roles and relationships what emerged from our London study of community care networks was a picture of multiple professional identities and team affiliations. They had, though, little or no emotional investment in these multiple identities, an overwhelmingly short-term instrumental approach to collaborative relationships and there was a radical individualization of work with very little evidence of any linkage between individual networks and relationships between teams (Trevillion 1996c).

Whereas the precepts of 'global awareness' might lead one to expect the forging of a new kind of interdisciplinary identity, we found scant evidence of any attempt to create a new integrated kind of community care professionalism. Multiple identities remained multiple identities and this was associated with a lack of emotional investment in attempts to connect these different figurations (Elias 1978, p.103). One could call this an *entrepreneurial culture*, characterized by a highly personalized but relatively impersonal work strategy and mode of interaction with others generating a number of very loosely connected loose-knit networks.

The Swedish network was associated with much higher levels of connectedness than the UK networks. While individual and person-centred networks were important in both countries there was a much higher degree of overlap between network systems in Stockholm than in London. The emphasis on relationships and mutual understanding was much higher in Sweden and while goal attainment was clearly important in both countries, it was only in London that this was translated into an instrumental attitude to network relationships. The Swedish practice culture could be described as one where there was a strong sense of a common network culture being constructed but on the basis of negotiation and with only a slight hint of pressure to conform.

When we met with representatives of the new collaborative organization in Stockholm, one of the talking points was what held this complex structure together. The answers we were given included trust, reciprocity, familiarity, and shared history/biography and opportunities for informal social interaction which extended to socializing outside the work context (Trevillion and Green 1998). Overall, we could call this a *relationship culture*, characterized by a close-knit network of strong personal affiliations.

What this brief comparison shows is that new forms of connectedness are becoming a characteristic feature of community care technology. The nature of this shift is quite marked in that it includes a movement away from the highly organized and prescriptive structures of conventional teamwork to more flexible, multi-agency patterns of collaboration and cooperation. Comparing UK and Swedish social workers also shows that a wide range of network possibilities and cultures can exist in the new environments currently being shaped by globalization. Entrepreneurial cultures and relationship cultures are two of the possible figurations or patterns of interdependency characteristic of the 'new organizations'. Each has its own type of subjectivity.

Researching changes in professional subjectivity

So far, the argument has been that concepts of culture and technology can help to resituate subjectivity in the context of globalization. But it could easily be pointed out that the generalizations so far produced provide only a limited picture of the mind-set of contemporary social workers. This is true. Subjectivity has to be situated within culture, but the two are not identical.

While most of the literature on culture tends to assume that individuals grow up within a particular culture and develop their sense of who they are through a process of extended socialization we cannot assume that this is the case with any kind of organizational culture. In particular, concepts of professional role, certain key values and expectations are likely to have been acquired prior to entering a particular organization and certainly prior to engaging in the kind of collaborative work involved in creating the new organizations associated with globalization.

Human beings are defined by their memories as much as by their contemporary experiences and no account of subjectivity which misses out this dimension can hope to be complete. Given the impossibility of factoring into any model, the diversity of biographies to be found in just one group of social workers, this makes the quest for an account of subjectivity appear to be foolhardy, at best.

However, there is no need to attempt to produce a comprehensive definition of subjectivity. The aim here is much more limited. I have been trying to explore the shifts in subjectivity associated with the new organizations and to explore these shifts in the context of cultures of interdependency. This is still a difficult task, but, nevertheless a manageable one.

The model taking shape is one in which the patterns of interdependency corresponding to a particular culture are represented in network terms and onto which the concept of the professional self is then mapped.

In relation to the two social work cultures that have just been been described, this model would generate a series of statements about the general tendency of those within the culture to behave towards other people in particular ways. I have given some indication of the kind of statements that could be made about subjectivity in an entrepreneurial culture and subjectivity in a relationship culture. Much more work on applying this model needs to be done before one could claim to be doing more than scratching the surface of the question of subjectivity. Nevertheless, I believe a start has been made.

Conclusion: the way forward

Globalization can be defined in many different ways and has many different kinds of consequences. However, one way in which all its different aspects come together is through changes in the patterns of interdependency within and between organizations. As far as social welfare organizations are concerned, the impact of globalization has been felt not only through changes in managerial style and approach and the increasing role of markets and quasi-markets, but also in the pattern of everyday relationships.

In order to grasp the way social workers currently experience their relationships with others and thus their own roles and identities we need to develop an account of the new subjectivities associated with globalization. The problem that has been identified, however, is that none of the traditional ways of thinking about professionalism and professional identity appear to be capable of generating adequate descriptions of what appears to be going on in contemporary European social work. In an attempt to solve this problem, a new model of subjectivity has been proposed based on the concepts of culture and technology. The result is a cultural model of subjectivity which is, at the same time, attuned to global processes and global systems, yet sceptical of rhetorical visions based on universal values and experiences. This model contains a view of the social worker as one whose subjectivity is constituted, at least partly, in and by the concrete interweaving and interdependencies of day-to-day social interaction and which is not synonymous with highly normative public pronouncements about professional identity or values.

In pursuing this line an argument has been made for an interactional 'turn' in studies of professionalism in social work and a more coherent attempt to connect the study of the professional subject with studies of social change and broader socio-economic and organizational debates.

Whilst the idea of globalization opens up an exciting new field for comparative European analyses, it simultaneously creates awkward, if not insoluble, problems in relation to research methodology which cannot be solved by conventional methods. Rather, what it suggests is the possibility of a systematic and comparative study of the relationship between felt experience, culture, technology and social network which would seek to explore the different figurations and subjectivities emerging in the context of globalization.

References

Barclay, P.M. (1982) Social Workers: Their Role and Tasks. London: NISW/Bedford Square Press/ NCVO.

Baudrillard, J. (1981) For a Political Economy of the Sign. St Louis: Telos Press.

Beresford, P. and Trevillion, S. (1995) Developing Skills for Community Care: A Collaborative Approach. Aldershot: Arena.

Best, S. and Kellner, D. (1991) Postmodern Theory: Critical Interrogations. Basingstoke: Macmillan.

Broadbent, J., Dietrich, M. and Roberts, J. (1997) The End of the Professions: The Re-Structuring of Professional Work. London: Routledge.

Cannan, C., Berry, L. and Lyons, K. (1992) Social Work in Europe. Basingstoke: Macmillan.

CCETSW (1989) Requirements and Regulations for the Diploma in Social Work. London: CCETSW, Paper 30.

Davies, M. (1981) The Essential Social Worker: A Guide to Positive Practice. London: Heinemann.

Dominelli, L. (1988) Anti-Racist Social Work. Basingstoke: BASW/Macmillan.

Dominelli, L. and Hoogvelt, A. (1996) 'Globalization and the technocratisation of social work.' Critical Social Policy, 16, 2, 45–62.

Elias, N. (1978) What is Sociology? London: Hutchinson.

Finn, C.B. (1996) 'Utilizing stakeholder strategies for positive outcomes.' In C. Hiexham (ed) Creating Collaborative Advantage. London: Sage.

Foucault, M. (1982) 'The subject and power.' In H.L. Dreyfus and P. Rabinow (eds) Michel Foucault: Beyond Structuralism and Hermeneutics. Chicago: University of Chicago Press.

Gay, B. (1996) 'Cross-sectoral partners: Collaborative alliances among business, government and communities.' In C. Hiexham (ed) Creating Collaborative Advantage. London: Sage.

Goffman, E. (1968) *Asylums: Essays on the Social Situation of Mental Patients and Other Inmates.* Harmondsworth: Penguin.

Gould, A. (1993) *Capitalist Welfare Systems: A Comparison of Japan, Britain and Sweden.* London: Longman.

Griffiths, R. (1988) *Community Care: Agenda for Action.* London: HMSO.

Hall, R.H. (1995) *Complex Organisations.* Aldershot: Dartmouth.

Jones, S. and Joss, R. (1995) 'Models of professionalism.' In M. Yelloly and M. Henkel. *Learning and Teaching in Social Work.* London: Jessica Kingsley Publishers.

Lewis, J. and Glennerster, H. (1996) *Implementing the New Community Care.* Buckingham: Open University Press.

Lorenz, W. (1994) *Social Work in a Changing Europe.* London: Routledge.

Macfarlane, R. and Laville, J.L. (1992) *Developing Community Partnerships in Europe: New Ways of Meeting Social Need in Europe.* Directory of Social Change/Calouste Gulbenkian Foundation.

Memedovic, O., Kuyvenhoven, A. and Molle, W.T.M. (eds) (1998) *Globalization of Labour Markets: Challenges, Adjustments and Policy Response in the European Union and Less Developed Countries.* Dordrecht, Netherlands: Kluwer Academic Publishers.

Mennell, S. (1974) *Sociological Theory: Uses and Unities.* Sunbury on Thames, Nelson.

Naisbitt, J. (1994) *Global Paradox: The Bigger the World Economy the More Powerful its Smallest Players.* London: Nicholas Brealey Publishing.

Olsson, S. (1987) 'Towards a transformation of the Swedish welfare state.' In R. Friedmann, R. Gilbert and M. Sherer (eds) *Modern Welfare States: A Comparative View of Trends and Prospects.* London: Wheatsheaf.

Peck, E. and Poxton, R. (1998) 'Health action zones: Towards a paradigm shift.' *Health and Health Care, 6,* 1, 7–12.

Robertson, R. (1992) *Globalization: Social Theory and Global Culture.* London: Sage.

Simic, P. (1995) 'What's in a word? From social worker to care manager.' *Practice, 7,* 3, 5–18.

Sutcliffe, F.E. (1968) Introduction to R. Descartes, *Discourse on Method and the Meditations* (translated by F.E. Sutcliffe). Harmondsworth: Penguin.

Trevillion, S. (1996a) 'Towards a comparative analysis of collaboration.' *Social Work in Europe, 3,* 1, 11–18.

Trevillion, S. (1996b) 'Hard choices in health care: Patients rights and public priorities.' *Social Work in Europe, 3,* 1, 37–39.

Trevillion, S. (1996c) 'Talking about collaboration.' *Research, Policy and Planning, 14,* 1, 96–101.

Trevillion, S. (1997) 'The Globalization of European Social Work.' *Social Work in Europe, 4,* 1, 1–9.

Trevillion, S. and Green, D. (1998) 'The co-operation concept in a team of Swedish social workers: applying grid and group to studies of community care.' In I.R. Edgar and A. Russell (eds) *The Anthropology of Welfare.* London: Routledge.

Van Liemt, G. (1998) 'Labour in the global economy challenge: Adjustment and policy response in the EU.' In O. Memedovic, A. Kuyvenhoven and W.T.M. Molle (eds) *Globalization of Labour Markets: Challenges, Adjustments and Policy Response in the EU.* Dordrecht, Netherlands: Kluver Academic Publishers.

Wallerstein, I. (1974) *The Modern World System.* New York: Academic Press.

Walls, G. (1994) 'Actors, legitimisation and cultures of social work.' *Scandinavian Journal of Social Welfare, 3,* 218–225.

Yelloly, M. and Henkel, M. (1995) *Learning and Teaching in Social Work.* London: Jessica Kingsley Publishers.

CHAPTER 4

Social Services and Contrary Cultures

John Baldock

Introduction: the cultural colonization of care

In the design and implementation of social policies, governments seek to work both with culture and to change it. Policy innovations that go beyond the limits of popular acceptance risk undermining political support and even the authority of the state. The eventual withdrawal of the Community Charge and of Unit Fines are examples which showed how even the radical Tory administrations of 1979–87 could be forced to backtrack. Mrs Thatcher famously argued that her policies worked 'with the grain of human nature'. In particular they sought to create a 'society in which government doesn't try to take responsibility away from the people' but gives them 'power to choose – to say for yourself what you want' (Conservative Party Manifesto 1992).

Choice has been one of the driving principles of the community care reforms of the last decade: the National Health and Community Care Act 1990; The Carers (Recognition and Services) Act 1995; The Community Care (Direct Payments) Act 1996. Together these, sometimes known as 'the New Community Care', have rapidly transformed the rules and procedures that govern access to state support for adults who need help with daily living. The vast majority of these people are old, most often in their eighties. Little consideration appears to have been given to whether the new polices fit with their expectations, values and practices, or with those of their families who will provide most of their care in the context of the new policies.

The arguments in this chapter are drawn from the observations of the author and Clare Ungerson of Southampton University when conducting research into the experiences of frail old people who have been exposed to the 'New Community Care'. Very little is known about how users understand the new policies and of their ability to integrate them into their lives. Indeed, we suggest that the experience and response to disability in great old age is largely 'unscripted': the culture provides no clear models of what to expect and what to do. As a result policy makers and others have projected into this 'empty territory' their own, often ideologically driven, conceptions of care and how it does and should work. The world of care, particularly the care of old people, has been colonized by a whole range of alternative discourses: those of the disability rights movement, the new managerialism, free marketeers, varieties of feminism and the carers lobby. Here we will focus on the first two, seeking to show how these discourses, more powerful and more articulate than frail old people themselves, have been able to present their conceptions of the right order of social care as the 'correct' or even 'real' one. However, research that directly observes the experiences of old people, and which listens to their accounts of their lives, finds relatively little in common with these various, colonizing discourses.

Thwarted attempts to rationalize the care of older people

The policy changes of the last decade have not succeeded as rapidly as their most senior managers would wish. Each year the Chief Inspector of Social Services publishes a report reviewing for the minister of health, and any members of the public willing to pay £20 for the report, the achievements of local authorities in meeting their social care obligations. 1998 saw the seventh and final report of the retiring chief inspector, Sir Herbert Laming (Department of Health 1998). Despite recording many achievements, there is no disguising a tone of frustration that pervades the document. It is very much a managerial frustration. As the summary records (p.8), 'most SSDs have planning structures and services that involve service users, carers and other agencies in shaping services' and only 'some have assessed whether existing services meet current or projected needs'.

Although much of the report is focused on failure to achieve acceptable standards in child protection services – and these are interpreted as managerial failings – a lesser part is taken up with similar concerns about services for older people:

> We meet many service users who do not know whether they have been assessed or whether they have a care manager whom they can contact. Staff have low expectations of the desire and ability of users and carers to participate in their assessment and care planning arrangements. Many users and carers do not have enough information to participate fully. (Department of Health 1998, p.23, para.3.17)

Sir Herbert Laming, interviewed at the time, appeared convinced that these problems are amenable to managerial resolution:

> I do not understand how managers can do their job effectively if case recording is poor and if there is no criteria for assessing whether a person's condition is improving. I read very few case files where we see the effect of supervision and management on decision-making … Management means management. By that I mean setting standards, having procedures, making sure that these standards are translated into action and having regular supervision and reviews. (Downey, 1998 p.10)

However, we would suggest that Sir Herbert is both too hard on local authority managers and too optimistic about the remedies he favours. Policy makers and managers tend to underestimate the social constraints that limit their effectiveness and which are beyond their control. Social care in particular is the site where the state comes into direct contact with the private and the intimate. Policy management will only achieve its goal if it is in tune with the deeply-rooted values and norms that govern the private order of people's lives. That is one reason why health and social care has traditionally taken place in institutions. Doctors and other public social carers find it much easier to get people to fit in with their (benevolent) objectives away from the powerful forces of home life. Home care services must take account of the material and ideological determinants of the private lives of old people; that is essentially of the culture of the home.

What are the basic characteristics of the culture that governs the lives of frail old people? We argue that one reason that policy design in this area has been able to proceed so vigorously is that no one knows the answer to this question – or even expects that they need to know it. The mechanics of the care of old people seem to be seen as banal and obvious and the lives into which it has to be integrated as uncomplicated and manageable. But this is to ignore growing evidence that old age is increasingly various and that personal care is far from a mundane activity. Reporting on their recent ESRC-funded study of the family life of old people, Phillipson et al. (1998) conclude that:

> … over the past 50 years we have moved from an old age experienced largely within the context of family groups, to one shaped by what may be termed 'personal communities'. These suggest a more 'voluntaristic' element in social relationships in old age … There are now many more different 'types' of older people than was the case in the 1950s, and many more different types of families. (Phillipson et al. 1988, p.4)

Because frail older people are weak and silent, and their care is mostly hidden behind the doors of thousands of private houses, it has been easy for outsiders to seek to impose their own logic and prescriptions about how the care system should work. The care of the elderly is an apparent cultural desert, easily invaded by other discourses. Policies are projected into what is seen as, at best, simple and, at worst, a vacuum. But then, as we seek to argue, they are met with an invisible opposition.

Our research experience

To a substantial extent the arguments offered in this chapter have grown out of our experience of following the care careers of a sample of old people who had suddenly been disabled by a stroke (Baldock and Ungerson 1994). Our sample had been small (32) and the research qualitative, designed to explore in detail with the old people and their carers how they were finding the experience of assessment and case management. Over their first six months of disability we interviewed the stroke survivors and their carers three times.

It is recognized in the methodological literature on qualitative interviewing that there is a high risk of what is sometimes called 'reactivity' or 'the reactive effect', the tendency of the interviewee to reflect the categories and causal connections that the interviewer is either suggesting or implying (Hoinville 1978). It is difficult to avoid this problem because of the very need to use language in conducting interviews and the fact that words come pre-loaded with assumptions about categories and connections between them. Clearly it is the job of an interviewer to avoid this form of influence as far as possible. However, in the course of many years interviewing old people and their carers we have become increasingly convinced that in understanding the experience of disability in old age this risk of a 'reactive effect' is particularly acute because very often the person being interviewed does not have access to a clear and established language to describe his/her (new) predicament and the way in which it is to be dealt with. As a result, when we have gone back and listened to the tapes of our interviews, or read the transcripts, we have found sections where, despite our best attempts at neutral language, there is clearly a gap between the concepts we assume will be used and those available to the interviewees. Some examples will shed light on this and provide some evidence.

We sought to find out, at the first interview after discharge, who people expected would help them do the things their new disability prevented them doing on their own. Later, once they had been at home for some time we explored who was helping them and in what ways. The approach we took was to ask, 'What problems do you foresee/face?' and 'Is anyone helping you with this?' In the later interviews where this approach had not borne the fruit we expected we can be heard to ask, somewhat illegitimately, 'Who is your main helper/carer?' But 'helper' or 'carer' were not always words and concepts that came readily to our sample. For example in one interview with a clearly housebound elderly man living on his own, while he had explained all the things that neighbours and others helped him with he still denied he needed help in any way. But we could not see how he was coping until, at the end of the interview, his daughter arrived to make his tea. It was she who was making his life possible but neither he nor she saw this in terms of helping or caring: she was just his daughter as she had always been.

The most immediate lesson we learnt was how inappropriate were the assumptions and expectations we had brought to the study. Despite our conscientious attempts to avoid prejudging what evidence we were going to get, it soon became clear that we in fact brought to the interviews a set of assumptions that were the product of our discipline, social policy: chiefly presumptions to do with access, choice and quality in public services. We expected that our respondents might offer criticisms of the services they received and the routes by which they had obtained them. We would not have been surprised to find them thwarted and angry about rigid rules and insensitive bureaucracy and form filling.

We were ready to record inequalities of access and problems of quality. But these are the traditional 'social administration' concerns of our subject. Instead we found that public or publicly-arranged services did not feature as distinct categories in most of our respondents' lives. Indeed, the only ones who used the concept of public service in a regular way were people who had formerly worked in one – in our research an ex-nurse and a retired schoolteacher.

The gap between the accounts of care given us by the service providers and by the recipients was made up of much more than differences over the facts of what had happened. The people in our sample talked of their lives with quite different meanings. Their use of words like 'care', 'help', 'problem' and 'need' showed that they were differently defined from the same terms used by the professionals, or even by us as researchers. As far as possible our respondents sought to define and understand their world after their stroke in the categories, understandings and activities of their previous lives. At the same time they were searching for new words and routines that would make their present predicaments more manageable. Much of the energy that drove the interviews, that compelled people to talk long and openly to us, was a search on the part of the stroke survivors and their carers for some confirmation from us that what they were doing, or not doing, was right. Particularly in the first few days after they had arrived home, people had little idea of what needed to be done or should be done. Many refused or did not recognize offers of help that were made to them. They appeared to be hoping that very soon their lives would return to the normality they had known before. Or if they expected help from any public source it was from their GP. It was usually their doctor who had initially diagnosed the stroke and had them admitted to hospital. They assumed he or she would now visit and resume oversight of their recovery. In fact we discovered that GPs very rarely play a role in the medical or social care of stroke patients once they are discharged back home. The GPs expect this will be managed by the hospital through regular visits to the consultants and the day hospital, together with support from the social services, and indeed this is formally a correct expectation.

As we followed our respondents over the next six months we observed them make what amounted to journeys across the landscape of care. For some these journeys ranged quite widely. Although our sample was very homogeneous in terms of income, education and occupational-class backgrounds, there were few common features to their experiences of the new disabilities other than the uncertainty and exploratory, even accidental, nature of the outcomes:

From an interview at three months after hospital discharge:

Q: Were there any options open to you? Did anyone give you any choice of help so that your husband could stay on at work?

A: Well, they did say something about the ... somebody, you know, three days, three times a day. But it was an awful lot to me to come all the way up here. Three times a day.

Q: Do you remember who suggested that?

A: The welfare lady I think. Was it Mary?

Q: Mary Stewart? Did she offer you that support?

A: Well no, she was thinking about it.

Q: Oh I see.

A: But it didn't go into detail. It was nothing like that. Where they were going to get it from I don't know.

Q: Since you have been home, have you found things easier or more difficult than you were expecting?

A: I think it was more difficult to begin with ... but as time's gone on ... *(Interrupted by husband: ... She couldn't walk when she came home. That was the trouble. She couldn't do anything.)*

This was the tone of most of our interviews. The categories we were schooled in – services, entitlement, choice, appropriateness – were not those used by our interviewees. The social topography of their worlds was quite differently perceived and classified. Most of all they had few expectations of how things would turn out and, where they did, these were rooted in the normality of their previous pre-stroke lives and their accumulated expectations and skills, now often rather inappropriate from our vantage point (see Baldock and Ungerson 1994 for a fuller account):

The same couple at six months after discharge:

Q: Do you think it would be useful to be getting any help from social services?

A: Not now, no. Not now. It's too late now. I mean we've got over ... over the first part. The hard part's gone.

Q: Do you get any help now?

A: No. The only thing she does now is go up to the hospital twice a week.

It becomes clear in the rest of the interview that the couple have only just mentioned the hospital attendances because they have not considered them as part of the wife's care. Indeed the trips are more of an obstacle to them, difficult to organize, but continued with out of deference to the doctors, who they feel wish to check on symptoms.

Further research-based evidence of an unscripted old age

In subsequent work with older people we have become more alert both to the ways in which they describe the order of their lives and to the risks that we might impose on them our own discourse and expectations. However, we believe we have continued to find evidence that older people, particularly the very old, do not often see their lives as ones that they manage or control, let alone engage in using a 'social care market'. Rather they describe lives which are very much focused on the present, open to chance and in which it is wise to follow the pre-scriptions of those who appear to have power or authority over them:

> If you can get your legs out of bed in the morning and stand up it's going to be a good day.

> Keep busy – librarian, tea lady, bingo caller.

> Sometimes I feel afraid. Loneliness makes you feel low. Will I wake up in the morning?

These are some responses from a small study of 41 people over 75 (some much older) living on their own (KCHCC 1999). The study was designed to explore their expectations of health and social services and in particular their views of the role their GP might play in organizing access to services. The research sought to compare the opinions of those who saw their GP frequently (more than twice in the last six months) with those who consulted more rarely (not at all in the last six months). Small discussion or 'focus groups' were used as a method of discovering their views in a way which might reduce the influence of a researcher's expectations.

These older 'survivors' were certainly not in their seventh age 'sans teeth, sans eyes, sans taste, sans everything' (*As You Like It*: II.vii.139) but there is some of what Shakespeare calls the 'second childishness' in that these people clearly did not believe that they were often in a position to demand or manage the help they needed, and, to a lesser extent, received. They refer frequently to the uncertainty that characterized their lives, to the abrupt changes that have flowed from illnesses, new disabilities and widowhood and the need simply to adapt to whatever help comes along:

> It's hit and miss, don't you agree? We just don't know about available help. They could provide a list of what is available. None of us know do we?

> It just depends on what happens. My neighbours are all right, but they're all at work. I'm the only one in about five houses. On my own all day.

> *What about the doctor?*

> No, it's not the doctor's job to make sure that you are looked after. Only go there when I'm poorly.

Some remarked that their GP had, often to their surprise, suggested or arranged some solution to a more social need. But this was regarded as exceptional and unpredictable. There was considerable anxiety not to appear to bother the doctor but an assumption that if something really serious happened then 'they' would arrange something. There was general agreement that the best way to maintain control over one's life was to avoid getting ill. It was often remarked that to demand attention and services was a risk to one's autonomy and to tempt fortune.

In a parallel focus group of six GPs asked to discuss their relationships with patients over 75, views that were complementary to, and in balance with, those of the patients were put forward. There were signs of a set of shared expectations amongst the doctors and the patients about the nature of their relationship. Both sides saw very old age almost as a game of chance in which it was often best to leave well alone. Neither side saw the GP as a 'gatekeeper' to be used to arrange access to other services:

> You mustn't create worries in people who are well. Often they are quite happy trekking along until someone tells them they are not safe ... they mustn't plug their kettle there ... and all of a sudden they think, 'Oh, I could break my hip' and while it's of course good to prevent that, it creates anxiety as well.

> I think to a certain extent everyone's got to be careful because these people are sort of chugging along in their nice little static system and you actually come round and find something like a loose stair carpet and think, great, let's get social services in to come and recarpet the house and to prevent them going in with a fractured neck or femur. And then you find the next week they are in with a fractured neck because they got a different coloured carpet.

> Well, the elderly people I see are often embarrassed to seek advice. They don't want to bother anyone. And social services and living allowances – it's all 'someone else, not me'. And I think we're putting too much pressure on them and they'll lose their autonomy and their self worth and their self support. Whereas you know, I wouldn't want to be a GP in 30 years' time because it would be a disaster ... they will want their allowances and their rails immediately.

> *So do you have a fear that, with the ageing of the population, the generation coming through will be more demanding?*

> (Everyone): Definitely, Yes, Absolutely awful.

There are clearly considerable methodological difficulties in relying on the research techniques used here to obtain the quotations appearing in this chapter, selected from transcripts of a small sample or from focus groups which may be unrepresentative. However, we are using them to suggest a limited and tentative hypothesis: that the nature of many people's experience of old age is one that is open and unscripted. If we are right, then we would suggest that more established research methods, for example sample surveys in which large numbers of people are asked large numbers of questions, may not be as meaningful as they appear. Clearly answers will be obtained and boxes will be ticked, generating 'hard data' that will get harder still when it is fed into computers and emerges aggregated into tables and figures. But we suspect that the questions asked largely have meaning from the service provision view of the world. Our experience of trying to enter the perspective of service users, particularly those for whom severe and sudden disability has disrupted all the routines and patterns of their lives, is that the usual classifications of care services and their division between the public, the voluntary, the private and the informal, often do not show up as distinct entities with specific purposes. Rather they are fitted in to people's changing lives, or left unrecognized and ignored, in a huge variety of ways that bear little resemblance to policymakers' conceptions.

Broader social explanations of an unscripted old age

While there are considerable methodological difficulties in establishing the thesis of the unscriptedness of old age through empirical observation, it is easier to point to broader social reasons why it is a likely thesis. There are material and ideological reasons why the people in our research samples might have found themselves without the language or experience to make sense easily of their situations.

Great old age and long lives in retirement are a relatively new phenomenon. As recently as the 1930s life expectancy for a man in Britain was less than sixty years and for a woman less than sixty five. The wider culture may not have access to realistic models of life in old age or the discourses to describe it. Dependency in old age has traditionally been hidden within institutional care, such as long-stay geriatric wards or more recently in nursing homes. Where care takes place at home, as it now mostly does (OPCS 1990) it is similarly cut off from the public gaze and when it has been revealed it has generally been described in terms of another discourse – to do with the plight of carers.

Furthermore, as the numbers of old people who require help have grown, there have been rapid changes in the policy response. This has made it difficult for a clear public conception to emerge of the usual modes of care and, perhaps more crucially, of the boundaries between public and private responsibility. First came the growth of local authority residential care in the 1950s and 1960s. In the 1980s and early 1990s private nursing homes took the larger role. More recently, the community care reforms are leading to an expansion of domiciliary provision in a context where state support is becoming more tightly rationed and the private and privately-funded sector is taking over. There is evidence that these changes mean that each new cohort of older people and their carers find themselves labouring under assumptions rooted in the past which now do not work. Social constructions of what is appropriate and normal in the balance of public and private provision are established over long periods. Yet the reality can be changed by social policy 'reform' at very short notice, and has been.

These difficulties are added to by the fact that the population of older people needing care is not a fixed one but subject to constant throughput. It can be estimated that about 50 per cent of older people who are bed-bound will die within a year and of those who are house-bound 50 per cent will die within three years (Baldock 1997). There is thus less opportunity for social learning. The relevant population is constantly added to by people who have relatively little appropriate knowledge.

Lastly amongst these material factors is the fact that ours is a society that sharply discounts the risk of needing help in old age. People believe it will not happen to them. They therefore make few or inappropriate preparations either materially through saving (Disney, Grundy and Johnson 1997) or emotionally and intellectually. This is not an unreasonable approach. The risks of losing one's independence through disability in old age are substantial but not overwhelming. The chances of maintaining one's autonomy are also high. More than half of people over 75 living in the community are able to report that they have no condition which limits their daily life (Goddard 1994). That one will avoid dependency in old age is not an unreasonable bet to make and this is reflected in images of old people in popular culture: more 'Last of the Summer Wine' or 'Steptoe and Son' than the more feared outcomes.

The relative openness of everyday life in old age, including the time of frailty that may come with it, is really only discovered by talking, or more particularly listening, to old people about their views of the future. But it is difficult to do so without imposing on the process cultural prescriptions about the sort of things old people ought to talk about. Many researchers have spent much time listening to old people and it has generated a large literature but one that is almost entirely focused on the past. To reminisce is what old people are expected to do. Until about the mid-century a huge proportion of personal memoirs called themselves 'reminiscences'. Other writers would see it as valuable duty to record the reminiscences of the great – for example Gorky recording those of the great Leo Tolstoy (Gorky 1920). Later, psychological theory argued, convincingly, that a person's personality and identity are essentially their aggregated memories (Eysenck and Frith 1977) and recalling the past came to be seen as therapeutic for old people (Coleman 1986; Norris 1988). Indeed a focus on the past became part of the process by which, sociologists of the 1960s and 1970s argued, old people began to 'disengage' from the present and prepare for death (Cumming 1961). This loading of cultural expectations and academic theory tends to discourage an alternative emphasis on the future and on planning and managing one's response to a long retirement and the particular adjustments that disabilities might bring. It is almost as if our culture is suggesting that a fatalistic stance is the most rational and the most acceptable approach to old age. But it leaves what old people have to get on with, the management of everyday life, rather open and rudderless. And, as we seek to show with two examples, it renders their lives and, to some extent their culture, open to 'invasion' by more powerful discourses, some of which enter under the banner of welfare.

The colonization of old age by alternative discourses

If the arguments set out so far are valid then the cultural territory that is old age, particularly disabled old age, is empty terrain and open to invasion by other discourses driven by other interests. The rest of this chapter seeks to show that this has happened, and that this may in part explain why other, more synthetic, conceptions of old age, particularly those expressed in public policy, do not achieve the goals they set themselves.

'Rights talk'

Over the last twenty years disability and the dependencies it is associated with have been a battleground of competing definitions of the 'problem' and its potential 'solutions'. Particularly in the United States, and to a lesser degree in Britain, the disability rights movement, in its many subtly different formations, has succeeded in redefining the meaning of handicap, showing that there are few necessary connections between a physical impairment and what were thought to be the inevitable and consequent social and economic disadvantages. A main battle was fought with medical conceptions of disability which tended to focus on a deficient individual rather than a disabling society (Campbell and Oliver 1996). The result has been significant legislation requiring a less disabling environment and outlawing various forms of discrimination.

These advances have mostly benefited younger people with stable long-term physical impairments. They have won at least greater opportunities for autonomy and control over their lives by obtaining new legal rights but also by influencing the vocabulary that is used in the politics of disability. It is no accident that disability rights activists are fussy, often strident, about the language that is used in discussing their issues. They are well aware that language can both imprison and liberate. Now people with impairments do not have to accept the life scripts that those with power over them used to prescribe: the limiting expectations of their families, carers and the doctors, social workers and other professionals who claimed to 'help' them. Young people with physical impairments can now access quite different and vastly more empowering scripts of how their lives may be led.

Similar but much smaller advances have been made in rescripting old age, particularly the part of it where one is still physically and financially autonomous: sometimes called the 'third age', usually of early retirement. Grey Panthers, the political clout of the AARP (The American Association of Retired People), and a growing popular entertainment literature (in magazines and on TV) about how to manage one's later years ('use it or lose it') all present older people with alternative images of ageing and the rights and powers it should entail. There has been less progress in rescripting the last years of old age when one may lose the ability to do the things one used normally to do and thus to get through the day unaided.

Paradoxically, it may in part be the very progress made by younger disabled people that has limited our understanding of disability and dependence in old age. The transference of the disability rights vocabulary to 'normal ageing' and the dependencies it brings is an example of colonization which has tended to import a whole range of solutions built upon the view that dependence is undesirable and that autonomy is to be won by controlling the care and carers one needs.

The particular risks of this discourse to the welfare of frail elderly people have been most carefully analysed by Diane Gibson:

> The dominant perspective might best be summarized as the maximally reducible model of dependency, and it characterizes almost all the literature in one form or the

other. There may be disagreement about how to get rid of it – transfer it from public to private, or private to public, restructure it, reinscribe it and so forth – but there is certainly agreement that it should be got rid of. But why? (Gibson 1998, p.205)

From her own research Gibson has shown that for many old people the reduction of dependency is neither particularly wanted by them nor possible, given their declining and unpredictable abilities. What is more important is the quality of their dependent relationships and the ways in which that quality can be monitored and ensured. 'Rights talk', she points out, risks creating systems that drive old people into unwanted, low quality autonomies. Certainly in our own study of older people who had suffered a stroke, there was a tendency amongst the providers to think in terms of a whole range of entitlements (to assessment, to case management, to disability allowances, to the right to choose from a range of providers) that were often not 'enjoyed' by our sample because of the uncertainties and insecurities they generated. In the cases of some even more frail people, they were often simply unaware that they were in receipt of these entitlements. The whole language of care used in policy and by the professional providers was unattached to the felt experiences of our sample and the words they used to describe their situations.

The 'new managerialism' and choice

Sir Herbert Laming's comments, quoted above, reflect his immersion in, and responsibility for, the ideology that currently dominates the UK's public personal social services. This involves a whole set of interacting ideas: the enabling state; the shift from direct provision to contracting out and managing the 'social care market'; setting targets and measuring outcomes; obtaining value for money; offering choice and consultation to users and their carers. This ideology has much to recommend it: it is clear about its goals and testing whether they are achieved; and it uses the language of consultation, entitlement and empowerment. For example, it has led to a continuing series of joint inspections of the performance of local authority social services conducted by the Audit Commission and the Social Services Inspectorate. Some excerpts from a recent summary report of the first 29 inspections gives a flavour of the approach:

What are Social Services for?

Social services are there to protect and empower vulnerable people. Councils can achieve these aims by working with individuals, by fostering communities that support people and by funding other organisations that help people. Councils are accountable for social services through a 'contract' which works at three levels:

- with citizens who use social services
- with communities that share responsibilities with councils; and
- with taxpayers who fund social services. (Audit Commission 1998, p.2)

What do users think?

Nearly three quarters of users and carers continue to rate services as excellent or good. Older people rate services more highly, as do women. Overall, this represents a high level of public satisfaction but individual council's scores for 'excellent or good' vary from 84 per cent to 59 per cent. (Audit Commission 1998, p.8)

Are services equally accessible to all?

There appears to be no consistent link between referrals, assessments and services either across councils, or indeed across different services within the same council. The Review Team cannot, therefore, reach any strong conclusions about targeting of services ... Services should be targeted on people who can benefit most ... However, councils are not collecting the information about need, or service effectiveness, to underpin their targeting strategies ... Neither citizens nor councils can easily judge whether services are hitting the relevant target. (Audit Commission 1998, p.11)

Taken together it is difficult to be sure what these observations amount to. They, and the report that contains them, which has a bright user-friendly look, amount to little more than an affirmation of the management approach (even culture) that they represent. This is a form of management by objectives but one which, on the report's own admission, has yet to succeed within its own terms. Their solution, found in this document and many others like it that emerge from the Audit Commission and the Social Services Inspectorate, is more of the same. Anyone who knows the history of social services management will know that the 'new managerialism' represents a deliberate effort on the part of the Department of Health to replace the professional social work culture that dominated the provision of social services until the mid-1980s. That approach, built upon the idea that a properly trained and socially committed social worker was the best judge of the appropriate allocation of services, was systematically discredited by research in the 1980s. It was frequently shown that local services were almost randomly allocated, had no clear objectives and produced no measured results that could be used to judge value for money (e.g. Audit Commission 1986). Within its own terms the 'new managerialism' is logical and had its own integrity. It is difficult to argue with attempts to find those most in need, assess them, arrange services and then measure the outcomes against the original intentions. However, our limited research amongst the ultimate recipients of social care services would suggest that they would not recognize many of the concepts that define the goals and methods of the 'new community care' and that even many of those who are in receipt of it do not know that they are. Gains may eventually be made and proven, but for the moment we would suggest that the 'new managerialism' mainly demonstrates the ease with which a new discourse, supported by powerful forces, can enter and appropriate the cultural space that contains the care of frail old people.

Conclusion

This is not a chapter that seeks with any confidence to prescribe what should be done to ensure that the growing numbers of frail old people over the next thirty years, amongst whom we may ourselves be counted, receive a better chance of care than is available today. We cannot quibble with the large amount of diligent research that has shown how too many needs are inappropriately dealt with or left unmet by any services. Neither do we question the motives of those who are seeking to remedy this situation. Rather we are simply seeking to show, on the basis of limited, qualitative research into how old people actually negotiate the problems of frailty, that both of Murphy's laws apply. Firstly, things are more complicated than they first appear, and secondly, what can go wrong usually will go wrong. The complexity is rooted in the relative novelty of a universal expectation that a substantial portion of one's life will be spent in retirement together with the less desired possibility that a further proportion will include dependency on others for help. Our culture does not provide much in the way of institutional forms and accepted norms of behaviour to support older people as they choose and construct their routes through what we have called an 'unscripted old age'. The risks this lack of a clear map gives rise to are mostly inevitable and unavoidable, but we suggest they are added to by the power of other interests to 'colonize' this unscripted territory of old age with their own, often weakly founded, interpretations of what is to be desired.

References

Audit Commission (1986) *Making a Reality of Community Care.* London: HMSO.

Audit Commission (1998) *Getting the Best From Social Services: Learning the Lesson From Joint Reviews.* Abingdon: Audit Commission Publications.

Baldock, J. (1997) 'Social care in old age: More than a funding problem.' *Social Policy and Administration, 31,* 1, 73–89.

Baldock, J. and Ungerson, C. (1994) *Becoming Consumers of Community Care: Households Within the Mixed Economy of Welfare.* Community Care into Practice Series. York: Joseph Rowntree Foundation.

Campbell, J. and Oliver, M. (1996) *Disability Politics, Understanding Our Past, Changing Our Future.* London: Routledge.

Coleman, P.G. (1986) *Ageing and Reminiscence Processes: Social and Clinical Implications.* London: Wiley.

Conservative Party Manifesto (1992) *The Best Future for Britain.* London: Conservative Central Office.

Cumming, E. (1961) *Growing Old: The Process of Disengagement.* New York: Basic Books.

Department of Health (1998) *Social Services Facing the Future. The Seventh Annual Report of the Chief Inspector of the Social Services Inspectorate 1997/98.* London: The Stationery Office.

Disney, R., Grundy, E. and Johnson, P. (1997) *The Dynamics of Retirement: Analyses of the Retirement Surveys.* Research Report No 72, Dept of Social Security. London: The Stationery Office.

Downey, R. (1998) 'Look back in anger.' interview with Sir Herbert Laming. *Community Care,* 25th June – 1st July 1998.

Eysenck, H. and Frith, C. (1977) *Reminiscence, Motivation, and Personality: A Case Study in Experimental Psychology.* London and New York: Plenum Press.

Gibson, D. (1998) *Aged Care: Old Policies, New Problems.* Cambridge: Cambridge University Press.

Goddard, E. (1994) *People Aged 65 and Over, A Study Carried Out On Behalf of the Department of Health As Part of the 1991 General Household Survey.* London: HMSO.

Gorky, M. (1920) *Reminiscences of Leo Nicolayevitch Tolstoy* (authorized translation by S. S. Koteliansky and L. Woolf). London: Hogarth Press.

Hoinville. G. (1978) *Survey Research Practice.* London: Heinemann Educational Books.

KCHCC (Kent Community Health Care Council) (1999) *A Consumer View of Primary Health Care Services for those Aged 75 and Over.* Maidstone: Community Health Care Council.

Norris, A. (1988) *Reminiscence With Elderly People.* Bicester: Winslow Press.

OPCS (1990) *Disabled Adults: Services, Transport and Employment, Disability Survey Report No 4.* London: HMSO.

Phillipson, C., Bernard, J., Phillips, J. and Ogg, J. (1998) *The Family and Community Life of Older People: Social Networks and Support in Three Urban Areas.* Report summary. University of Keele: Dept. of Applied Social Studies.

PART II

Researching Welfare as Culture

Introduction to Part II

Andrew Cooper

The comparative study of European welfare systems has traditionally been grounded in research methodologies suited to the task of establishing or revealing variations in the structure of welfare states at the macro level. It is only more recently, and partly as a consequence of the momentum towards greater European integration, that researchers have begun to deploy qualitative methods in cross-national, comparative research. This development has had a direct bearing upon the 'rediscovery of culture' as a key dimension in the constitution of welfare practices, ideologies and systems. The majority of papers in this section derive from this latter, emergent tradition, while Mike Hornsby-Smith's belongs recognizably within the former, drawing as it does upon Esping-Andersen's seminal work in the elaboration of welfare typologies as well as the massive European social values survey. Although the balance of contributions is uneven, the juxtaposition is instructive since it is a feature of comparative micro studies that they must find some way of organizing the study of similarities and differences by reference to macro variables at the level of the nation, region or some other superordinate framework. There are, for example, possible explanatory links between Hornsby-Smith's discussion of those societies which seem to legitimate citizens' rights to social welfare and protection, and Rachael Hetherington's discovery of the differential experience and attitude of French and English parents who come into contact with child protection services.

Both Hetherington's paper and my own contribution reflect work undertaken as part of a programme of studies of child protection in a number of European countries, although both the present papers concentrate solely on Anglo-French comparison. One project sought to induce a reflexive self-awareness among welfare professionals in the two countries by exposing them, through video and interview material, to the practices and assumptions of their counterparts; practioners in different countries were seen (and saw themselves) to be dealing with an identical, artificial case in different ways. Another (Hetherington's) involved the 'retranscription' of parents' narratives into a form they might have taken across the channel. This research enabled research subjects – social work practitioners and 'users' – to engage with their own experience by encountering the national 'other'; it also allowed thickly textured data to emerge from the lived experience of social actors in different welfare regimes. It is this combination which enables culture to emerge as an irreducible dimension of the production and reproduction of welfare practice in different countries. Identical or very similar initial conditions are shown to give rise to rapidly and widely divergent processes and outcomes explicable only in terms of their embeddedness in a complex field of social, political, historical, legal and ideological variables.

The development of plausible and intelligible interpretations of case studies at this level may be a process akin to orthodox ethnographic or anthropological analysis in which the primary aim is the identification of a set of internal relations among observed phenomena which give coherence to the new and unfamiliar phenomena encountered by the field worker. The chapters by Prue Chamberlayne, Antonella Spanò, and Eli Tejero and Laura Torrabadella derive from related research projects drawing on the biographical methods developed over the last twenty years by sociological researchers including Daniel Bertaux, Martin Kohli and Fritz Schütze. This method proceeds inductively from the particular details of reported biography to an analysis of the subject's life conceived as a strategic accommodation to a set of social and cultural possibilities and constraints. It constitutes a powerful, empirically based assault on the traditional sociological problematic of 'agency' and 'structure'. As Tejero and Torrabadella argue in their contribution, the life strategies of the women they took as their research subjects reveal not only the shaping forces of external social circumstances but also the activity of the subjects in creating new ideological and cultural spaces for disadvantaged women. In turn, Chamberlayne's paper demonstrates how strong empirical generalizations start to emerge from the aggregation of quite small numbers of case studies, so that the distinctive cultural forms assumed by welfare regimes in different countries take shape as something constituting but also constituted by the individual life lived in the matrix of social time and space. Apart from the intrinsic interest of their various findings, the papers in this section are compelling examples of exactly the kind of creative effort required to synthesize macro- and micro-level research (Freeman and Rustin, above).

Against this background, it is possible to argue that certain assumptions of the founding tradition of positivist, cross-national comparative research no longer hold water. To compare outcomes in welfare interventions across national boundaries without first researching and defining the cultural norms which shape the day-to-day intentions of welfare professionals – let alone the equally significant everyday expectations of recipient users – is no longer defensible. Variations in national frameworks of child protection (both legal and cultural) mean that certain options available in one country are simply unavailable by definition in others; to some extent, therefore, a kind of teleology operates to alter professional actors' conceptions of apparently identical initial conditions and how they might be managed. The subsequent evolution of case careers can only be understood by reference to the respective 'futures' differentially available for them. One instance of this is the judicial and cultural valorization of child adoption in the United Kingdom, and its more or less complete absence in France: the availability or unavailability of such an outcome acts to alter practice behaviour across a whole range of potential decisions and subjective responses by both professionals and parents in child welfare cases. Cross-national evaluations can only be severely distorted unless such factors are taken fully into account.

However, these observations are not intended to signal anything as straightforward as a rapprochement between an old positivism and a new qualitative and culturally sensitive methodology. For policy, the stance implied in these papers is more radical. Reading those which draw on biographical methods, one cannot but be moved by the stories, by their affective, and dare it be said, tragic as well as hopeful dimensions. What are we to make of this, if we take it seriously? That feeling, empathy and concern for the predicaments of other people might be an engine of social policy? In Britain at least, where we seem to have embarked upon an era of content-free social policy, in which talk of consumer satisfaction surveys are the nearest one comes to evidence that sentient persons might be what all the fuss is about, such thoughts are more unthinkable now than they were ten or even twenty years ago. In this sense, we are living through change processes bigger than any political party programme currently has the courage to embrace. But the challenge for policy, which we take up in more detail in our closing chapter, is located exactly at the point of contact between the suffering and vicissitudes of lives lived in 'risk societies' and the responsibilities of those with the political power and resources to respond. In our view, policy can no longer be led from the 'top', any more than it can be directed exclusively by those on the dispossessed margins; a new kind of meeting point, and capacity for dialogue, capable of both human identification and structured action, is required. In this way the methodological innovations described in these chapters seem to point beyond themselves, to the possibility of engagement with radical forms of uncertainty in human affairs.

CHAPTER 5

Anxiety and Child Protection Work in Two National Systems

Andrew Cooper

Introduction

Child protection social work gives rise to intense anxiety in those who practise it. In England and Wales we now take this so much for granted that it has become hard to ask intelligent sounding questions about why it should be so. The inability to ask questions would not matter so much if all was well with our system of child protection work, but it is not. Arguably, of course, these considerations are related; the climate of professional impotence and defensiveness attenuates our capacity for self-examination, which in turn feeds our helplessness and increases our anxiety. It is harder to stand outside and evaluate with a fresh eye. The vicious circles and closed systems of our current situation have been well described by some recent commentators (Preston-Shoot and Agass 1990) who conclude that '…the now urgent need is to communicate about the communication, to assume a meta position and focus on the system' (p.115).

Anxiety arising from practice encounters is part of all social work and an aspect of the experience of all practitioners; part of the importance of psycho-dynamic understanding in social work is to teach us that anxiety will not go away, that we must learn the capacity to tolerate it, and that it is more destructive when denied than when faced. But to what extent are the pressures experienced by today's child protection workers inevitable; part of the reality which must be tolerated for the sake of continuing to do the job?

A project which set out to compare the child protection system of England and Wales with that of France may help to shed light on this question. One of the unanticipated outcomes of the project, which was undertaken jointly with French researchers and practitioners, was the way in which participants found themselves taking up a 'meta' position on their own system by virtue of increased understanding of practice realities within an alternative one. Put simply, this was an experience of doing a 'double-take' and seeing that 'it really can be different'. This insight ranged over many aspects of work within the two systems, but the body of this chapter concerns the creation, maintenance and management of professional anxiety within specific systems of social work practice.

The work of Menzies Lyth (1988, 1990) offers a developed psychoanalytic account of the way in which intra-psychic anxiety can be mobilized by the primary task of caring, and if not contained by the organization in a helpful way, lead to the creation of socially structured defence mechanisms. Menzies Lyth stresses the process of externalization of defences, so that in effect unconscious dynamics originating in the inner world of individuals engaged in a common task end by significantly shaping the micro-social structures in which they work. The present chapter aims to complement this account by showing how social structures, in the particular form of two different child protection systems, can create different and more or less fertile conditions for the mobilization and management of anxiety and unconscious phantasy in practitioners. Thus the paper aims to illustrate how macro-social structure intersects with the micro processes described by Menzies Lyth, to provide a more comprehensive account of the nature and origins of professional anxiety in the child protection task.

However, the different 'systems' of protection within which French and English practitioners work, and with which children and parents become engaged, are not simply structural variations on a common theme; the character of the two systems – the principles, values, models of practice, available decisions, pathways and 'outcomes' which constitute them – cannot be understood or explained in isolation from what we term 'culture'. The implicit and explicit rules and norms of behaviour which organize the operation of systems of this kind are themselves expressions of culture, and constitutive of it. Part of the wider thesis implied by the present chapter, and elaborated in other publications arising from this research programme (including Rachael Hetherington's contribution to this book, see Chapter 6), is that we can 'read off' something of the broader culture of the society from how it finds expression at the micro or meso levels. As Richard Freeman and Michael Rustin argue in their introduction to the present collection, 'For culture is made visible at the micro level: in organizations, in meetings, conferences and consultations, in interactions between people' (see Introduction).

The design of the research

In this study data was collected in three ways. First, the same fictional case study involving child protection concerns – but neutral with respect to the systems of the two countries – was given to two groups of practitioners from each country, who were involved in child protection work. At each of four stages in the evolution of the case, individual questionnaires were completed, recording information about what action would have been taken, why this intervention was chosen, and what concepts or ideas informed the choice. Second, each group took part in a video-recorded discussion about the case and wider issues of child protection work. Third, one video from each country was dubbed and sent to the other country; the groups reassembled and after watching the video of their colleagues across the channel, took part in a tape-recorded discussion about their reactions to what they had seen; the discussion was structured to focus on what they found similar, different, or surprising about their colleagues' response to the same case material.

One French group of practitioners (F1) consisted of a team of workers from a voluntary organization (JCLT) in Beauvais, whose mandate is to undertake statutory child care work under the direction of the Children's Judge (*Juge des Enfants*). The other (F2) comprised workers from other parts of the system, particularly those employed by the *Direction d'Actions Sanitaire et Sociale* (DASS), which is roughly equivalent to a local authority social services department; workers in this latter group are responsible for identifying possible abuse and making referrals to the Children's Judge, but they do not implement judicial orders. The first English group (E1) consisted largely of local authority social workers with direct responsibility for child protection work, and the second (E2) largely of practitioners, such as family placement workers and family centre workers with direct involvement in statutory child protection work, but not carrying first-line responsibility.

Care and control in the two systems

Some understanding of the differences between the two systems of child protection is necessary in order to appreciate the findings of the research. First, from a legal standpoint the French system can be viewed as inquisitorial or investigative, whereas the English one is adversarial. The Children's Judge is the central legal figure in child protection and juvenile delinquency work in France, but the informal hearing or 'audience' conducted by the Judge is not centrally concerned with guilt or innocence, or even with evaluating evidence. This means that for French social workers child protection assessments entail gathering information, rather than evidence to be presented in court subject to rules of admissibility as in England, and that the Judge is concerned with understanding the case at least as much as with administering the legal process (King and Piper 1990, p.136).

The French system places considerable emphasis on the welfare of the child and much less on his or her rights, whereas in England and Wales the reverse is the case. The French system is comparatively informal and accessible in comparison to the English one; normally in child protection cases the Children's Judge will see children and families in his or her office, without ceremonial robes and without lawyers, although the social worker is often present, especially if a statutory order is being recommended or reviewed, as it must be every six months. Children, parents and social workers can approach a Children's Judge at any time. All of this is in stark contrast to the formality and inaccessibility of the English system, and makes it difficult to compare the *Juge des Enfants* directly with an English Magistrate or High Court Judge.

Finally, the division of professional labour is significantly different in the two systems, both within the social work part of the system, and between the law and social work. In France social workers responsible for implementing statutory orders normally work in a different part of the system from those responsible for identifying and referring child abuse cases into the legal domain. The situation in Beauvais, where we conducted the research, is fairly typical: the voluntary organization with whom we worked (JCLT) is contracted by the local authority (*Conseil Générale*) to undertake statutory work and operates as a separate '*service d'AEMO*' (*Action Educative en Milieu Ouvert*).

Once a statutory order has been made, the Children's Judge retains responsibility for and involvement with the case; social workers are accountable to the Judge, carry out his or her directions and ensure that new information is passed back. In England where there are grounds for suspecting abuse but insufficient evidence, practitioners carry a heavy responsibility which is not matched by their power to take action. For its part, the court has considerable power in making dispositions about cases but it carries no responsibility for a case where there is insufficient 'evidence' or for what may happen after an order is made.

Thus the relationship between 'care' and 'control' in French child protection work has quite different institutional manifestations from those in England. Social work and the law must and do collaborate. The Children's Judge is trained to think and act almost as much in welfare as in legal terms. In a well-known French text, aptly titled 'The Children's Judge – To Punish or Protect?', the author who is himself a *Juge des Enfants* writes:

> How does the judge assess the likely danger to a child? … Medico-psychosocial assessment has a legitimacy different from but equal to that of the judge. The judge's assessment and the medico-psychosocial assessment are interactive. The question deserves to be approached according to a dynamic model. (Baudoin 1990, p.78)

The author continues with a sophisticated discussion of the delicate balance Children's Judges must strike between implementing the law and obtaining the cooperation of reluctant parents and children; of managing the fluid boundary between his role and those of the welfare services; of the strategic and even therapeutic use of his authority. Rather than make elaborate attempts to elicit confessions from abusing parents, or gain their reluctant consent to a placement, a firm statement that he will not listen to denials and that his job is to ensure the safety of the child:

> … is much more reassuring for them, and the absence of protest often indicates an implicit acceptance of the facts and a tacit acceptance of the statutory measures for the child's protection which they secretly want, but cannot ask for.

In the end the best guarantee for both parents and children, and of effective implementation of the statutory order:

> ... rests with the Judge's competence, and his ability to make use of the competence of his partners – doctors, psychologists, social workers and so on. (Baudouin 1990, p.108)

The frequently noted paternalism of the French system of justice is clearly visible in even these short extracts. In our research, English practitioners were both astonished at the uncircumscribed power of the Judge and the absence of formal procedure for guaranteeing the rights of both parents and children, and simultaneously envious of the apparent structural integration of the law with social work as well as the ease of access which social workers have to the legal domain. By and large 'care and control' in the French system seem to be united in the figure of the Children's Judge (Ely and Stanley 1990).

In England and Wales, when it seems there is a need to take legal measures to protect a child, social workers are likely to find themselves in immediate institutionalized conflict with the parents, and possibly also with the law. In effect, intra-familial conflict is exported into the various organizations and representatives of the state and the law, who then reconvene in court for an institutionalized family argument (Cooper *et al.* 1992b). Despite its emphasis on partnership, in some respects the Children Act (1989) exacerbated this situation, by assigning more rights to more individuals in an attempt to resolve the problem of conflict of rights. In England 'care and control' tend to be easily sundered as a result of this process of institutionalized polarization, which creates a false dichotomy between the values and practices of the law and of social work. 'What emerges is a "tug-of-war" image, or alternatively a system embodying conflicting imperatives of welfare and justice.' And so:

> Role insecurity, reflected in either defensive or omnipotent practice, is the outcome. Rather than the creative solution, which requires practitioners to hold and resolve the tensions in each case, refuge is sought in an over emphasis on one or other polarity. (Braye and Preston-Shoot 1990, pp.336–338)

Anxiety and child protection work in the research findings

The case study which was given to all four participating groups described a family situation with gradually escalating concern in the welfare network, and an accumulation of possible indicators of child abuse; however, the parents had become uncooperative, and the adolescent girl who had hinted at an over-intimate relationship with her stepfather, would not elaborate further.

Questionnaire responses were administered at each of the four stages of the case study, and subsequent group discussions were structured to focus partly on how groups thought they could or should proceed after stage four. The evolution of anxiety and the level it attained varied significantly among groups, but according to a pattern which makes sense in terms of the different distributions of the groups' responsibility for child protection and power to act within their system (Cooper *et al.* 1992a).

Group E1, which contained mostly local authority practitioners, were more anxious and seemed to feel more impotent than their colleagues in E2, who were from settings with less direct responsibility for child protection work. Nevertheless, by stage four of the study both groups felt powerless to act and anxious because of their responsibility for the welfare of the children. On viewing the video discussion of E1, the second French group (F2) identified with the predicament of the English workers to a much greater extent than did F1. In contrast the latter were struck by the preoccupation of their English colleagues with 'pressures' and the anxiety associated with their responsibility. F1 appeared comparatively free of anxiety and only after some encouragement agreed that they would be likely to feel some pressure from other agencies to act or make a referral to the Judge. It will be recalled that F1 comprised the *service d'AEMO* practitioners who work under the authority of the Children's Judge, while F2 mainly consisted of generic and non-statutory workers who are responsible for referring suspected abuse to the Children's Judge.

An analysis of this data in terms of structure suggests that:

1. The greatest degree of anxiety is carried by English child protection workers who remain responsible for child protection cases before and after referral to the courts. This may be true both in cases where there is sufficient evidence to prove abuse and in those where there is not.

2. A comparable degree of anxiety is carried by French *assistants social de secteur* and *éducateurs d'ASE* who are responsible for referring cases of suspected abuse to the Children's Judge. However, their level of anxiety appears to be less acute, because they have much easier access to the judicial arena than their English counterparts who are always dependent on having sufficient evidence to make such a referral. In France anxiety for these workers is partly connected to recent prosecutions for failure to refer such cases in time (Cervi 1991). There have been no public enquiries or child abuse 'scandals' in France comparable to Cleveland or the Orkneys, but the prosecutions represent a similar kind of public pressure.

3. English family centre workers and French AEMO workers appear to carry the least anxiety, because ultimate responsibility rests elsewhere, in England with the local authority worker and in France with the Juge des Enfants. Of course these workers are confronted at times with difficult decisions about suspected abuse; the point in the present context is that overall distribution of anxiety can be understood as structurally determined.

The origins of anxiety in child protection work

We suggest that anxiety in child protection workers originates from four discrete but interlocking sites. The contribution of our research is in clarifying the areas of intersection, and showing how different professional structures and systems of management create better or worse conditions in which anxiety can flourish or be appropriately contained.

The child and the abusing parents

Abused children have been subject to one form or another of physical, sexual or emotional violence. Physical harm, bodily invasion, transgression of boundaries, or fear and anxiety arising from neglect are the realities within abusing families. Abusing parents are likely to have strong or aggressive defences against knowing about these realities, particularly when first faced with an outsider who is enquiring or investigating.

Whatever the child protection worker's own capacity for receiving and tolerating this knowledge, contact with families will give rise to powerful and primitive feelings, for example rage, fear, repulsion or eroticism. Strong identifications may be mobilized, and strong defences against aggression and 'knowing'.

The worker

The strength of recent psychodynamic work in this area is that it stresses the inter-active or systemic character of the processes involved. A focus on the way in which workers react defensively to contact with child abuse does not have to imply personal pathology. Rather:

> ... in each one of us, a defensive system arises in the form of a primitive counter-transference which is capable of destroying those efficient reactions which could be used for the treatment and protection of the endangered child. This dynamic problem will always exist, whatever the strength of the judicial protections system (Hadjiisky 1987, p.32)

Mattinson and Sinclair's (1979) study examined the role of projective identification in creating the 'reflection process' wherein the worker's behaviour comes to mirror that of the clients; this work has been fruitfully extended in a recent major study of inter-agency dynamics in marital work (Woodhouse and Pengelly 1991). Nevertheless, it is clear that in these dynamics the practitioner's own capacity to experience anxiety is powerfully mobilized.

The organization and the professional network

At the micro-social level, Menzies Lyth (1990) stresses the role of anxiety and collective defences against anxiety in shaping the organization within which practitioners work:

> In developing a structure, culture and mode of functioning, a social organisation is influenced by a number of interacting factors, crucial among which is its primary task ... The need of the members of the organisation to use it in the struggle

against anxiety leads to the development of socially structured defense mechanisms, which appear as elements in the structure, culture and mode of functioning of the organisation (p.443)

This line of thought has been extended by practitioners and theorists in a number of directions, including analysis of how unconscious processes influence the functioning of professional networks. Here it is the socially and structurally given divisions between professional groups and organizations which are mobilized in service of the defence of splitting. Woodhouse and Pengelly (1991) offer an astute discussion of the operation of such processes among the professional and gender groupings at the centre of the Cleveland crisis.

Writing about 'interprofessional dysfunction' Will and Baird (1984) point to the interaction of three variables, of which the first two are comparable to those discussed above; the third they describe as 'real interprofessional vulnerabilities (which) provide lines of least resistance along which mirroring may occur' (p.289). Their analysis is focused on tensions in philosophies and values, agency perspectives in relation to task and responsibility, and differential status of professional groups; in examining macro-level systems and their relationship to the production of anxiety, the notion of 'lines of least resistance' is an equally potent one.

The child protection process

As a force shaping the dynamics of anxiety in social work practice, the nature of the larger social formation in which practice occurs remains largely unexamined. Although Menzies Lyth acknowledges the explanatory limits of her thesis about the emergence of socially constructed defence mechanisms, it is a theoretical weakness characteristic of psychoanalytic forays into the social, that the latter is understood solely as the externalization or collectivization of intra-psychic processes.

The remainder of this chapter is devoted to exploring how the structure of the English and French child protection systems seem to engender different possibilities for the emergence, growth and containment of professional anxiety with respect to the primary task of trying to protect children.

Considered as a social structure, a system of child protection, or its parts, may well become the repository of collective defence mechanisms and be manipulated in the service of defending against corporate anxiety; but it can also serve more or less effectively as an appropriate container of anxiety. Whether and how it does this will be a function of the 'fit' between its internal structure and the dynamics of anxiety associated with the job of protecting children. The ambivalence to the concept of 'defence' in this context is clear in the research material we gathered.

The social structuring of anxiety

The different distributions of power and responsibility between the social work and legal parts of the two child protection systems, and the ease of access from one part of the system to the other, seem to significantly determine the scope for development of professional anxiety. Where power and responsibility for the primary task are structurally disconnected from each other, and where there is difficulty about access from the social work to the legal part of the system, then the scope for anxiety increases in particular ways. This manifests itself as both a blockage to the possibility of conflict resolution, and as a lack of containment with destructive potential for workers.

Blockage

In their questionnaire and discussion responses to the case study, English workers clearly felt that they were left with responsibility for the welfare of the children but, lacking the evidence, no power to act to protect them. This immobilized them and made them anxious:

> I think there's this worry about what is actually going on in the home, when nobody's telling us and we haven't got any proper evidence; particularly as the family are resistant to our help ... It's very difficult when we haven't actually got the evidence to remove the children ... I think there would be a lot of pressures on us from other agencies to remove them possibly. (E1)

Here the pressure to act is both 'internal' and 'external'; but it is the inability to meet the legal criteria which causes paralysis. In response to a question about who is responsible for what concerns in such a situation, the reply in E2 is unequivocal:

> Invariably social services. They are left with it because you've got the statutory obligation to try and do something.

In contrast, after watching the discussion of their French colleagues, both English groups commented at some length on their counterparts' confidence in the possibility of seeking resolution of the case through negotiation; the French workers clearly felt that the possibility of both the Judge and the parents and the Judge and the child entering such a 'negotiation' was realistic, and they also saw judicial intervention as potentially enabling negotiation between the family and the workers themselves. Implicit in this was the French workers' confidence in the Children's Judge:

> ... they didn't seem to have to panic; A needs to be done, B needs to be done, if not we refer it to the Children's Judge, and it's all trying to get things done in a negotiated way even though the judiciary was involved ...

> They didn't seem concerned about the repercussions of their decisions; they seemed to have confidence in the Judge ...

> They made a distinction between pressure and negotiation, most of them saying that though people might have different views, they would negotiate and come to

some decision between them, and they seemed sure that that would happen, that it was something that could be resolved. (E1)

But what exactly is the nature of the anxiety which the English workers carry by virtue of their inability to 'enter negotiation' with the judicial domain and effect a 'resolution' of the conflicts in the case? We discerned a set of complex and ambivalent feelings here, which it is worth analysing in some detail.

Workers in E1 reacted quite enviously to their French counterparts' 'freedom from evidence gathering', and as one participant also said, the early encounter with the Judge might:

> ... clarify a few issues – if I'd misunderstood certain things I'd feel a bit safer ...

While those in E2 also commented at some length on the lack of focus on evidence in the French discussion, they were concerned that French workers seemed 'judgemental' about the family, and saw the role of evidence and legal process in the English system serving both to protect families from unfounded allegations and to protect workers from accusations of bringing such allegations. This difference of emphasis may reflect the composition of the groups: E2 largely comprised workers without direct child protection case responsibility, who may have felt freer to think about protecting families from abuses of power than their colleagues in E1 who are more preoccupied with protecting themselves from either failing to intervene or being over-zealous in doing so.

A central theme in E2's original group discussion following questionnaire completion was a robust debate about the 'right' to intervene in the case; some participants stressed the need to find a way to do so in the interests of the children and in view of the accumulated indicators of abuse, while others felt strongly that there was an absence of evidence to support an intervention.

> It sounds like a weird situation where there's these people saying, 'Look, I'm very depressed, I need help, someone to do something', and we're saying, 'Well ... There is no physical evidence of abuse to that four year old.'

Or as another participant poignantly summarized it:

> You just ... you shouldn't be destroying families without evidence.

Lack of containment

Destroying families without evidence and wanting early legal intervention as protection against misunderstandings are preoccupations that speak eloquently of the way in which the English system of child protection allows professional anxiety to be displaced away from the intended object of protection, namely children, onto workers themselves. Workers appear to feel that they are either objects of potential persecution, or are themselves potential persecutors. In either case it is reasonable to speculate that the concern which English workers felt about the apparent lack of legal constraint on the powers of the French Children's Judge represented anxiety about the removal of a defence against the potential destructiveness of social work intervention in child protection work. Who or what will prevent me doing something terrible to this family?

The paradox of this situation is acute; the very same rules of evidence which deny social workers the power to act on their reality-based anxiety about children, and leave them responsible for genuinely anxiety-provoking situations, are invoked by them as a form of protection against both the psychic anxiety involved in 'destroying families' if they do act, and the anticipated public blame if they do not and some harm comes to a child. As a defence against anxiety, the reliance on anxiety in our system clearly does not work. Why not, and what might be the difference in the French system?

Amongst the elements of the 'primitive counter-transference' which Hadjiisky (1987) describes as arising in child protection workers, we assume there will be a mobilization of the basic oedipal wish to 'break up the parents' and dominate the family scene, alongside the corresponding fear of this impulse. The image of 'breaking up families' occurs repeatedly in the discourse of the English workers in our study, in a way that seems taken for granted; writing about the Cleveland affair, Woodhouse and Pengelly remark on the:

> ... kind and quality of unconscious phantasies to which child sexual abuse is likely to speak in any practitioner ... a primitive world that is associated with the longing to possess and be possessed by the parents. (1991, p.251)

It is our belief that the crucial factor in understanding how these processes are translated in different child protection systems is whether the judicial system with which social workers collaborate is itself experienced by them as benign or malign, as an understanding authority or as a punitive one; in the end whether it enables social workers to distinguish between the realistic need to intervene in families in the best interests of children, and the wanton, arbitrary acting out of destructive impulses.

As Hadjiisky suggests, child protection social workers operating under optimum conditions tend to find themselves in the grip of counter-transference reactions, identifying with either the abused and persecuted child, or defensively with the abusing and persecuting parent; that is, they experience themselves as either persecuted or persecuting, and frequently both; if in addition the authority which legitimates their actions (the law and the court) is itself experienced as arbitrary, hostile, and judgemental, this will severely exacerbate tendencies towards self-blame, doubt, and critical self-examination in social workers even when they believe they are doing the right thing in terms of social work values and principles. The situation is analogous to living in the shadow of a too harsh superego; reality-based doubt and anxiety rooted in 'concern for the object' is fused with and obliterated by an irrational sense of generalized guilt and fear of 'getting it wrong'.

Thus there is an irony in English practitioners seeing their French counterparts as 'judgemental', as though their own task can be performed without making judgements about families. Under attack by the courts and the public for 'getting it wrong', it is understandable that English practitioners come to construct 'evidence gathering' as a value-neutral and technical activity, and want to hand over the responsibility of 'making judgements' to the court. At this point two varieties of defence can be called upon – identifying with the court as the aggressor, if the courts endorse an application to 'break up the family' ('We merely submitted the evidence, the court actually decided'), or abdicating responsibility for the process of making judgements if the application is rejected ('It's the court's decision, we did our best'). But neither defensive manoeuvre really works because in both cases the court, having made its decision, hands back responsibility for the case to the social worker, leaving them to wrestle with the consequences of one variety or another of felt destructive action.

It appears to us that the structural relationship between the social work and legal parts of the English system does not readily enable child protection workers to manage their own authority; authority is too easily experienced as destructiveness. Another way of putting this is to say that social workers deserve, and need, to be protected from external blame; the potential for self-blame and guilt, transferred from and activated by the families themselves, is already great enough.

Musing about the climate of French child protection work, one E2 participant said, 'They must have children who die' but concluded that perhaps the French public blame the parents, not the social workers. Irrespective of the real situation in France, this is a telling remark because it assumes that someone somewhere is going to be blamed. But it was clear to English workers that the Children's Judge was not perceived by the French as threatening in this respect; rather the emphasis on scope for negotiation, and ease of access to the judiciary, was linked to a general perception of these French AEMO workers as carrying less of a burden of responsibility:

> There was a willingness to involve the judicial system very early on ... It almost felt to me like some of the heavy individual responsibility a social worker might carry in managing a case was not here ... (E1)

In E2 a participant commented on the need to 'take away some of the heavy responsibility of the worker on the ground', and another agreed saying that '... we are more powerful than they (French social workers) are and that is not a good thing.'

In the French system the Children's Judge not only retains responsibility for the case after a statutory order is made, but shares with social workers the responsibility for both the care and control dimensions of the child protection task. The social work part of the system (l'éducatif) receives a 'mandate' from the Judge to implement a social work task (mission éducative), but as Baudouin (1990, p.107) observes, 'If the parents oppose the judge's decision, but end up abiding by it, it is with respect to the judge that they will eventually express their resentment'!

Children's Judges' training and daily practice generate a very different cultural set of role requirements from those ordinarily associated with the judiciary. These include:

> ... a working knowledge of child development, skills of communication with children, familiarity with recent research by child specialists ... and an acquaintance with the range of facilities offered within their own jurisdiction which aim to help children with particular problems. (King and Piper 1990, p.144)

Judicial contact with the reality of the social work task, and shared responsibility for its success and vice versa, means that structurally the 'critical and judging faculty' is in dialogue with the 'helping and concerned' faculty. There is the possibility of mutual identification, including identification by social workers with the rule of law. Each may modify and temper the other, and prevent over-identification with either the persecuted or the persecuting elements in the child abuse dynamic. This containing and reality-oriented function will extend to the experience of social workers themselves, in the task of managing their own anxieties and destructive phantasies, and thereby give them a capacity for dealing effectively and thoughtfully with child abuse itself. Writing about the superego, Winnicott said:

> A sense of guilt therefore implies that the ego is coming to terms with the superego. Anxiety has matured into guilt. (1965, p.18)

Out of this emerges the capacity to tell right from wrong, which is at the heart of intervening in abusive families.

It is the argument of this chapter that the structural split between the social work and legal part of the English child protection system represents a 'line of least resistance', now opened into a fissure, which simultaneously cannot be bridged when necessary and becomes a channel along which the unconscious anxiety of social workers flows and proliferates. Social work is stuck on one side managing both the care and control dimensions of child protection work, while the law is on the other disposing of judgements from a safe distance. The structural integration of these dimensions in the French system would seem to preclude the possibility of social work and the law ever being able to enter into the kind of persecutor–victim dynamic which increasingly characterizes their relationship in England and Wales.

Who cares for the Judge?

In the course of our collaboration we became aware as a research team of a tendency for representatives of each country to idealize the system and practices of the other. No doubt there are difficulties with the French way of doing things, and certainly they see many positive features in English practice. But, as English researchers we found ourselves posed with a new question about the structure and functioning of the French system, which is relevant to the wider task implicit in the present paper – the search for a better balance among the many factors which must contribute to an effective system of child protection. In the end it is unclear whether the French system contains professional anxiety better in some absolute way, or merely redistributes it, or both. Perhaps the Children's Judge performs a parallel role to English child protection workers in being a carrier of anxiety and unresolved family conflict? Our English research participants were certainly aware of the power invested in this figure:

> Well, it is investing a tremendous amount of authority and trust in that Judge, making him all things to all people (E1)

or as one E2 participant put it:

> the great wise one ...

But if there is a single lesson to be learned from the analysis advanced in this chapter, it is that if social work and the law are both to retain a stake in child protection work, they must recognize their full interdependence in this matter; and if we wish to ask that in accepting greater responsibility for the complexity and uncertainty of this work, the law take better care of social workers, we cannot then abdicate all concern for the practitioners of law. Unless as King and Piper (1990) hint, it would be better to remove child protection from the ambit of the law altogether. Subsequent research into the role of Children's Judges in France revealed rather what we had expected, namely that they seem to act as a locus of conflict for the various competing and warring parties to child care cases, and to suffer from a sense of professional isolation as a consequence (Cooper *et al.* 1995). But comparative work on the child protection structures, systems and cultures of several other European countries has revealed that they all have more permeable boundaries between the administrative and the judicial domains of protection than does England and Wales (Hetherington *et al.* 1997). Sometimes this boundary is managed by an institution, as with the Mediation Committee in Flanders or the Children's Panel in Scotland, and sometimes by an individual in a role like the Children's Judge; but in every case the authority of professionals to intervene in cases where they assess children to be at risk is more fully and easily legitimated than in England.

Cultures of subjectivity

For children, parents and professionals alike the experience of being an actor within the system, or within the institutions of the system, is differentiated in different countries by a range of system-specific factors, of which the place of *relationships* in the exercise of authority and decision-making, and in effecting mediation or negotiated solutions to family problems, is key. France is an extreme instance in which considerable power is conferred upon one individual, who is nevertheless required to use his or her office (literally and figuratively) to create a formal social space within which relationships of power, authority, responsibility, obligation and dependency are negotiated and renegotiated in the interests of the welfare of children. In this setting, the Judge is understood by all concerned to embody both the authority and the protection of the state in its relationship to citizens and families, which are understood in turn to be the bedrock upon which the state exists and reproduces itself. Thus, the 'culture' of institutional relationships to be found in the *audience* with the Judge, between social workers and Judges, and between social workers and families, is the expression of a particular global social contract between the state, the individual child and the family; equally every time this culture of relationships is enacted, the particular state cultural formation which we may recognize as characteristically 'French' is reaffirmed and reproduced.

The same analysis is possible in the articulation between cultural and state formations in England and Wales. Here the concept of the residual state as set apart from the private domain of the family and civil society, into which it must not transgress unless there is transgression, typically calls for not a negotiation at its boundary but a contest over the 'right' to intervene and seize authority within the Englishman's castle. Seen in this light, the professional anxiety carried by English social workers is as much the manifestation of a political task with which they are charged – the maintenance of appropriate state-family boundaries – as it is an expression of the transferred and projected psychodynamics of abusing families. In fact, this chapter has been devoted to arguing that in both countries concerned, it is both of these; the possibility that the comparative 'containment' of professional anxiety afforded by the French model may reflect a greater degree of general social cohesion within an inclusive state formation, and the lack of containment experienced in England with a corresponding failure of social integration, may afford interesting possibilities for further comparative research into cultures of subjectivity.

Note

The present chapter is an amended version of a paper originally published in *Journal of Social Work Practice, 6*, 2, Autumn 1992, under the same title.

References

Baudoin, J.M. (1990) *Le Juge des Enfants – Punir ou Proteger?* Paris: ESF editeur.

Braye, S. and Preston-Shoot, M. (1990) 'On teaching and applying the law in social work: It is not that simple.' *British Journal of Social Work, 20*, 333–353.

Cervi, B. (1991) 'Where families come first.' *Community Care, 88*, 16–18.

Cooper, A., Freund V., Grevot, A., Hetherington, R. and Pitts, J. (1992a) *The Social Work Role in Child Protection*. London: Wilthe Press.

Cooper, A., Grevot, A., Hetherington, R. and Pitts, J. (1992b) 'La protection de l'enfance en Angleterre, et en France, elements de base d'une comparison entre les deux systèmes.' *Actes du Colloque: Autorité Responsabilité Parentale Et Protection De l'Enfant* (Confrontations Européennes Regionales, Lyons, France).

Cooper, A., Pitts, J., Hetherington, R., Baistow, K. and Spriggs, A. (1995) *Positive Child Protection: A View from Abroad.* Lyme Regis: Russell House Publishing.

Ely, P. and Stanley, C. (1990) *The French Alternative: Delinquency and Child Protection in France.* London: NACRO.

Hadjiisky, E. (1987) 'On first contact with child abuse and neglect.' *Journal of Social Work Practice, 3,* 31–37.

Hetherington, R.; Cooper, A.; Smith, P. and Wilford, G. (1997) *Protecting Children: Messages from Europe.* Lyme Regis: Russell House Publishing.

King, M. and Piper (1990) *How the Law Thinks about Children.* Aldershot: Gower.

Mattinson, J. and Sinclair, I. (1979) *Mate and Stalemate.* Oxford: Blackwell.

Menzies Lyth, I. (1988) *Containing Anxiety in Institutions: Selected Essays,* Volume 1. London: Free Association Books.

Menzies Lyth, I. (1990) 'Social systems as a defense against anxiety.' In E. Tryst and H. Murray (eds) *The Social Engagement of Social Science.* London: Free Association Books.

Preston-Shoot, M. and Agass, D. (1990) *Making Sense of Social Work.* London: Macmillan.

Will, D. and Baird, D. (1984) 'An integrated approach to dysfunction in interprofessional system.' *Journal of Family Therapy, 6,* 275–290.

Winnicott, D. (1965) 'Psycho-analysis and the sense of guilt.' In *The Maturational Process and the Facilitating Environment.* London: Hogarth Press.

Woodhouse, D. and Pengelly, P. (1991) *Anxiety and the Dynamics of Collaboration.* Aberdeen: Aberdeen University Press.

CHAPTER 6

Parents' Experiences of Child Welfare in England and France

Getting Help and Having Rights

Rachael Hetherington

Introduction

This chapter is an account of certain aspects of a research project comparing the experiences of parents who have been involved with the child welfare or child protection services in France and in England. It is part of a series of comparative studies focused on systems of child welfare and child protection in Europe, which have looked in most detail at France and England (Cooper *et al.* 1995; Hetherington 1994; Baistow and Hetherington 1998), and also at systems in a range of other European countries (Hetherington *et al.* 1997). The rationale for embarking on comparative research was twofold. In the first place we were curious to know how similar problems were dealt with in different countries. It was accepted that child maltreatment took place in other European nations, but the information available in the UK about responses to this was limited. There were either very generalized descriptions of systems or very specific descriptions of small treatment programmes. We were interested in the more mundane and day-to-day aspects of social work intervention, and the structures that supported this. How did the systems function in practice? What journey did the family make to get into a treatment programme? In the second place, we thought that there were many problems in the approach to child protection in England, and that one of these was a feeling of helplessness and being stuck. We looked across the Channel for a new perspective that might enable change in this country, rather as a family might ask a family therapist to introduce a reframing of problems that would enable a systemic shift in the interaction of the family. We were not looking for *better* ways of handling the problems of child maltreatment, but for *different* ones.

The process of comparison

An integral part of the research from the start has been the importance of participation, of parallel work in each country, and of discussion between the researchers from different countries. Everyone involved has been both research subject and researcher at the same time. Each stage of the research has produced two reports, one in France and one in England. These are not solely descriptions of the English system for France, and of the French system for England. The French reports give a new picture of the French system because it is seen through its difference from England and the English reports do the same in its difference from France. Identification of sameness and difference becomes a process by which a familiar landscape begins to look different as light falls on it from a new angle. Whether the chapters in this book are explicitly about comparisons or not, an implicit comparison takes place when we hear about a different way of doing things or hear a theory applied in a different culture from our own. We gain knowledge of another system or another way of looking at things; we also develop a new perspective on our own system or way of looking at things.

Bateson describes how all information is ultimately based on comparison:

> It takes at least two somethings to create a difference. To produce news of difference, i.e. information, there must be two entities (real or imagined) such that the difference between them can be immanent in their mutual relationship. (Bateson 1979, p.78).

The product of studying the system of another country (or a parallel system within the same country, see, for example, Antonella Spanò's research described in Introduction3) is therefore twofold: information about the other system, and 'news of difference' which is new information about the first system. It is important to resist competitive comparative hierarchies of better and worse, because these do not give 'news of difference'.

Making comparisons – culture and ideology

There was one unexpected aspect to our research which declared itself early in the first phase, and that was the extent to which we found ourselves studying aspects of cultural difference, and the importance of the particular aspect of culture with which we were engaged. Studying systems of child welfare and child protection involves looking at the interface between the family, the state and the individual. It entails a consideration of:

- the nature of the family in the culture in question;
- the relationship between the responsibilities for the bringing up of children held by the family and those held by the state;
- the expectations that are held by individuals about this relationship.

Ethnographic definitions of culture vary; see, for example, Thomas (1993) or Taylor (1995), but it seems safe to say that these particular relationships would be seen as aspects of culture according to any definition. In our research therefore we have been studying a particular aspect of the relationship between child welfare and culture. We have been looking at different examples of the way this relationship is played out in different European countries with regard to the roles of family and state in the bringing up of children and in the face of child maltreatment. The research with parents demonstrates some aspects of the ways in which culture can affect the experience of child welfare services.

The research setting

The research with social workers

Earlier phases of this research have been published elsewhere (Cooper *et al*. 1995; Hetherington 1994). The starting point of the research was a comparison of the child welfare and child protection systems in France and England from the point of view of the social workers who operate them. From this research we learnt about the legal and administrative structures of each other's systems and about the experience of the social workers in working with these structures. We gathered our information through the experience of English and French social workers who heard about each other's systems and working life, and shared their reflections on this with us as researchers. From this we got a view of a shifting, dynamic relationship between professional culture, national culture, and the ideologies and structures which both expressed and shaped these cultures. However, this was only one view of the situation. Other players in the game would be likely to see things very differently and different comparisons might emerge.

The research with the parents

The current project therefore aimed to move on from the views and reflections of social workers to those of the family. In both countries, we wanted to hear what the families thought and felt about the services available to them (or, in some cases, imposed on them). We then wanted to make a range of comparisons between them. Some of these were comparisons about resources, some were about the impact of the experience on those involved, some were about the underlying assumptions that were being made by the families and by ourselves. There is some previous research on the experience of families in England, but this is mainly very specifically targeted on the experience of child protection procedures (Hooper 1992; Howitt 1992; Prosser 1992; Lindley 1994; Cleaver and Freeman 1995; Farmer and Owen 1995). There is very little previous research in France. When the focus was on social workers, we felt that we knew from our own experience what the social workers were likely to feel about their own systems; what we wanted to explore was what they might feel about another system. We had less idea what families might feel about their own system. We aimed very broadly, to discover what the families we interviewed thought and felt about their experience, to hear their stories, and to use comparisons with experiences in another system to try to make sense of these stories.

Methodology

Research design

The original proposal was to interview 20 families; in 8 families we would interview a child, in 12 we would interview the parents. We intended to interview each family twice. On the first occasion, we would learn their story. On the second occasion we would 'translate' their stories as they might have happened within the structures of the other country; we would tell them what their experience might have been in the other country, and ask them for their reflections on the differences. This plan was modified in three respects. First, we did not have sufficient resources to interview children. The experience of the interview was potentially distressing for the children, and we had no capacity to follow up any problems that might arise. Second, we were not able to carry out any of the second interviews in France, and only with five families in England. Third, we had to reduce the number of families interviewed to thirteen in each country, owing to difficulties in recruiting the families. The methodology is discussed in more detail in the French and English research reports (Freund *et al.* 1995; Baistow *et al.* 1996). In England we also met a group of four mothers who did not wish to be interviewed individually, but did wish their views to be heard as a group.

Data collection

We left it to the families concerned to decide who in the family should be involved in the research. In most of the families, and in all the English families, the mother was the parent interviewed. The interviews were unstructured. The interviewees were asked for their account of what had happened, what their experience had been of the ways in which social workers and other professionals had acted, what their experience of the courts had been (where relevant) and what they felt about their experiences. The starting point of the story and the sequence of events was left to them. The interviewers had a checklist of aspects of the story that should be covered if possible. Questions could be used to elicit further information to cover these points if necessary, but it was usually the case that questions were only needed for clarification or to encourage further detail around a point already mentioned. The interviews were recorded but not transcribed. An account of the interview was then written.

The qualitative approach

All stages of the project have followed a qualitative and reflexive research design, but with variations. The first phase of the research used a case example as the starting point of a focus group discussion. The second phase, which paired social workers from France and England, was a back-to-back ethnographic survey, in which the research participants were at the same time both the research subjects and the researchers. This design was interesting in that it went some way to meeting certain criticisms of ethnographic research. The account was not 'mono-logic' (Bakhtin 1981) because each researcher's account of the 'other' was balanced by the 'other's' account of the researcher. As David Rose (1990) describes, it created a 'reversal', an 'implicit critique, the reversal of perspectives, the critique of the ethnographer by those for whom the ethnographer had to pro-vide the framing discourse' (Rose 1990, p.38). In other words, while the English social workers may have approached the French social workers in the same spirit of inquiry with which Malinowski approached the Trobriand Islanders, the French were at the same time approaching the English in the same way.

The third phase of the research, the work with families, adopted a biographical approach. In the few second interviews which we were able to undertake, when we told the English participants what might have happened to them in France, and asked for their thoughts about this different system, we were attempting to develop the reflexive use of research subjects as both experts and participants. Where we were able to carry out these interviews, we had useful feedback from the participants. It was enough to make us feel that there would be a great deal to learn from an extension of this aspect of the research, but the financial and logistical problems are great. We would like to have been able to involve the families more actively in the research process.

Our aim was to give a voice to the parents in commenting on the differences between two systems. We wanted to know what might seem important to them, what, in their own system, they might want to keep or to get rid of. This would give us a different perspective from that of the researchers, and introduce a parental perspective on difference and priorities. We then would have had three levels of data: the initial 'stories' (and the analysis of their content), the 'translations' of the stories into another system, and the parents' commentary on their own story 'translated'.

The few interviews that we were able to undertake with the English parents provided an interesting but incomplete commentary on the reflections of the social workers in the earlier project. Qualitative research is bound to create some change in the object of the research. Indeed, that may well be an important factor in the researcher's intentions. Both in the earlier research with social workers and in this project, we wanted to give our participants information about difference that could lead them to develop new ideas, opinions or understandings about their own situation. This was the ultimate goal of our research.

The position of the researcher

The researchers brought with them to the project their previous experience as social workers and their previous experience of cross-national research and cross-national comparisons. These elements also contributed to our perceptions and our understanding of the stories that we heard. In both countries, at least one of the researchers was a practising social worker; for them, interviewing a family was familiar territory. What was striking was the subjective difference in the experience of these interviews, and the difference in emotional content. All the interviewers remarked on the quality of the information received. The accounts given by the parents of their experience were rich and vivid. In these interviews, there was a different quality, both to the information that the families gave and to the process, from the interviews that the researchers were used to as social workers. It was not that the information was necessarily objectively different, but that the manner of conveying information, and the affective tone of the interviews, was different. The engagement of the teller of the story was complete. The response of the parents in both countries to a research interview compared to a social work interview seemed to be the same. It is an important reminder of the effect of the context of the social work interview on the message that parents are able to convey to the social worker.

Findings

The data

There were thirteen accounts from each country of the experiences of parents who had been in contact in some way with the child welfare or child protection systems, and one account of a group interview in England. These accounts covered a wide range of experience from very limited encounters, or attempts to get help, to children who were being placed in long-term care (in two English cases, being placed for adoption). We did not attempt to match families in terms of their experience within their systems; we knew from previous research experience that this would not be possible because the systems differed too much. Where equivalence could be found was in the subjective experiences of difficulty that the parents felt. In both countries, there were parents struggling with teenagers, parents unable to cope with small children in circumstances of chaos and poverty, parents involved with the social work system, the healthcare system and the legal system, parents with children in placements and parents who wanted their children to be in placements. The thirteen families in each country covered a range of social situations, family structures, ages of children and types of problem.

The data was analysed in terms of both the practical (for example, what services were offered) and the subjective (did the social worker see your problem the same way as you did?). From this certain themes emerged. The theme on which I will concentrate here is the experience and expectations of getting help.

Getting help

In both countries, at the initial contact with the services, most parents were asking for help. Sometimes the contact was suggested by others, but the need for help was not then disputed. In both countries, parents were asking for a combination of practical, material and psychological help. However, differences in structures led to differences in the way that help was experienced.

FIRST CONTACT

In France, the equivalent service to the English health visiting service is the *Protection Maternelle et Infantile* (PMI). The PMI/health visitor referral was not the only point of entry for our families, but it was a common one. In France, the PMI is part of the same multidisciplinary team of the local authority service as the social work service, and referral by the PMI to the social services is straightforward. In England, referral by a health visitor to the social services department is more complicated, and parents were aware that the social services might not act on a health visitor's referral. Another important difference at the point of entry to the system is that in France an *Assistant Social de Secteur* (generic area team social worker) has a specific 'patch' and a specific population, so that a parent asking for help knows from the start who the social worker is. English social services nearly all operate a duty system, and several of the English mothers were eloquent about the frustrations of repeating their story to many different duty social workers. Getting to the first stage of asking for help seemed to be relatively more complicated for the English families.

THE GROUNDS FOR GETTING HELP

One mother was not referred to social services by her health visitor, although her story was similar to others who were. The health visitor found an alternative resource by referring her to a community psychiatric nurse. When this mother did approach social services for help over a nursery place, she was told that she could not have a nursery place unless her child was at risk. This illustrates one of the most important and fundamental differences between the French and English systems, a conceptual difference about the grounds for the provision of services.

The services for children and families in France are basically 'open door' services. None of the French families had difficulty in getting some response from the service or in getting some level of help; it may not have worked well, it was not always what they wanted, but it was offered and given a try. In most cases, the starting point was some form of *action éducatif*, offering parent, or parent and child, the opportunity for emotional support as well as practical help.

In England, services for children and families were offered according to categories; services were available for children 'in need', or for children 'at risk'. (At the time the research was undertaken, the integration of 'family support' and 'child protection' was not even on the agenda; it is debatable whether this integration has yet led to any changes on the ground). Because of financial restrictions, the definition of need is restricted, and parents felt that in reality there was very little help on offer unless a child was 'at risk'. This created considerable problems for the parents in getting help. They had to tread a narrow path between managing too well and not being in need, and managing so badly that their child was 'at risk', at which point their perception was that they were at risk of having the child removed:

What have you got to do, kill your kids before they help you? You're telling them you need help.

We don't go to these people easily, we go in desperation.

RESOURCES

There is a question here of differences in resources. Not only do French social services seem to be better resourced in terms of staff time, but there are other important universal resources for families. There is nursery provision for virtually all children from three years, and the French benefits system is certainly more generous than the English, especially where families are concerned (Cooper *et al.* 1995). However, it is not only a question of the quantity of resources, but of how parents can get access to them. Some of the English families were receiving resources on a considerable scale, but the context was one of compulsion. The release of resources was not triggered by the parents' request for help, or the parents' definition of need, but by the social workers' definition of risk.

Faced with these hurdles, English parents had a variety of strategies for getting help. One mother, who referred herself to social services because she was hitting her eldest child, accepted that her children should be registered because the social worker advised that it would make it easier to get resources. This mother was always anxious that her children would be taken away from her, but accepted the help she was offered, and appreciated the extra help she got after registration:

> I just went along with whatever they said because they know what's best. That's the only way to get the help that I'm getting now, to let them be on the register.

She was able to arrive at an understanding with the social worker; she described going down to Social Services, asking for the children to be fostered because she couldn't cope, but now, 'Sally knows that's not what I want but it's just the way that I cry for help.'

Another mother in a similar situation but with a more forthright approach seemed to be less successful in getting help. She was told that she was able to manage without help:

> but believe me when you are on the verge of a nervous breakdown, the last thing you want is someone forcing you to be even more responsible than you've been in the past.

Whatever the strategy adopted, getting help seemed to entail calculation and a balancing of advantage and disadvantage.

There were no comparable comments from the French families. The parents seemed to think that there was some initial agreement between themselves and the social worker over the nature of the problem with which help was needed (although not necessarily over the solution). The fact that children did not have to be 'at risk' meant that there was not a need to define any level of parenting failure, so that there was more chance of social worker and parents being able at least to start their relationship on the basis of a common definition of the problem. There were no reflections of the kind of games playing that both social workers and parents had to subscribe to in England in order to get resources.

THE RIGHT TO HELP

Quite apart from the difficulty of getting help in England, there were indications that the parents did not feel they had any specific right to help. There was an assumption that it would leave you feeling bad. Getting help from voluntary organizations was viewed more positively. Experiences with voluntary organizations were not uniformly good, but they were mainly good, and very different from the relationships with social services departments. All the parents who had voluntary organization contacts were quite clear that these were not local authority social services department workers, even if they had been referred to the voluntary organization by the social services department. Social services was an arm of the state, and the state was there to keep you in line, not to help you; voluntary agencies were there to help you; they might not always get it right, but that was their reason for being there.

The French parents seemed to take for granted that they should and would be offered help. They were not always satisfied with the help given, but they seemed to be confident that it would be forthcoming. They made no distinction between help from social services and from voluntary organizations, and it was not always possible to tell where the social workers were based.

The structure of the services in the two countries seemed likely to be a factor in the difference in experience of parents in the two countries. But it was possible that the difference in structure and the difference in experience both followed from the same underlying cultural assumptions. We speculated that the attitude of English parents to getting help, their lack of any confidence in getting help, and their lack of an expectation that help was their due, may have been connected to a very different set of expectations about the relationship between the state and the people. The relationship between the state and the people in England, not being anchored by a written constitution, is heavily rights based. In default of a written constitution, the ability to challenge the governing system in the courts as equals before the law is crucial. But if you can challenge the governing system *as an equal*, you are in difficulties when you need to ask it for help. By contrast the French parents were able to assume that help would be forthcoming. We speculated that this might be the product of a different relationship with the state, part of which was the greater clarity of the reciprocal responsibilities between citizen and state which are outlined in the French Civil Code.

The French families also assumed that they could have some say in the form that help took. One French mother described having been offered sessions with a psychologist when her son was on a supervision order and being seen by an *éducateur* (specialist social worker). She refused the sessions 'because it did my head in', but this did not affect the help that was offered to her son. By contrast, an English mother attended sessions in a family centre initially because she thought that otherwise her child would be taken away and latterly in order to get the social services to pay for a child minder while she did a training course. This mother felt that she had to bargain for resources and that she had few rights.

Another area in which French parents plainly had more control than English parents was over the nature of the placement of a child away from home. In the first place, to ask for a placement seemed, in France, to be considered as reasonable. Thus, in France, the parents' requests for placement were usually accepted. By contrast, an English mother was refused a placement for her son at a time when her partner was violent and her son was showing considerable behavioural problems. In the second place, parents in France have more rights to a choice over the nature of the placement. One mother turned down a suggestion of a foster placement from the child and family guidance clinic (CMPP – *Centre Medico-Psycho-Pédagogic*), but requested a residential placement through the social services, which was then arranged. Several of the English mothers had disagreements with their social workers about their child's placement, but had no rights in the situation. This lack of rights over placement reached its extreme in the two cases where children were being placed for adoption against their mothers' wishes.

Having legal rights

Given the high profile of the law in the English child welfare system, we had some expectation that English parents would have strong views on their rights. The parents' experience of their rights and their feelings about rights were areas we were specifically interested in exploring. We thought that there might be differences between the expectations of French families and English families with regard to legal rights and the role of the law in child protection. We did find differences, but not of the kind that we had expected.

The English parents usually gave quite a clear picture of the administrative and legal structures within which the system operated. When it was not clear, the situations suggest that this may have been due to the fact that mothers may not have wished to go into details that would label them as bad parents, for example if a child was registered. On the whole, the parents were clear about the location of the different professionals they had had dealings with, they knew the role of the judge or magistrates within the legal system and they knew how things had got to their present state. They referred to explanations of procedure that had been given them by social workers, for example explanations about what would happen at a child protection conference. The French parents seemed to be less clear about the workings of their system. It was not noted by them whether an *éducateur* was employed by the local authority or a voluntary organization. They were often confused about the introduction of the Children's Judge on to the scene, and did not always seem to be aware that it was going to happen. They were unclear about the location of power in relation to some of the placements; in spite of the right of choice that parents theoretically had over placement, there were instances of placements being altered with little or no consultation.

English parents did introduce the idea of rights into their stories more than the French parents. However, the rights they talked about were the rights they felt that they did *not* have, the right to help. They did not talk about the right to bring up their child as they thought best, or the right not to be interfered with by the state. If anything, they wanted more intervention, not less. They were more concerned about the lack of support that they got from the state and the fact that the support was not given until too late. Their concern was for the welfare of their children and their focus was on continuing to care for their children. Their experience of the legalistic English child protection system was not that it gave them rights, but of how much power it gave to others. One mother, who had been subject to a child protection investigation, said that it made her feel powerless and out of control. She had no say in what was happening. There had not been a child protection conference (because they had cooperated), but the possibility had been discussed, and this had been very frightening. 'It makes you realize how powerful they are.' One mother fighting the adoption of her child, another fighting to continue to have contact with her child, talked in terms of need – the child's need for family, their need for help – rather than rights. They felt powerless and wanted help.

French parents did not talk about having a right to help. It did not appear to be an issue; they seemed confident in claiming help. They did not talk about rights to non-intervention, or rights to bring up their children, but about the particular actions of individuals, with which they might disagree and argue, sometimes successfully, sometimes not. One mother, who had had experience of Children's Judges both as a child in care and as a mother, said that she was against them because:

> ...they are useless, they break up families; but I am for them as well because in certain situations that's necessary, like when Mathilde was placed, I couldn't have managed with two children.

Referring again to a Children's Judge, with whom she disagreed, she said, 'but there are no stupid jobs, there are only stupid people'. In spite of disagreements with judges and social workers, and in spite of the confusions which several seemed to have about the powers of judges and social workers, the French parents seemed to be more in accord with their system than the English.

The fundamental concerns of both French and English parents seemed to be the same. They were not about rights as such, but about getting help that would enable them to bring up their children and maintain the family. Where children were in long-term placement the concerns were no different, and in both countries there was a strong sense that the child and parent remained 'family' to each other.

Conclusion

The English and French parents who took part in this research had similar problems. They also had similar definitions of the kind of help that they wanted. They wanted practical help, but they also wanted emotional support. They wanted to be listened to, and to be able to discuss what help they were being offered. Their experience of the child welfare system in their respective countries was considerably different. Resources were not equivalent between the two countries, but differences in the administrative and legal structures were also important. With equal resources, the experiences of the parents would still have been different.

There were also cultural differences that could be seen either as a response to these differing structures and resources, or as the product of the very values and ideologies that formed those structures and provided those resources. The parents had different expectations of the services. English parents had lower expectations of being helped, and seemed less sure of having any right to help. There was nothing to suggest that other rights were a major concern for parents in either country. Even those parents who were most in conflict with the system, and who were opposing the legal situation, talked in terms of the child's welfare and not of their rights, or of the child's rights. They talked about feeling powerless, but did not make any connection between power and rights. For the parents in both countries, the predominant discourse was a welfare discourse.

In the earlier research with social workers in both countries, we had seen that social workers in France worked almost entirely within a welfare discourse, while English social workers were increasingly having to work in a legal discourse, moving with some difficulty between welfare concepts and rights concepts (Cooper *et al.* 1995; King and Trowell 1992). In France, the justice system for children also works largely in a welfare discourse (King and Piper 1995). In England, the justice system, although slightly modified by the Children Act 1989, essentially operates in a legal discourse.

Diagrammatically, you could place the different players on a continuum in relation to their predominant use of welfare or rights concepts (Figure 9.1).

This diagram situates French social workers and the Children's Judge close to families. Thus, although the social workers from both countries share a professional culture, French social workers are closer to the families they work with than English social workers. The pull towards the legal discourse redirects the efforts of the English workers away from the things that matter to the parents they are working with.

There was a lot of common ground between the English cases and the French cases in the reactions of the parents to their experiences. What broke new ground for us was the configuration of the similarities and differences between the English and the French cases. What we think we have seen exemplified is that:

- The English parents did not feel that they had a right to help from the state (although they may have felt that they needed help). The French parents expected help.

- The English and French parents who were in difficulties were primarily concerned with issues of welfare and not of rights.

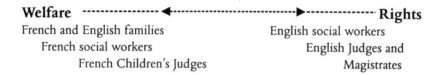

Welfare ---------------- ◄----------------------------► ---------------- **Rights**

French and English families	English social workers
French social workers	English Judges and
French Children's Judges	Magistrates

Figure 9.1 The welfare–rights continuum in England and France.

We had learnt from earlier research that the construction of child welfare in England required English social workers to be concerned with rights as well as welfare, which gave them a different agenda from English parents. The English social workers' concern with rights means that they explain the English system very carefully to English parents. The English parents therefore had a good under-standing of their system, but they did not seem to feel any ownership of the system. French social workers are mainly concerned with welfare and less con-cerned with rights. They are more likely to have the same agenda as French parents. This lack of concern with rights resulted in less clarity for the French par-ents, who often seemed unsure about their rights. But the French parents seemed to accept the legitimacy of their system, even when they disagree with its actions.

Thus the rights-based philosophy of English culture seems to affect both our view of the family and the experience of families. The concepts of less eligibility and the deserving or (more frequently) undeserving poor are notoriously very persistent. The citizen as consumer (Silberman 1996) is expected to share this attitude to independence and rights with the state. But the families who need help, for whatever reason, whether economic or social, are not citizens as consumer; they are excluded from this domain, and they look for help not rights.

This mismatch of concerns may help to explain the unpopularity of both social workers and the child welfare system in England at present, and of the greater acceptance of social workers in France. Earlier in this chapter I referred to our speculations about the relationship between the lack of a written constitution and the problems of getting help. The difficulties that the English parents experienced in getting help with child-rearing problems seem to point to differing expectations within English society about the role of the state in supporting parenting. Paradoxically, perhaps it is not parents but the state that worries about parental rights and state intervention. Parents worry about their children's needs.

Acknowledgements

The author would like to acknowledge the contribution of other members of the research team, Karen Baistow, Veronique Freund, Alain Grevot, Angela Spriggs and Margaret Yelloly, who jointly undertook the data collection and analysis. The conclusions drawn in this chapter are the responsibility of the author.

References

Baistow, K.; Hetherington, R.; Spriggs, A.; Yelloly, M. Freund, V. and Greust, A. (1996) *Parents Speaking: Anglo-French Perceptions of Child Welfare Interventions.* London: Centre for Comparative Social Work Studies, Brunel University.

Baistow, K. and Hetherington, R. (1998) 'Parents' experience of child welfare interventions: An Anglo-French comparison.' *Children and Society, 12*, 113–124.

Bakhtin, M.M. (1981) *The Dialogic Imagination.* Houston, TX: University of Texas Press.

Bateson, G. (1979) *Mind and Nature, a Necessary Unity.* London: Wildwood House.

Cleaver, H. and Freeman, P. (1995) *Parental Perspectives in Cases of Suspected Child Abuse.* London: HMSO.

Cooper, A., Baistow, K., Hetherington, R., Pitts, J. and Spriggs, A. (1995) *Positive Child Protection: A View from Abroad.* Lyme Regis: Russell House Publishing.

Farmer, E. and Owen, M. (1995) *Child Protection Practice: Private Risks and Public Remedies.* London: HMSO.

Freund, V.; Grevot, A.; Baistow, K.; Hetherington, R.; Spriggs, A. and Yelloly, M. (1995) *Les Strategies des Familles et leur Representations de l'Intervention Sociale et Judiciare de Protection de l'Enfance. Comparaison Franco-Anglais.* Paris: JCLT.

Hetherington, R. (1994) 'TransManche partnerships.' *Adoption and Fostering, 18,* 3.

Hetherington, R., Cooper, A., Smith, P. and Wilford, G. (1997) *Protecting Children: Messages from Europe.* Lyme Regis: Russell House Publishing.

Hooper, C.A. (1992) *Mothers Surviving Child Sexual Abuse.* London: Tavistock/Routledge.

Howitt, D. (1992) *Child Abuse Errors; When Good Intentions Go Wrong.* London: Harvester Wheatsheaf.

King, M. and Piper, C. (1995) *How the Law Thinks About Children.* London: Gower.

King, M. and Trowell, J. (1992) *Children's Welfare and the Law: The Limits of Legal Intervention.* London: Sage.

Lindley, B. (1994) *On the Receiving End. Families Experience of the Court Process.* London: Family Rights Group.

Prosser, J. (1992) *Child Abuse Investigations; The Families' Perspective, A Case Study of 30 Families.* Essex: PAIN (Parents Against Injustice).

Rose, D. (1990) *Living the Ethnographic Life.* London: Sage.

Silberman, M. (1996) 'The revenge of civil society. State, nation and society in France.' In D. Cesari and M. Fulbrook *Citizenship, Nationality and Migration in Europe.* London: Routledge.

Taylor, S. (1995) 'Feminist classroom practice and cultural politics.' In J. Holland *et al. Debates and Issues in Feminist Research and Pedagogy.* Multilingual Matters Ltd and Buckingham: Open University Press.

Thomas, J. (1993) *Doing Critical Ethnography.* London: Sage.

CHAPTER 7

Family Relationships in Democratic Spain

Cultural Change From a Biographical Perspective

Elisabet Tejero and Laura Torrabadella

Introduction

Value systems and cultural differences in family issues have become a focus of increasing interest in comparative policy studies and classification of welfare regimes. More specifically, they have been introduced as an explanatory variable for delineating the Southern type of welfare model. The role played by the family within this is presented as a distinctive dimension for social integration, and therefore for the maintenance of the welfare system in the meridional countries. In Spain, the speed of the political, social and economic transformations brought about by the shift from a dictatorial state to a democracy is a crucial element for interpreting the degree of change in family relationships and the norms, values and imagery which underpin them. Changing family relationships, however, cannot be understood without examining changes in gender and intergenerational relationships.

The aim of this chapter is to explore the complexity of Spanish cultural change in the field of gender and intergenerational relationships from a biographical approach. According to this aim, by 'culture' we refer to 'values, practices, emotions and artefacts, as well as institutions and "ways of doing things"' (Introduction), in which family relationships are immersed. Through the analysis of Carolina's life story the lived experience and meaning of welfare comes to the surface, thus allowing us to enrich and contribute with a different perspective to the current debate on the integrating role of the 'southern family model'.

Carolina, a Catalan woman born in 1950 to a coalmining family from a small province next to Catalonia, belongs to what we could call the 'generation of the transition'. (By this, we refer to an age group socialized during the 1960s and 1970s, that is, within a period of economic, political and cultural change for Catalonia, as one of the most industrialized regions in Spain.) Throughout these twenty years Carolina's generation has lived through the changes from an autarchic system to a modernized industrial capitalism, and from a dictatorship regime to a pluralist democratic political system. Culturally speaking, this generation has borne witness to how traditional, Catholic and conservative values in family and patriarchal relationships began to be put in crisis, thus opening legally and socially recognized new forms of family organization. After fourteen years of domestic abuse against her and her three daughters Carolina divorced her husband. Through a child-oriented strategy and an active community involvement against domestic violence Carolina was able to re-orient her biography towards a more autonomous way of living. She is currently working in the casual sector as a cleaning lady.

We offer first an overview of the 'familist' nature of the Spanish welfare state within the meridional model of welfare states by focusing on the historical development of Spain from the late Franco dictatorship until the present day. Furthermore, a variety of analytical tools are presented for analysing Carolina's case. Through her life-story the reader will identify how different welfare resources such as family and community allow individuals to deal with biographical ruptures, thus generating new ways of social integration and change. However, as we will see, new forms of biographical costs and social conflict emerge as a result of changing roles of the family. Our hypothesis is that the role played by family relationships in Spain, and possibly in other southern countries, cannot be understood as a 'remnant of the past'. Instead, it reveals a new cultural dimension of social life which, by combining traditional and modern assumptions and social practices, posits new challenges to cross-national research on welfare and social policy. Finally, the case will allow us to make some concluding remarks on the tension between social change and biographical strategies.

Family relationships in Spain within the meridional model of welfare states

The role of the family in the organization of welfare in Southern Europe

Recent comparative research on welfare states is aimed at exploring the diversity and plurality of models of their construction and development. The most recent studies locate Spain in the so-called 'meridional model' of welfare states, together with Greece, Italy and Portugal (Ferrera 1995; Giner 1995; Sarasa and Moreno 1995). However, the existing differences between this group of countries, and even between different regions within the country, have been underlined too (Saraceno 1995).

The meridional countries share a high degree of polarization of social protection. The coverage for those in the skilled/professional workforce contrasts strongly with those in social groups involved in the unskilled/casual labour force. The distinguishing feature, though, which reinforces the argument of an autonomous meridional model, is the role played by the family. Family is defined as a 'camera of social compensation' (Ferrera 1995) due to its elasticity to change.

The integrating role played by family is also stressed when conceptualizing the Spanish welfare state. The Spanish welfare state has been defined as a model of 'precarious integration' (Aguilar, Gaviria and Laparra 1995). Whereas the use of the term 'precarious' refers to the rudimentary nature of social policies, 'integration' is achieved by the role played mainly by the family in a context of low welfare protection, unemployment, the black economy and temporary working conditions.

Feminist critiques have drawn attention to the role of the family not only as a specificity of the meridional model, but as a distinguishing criterion for understanding welfare state formations in Europe (Balbo 1983; Saraceno 1995). They have emphasized the interrelationship of the family, the state and the market, thus 'gendering welfare states' (Sainsbury 1994). The ideology or cultural patterns embedded in family practices are heavily conditioned by the kind of incentives and ideologies from the state, which in the meridional context conceives the family as a unit of solidarity. Rather than promoting a male 'breadwinner model' (Lewis 1992) the state, through its social policies, encourages the interdependency or solidarity between family members and kin, thus hiding the sexual division of unpaid labour. This is what Saraceno (1995) calls 'ambivalent familism'.

By *familism* we understand the ideological assumptions which underpin family relationships, based on strong family ties or family-oriented values and attitudes. In other words, familism is an ideological construct according to which family is considered as a moral good *per se*. As we can see, not only family relationships, but familism itself have been conceptualized – among other 'cultural variables' such as religion – as a fruitful criterion through which different types of family models in different welfare states can be distinguished. By doing this, the key role of the cultural dimension in comparative research on welfare has been recognized, thus going beyond those approaches restricted to socio-economic and political explanations.

Our conception of *family* combines both a 'strategic' and a 'dynamic–relational' perspective. (Even though the use of the term 'family' tends to be easily objectified and reified, it will be used here in order to avoid over-long formulations.) A dynamic–relational approach sees family as a social space of changing gender and intergenerational relationships and conflict, rather than as a homogeneous entity without different interests in its core. According to the strategic perspective, family is not only to be understood as an institution, but also as a *mechanism* through which other social spheres operate. The state, economic and social agents strategically rely on family solidarity (that is, basically on female unpaid labour) for facing contemporary processes of change. At the same time families develop different strategies, using resources coming from other social spheres, in order to adapt to change. Furthermore, families are not only recipients of the changes which are taking place in other social spheres such as the state, the labour market or the community, but are at the same time impacting on these spheres; thus the family becomes an agent of social change. However, in order to capture the qualitative elements of this change, we find it necessary to focus less on a structural and more on a dynamic and relational approach to family. This will lead us to the empirical analysis of a biography.

According to this perspective, we need to consider how gender and generation coordinate with social and cultural change and conflict. By 'gender' we mean the social constructions which confer on individuals an unequal position in society depending on their sex (Moore 1991). In a patriarchal and capitalist order, individuals' strategies within the family are conditioned by the gendered nature of social roles. Yet, changes in gender strategies cannot be entirely understood without the generational frame in which they take place. Taking 'generation' into account allows us to see how processes of cultural transition – in terms of changes of lifestyles, political regimes or common values and practices – have an impact on family and gender relationships. By 'generation' we understand a specific age group socialized in the same historical period. The use of this variable helps us to make operative the link between biography, history and structures (Feixa 1998).

Familism within the construction process of the Spanish welfare state

Family relationships have suffered a rapid transformation in accordance with the overall major social, economic, political and cultural changes in Spain in the shift from an 'authoritarian welfare regime' to a 'democratic welfare state' (according to Rodríguez Cabrero's terms, 1995). The speed of this change has had important ideological and cultural consequences for the Spanish population. Three periods of recent Spanish history will be referred to in order to illustrate the changing dimension of cultural and social development in the field of gender and family relationships. These are the *desarrollismo*, the political transition and the consolidation of democracy. (*Desarrollismo* comes from 'desarrollar', the Spanish word for 'to develop'. It refers to the quick and radical economic growth based on an industrial development due to the setting up of foreign enterprises, and the massive urbanization process in the most populated and richest cities of Spain.)

The construction of the Spanish welfare state has its origins within the last period of Franco's dictatorship, and more specifically from 1960 to 1975. During these years, the Spanish economy was liberated from the interventionism of the autocratic period by joining the Fordist process of the world economy, though in a subordinate position. Within this period, called *desarrollismo*, the social security system, which had been created in 1963, became more extensive. However, the rigid link between social security and employment implied a gendered segregation in social protection, since it was mainly oriented towards male industrial workers, and through them, towards their families. In short, welfare policies and therefore the institutional definition of welfare, was built on the relationship between family and the labour market, thus reproducing the logic of a 'strong male breadwinner' model (in the sense of Lewis 1992).

The institutional definition of family in the Catholic Spain of Franco was based on the unity and indissolubility of the family as a basic cell of society, and the domestic-familial sphere as the 'natural' place for women. According to the Catholic normative view, women's destiny was marriage, and marriage was oriented to procreation. Sexual purity and marital fidelity were two cultural rules which had to be followed. Women were legally obliged to leave their jobs as soon as they married, and received a 'dowry' from the enterprise as a symbolic compensation. Even though this law was abolished in 1961, women's withdrawal from the labour market once they got married had become a cultural pattern (García-Nieto 1993). During the 1960s and 1970s women's participation in the labour market increased substantially, due to the demand for labour in the industrial sector (Garrido 1992). Women of working class origin continued to work, yet in a more visible way, as waged workers. The traditional image of family and moral values began to be brought into question. However, women's roles in Spain, as probably elsewhere, changed notably faster and even provoked the start of the change in family practices.

After Franco's death in 1975 the general election of 1977, won by the centrist party UCD (Union of the Democratic Center), and the Spanish Basic Law of 1978 introduced a new institutional frame. This political transition substantially changed the nature of state intervention. The Spanish National Health Service and the Spanish National Social Security System, two of the most significant universal measures put forward in that year, played major roles in modifying women's position in relation to the state. In legal terms, the transition had a special impact on gender equality. One of the most important achievements of this period was the passing of the Divorce Law in 1981. In spite of the reactionary attitudes of conservative sectors of Spanish society, the high rates of divorce in the first years of democracy (Flaquer 1990; Alberdi 1994) revealed the high degree of cultural change in regard to modernizing assumptions about family relationships. This emergent social and cultural change, accompanied by a renewed discourse on female emancipation promoted ideals of equality and freedom which had an impact on the cultural openness of Spanish society and, more specifically, on the cultural acceptance of more flexible family relationships. (The original wave of discourse on female emancipation occurred during the Second Spanish Republic (from 1931 to 1936) with the Suffrage movement.) However, the new cultural environment coincided with the economic crisis of the late 1970s and the beginning of the 1980s. As a result, the modern ideas introduced by the first years of democratization grew faster than the economic openings for most of the population. Against the high level of female incorporation into the labour market during the previous period, the transition years represented a decrease of the activity rate for women, thus showing how fluctuating and functional the female workforce was for the needs of the labour market.

The electoral victory of the social democratic party (PSOE) in 1982 opened up the consolidation of democracy which has lasted up to the present day. The modernization of the economy promoted by the first socialist government, however, led to high rates of unemployment. The modernization process coexisted with the structural black economy of the Spanish labour market, and did not prevent the high rates of women's participation in this. Different policy measures were carried forward in order to address the unequal effects of economic modernization.

The main thrust towards democracy was expressed in socio-political processes such as the universalization of services, through which health and education have been the most favoured fields of intervention. The passing of the Law of Non-Contributive Pensions of 1990 followed this universal logic by covering large sectors of the Spanish population who had not been protected until that moment. The most significant beneficiaries of this law are women, who have traditionally formed an unprotected sector of Spanish population. However, these policy measures reinforce the welfare mentality of non-contributive pensions, and the subsequent 'second-class citizenship' for the most vulnerable groups such as lone mothers (Carrasco et al. 1998). The Spanish approach to supporting the specific group of lone mothers is not through designated benefits, but through the provisions that exist for all families with children. Accordingly, support received by lone mothers is based on their status as wives, mothers and/or heads of poor families.

The socialist government introduced significant measures aimed at equality between the sexes, as represented by the creation in 1983 of the *Instituto de la Mujer* (Institute for Women), which so far has promoted three different Plans for Equality of Opportunities for Women. Following the work of other European feminist scholars such as Hernes (1990), experts in Spain have defined Spanish feminism as being of an institutional nature – *Feminismo de Estado* (state feminism) – and hardly having an impact on the cultural practices of the population of both sexes (Astelarra 1990). Furthermore, the lack of solid measures to support the family, and extremely low public expenditure on the family, locates Spanish family policies within the poorest in Western Europe. One of the explanations for this paradox must be found, according to some authors (Guillén 1997), in the conservative connotation which 'family' has historically had under the Franco regime.

Parallel to these social policy processes, new forms of family have developed during these years in Spain, though to a very modest degree. The greater cultural acceptance of different ways of structuring a family, brought by the rapid political and legal change into democracy, does not match with the statistical data provided by recent studies of changes in family lifestyles. Cross-national research on southern Europe shows how Spain (like other southern European countries) has a family culture based on strong family values, such as child-oriented attitudes, a high degree of cross-generational cohabitation, a strong institutionalization of marriage and very low divorce rates. At the same time, though, Spain also has one of the lowest fertility rates in Europe, a higher average age of marriage, a steady increase in lone parenthood and other family practices labelled as 'modern' (Jurado and Naldini 1996). The coexistence of what are considered to be 'traditional' and 'modern' family practices and values is taken as an argument for the specificity of the 'southern European family' in accordance with the theses about a specific Southern model of welfare state. This brings us to the following section, in which we will try to show how the coexistence between the 'old' and the 'new' can also converge in one person's path in life.

The analysis of Carolina's case follows the principles of the biographical interpretative method. This method is based on the principles of hermeneutical case-reconstruction as first developed by Oevermann (1983), Schütze (1983), and subsequently by Rosenthal (1993), Fischer-Rosenthal (1997) and Breckner (1997). The main focus of this method is to analytically distinguish the *lived history* and the *told story*. The first is based on the 'reconstruction of the biographical meanings of events at the time they happened, and the reconstruction of the chronological sequence of experiences in which they occurred' (Breckner 1997). The second is based on the 'reconstruction of the present meanings of experiences and the reconstruction of the temporal order of the life-story in the present time of narrating' (Rosenthal 1993). The main function of 'history' is to constitute a 'we' by sharing interpretations and modes of understanding of the past within a family, a group, a class etc. and building up continuities reaching beyond our lifetime which connect us to the previous and following generations '… A life story refers even if socially prestructured and institutionalized as a form, to the social history of a person focused on his or her lifetime out of the perspective of an "I"' (Breckner 1997).

Carolina's case: 'I've always existed for the sake of someone'

Carolina's life trajectory is structured by the experience of domestic abuse, which took place during fourteen years of marital subjection. Her biography takes place within the frame of a female working class, and a traditional caring role within the family history. Both dimensions allow us to interpret Carolina's position as a sub-ordinate one within the Spanish social structure. Yet, Carolina was socialized in the limits of the traditional gender and family values represented by the Franco dictatorship, and the emerging feminist values which introduced more equal and democratic gender and family relationships in the public arena. This changing context will become a significant resource for her to face biographical conflicts and ruptures.

Carolina presents herself in her life as both a strong surviving victim of several biographical events, especially of domestic abuse, and as a fighter for her daughters' future. Both elements will give us the clue to understanding her present biographical strategy. The autonomy gained through divorce allows her to feel legitimated to claim her daughters' rights and well-being. In other words: the function of Carolina's self-presentation as a 'surviving victim' is to show the limits placed on herself – but not on her daughters – in starting a new kind of life. As she points out in a later sequence: 'I've missed the train but maybe it's not too late for them'. We will see that this does not prevent her from offering a picture of sacrifice regarding her own past and future.

Family uprooting: the context of the post-war period

Carolina, born in 1950 in a coalmining town, was the youngest of six siblings, three of whom died at a very early age. Carolina's birth year symbolizes the ashes of the Spanish post-war period, with extremely hard living conditions for most of the population. During these years large numbers of families surviving in precarious conditions in the countryside fled to the most industrialized cities, seeking new opportunities. As she herself describes:

> children in those times worked very hard ... when I see pictures of the Third World on TV I always think of myself, because we were undernourished and overworked. The thing is that we came from the post-war and that was not easy.

Significantly, Carolina starts the interview recalling her own birth, in which she introduces herself as the youngest of three surviving children. Her father, ill with silicosis due to his coalmining activity, had to migrate to Zaragoza, a medium-sized city, and with him all the family. He died when Carolina was seven years old. This was a decisive biographical event which speeded family disintegration. At the age of twelve Carolina was sent to work as a maid far from her mother and brothers, and like many other children at that time, soon developed a 'breadwinner role' by sending her wage to her mother. As expressed by Carolina: 'my mother was convinced that parents had children in order to have a kind of life insurance.'

Carolina presents this chapter of her life in terms of being a victim of her immediate social environment marked by poverty, non-communication and uprooting within the family relationships:

> (I had) no childhood, no family; I've always been for the sake of someone. I started my own family when I had my daughters ... In those times parents used to hit their children ... but it was so painful for me that I promised myself never to hit my own children, and so it has been.

Interestingly, Carolina avoids blaming her family directly. She uses the historical context of 'those times' for justifying her mother's violent behaviour, and abandonment. Carolina describes one of the most painful experiences in her life:

My mother had a very strong personality, what she said had to be done, she was an aggressive person, she was like this. It is now very painful for me to talk about this, since she died of Alzheimer's one year ago. She was unable to love, she only lived for herself, I cried a lot because I couldn't have her. (From her own perspective of now being a mother Carolina wonders) how could she sleep in peace while knowing I was so far away?

These childhood experiences shape Carolina's lack of parental references, something of which she is very aware: 'without having a family I had to survive as I could, without having any point of reference...' For this reason it is easy to imagine Carolina's feeling of orphanhood and understand better the latent meaning of her initial sentence: 'I'm the youngest of three surviving children.'

From Carolina's educational and professional path in the city to starting a family: the experience of violence. The years of 'desarrollismo'

At the age of fourteen Carolina moved alone to Barcelona to live in a female boarding house and work in the industrial sector. In contrast to her previous enclosure in the domestic sphere, her relationship with the formal sector of the labour market and the fact of living together with other women of her age acted as a new socializing and integrating mechanism for Carolina: 'life with my friends and colleagues, going dancing and so on, was the typical life of a young girl.' This period represented a discovering of youth for Carolina, which contrasts with the absence of childhood. It was a chance for her to participate in the broader community and social life, beyond the boundaries of the domestic-familial sphere.

Carolina had the opportunity to start primary studies in night school, which enabled her to get the primary School Certificate. During the day, she worked in a factory. It was a time of increasing incorporation of Spanish women into activity. Carolina evaluates this period as a very enriching one:

It was one of the best times of my life: my job, my colleagues, the possibility to be independent ... I had a strong desire to learn things, even though I could never attain a good education. I don't know how clever we were, but we were able to improve within the factory ... I managed to have a specialization.

In this sequence, Carolina presents that stage of her life as an opportunity to become emancipated and skilled. However, this reconstruction of the past must be understood from the (narrative) perspective of the present. During the years of *desarrollismo*, feminist ideas were still absent in the public discourse, even though it was for some women the first opening to the public sphere. Now, though, Carolina has already absorbed the feminist discourse through which she can re-interpret this biographical period. With regard to the link between education and work, Carolina is recognizing the occupational opportunities of the years of *desarrollismo*, when compared with the present difficulties of improving working conditions in the labour market.

As we will see next, Carolina's emancipatory trajectory within an emerging (economically) favourable context is interrupted by her return to the familial-domestic sphere. In 1970, when Carolina was twenty, her youngest brother died and she left her job to take care of her sister-in-law and nephews: 'I decided to go to my sister-in-law's place in order to help her. I love her a lot, but by that time I didn't know her. Now I adore them, perhaps they are my point of reference.' This event shows how a family pattern would operate through her whole life. More specifically, by reconstructing the kin links Carolina may have compensated for her own lack of parental references. Three years later, though, Carolina made an attempt to resume her previous job. The attempt failed, however, due to the unstable political climate of the last years of dictatorship and the oil crisis affecting the industrial sector, which caused a slump in the rates of activity for the female workforce, and therefore of incorporation into the labour market (Garrido 1992).

Carolina reconstructs this period of exclusion from the labour market and of caring for her kin during these three years as a contradiction. On the one hand, she justifies her role as carer by pointing out her moral duty towards the family links. On the other hand, she acknowledges that her decision may have interrupted a potentially interesting path for her:

> When my father died my brother protected me, making life easier for me. I felt then that I owed him something, and that's why I took care of his family ... I've always existed for the sake of someone ... I don't regret it, but somehow, it cut off a lot of things.

Carolina's statement regarding her commitment to the family points to the core of the gender conflict in which Carolina is immersed, that is, the power of the (socially constructed) moral duty of care, which keeps her trapped and subordinate in both the productive and reproductive spheres. As pointed out above, Carolina had to assume from an early age not only a breadwinner role but an adult role as care-giver. This was to become an orienting principle of her future trajectory and strategies. Here again, the underlying message of this sequence is her lost opportunity of emancipation ('it cut off a lot of things') which can only be understood as a reconstruction from her present socio-economically vulnerable situation.

Carolina then resumed her domestic role in the casual labour force, this time working as a maid for a theatrical entrepreneur. Two years later, in 1975, she married and left this job. This event represents a highly characteristic relationship of the female population in Spain towards the labour market. Marriage for Carolina is experienced as the opportunity to have a family of her own and compensate for the lack of family unity during childhood.

When narrating the story of her marriage she follows the scheme of a happy marriage which soon becomes a hell, due to her husband's aggression:

I married madly in love. It was just me and him, but insults and aggression gradually increased. The first time he tried to strangle me I asked him if he thought this was normal, and he answered that he was aware of not being normal. He didn't know what had happened, it is as if he had two personalities ... I didn't want to live like this, but he never accepted an agreed separation. He wanted us to stay together at any price. It was the time when men were men; they dominated the situation and those who lived with them had to accept their way of being ... from that moment on I had a bitter life and I'm still asking myself how I could have endured that situation for so many years ... What are the causes for arriving at a situation like this? One wants things to go well and that's why you hold on ... firstly, because life has not been easy and, secondly, because you wish from the depth of your soul that the relationship will work ... but wishing is not enough.

Carolina starts constructing the story of her marriage through the modern meaning of a partner relationship, namely, marrying in love and building a 'happy family'. But with the appearance of domestic violence this myth falls apart. Once again, the historical context becomes a resource for Carolina to explain her subordinate position as married woman, and her incapacity to break away during fourteen years of domestic violence.

The use of a collective subject and the 'pedagogic' form of the sequence has the function of making socially understandable how difficult it is for women to get away from a situation of domestic abuse: 'When women find themselves at the first stage of violence they're so blocked and feel so bad that it is impossible, impossible to make them understand how to deal with the situation.' By doing this Carolina reveals her own political commitment and her own understanding of domestic violence, from the perspective of women suffering the same problem.

The experience of divorce: the political transition

Carolina qualifies domestic abuse as a vicious circle, as a trap for her and for her daughters, who have also been victims of domestic violence:

With that man there was no way to come to an end. After a violent episode I used to tell him that I would lose my fear and leave him, and then he answered that he loved me more than his own life; and it seemed he was being sincere, but then everything started again. It was a circle from which it was difficult to escape.

The consequence of violence for her daughters led her to a first and failed attempt to divorce, four years after the Divorce Law of 1981 had been passed. This law implied a recognition of the family as a possible arena of conflict and represented a turning point towards democracy in the sense that it reflected the cultural change regarding family and gender relationships within the Spain of political transition. In 1985 Carolina decided to ask for divorce but: 'One night he came home with a knife and destroyed all the furniture, and he told me that I had to withdraw the demand for a divorce or he would kill the four of us. I was terrified and I withdrew it.'

In 1990, after a major physical assault, Carolina escaped from home with her daughters, and contacted the same feminist lawyer who had dealt with her first demand for divorce five years before. This lawyer belonged to a group of feminist lawyers who played a significant role in assessing abused women during the political transition. Carolina sought refuge in one of the newly created public shelters for abused women. Finally she divorced and was given the custody of her daughters, though 'visiting rights' were to be granted to her ex-husband:

> When Susana (oldest daughter) was eleven my husband not only battered me, but also her; it was a tremendous assault. One day after, I told him that it could not continue like this. When giving breakfast to my youngest daughter he took a knife and tried to threaten me. I thought this was my last day. I took my daughters and left.

This chapter of Carolina's life is reconstructed as a 'successful' attempt to break the vicious circle of violence, but it also reflects the high cost she has had to pay for it:

> He spoiled not only my life but also that of my daughters. So, I had to fight for them, especially for the oldest. He pushes you into the corner but he has his own frustrations too. I see that it is an absurd situation, but still today I can't hate him. Even more: I could never start another serious relationship.

Carolina's reflections on the fight are permeated with an ambiguous feeling of guilt and shame regarding her daughters. Subjectively, the experience of domestic abuse embraces a more extended time span, in the sense that it constitutes a 'presence' for future episodes and biographical strategies for her as well as for the generation of her daughters. A contradictory feeling towards her husband underlies the sequence too. From a present perspective, Carolina tries to find a balance between understanding her ex-husband as an aggressor or victimizer and as a victim of his own circumstances. As shown in most of the cases of victims of domestic abuse, feelings of anger coexist with feelings of guilt regarding the children (Pérez del Campo Noriega 1995). Significantly, Carolina rejects the possibility of starting a new relationship. Her recognition of feelings of fidelity have to be framed in her Catholic family pattern. In that sense we can interpret her symbolic status as a 'still married' woman.

Lone motherhood and community commitment. The consolidation of democracy

After one year in the public shelter Carolina started a new life with a new family status as lone mother. She resumed her working life in the black economy as a cleaning lady and combined her family and worker roles with a new community role. In 1992, Carolina, together with other women from the public shelter, set up a self-help group for abused women, the first of its kind in Barcelona. We can assert the permeability of the feminist discourse (newly arrived in the public arena) in Carolina's evaluation of the self-help group:

> Living together in the public shelter with other women and children was very hard. Sometimes we felt confined, but when we left the shelter we realized that we felt much more comfortable amongst ourselves than with other people, most of whom considered our situation as a personal problem. Then we decided to set up the self-help group. In my case the group has been very helpful in working out many things by reflecting and communicating with each other. The group has helped me to make big changes, such as regain my self-esteem, to work out the 'whys' and 'hows' and to focus on my daughters growing up.

Carolina presents the group as a necessary arena of communication, in a social context which cannot fully understand a very serious problem: 'Many of my friends and relatives said: you are alone with your daughters, so you will go back to him. I believe your story, because you're saying it to me, but it's incredible.' She presents the community work in the group as a way of fighting against the invisibility of patriarchal violence, caused by the social perception and definition of marriage as a 'private issue'. Moreover, the group helps her to work out the meaning of her new family status as lone mother. Carolina expresses her need for support for facing lone motherhood:

> After sixteen hours of work you must be strong: play with the youngest daughter, help the oldest to do homework and listen to the other's school day; then do the dishes. And it is not easy, in fact it's horrible. The group has helped me a lot to work out these kinds of things.

More specifically, the self-help group is a tool through which she tries to prevent her daughters from falling into the same trap: 'I don't understand Susana because she's a sensitive girl, but sometimes she reacts like her father. I talked to one of the members and she told me that this was normal.' Therefore Carolina's involvement in the self-help group could be understood as a 'female repair strategy' towards her daughters, in the sense that she extends her role as caregiver and fighter for her family to the community. The 'we' perspective, previously linked to the family, becomes a politicized community-oriented 'we'. The fact of resignifying the sphere of care (culture of care) could be interpreted as a 'feminist strategy' from the perspective of the post-modern strand of 'feminism of difference'. (This strand of feminism, with special impact in countries like France and Italy, has tried to resignify and positively evaluate the 'traditionally female' attributes.) Finally, we can see here how the autobiographical narration used in the dynamics of interaction among the members of the self-help group can be converted into a tool for political action. Effectively, Carolina could convert the legal and cultural resources and reforms from the democratic system of a modern 'State of Rights' into biographical resources towards a liberating strategy, for her and other women: 'I'll fight as much as I can, for helping other women like me, this is clear to me.'

However, Carolina, like most of the housewives depending on a breadwinner for their subsistence, has an extremely vulnerable position after divorce. On the one hand, she opted for the black economy as the only alternative she had if she wanted to have some income to cover the needs of her family and have some time for being with her daughters. On the other hand (after seven years taking care of her daughters) she decided to apply for a proper job in a factory, but had to forfeit her wish. Carolina describes this vicious circle of discrimination in the labour market as follows:

> After divorce I was forty-one and I didn't want to work in a company, because I felt that I couldn't separate from my daughters so many hours every day. I decided to take this kind of job (as a cleaning lady) because it allowed me to have lunch with them and talk to them. Now I'm forty-seven, and I would like to get another job, but now in companies they ask you if you are a lone mother, and when I say yes, they say that they are afraid of absenteeism. They don't understand that it is lone mothers especially who can't allow themselves to fail in this regard. So, reality is like this, and therefore the only thing left is to work and work and fight ...

Being a cleaning lady in Spain implies working in the black economy and therefore being without any right to unemployment benefits, health insurance or old-age pension. Carolina has therefore started to pay for a private pension. Her ex-husband is legally obliged to send Carolina a monthly amount for their third daughter, who is still a minor. However, Carolina is actually responsible for her three daughters and cannot rely on her ex-husband's contribution. In terms of state benefits, Carolina has only received a grant for the schooling of her daughters. She expresses her fears on her future very clearly:

> In order to live as a lone mother you must be very strong. You must face everything on your own. You are on your own and you have to survive, make decisions, maintain a household, everything. Being a lone mother is a job in itself. Up to now I've managed quite well, but from now on ... what will happen when I cannot work any longer? What happens if I break my leg? As you may imagine, many women don't feel capable because the support that they receive from society is nothing.

To conclude, we can say that Carolina finds herself in a reflective period of her life for different reasons. First, the depth of the biographical impact of violence on her self-esteem and dignity as a human being makes it impossible for her to experience the question of violence as a closed issue. Second, she is reflecting on her future by linking it to the future of her daughters. Through these experiences Carolina is trying to find a new meaning for family relationships based on an exchange of experiences, opinions and dialogue, which was an unknown pattern for her as a child. In order to fulfil her ideal of the family she is aware that she has to make an extra effort to bridge the generational gap with her daughters through communication and education:

> I want my daughters to have those things which I couldn't have. I try to read as much as possible in order to follow my daughters, to communicate with them and be able to express our feelings. That's a family for me. I see them as having good prospects; I see them strong and prepared to adapt to life, and to find a way out

whatever happens to them ... my own future is obviously blacker, since I'm getting older ... but if I get a better future for my daughters, an important task will have been achieved.

Conclusion

Carolina's strategy – of liberation from a problem of oppressive gender relationships – implies, as we have seen, an active involvement in the community sphere, thus breaking with the social trap of considering violence as a private issue. Her politicization based on women's collective solidarity and feminist awareness must be understood within the new socio-legal and cultural framework on gender and family relationships, brought about by the democratization process. A new cultural sphere of communication has made it possible for Carolina to feel culturally legitimized to claim her rights from a public platform, and more specifically for her daughters' rights, whom she is trying to socialize as 'citizens'. Significantly, for Carolina – as a member of the generation of the transition – the meaning of citizenship has to be worked out starting from nothing, whereas for the generation of Carolina's daughters this concept is sustained by a frame of rights, crucial reforms, and benefits developed within democracy.

Carolina's strategy based on the mediation between the family and the community demonstrates how the gendered construction of an autonomous subject is an insufficient theoretical frame for explaining the experience of citizenship and welfare. The mediation between social spheres has been characterized as a traditional 'female' cultural pattern when defining women's labour. Possibly, this (gendered) cultural pattern might be a useful resource for integration and liberation. The path of Carolina's life contrasts with the model of female emancipation presented by Spanish mainstream literature, according to which women's entrance into the labour market is the only way to combat gender inequalities. Carolina's case illustrates how 'emancipation' does not have to follow a single path (via labour market). Instead, her 'emancipation' implies a future-oriented strategy for the well-being of her daughters within a communicative and emotionally supporting context. Through Carolina's case we have a more complex but probably a more accurate idea of agency, understood not as an isolated struggle for autonomy, but in relation to other groups.

Carolina's relationship to the welfare state cannot be understood without bearing in mind her belonging to the generation of the transition: for the first time the state provided some minimum resources to find a way out from marital subordination. Beyond the 'welfare' provided by the state, welfare as such cannot be understood without integrating the emotional and moral guidelines which impregnate an individual's experiences and actions. It is the lived experience of welfare which contributes to a more accurate understanding of welfare *in* the system, rather than welfare *of* the system.

The family orientation of Carolina's life strategy acts as a factor of integration, both for her and her daughters. Even though the values, assumptions and norms of family and gender relationships in recent Spanish history have opened and democratized, there are still many conflicts operating. As we have seen, Carolina has always defended and acted according to the permanence of family solidarity and loyalty in spite of the high costs that this strategy has had for her. In other words, she has been able to adapt her 'old' family pattern of orientation into a 'new' status of lone mother in the present. Nevertheless she has not broken the cultural rule of fidelity towards her ex-husband. In symbolic terms, therefore, she is still married and therefore too damaged to think of the possibility of a new partner relationship.

After the breakdown of her marriage, Carolina's priority has been to reproduce the ideal of family as a unit of solidarity, communication and reciprocity, yet assuming the responsibility of this family project on her own. She has prioritized cohesion and integration within the family against her own experience of family rupture throughout her life. In order to do that, she has had to change and reconvert her role as breadwinner and mother, and simultaneously develop the roles of educator and highly committed community member. This multiplicity of roles reveals the social dimension of an individual's strategy, which is in the end a strategy oriented towards social integration. The meaning of this integration via family is a result of the 'I'-perspective inevitably linked with the 'family-we' and the 'community-we'. In this sense, from Carolina's case analysis we derive a concept of family that has to be understood not only as a fundamental tool of socialization, but as an agent that constructs identity. Her status as lone mother is lived as a contingency and not as an obstacle for developing her ideal of family.

However, the potentialities of integration and change via the family have to be carefully contextualized, in order to understand the limits of their impact. Carolina's family-centred strategy reproduces class and gender inequalities – she is still confronted with the lack of rights derived from working in the black labour market, and with her precarious status as citizen in the contribution-based Spanish welfare state. As she grows old the precariousness of her situation will increase, making her more vulnerable. Therefore, in spite of her proactive and creative strategy towards social integration through family and community, her position regarding the state and the market is still one of subordination. The precarious or rudimentary nature of the Spanish welfare state is reflected in a perverse contradiction: the same social policies which enable women to divorce do not contribute to providing them with a minimum of security and welfare in their new status as divorced women and lone mothers. With this we can see the complex nature of social change.

A further aspect of this complexity is also reflected in Carolina's trajectory as a member of the transition generation. Her case illustrates that change does not follow a single path, but rather is constructed by combining different resources from the past (e.g. traditional values, biographical ruptures), the present (e.g. democracy) and the future (e.g. hope for her daughters). Furthermore, Carolina's case reveals how gender emancipation and family strategies are not of contradictory natures. As we have seen, a family pattern based on traditional values can perfectly coexist with a longing for gender equality, as long as the first is able to be modified. In terms of social policy, therefore, the challenge would be to combine gender equality and sensitive gender approaches with family-supporting policies. In Spain during the period of democracy, this has been regarded as somewhat contradictory, because of the authoritarian connotations of family policies during the Franco regime.

When studying the role of the family in European societies, we find it much more fruitful to explore family relationships – both in terms of assumptions and practices – than the 'family' as an institution. Family relationships are being transformed with society, not only by adapting to social change, but by becoming a cause of change themselves. The specificity of this change, as we have seen from a biographical and generational perspective, is the re-functionalization of traditional cultural patterns within a new cultural context of values. As we have attempted to demonstrate in this chapter, the family in Spain can neither simply be conceived as a supporting and resisting cushion to fall upon in a context of change, nor as an institution in a process of decay in a context of increasing de-standardization and individualization of social relationships. More interestingly, new forms of family and kin relationships, both at a partnership and parenthood/motherhood level, seem to be emerging by combining traditional, modern and post-modern patterns of orientation and action. In this sense, social policy concepts should be sensitive to the biographical transitions which illustrate new gender relationships within family and society.

The challenges posited by the transformation of the Spanish welfare state, which seem to be leading the family to play a more crucial role in the future, contrast with the State's image of the family, which is reflected in its social policies, as a spontaneous provider of welfare. In this sense, it is important not to romanticize the informal sector or to see family and community-based strategies as the panacea for welfare. The recent trends towards privatization and residualized welfare assistance in a context of precariousness in the labour market in the Spain of the 1990s makes evident the risk of progressively attributing to family more responsibilities for social integration and welfare. It is an open debate whether a major role of the state or the interdependence between the state, the labour market, the family and the community could enable families to become a less vulnerable resource of integration for the generation of the children of democracy.

Note

This chapter is based on the work developed in the SOSTRIS (Social Strategies in Risk Societies) research project, funded by the IV TSER Programme of the European Union (1994–1998) on social exclusion and integration processes. More specifically, the aim of the Sostris project is to explore the processes of social transformation through biographical strategies within the framework of seven European countries (Great Britain, Germany, France, Greece, Sweden, Italy and Spain). Six exemplar categories for researching biographical risk have been studied. These are: unemployed young graduates; unqualified youth; ex-industrial workers; early retired; migrants and/or ethnic minorities; and lone parents. The case analysis presented here belongs to the category of lone parents and has been worked in depth by the Spanish team (Autonomous University of Barcelona).

Acknowledgements

Our warmest thanks to Mònica Nadal, Pilar Carrasquer and Gavin Burke for their intellectual and personal support.

References

Aguilar, M., Gaviria, M. and Laparra, M. (1995) 'Exclusión social y políticas de integración en la Comunidad de Madrid.' *ES*, 12, 217–232.

Alberdi, I (1994) *La situación de la familia en España*. Madrid: Ministerio de Asuntos Sociales.

Astelarra, J. (ed) (1990) *Participación política de las mujeres*. Madrid: Siglo XXI.

Balbo, L. (1983) 'The servicing work of women and the capitalist state.' *Political Power and Social Theory, 3.*

Breckner, R. (1997) 'The use of "history" in the process of constructing European East–West migration biographies.' Paper given at the ESA Conference in Colchester, Essex.

Carrasco, C., Alabart, A., Mayordomo, M. and Montagut, T. (1998) *Mujeres, trabajos y políticas sociales: una aproximación al caso español*. Madrid: Ministerio de Trabajo y Asuntos Sociales.

Feixa, C. (1998) *De Jóvenes, Bandas y Tribus*. Barcelona: Ariel.

Ferrera, M. (1995) 'Los estados del bienestar del sur en la Europa social.' In S. Sarasa and L. Moreno (eds) *El Estado del Bienestar en la Europa del Sur*. Madrid: CSIC.

Fischer-Rosenthal, W. (1997) 'How to fix lives. Biographical work and biographical structuring in present time societies.' Paper given at the workshop *Subjectivity revisited* in London.

Flaquer, L. (1990) 'La familia española: Cambio y perspectivas.' In S. Giner (ed) *España: Sociedad y Política*. Madrid: Espasa Calpe.

García-Nieto, M. (1993) 'Trabajo y oposición popular de las mujeres durante la dictadura franquista.' In G. Duby and M. Perrot (dir) *Historia de las mujeres. El siglo XX*. Madrid: Taurus.

Garrido, L.J. (1992) *Las dos Biografías de la Mujer en España*. Madrid: Ministerio de Asuntos Sociales.

Giner, S. (1995) 'La modernización de la Europa meridional: Una interpretación sociológica.' In S. Sarasa and L. Moreno (eds) *El Estado del Bienestar en la Europa del Sur*. Madrid: CSIC.

Guillén, A (1997) 'Regímenes de bienestar y roles familiares: Un análisis del caso español.' *Papers, 53*, 45–63.

Hernes, E. (1990) *El Poder de las Mujeres y el Estado de Bienestar*. Madrid: Vindicación Feminista.

Jurado, T. and Naldini, M. (1996) 'Is the South so different? Italian and Spanish families in comparative perspective.' *South European Society and Politics, 1*, 3, 43–66.

Lewis, J. (1992) 'Gender and the development of welfare regimes.' *Journal of European Social Policy, 2*, 3.

Moore, H.L. (1991) *Antropología y Feminismo*. Madrid: Cátedra. Col. Feminismos.

Oevermann, U. (1983) 'Zur Sache: Die Bedeutung von Adornos methodologischem Selbstverständnis für die Begründung einer materialen soziologischen Strukturanalyse.' In L.V. Friedeburg and J. Habermas (eds) *Adorno-Konferenz 1983*. Frankfurt a.M.: Suhrkamp.

Pérez del Campo Noriega, A. (1995) 'Una cuestión incomprendida.' In *Cuadernos inacabados*. Madrid: horas y HORAS.

Rodríguez Cabrero, G. (1995) 'La política social en España.' In S. Sarasa and L. Moreno (eds) *El Estado del Bienestar en la Europa del Sur*. Madrid: CSIC.

Rosenthal, G. (1993) 'Reconstruction of life stories. Principles of selection in generating stories for narrative biographical interviews.' In R. Josselson and A. Liehlich (eds) *The Narrative Study of Lives*. London: Sage.

Sainsbury, D. (1994) *Gendering Welfare States*. London: Sage.

Saraceno, C. (1995) 'Familismo ambivalente y clientelismo categórico en el estado del bienestar italiano.' In S. Sarasa and L. Moreno (eds) *El Estado del Bienestar en la Europa del Sur*. Madrid: CSIC.

Sarasa, S. and Moreno, L. (1995) 'Existe un estado del bienestar propio de la Europa meridional?' In S. Sarasa and L. Moreno (eds) *El Estado del Bienestar en la Europa del Sur*. Madrid: CSIC.

Schütze, F. (1983) 'Biographieforschung und narratives interview.' *Neue Praxis, 3*, 283–294.

Further reading

Adelantado, P.; Bonal, X.; Brugué, J.; Gomà, R.; Noguera, J.A.; Rambla, X.; Sáez, L.; Sensat, N. and Varella, R. (1998) 'Las relaciones entre política social y estructura social: Una propuesta teórica.' *Working Paper 1*, Seminari d'Anàlisi de Polítiques Socials UAB.

Alberdi, I (1998) 'La nueva familia democrática.' *Temas para el debate, 38*, 38–43.

Esping-Andersen, G. (1990) *Los Tres Mundos del Estado del Bienstar*. València: Alfons el Magnànim.

Flaquer, L. (1998) *El Destino de la Familia*. Barcelona: Ariel.

Iglessias de Ussel (1997) 'Crisis y vitalidad de la familia.' *Revista de Occidente, 199*, 21–34.

Molinero, C. and Ysàs, P. (1992) *El Règim Franquista. Feixisme, Modernització i Consens*. Girona: Eumo Editorial.

Roca, J. (1996) *De la Pureza a la Maternidad. La Construcción del Género Femenino en la Posguerra Española*. Madrid: Ministerio de Educación y Cultura.

Singly, F. (1996) *Le Soi, le Couple et la Famille*. Paris: Nathan.

Théry, I. (1997) 'Diferencia de sexos y diferencia de generaciones: La institución familiar sin herederos.' *Revista de Occidente 199*, 35–62.

Varella, R. and Sensat, N. (1998) 'Las políticas dirigidas a las mujeres: La acción pública para la igualdad entre los sexos.' In: R. Gomà and J. Subirats (eds) *Políticas Públicas en España*. Barcelona: Ariel Ciencia Política.

CHAPTER 8

Cultural Analysis of the Informal Sphere

Prue Chamberlayne

One of the challenges which arises from the new subjective and cultural turn in social policy is to create a language within social science which is capable of exploring and comparing feeling and emotionality in welfare situations. A similar challenge occurs in the sphere of social relationships within the informal sphere. For while the importance of the intermediate arena as a cultural resource in everyday life is now being recognized in the new focus on 'social capital', the 'third sector', 'informal networks', and the like, the concepts and language to grasp such social dynamics are sadly lacking.

It may be that the problem is worse from an Anglo-Saxon social policy perspective, forged as it mainly is by Fabian positivism. Fortunately, one of the consequences of Europeanization and the rapid spread of comparative research is the widening of repertoires of analysis and the highlighting of contrasting intellectual heritages. Comparison of informal welfare cultures, for example, exposes the gulf between an Anglo-Saxon discourse concerning public–private relations and a Continental discourse concerned with 'the social'. While descriptively concerned with the same terrain, the concepts are rooted in different sociological and political traditions and difficult to work between. On the other hand they bring different strengths, so that they make a powerful combination, if only a working hybrid language can be found.

This chapter presents findings from a cross-national project which has drawn from both liberal and Continental traditions in making an analysis of caring in the informal sphere in West and East Germany and Britain. The research was based on biographical interviews with carers in three cities (Bremen, Leipzig and London). The interviews were conducted in 1992 in East and West Germany, and in 1995 in Britain. (The terms 'West Germany' and 'East Germany' are used throughout, which may seem anomalous in the post-unification context. The device is used to highlight differences between the two systems, many of which endure as cultural forms in 'the two Germanies'. The term 'Continental' refers here to West European political thought, and particularly French, German and Italian. The argument does not apply to East German state socialism.)

The focus of the project is on the way relationships between the private and public spheres are structured differently and played out in caring strategies in the three societies, creating situations in which carers are 'pulled into' and restricted to the domestic sphere or, alternately, more actively connected with the outside world. As a small-scale study the sample lays no claims to representativeness. The sample was recruited through a variety of sources, with the aim of maximizing contrast. Clearly there are likely to be regional, urban–rural and ethnic differences in all three societies, which are not captured in this study.

The project is concerned with the paradoxical contrast between formal policies and the carers' practices in everyday situations, and the extent to which those 'practices' can be construed as 'cultural patterns', even when they appear as structurally determined. Culture and structure are closely intertwined, but when structural determinants produce consequences for identities, everyday strategies and social relationships, then a cultural pattern has emerged, particularly if it has an enduring and reproducible character. I am here using 'culture' in the sense of patterns of everyday action and orientation. In speaking of 'cultures of the informal sphere' I am particularly interested in orientations and dispositions towards the public and private spheres and ways of trafficking between them.

The chapter begins with a review of the conceptual resources which are available to such an analysis, particularly within contrasting liberal and Continental traditions and within various disciplines. This section also discusses the bearing on the position of carers of theories of modernization. The second section presents case studies from the three societies, in a cumulative process of comparison which 'hovers low over the data' (Geertz 1975). The cases selected here are the same as in our forthcoming book, where they will be more fully presented. Six maximally contrasting cases are presented for each society (five in the case of East Germany), out of a total of seventy-five overall. For a fuller account of the study see King and Chamberlayne (1996) and Chamberlayne and King (1997). The third section moves on to the implications of the findings and of a biographical approach for policy interventions.

Conceptual resources

It is arguable that liberal individualism, unlike Durkheimian and Social Catholic traditions, cannot conceive of 'the social fabric' of society, that liberalism has 'lost' the social world (Rustin and Rix 1997). (Clearly 'Durkheimian and Social Catholic' thinking does not exhaust 'Continental' traditions of thought. I am necessarily using broadbrush categories here. A more differentiated comparison of Continental approaches to 'the social' would also be helpful.) While this may be true of the cognate disciplines of social policy and political science, it is not the case in anthropology, nor in the new social movement politics. Indeed, one of the effects of the new cultural turn in British social policy, which has been additionally impelled by comparative research encounters, has been the reforging of social policy's disciplinary alliances, and the rediscovery of its affinities with anthropology and social interactionism.

For decades, attempts in Britain to focus on 'the social sphere' in social policy have remained marginalized (Abrams *et al.* 1989; Bulmer 1987). Indeed, Abrams concluded that the formal and informal spheres of welfare were fundamentally incompatible, that formal interventions could only work against the essential spontaneity of informal exchanges (Bulmer 1987). Writing from a feminist perspective, Riley (1988) traces the way in which 'the social' has been constantly walled off from 'the political'. The 'social', which emerged within new forms of welfare and philanthropy in the nineteenth century, 'enmeshed' women and gave them a new point of access to the public sphere. Anthropological studies, in contrast to political science, have long regarded the sphere of informal social networks as a crucible of relations of power in the wider society (Hann and Dunn 1996). But anthropology, which has become well-established in medical sociology, has remained ancillary to British social policy, as have community studies generally (Frankenberg 1966). (The argument that community work should be placed on an equal footing with case work in British social work training was decisively lost in the 1970s.)

In contrast to liberal individualism, Continental traditions tend to see the individual as realized and enhanced by social relationships, particularly those in the informal sphere (see the argument on Social Catholicism in Introduction2). This much is common to Durkheimian and phenomenological modes of thought. German social policy of the 1980s and 1990s abounds with appeals for a revitalization of the system of subsidiarity, a state-free terrain of 'self-help' in which socio-political actors can work on the social order on the basis of their own social goals, creating a 'new grammar of life-forms', in which the provision of services seeks to generate a sense of belonging among excluded groups (Plaschke, 1984; Heinze and Olk 1984). This concern to enhance moral agency echoes the argument of Habermas (1987) that social systems have become disconnected from life worlds.

It is no coincidence that the main comparative literature on the informal sphere and the third sector emanates from the European continent (Oyen 1986; Evers and Nowotny 1987; Evers 1988). It might be argued that communitarianism, which has developed as a critique of extreme individualism in the liberal tradition, represents an attempt to reconstruct the relationship between the individual and collective life, a perspective on 'the social'. Based within the liberal framework, however, it is still grounded in concepts of individualism. As Fraser and Lacey (1993) argue, moreover, by lacking any critique of gender or class aspects of 'community' it falls into conservative rationalization of the status quo. Other writers have pointed to its normative moralizing about family responsibilities (Kraemer and Roberts 1996).

Donati (1995) defines the crisis of the welfare state as the need to renegotiate public-private relations, to address the everyday problems of un- and under-used people, and for the welfare state to shift from centralistic solidarities to intermediate and primary institutions, including familial, amical and neighbourhood networks, and to a notion of 'relational citizenship'. Yet if a strength of continental European sociology and social policy lies in its provision of a language of socially-related subjective action, a counterpart strength arises in Anglo-Saxon attention to structures of power and difference (Fraser 1995; Thompson 1990). While in many ways German social policy emphasis on 'self-help' sounds remarkably parallel to British social policy language of 'empowerment' and 'citizenship', there remains in Britain more emphasis on individual rights and benefits as a means to personal autonomy, as compared with an emphasis on subjective and relational processes in Continental social policy (Zapf 1986; Donati 1995; Rosanvallon 1988). It may be, therefore, that while Continental social policy has a language which can more fully describe the sphere of informal cultures of welfare, the Anglo-Saxon traditions offer a means of its political evaluation.

If conceptualizing 'the social' and the intersection of public and private worlds is one resource in analysis of the informal sphere, concepts of subjectivity and the sense of self are another essential component. This is certainly so in an action or cultural approach which is interested in strategies of everyday life, a combined analysis of experience, belonging, agency and social structural position. Wright Mills regarded 'the critical and imaginative conjuncture between the public and the private in sociological research' as a key locus of social and political change (Morris and Lyon 1996, p.3), while the history of gendered and contested shaping and reshaping of public–private relations is a strong theme in feminist writing (Pateman 1989; Fraser 1995). Feminist literature on caring has also long sought to bridge the worlds of social roles and personal meaning, or task and feeling, by transcending the divisions between social policy and psychology (Finch and Groves 1983).

This debate continues in a new guise in debates in British social theory concerning agency and structure, and reflexivity, identity and autonomy; yet capturing the articulation between the personal and the social remains elusive (Giddens 1990; Archer 1996; Shilling 1997). Sociological approaches to subjectivity and identity have tended to be both constructivist and cognitive. Socially constructed representations within discourse analysis pay little attention to the sense of self which operates in both self-directed action and in inner worlds of emotion and feeling, and have little purchase on coping strategies and experiences of everyday life. An 'over-cognitive' approach to autonomy and intimacy assumes creative personal mastery of deep-set emotional and personal dynamics. As Shilling puts it, 'the idea that human agents possess senses, sensualities and physical habits that have been *partially* socialised, but that *continue to shape* as well as be shaped by social structures, remains marginalised' (1997, p.738).

Yet for purposes of intervening in social life, social policy requires a theoretical language of the self and personal meaning. As Williams and Pillinger (1996) argue:

> We need to tease out the differences between people's subjectivity – their understanding of their own experiences, their identity – their sense of belonging, their agency – the capacity to act individually or collectively, and their social position – and the objective interpretation of that person's position. In addition we need to relate these to the social topography of welfare risks and needs. (p.3)

In their study of young mothers, Bell and Ribbens (1994) argue the significance of analysing informal networks, partly to make women more visible, but also to provide the 'missing link' in the chain of structure, consciousness and action. Like Mills, and drawing on anthropological approaches to civil society and the informal sphere, they assert the political significance of the private sphere in women's modelling of relations with the outer public world to family members. They also point to the importance of informal networks in both empowering and constraining power relations within the family.

Such an approach challenges the Marxist view that domestic roles 'confine' women to the narrow world of the home, and that emancipation is only possible through wider social and collective engagement in the world of employment and politics. This 'universalist' thesis, even as applied to industrial societies, neglects social and historical variations in the extent to which households and household members have been isolated from wider social exchange and have differed in their forms of outside engagement. In Banfield's (1958) thesis of 'amoral familism' in southern Italy in the 1950s, a strong version of the narrowing effects of family confinement is contingent upon a particular context of economic backwardness and political hierarchy. Balbo (1987) writing in the contrasting context of developed welfare systems (including Italy), points to the 'modern' role of women in mediating and negotiating relationships between family members and outside agencies of provision. The transferability of such domestic skills to the modern labour market, she argues, has catapulted women from the periphery to the centre of society. While there has undoubtedly always been great diversity in the degree to which domestic roles were separated from the outside world (for example, from the 1880s to the 1920s German bourgeois feminism used the notion of 'spiritual motherliness' (geistige Mütterlichkeit) to claim gendered access to the public sphere, with monopoly control over education and welfare work (Chamberlayne 1990a), Balbo's analysis suggests a 'modern' scenario of strong connection between public and private worlds, with mediations in the informal sphere playing a critical part in the development of personal capacities. It is arguable that a key characteristic of post-modern society is the striking of a new balance between roles in the public and private spheres. One of the points of interest in the *Cultures of Care* study is the extent to which welfare systems promoted such 'new roles', or cemented carers in domestic confinement, as Cinderellas of modernity. Certainly carers seem left out of the gender equality which Giddens (1991) and Beck (1992) identify as the hallmark of modernity, based in outside employment and more autonomous personal lives.

In the *Cultures of Care* study we found a powerful sense of home ties and of family responsibilities and identities in all three societies. Both women carers and male spouse carers were determined to sustain central caring roles, including in circumstances of great personal sacrifice. In all three societies there were some carers who were mainly confined to the home sphere, some who were more outwardly-oriented, and some who were torn between home and the outside world. However, the interplay of personal factors/family pressures and service contexts which produced a particular orientation was markedly different in each society, as were the individual motivations for each strategy. This resulted in characteristic forms of engagement in both the public and the private spheres in each society.

Curiously, in the emergent process of defining such 'characteristic cultures' the variations between cases in each country were often as helpful as the contrasts between societies, since the carers who resisted or worked around particular constraints and pressures often highlighted those very structures. The next section, in which five or six cases are presented from each society, aims to show both how the detail and richness of specific case studies illuminates particular cultural dynamics, and how a point of convincing 'saturation' has been reached in making statements about particular cultural patterns.

The research was based on narrative interviews with about twenty to twenty-five carers in three cities. The initial question invited an open account of the caring situation, how it started and developed, forms of support which were available and which the carer might have liked, and what the experience meant to her/him personally. The analysis followed interpretive methods which compared the lived and the told life story, in the style developed by Gabriele Rosenthal, producing holistic or gestalt-like case studies of caring situations and strategies. The interpretation proceeded sequentially, hypothesizing what might come next in both the pattern of the life and structure of the narrative text, in an action frame of reference. This method of analysis involves a process of double reconstruction, in the manner of the double hermeneutic: in the analysis the researcher 'reconstructs' the lived life and the told story, which the interviewee has reconstructed within the interview (Rosenthal 1993; Chamberlayne and King 1996).

The West German cases

The West German informal sphere of caring was characterized by weak ties out-side the home, whether with services, employment, informal networks, or wider family situations. A 'pull into the home' results both from the strength of tradi-tional family ideologies and divisions of labour, and from the channelling of relatively generous and thereby de-politicizing services and benefits into the home. Beyond such structural determinants of home-orientedness, the case stud-ies show the extent to which active individual decisions play into this pattern. 'Modern' social carers who actively mobilize and negotiate outside services are the exception in West Germany; isolation and confinement are the more likely reality.

The two most home-oriented carers are both entrapped in closed and isolated caring situations. Frau Jakob (60), in deciding to bring her dying husband back home from hospital, is acting in continuity with her lifelong role in family service. However she is also bitterly disappointed by a lack of family support. She has not grasped the shift in family structures, from extended to nuclear patterns, which has taken place in her own lifetime, and still embraces the anachronistic philosophy of 'traditional familism' which continues in much official and popular ideology. The self-willed nature of her isolation is symbolized in her decision (made with her husband, who dies between the two interviews) to opt for an anonymized grave, which will spare others the 'trouble' of looking after the grave, but which also punishes her brother-in-law for his neglect of his brother. By this means he is denied the opportunity to mourn at his brother's graveside.

Frau Hamann (35) has opted to abandon her own professional career, family and friends to make a family life with a divorcing man in a family practice. A disabled child only compounds her isolation, since in the eyes of her in-laws her medical skills make her the 'perfect' carer. Frau Hamann has seemingly been driven to this marriage by some inner need which may well be fed by traditional ideology, but not by her 'beliefs' as such. She might well have anticipated the closed nature of the culture and structure she was entering, but the situation closed around her rather than being her active choice. At the time of the interviews she was in a state of rather passive despair.

The two 'torn' cases exemplify a similar cultural dynamic of family closure. Frau Luchtig (50) has wrestled with a lifetime's subordination to her mother, in the family grocery, as her tenant, and more recently as her carer. Latterly she has actively and ingeniously seized every opportunity to pursue independent craft and musical interests which she has built up in lieu of education, but the scope is limited, mainly by her mother's refusal to accept more outside services, which are available. Further restrictions impend on her, from her mother's increasing frailty and her husband's likely early retirement. Frau Hegemann (45), by contrast, whose husband has rapidly deteriorating multiple sclerosis, is a more passive personality. In the early stages of the disability the Hegemanns continued with their three children as a 'normal' family, and Herr Hegemann, a former policeman, enjoyed his public activity and status as leader of a self-help group. But Frau Hegemann, despite her role as breadwinner (she is a clerical worker) and now as family representative in the self-help group shows no enthusiasm for these outside roles, or for the independence or opportunities for self-development which they might bring. She seems frozen in a strategy of day-to-day living, which worked well in the past, but which is clearly inadequate now, in relation to her demanding adult children or to her husband's condition.

It may seem that biographical methods, by stressing actions and decisions as in the presentation of these four cases, omit pressures of the system from view. However a comparison with the West German carers who are more outwardly connected bring structural and cultural pressures more clearly into focus.

Both Frau Mahler (31) and Frau Alexander (35) exploit the relative generosity of West German benefits by innovative strategies which allow mobility and flexibility in conducting their lives. The Alexanders, members of a biker milieu, buy a campervan which can accommodate their 14-year-old son's breathing and other apparatus, in order to maintain their mobility and sociability in the evenings and at weekends. Helped financially by fostering a disabled daughter, the Mahlers are able to move to a larger, more collective house, which will combine their personal and professional interests. Through their own employment experience they have cooperative and proactive links with social workers, whereas Frau Alexander's confident but combative relationships with medical personnel has been achieved through long and bitter struggles. These carers are thus working the West German system, manipulating it for their own goals, even challenging its official purposes, certainly stretching its constraints. They operate as husband-and-wife teams and belong to wide networks of friends. Personal and public lifestyles are closely linked in the case of the Mahlers, so that the boundaries of family privacy, which are rather strongly enforced in the other cases, are largely transcended. The Mahlers even talk freely and openly of emotional experiences, while Frau Alexander, who regards the unsayability of the anguish of caring as the main reason why carer groups fail, is still biting back her inner pain:

> You have to sort out your own problems first before talking about it or before you could come out of yourself somewhere.

Rather than being bound by the conservative ideology which typifies the male breadwinner model of West German welfare (Lewis 1992), the Mahlers and the Alexanders are influenced by alternative thinking in West Germany, although neither defines their actions as political. In the case of the Mahlers, class as well as public/private boundaries are transcended (Herr Mahler moved from ship to residential work), and the Alexanders come from a sparse and generationally widely-spaced family as well as a culturally marginal and oppositional milieu. Thus the more outwardly-connected families, in which the carers are also younger, have 'escaped' the traditional family hierarchies and divisions of class, generation, gender and 'privacy' which enclose the other cases. Their networks are characterized by horizontality, flexibility and trust, recalling the structures which underlay Putnam's (1993) definition of 'civic competence' in his study of cooperative relationships in Northern Italy. (A different location, and especially Berlin, might have yielded a stronger representation of 'alternative' carers. On seeking out interviewees we were seeking variation in referring agency or self-help group, and in types of disability and household structure, rather than representativeness. Case study comparisons often seek out maximally contrasting rather than 'representative' cases.)

East Germany

Among the East German carers outer-connectedness is the dominant cultural dynamic, and the privatizing effect of the West German system is virtually absent. Here the norms of full women's employment and of public provision, determination to maximize rights under German unification, and the strong web of informal networking produce a cultural dynamic of outward-orientedness, which is only rarely defied, as in the exceptional case of Herr Speyer. The focus on outside services and employment are 'intended' by official state socialist policies, to the extent that there are no public representations of women in domestic roles (Doelling 1991). By contrast, the strength of informal and familial networks of support and exchange result from 'unintended' workings of the system, such as inadequacies in the sphere of consumption and the meaninglessness of the public sphere. This flies in the face of western theories of totalitarianism, which emphasize atomization and social disintegration in state socialist societies (Keane 1988; Chamberlayne 1990b). By contrast, some Central European sociologists see in the informal networks of state socialism the potential infrastructures for post-modern formations (Hankiss 1990).

That the most outwardly-oriented East and West Germans are similar – one feels the Mahlers might get along with the Gruens, and the Alexanders with the Meissners – is perhaps not surprising. All four couples are relatively young, although Frau Meissner's daughter is now 21 years old. The Gruens (mid-20s), like the Mahlers, are in the caring professions; Herr Gruen is studying theology, and Frau Gruen is shifting her training from nursing to social pedagogy. Both are intensely involved in the care and education of their highly disabled six-year-old son, deeply empathetic with him and reflective of their own understanding of disability and learning difficulties. The Gruens, who are from a dissident church milieu, have also sought out sympathetic medical and educational personnel, and maintained a wide circle of friends who help relieve them and accompany them on weekend and holiday trips to the country – several wheelchairs have been worn out in the process. Contrary to the Mahlers, though, and perhaps because of their East German context, they are wary of the boundaries of privacy. In the interview they (rather unsuccessfully) use each other and the child to fend off free-flowing talk, and they do not respond for a second interview. Like other East German carers, the Gruens have sought out sympathetic medical and educational personnel. They are supported by friends more than family – Frau Gruen's mother tends to be into 'pity' – and they quite envisage that Joe will go to a boarding school in years to come: 'if they don't do away with everything – they're cutting things like crazy'.

Frau Meissner (41) is a divorced woman who has largely operated as a single parent, but always maintained the active cooperation of her ex-husband – she even shares a garden with him and his new family, to the astonishment of the neighbours. She has a long and intensive experience of challenging authorities. By lobbying sympathetic headteachers and enlisting support from other local influentials she defied the official designation of her disabled and incontinent daughter to residential care. Insisting on integrated schooling, she has accompanied her during the school day and on school trips, eventually becoming trained as a school nurse. Thus although Frau Meissner gave up work to look after her daughter, in doing so she maintained the outward orientation of an employed woman. More recently she and her husband have fought for their daughter to be trained in the post office and shared the necessary transport. Frau Meissner has campaigned for GDR participation in the Olympics for Disabled, runs discos for disabled youngsters in Leipzig, and has taken her daughter with other friends in wheelchairs on holiday in America, to which they intend to return, 'to ride down highway 66'. She does not regard herself as political – she is simply busy and active; in her words, 'it just happened'. She is part and parcel of East German network society, often adeptly insinuating herself into supporting positions rather than engaging in direct confrontation. By soliciting help and accompanying Katrin into outside situations she has forged a bridgehead to wider social engagement. Her teacher colleagues met the tram every morning to help her lift the wheelchair down. Like Frau Alexander, she started meekly from low-grade clerical work and it is through fighting for her disabled child and for her right to remain attached to that child that she has gained her personal strength and competence. (In the process of hypothesizing about the early stages of this case, the research team felt convinced that a pattern of over-dependency would develop, that Frau Meissner was clinging onto her daughter for her own emotional needs. This proved quite false.)

A notable difference between West and East German systems lay in the opposite impulses attendant on disability. In West Germany, since disability payments advance with the severity of the disability, the pressure is to exaggerate the condition. In East Germany the pressure was to underrate the severity of the disability, since those considered less disabled received education, training, guaranteed workplaces and salaries, whereas those considered 'incapable of development' (*föerderunfähig*) were consigned to residential warehousing.

In the next two 'torn' cases in East Germany the same outward propulsion is in evidence. Perhaps it is even intensified by the process of German unification, in which retraining and maintaining employment, together with inquiries and negotiating for new welfare and disability rights, are experienced as priorities. At the heart of both these cases is a difficult emotional struggle against patriarchy in which the forces of outward propulsion support the personal impulse for greater independence. We have already seen the opposite pattern in West Germany, where 'system forces' might well intensify problems of emotional dependency and subordination.

In the first interview, Frau Arnd (23), a single parent, has been pulled back into the confining arena of her parental home, in which her grandmother also lives. This arises from her decision to get retrained from kitchen work, from which she has been made redundant, to public employment, which will give lifelong protection. Her father's mission to save his daughter from becoming 'a social case, one which would stay in the records', fortifies his patriarchal tendencies. Interviewed in the company of the parents, Frau Arnd describes the tension in the small flat when everyone comes home from work: 'everyone has something else, and then such a child, one has a lot to do, either there's an explosion, or a real rumpus ... We subordinate ourselves, and grandfather always has the say with us ... We all have our feet under his table.' At weekends she returns to her own flat on an estate, where she feels lonely on occasion, but where she meets friends, several of whom have disabled children and are connected with *Lebenshilfe*, a campaigning organization for people with mental disabilities. Through these contacts Claus goes to an integrated crèche and then a small kindergarten group with specialized staff; through the group she is supported by a lawyer who is appealing against reductions in the benefit level. Meetings with these friends are described in a notably more relaxed way: 'We're pleased when the children are together and we can talk together. Now it's winter we all meet in the flat, and all three boys are lively, there's a real rumpus sometimes, but one can easily tolerate that.'

By the time of the second interview Frau Arnd has completed her qualification, has secured a job and is permanently back in her flat, although she meets her family frequently, not least on the child's insistence. It is also striking that despite Frau Arnd's young age, lack of education and experience, and despite the family's feeling traumatized both by the disability and the new social system, they have succeeded in accessing good services. Despite the drastic deterioration of medical services around the time of unification, exacerbated by the exodus of personnel, a well-known cardiologist performed an operation on the child early on, and the family benefited from a good physiotherapist and good social worker. Thus their fortress family is not closed off, rather from it they sally forth in combat and determination, helped by networks of information, a rights-conscious culture, and their own anger.

Michael Hofmann (1991) argues that values of equality and participation, despite the cynicism of officialdom, permeated East German society, and were particularly asserted in arenas outside the close surveillance of the party, such as health and welfare. (Party organization was centred on the workplace, leaving public and neighbourhood services somewhat more free (Chamberlayne 1990b).) Indeed, the informal networks of mutual support and information among elderly and disabled people and their shared understandings of the failures and hypocrisies of the system amounted to a 'quiet social movement'. Party claims to socialist superiority in satisfying human needs fuelled a rights-consciousness in the population and enraged those most dependent on welfare services. Perhaps this latent anger, as well as the generalized sense of threat and insecurity which accompanied unification, explains the determined, even manic, fashion in which East Germans set about mastering the new welfare regulations and entitlements, as in the case of Frau Blau (60).

Frau Blau's husband, a transport engineer, had a stroke following his lay-off and is only slowly recovering his speech and movement. As in the case of the Arnd family, Frau Blau's anger at disability and unification are intertwined; her response is to do battle with the external world for benefits, equipment, spa cures and holidays. This ceaseless fight for rights continues the couple's earlier pattern of struggles in the GDR to get a telephone or a car, and is doubtless aided by Frau Blau's professional experience as administrator of supplies in a textile firm. The impulse to 'get out' is amplified by the bitter foreshortening of the opportunities to travel in their retirement. Despite Frau Blau's frequent sorties, she feels both confined and exposed: 'Hmm, (sighs) like in a bell-jar. (Pause) Life goes on outside and we just watch. (Long pause).'

But the outward thrust is not the only impulse. Despite working, Frau Blau has been quite a traditional wife, and has cared for her mother and her daughter, and the shift to full-time care confronts her with her dependency and subordination in the marriage. Asked if she would accept an afternoon or day's respite care she says:

> Yes, now yes, a year ago I said, 'No I won't do that, I don't want that', but today I see through that. Basically I don't get five minutes to myself. Sometimes I feel wiped out. He can't help it, but he's like a limpet, he takes me over completely and utterly. Before we liked going to a concert, to the opera – that is all gone.

Underlying her account of her struggle for rights in the public domain is the scary reshaping of her identity as a woman and as a wife, and therefore of their partnership:

> Frau Blau: (Pause) Through this I have become much more independent, more independent than …
>
> Herr Blau: You were like this before.

Frau Blau: But not like this, Hans-Otto. I have to represent us completely to the outside world ... (pause) and I have to check myself sometimes, because I am out there alone, but I am still (saying) 'we'.

The point is that while Frau Arnd and Frau Blau are in part pulled back into the home by caring, they maintain a strong and more dominant orientation to the outside world. This outward orientation may not act as a bridge to wider social activity or involve the spread of friendships and contacts as in the case of Frau Meissner and the Gruens, but it is in marked contrast to the home orientation of the West German caring situations and strategies.

This is not to say that the 'home-orientation' cannot be found in East Germany. Indeed we did have one such case, an older man of 60, former lorry driver who had taken over his wife's family's taxi-business. His response to his wife's epilepsy, which started with the birth of their first daughter, worsened with the second, and has by now destroyed three-quarters of her brain, has been to blockade himself in with her in the private sphere, refusing not only residential options but any help beyond an hour's nursing care. Presenting himself as a heroic Atlas figure, honouring conjugal responsibilities, he downplays the support of his daughters. In many ways he is like West German Frau Jakob who insisted on caring alone for her terminally ill husband. Both are older people, though no older than Frau Blau, whose dynamic is quite different. In the East German context Herr Speyer is making a double protest, against both male roles and the political norms of collective provision. It was not a dynamic which arose in any of the other East German cases – it is rather a contrasting case which highlights the more typical pattern of outward-orientedness.

The British carers

The British carers lie between the extremes of the West German 'pull into' and East German 'push out of' the home. They have for many years combined caring, employment and wider voluntary and social activity. Nevertheless the dominant British cultural dynamic is towards home solutions, although the routes by which British and West German carers find themselves centred in the private sphere are different. Part-time work, daycentres, respite care, voluntary and self-help groups exist in greater measure than in West Germany, but the context of welfare cutbacks and fragmentation in the 1980s and 1990s turns carers in on their own resources and intensifies intergenerational dependencies. So despite phases of outside social engagement and more active support in caring tasks from husbands than in West Germany, the British carers tend to fall back into family traditions, even those from which they have previously escaped. Carers' groups, to which several of our interviewees belonged, operated more as an extension of the private sphere, providing solace, 'a laugh' and basic information, than as a bridgehead to wider contacts or to more transformative action (Williams 1993). This confirmed the thesis that carers groups in Britain have become incorporated rather than radicalized (Barnes 1997, p.162; Gordon and Donald 1993, p.167). The contrast between caring and disability groups is instructive. Both groups shared a common base of demands in the 1970s, but through the 1980s and 1990s, following community care legislation, carers' groups have often been set up by local authorities, also for formal requirements of consultation, whereas disability groups have remained more independent. National carers' groups, which campaign for better finance and support, do not challenge the basic terms of caring, while disability groups, which are also more diverse, operate from a more challenging political platform (Oliver 1990; Morris 1993).

Mrs Buckley (55) is emblematic of these processes. Coming from a large Catholic East End family, she initially defied her family's prolonged child-bearing norms through a successful and mobile career. On giving birth to a disabled daughter in her thirties she started on a long career of struggles for appropriate referrals. And despite repeated health crises in which she stopped work, she valiantly regained employment, in which she was actively supported by medical personnel at a specialist children's hospital, and continued her involvement in voluntary groups. In Melanie's late teens, however, in the shift from education to adult services and the context of the cost-cutting 1990s, there is no such support. Reduced day centre schedules are difficult to reconcile with employment. Moreover, Melanie's gynaecological problems have excluded Mr Buckley from the direct caring role he used to play, at home as well as in public places. A friend's car accident is the final straw for Mrs Buckley:

> I was so upset about that and I thought, 'Oh I'll pack up work.' I did it on the spur of the moment ... I did feel a bit, not bitter towards her (Melanie), but I just feel sometimes, 'Oh, why did I have to pack up my job, because I liked it.'

Thus there is a service void around Mrs Buckley in a period in which she needs active and positive support to find good alternatives for Melanie.

Mrs Rushton (60), whose husband is now in the later stages of a twenty-year muscular generative disease, refuses repeated offers of additional night nursing. He attends a day centre, and they both belong to a carers' group. Mrs Rushton's caring duties begin several hours before the ambulance arrives – 'I've been seeing to his enemas, I've been feeding him, I've been shaving him, I've been washing him' – and continue throughout the evening and night, with constant bickering over the practical procedures. Mrs Rushton feels patronized and undervalued, and trapped in the daily routines. Yet she wants to maintain control over her privacy, possibly to keep private their conflictual relationship:

> Your life is run without you having any say in it. You are beholden to them and also you have people coming in a home. I sometimes feel I am taken over, you know they come in ... but it's shared, it's not my personal private place ... they're coming in on my personal privacy.

Like Mrs Buckley, Mrs Rushton appears to need firm and sensitive help, particularly with relationship issues. Yet there is no mention of such initiatives, either from social services or the nursing personnel.

The intertwining of personal and public factors and the effectiveness of personally supportive advice from a social worker is shown in the case of Mrs Rajan (35), who remained closed off from outside help for eleven years. During that time her shame and despair at having a disabled son, the lack of confidence in medical personnel who had said her son would die, her mother's successful use of traditional Indian medicine to save him, and her difficult adjustment from a female-dominated extensive family to a predominantly male and nuclear-family structure all combined to keep her locked in the strategy of family closure which characterized her own childhood in East Africa. Racist experiences in Britain may well have compounded her response. But with the medical support around her second son's birth came a friendly social worker with offers of respite care and future fostering, and later on an invitation from her second son's headteacher to do ancillary classroom work and some training, which she has taken up enthusiastically, alongside a range of community activities.

In Mrs Rajan's case the initiative for a greater outward-orientedness seems to have come from a social worker, although her new inner preparedness for more sociability was also crucial. Mediating interventions are perhaps all the more critical in a precarious and patchy system in which great personal determination and fortitude are needed to access good quality provision. In West Germany good quality home-based services are much more amply provided, with psychologists and physiotherapists doing intensive domicilary work at an early stage. For equivalent aged British children, carers need to be far more outgoing, as in the case of the East Germans.

It also seems that, in contrast with the East German system, the absence of structural and cultural support for outer-connectedness leaves carers in Britain in a situation in which personal dependencies and dilemmas become particularly problematic and anxiety-making.

As among the West German cases, the more outwardly oriented cases in Britain appear somewhat 'exceptional'. In the British study both are men. In West Germany the outwardly oriented cases 'escaped' the full force of the 'pull into the home' by belonging to marginal or alternative milieus, whereas the British cases escaped the dynamic of 'home solutions' by their gendered 'outward' response. They are interesting in showing the social infrastructures which can be drawn on by carers in Britain. Mr Allahm (65), a senior professional who has travelled and lived throughout the world and has a wife now suffering from an advanced degenerative disease, uses his professional skills to buy in substitute care, and to arrange visits and support from church members. Drawing on his long experience of creating 'home' abroad among expatriates, he has even established a new church group in which he and others like him will have spiritual support in caring and loss. Thus alongside arranging his wife's care he is creating a substitute community for his far-flung family, and for the wife he has loved so dearly. This allows a fluidity between public and private spheres, in which outside help is accepted in and spiritual needs are taken outside. Mr Merton (44) is likewise intensively engaged in social groups which are largely of his own making. A former seaman, so also widely travelled, he staves off the debilitating effects of his own epilepsy through a marriage with a disability activist in which the two partners can sustain each other. In this case the militant campaigning and advice work leads to a heavy invasion of private space, so much so that Mr Merton has to lock himself in his room with the phone off to get an hour's peace.

Implications for policy

The study reveals consistently different patterns of action in the three societies. To some extent a generational change is evident; in general the younger carers are more outwardly-oriented, less consumed by domesticity, more able to hold on to past identities and future horizons. Yet it is cultural as well as structural forces which pinion West German Frau Hamann (35) in her husband's family, and which give much less well resourced East German Frau Arnd (23) an escape from her patriarchal family. Different political cultures of caring explain the different responses, of retreat and proactivism, to poor services in Britain and East Germany.

All the carers would benefit from supportive interventions in the alleviation of their distress and pain. But while the 'outwardly-oriented' carers have wide resources on which to draw and are more actively oriented to the future and to changes in their responsibilities, the home-oriented and torn carers in West Germany and Britain are more likely to be in retreat from wider and more proactive activity, and become vulnerable to crisis, given the changing circumstances of disability and life course positions. Such carers are in need of firm and sensitive support in mediating both their relationships with the outside world and and their family dependencies. But despite the professional emphasis on self-help in West Germany and on empowerment in Britain, this kind of intensive inter-personal support seems unlikely to be provided.

There is a striking contradiction in this study between formal ideologies and everyday practices. The West German system of subsidiarity, backed by the resources of the social state, claims to deliver social solidarity and a tight interweaving of formal and informal sectors, yet it often plainly fails to do so. Rather it is the 'family' component within the philosophy of subsidiarity which exerts the strongest pull, often leaving carers trapped and isolated. (Subsidiarity is defined as delegating responsibility to the lowest level of society capable of bearing it, so that maximizing family responsibility accords with the system — often with disastrous consequences, as we have seen.) Britain, despite its neo-liberal philosophy, maintains a broader web of social relationships, and perhaps the voluntary tradition is a form of resistance to liberal individualism. But informal support in Britain does not substitute for structural provision. Indeed, the study relativizes the meaning and significance of 'empowerment' and movements for 'self help' in Britain and West Germany. In either context carers' groups are only 'empowering' in the sense of maintaining minimally adequate situations, combating a defeatism which is service-induced. Welfare systems are faced with the need to remedy a social incapacity which is of their own making. In different structural and cultural conditions there would have been no need for such 'empowerment'.

In East Germany, 'empowerment' derives from wider social infrastructures, notably the employment model for women, an egalitarian ethos, and the strength of informal networks. It is ironic that East Germany, which denied the legality of civil society, produced the most active forms of informal civic engagement, at least in the field of caring. It may well be that the meaninglessness of formal politics and the repression of civil society in East Germany pushed active social engagement down to informal levels, such as 'work' and 'house collectives', where a need for human communication spilled out regardless of official attempts at surveillance (Pollack 1992; Chamberlayne 1995, p.28). Perhaps the subversion of official dogmas is itself a means of spiritual survival. The 'social levelling' within East Germany also facilitated the exchange of social advice, such as benefited Frau Arnd.

It is not a question of replicating the East German situation elsewhere, but of identifying some of the wider determinants and components of a more energized and supportive culture in the informal sphere. The study suggests the need for a different relationship between social lives and welfare services, one which will strengthen human relatedness and operate in a context of trust.

Conclusion

The *Cultures of Care* study highlights the social vibrancy and creativity which accompanies more outward-oriented models of caring, and the efficacy of such energy in challenging and reshaping existing systems. It is by such positive agency and 'signifying practices', including by those in modest positions, that the cultural standards set by dominant meaning systems become stretched and generate new realities (Kochuyt 1997, p.13). Here we see relational 'subjects' rather than 'individuals' in action: 'the capacity of that actor to oppose cultural and political domination, to be involved and to transform his or her own social environment' (Hamel 1995, p.245). In the outward-oriented model we also see the potential for equality between carers and professionals, through the gaining of social competence among lay experts. The study also makes it clear that where social trust and 'the social' are denser and social capital is richer, carers can become more resourceful in seeking out tailor-made support, so that less welfare intervention is needed. Thus it is the wider social relations which give rise to particular imagined worlds in which such actions are possible and indeed socially engendered – or foreclosed on. Sensitivity to such 'social relations' goes well beyond the usual parameters of social policy, which tends to operate with 'thin' knowledge of social systems. This study suggests the need for more culturally and sociologically specified accounts of social situations and contexts.

This approach returns social policy to a focus on the actor, meaning, and 'society', and away from post-modern emphasis on the 'individual', 'rights', and 'tasks' (Howe 1994; Nolan, Grant and Keady 1996). As Gordon and Donald (1993) argue, the exploration of hidden social capacities requires an action approach. Biographical methods also have the advantage of accessing 'unconscious or latent meanings (which) manifest themselves behind the backs of the subjects' (Oevermann *et al.* 1987). In this way the analysis is not restricted to the conscious intentions of the actor, but explores underlying patterns of behaviour and practice, both at the level of hidden family histories and as structurally induced by wider social practices.

As Frazer and Lacey (1995) argue, interpretive methods dissolve the liberal dichotomy between individual and society. This poses a great challenge to traditional social policy, with its top-down Fabian focus on centrally administered 'provisions', which pay no regard either to individual subjectivity or to socio-cultural milieus. Then comes the problem of lack of appropriate discursive language, together with, as Fraser (1995) and McCulloch (1997) put it, a great deal of contending to be done over boundaries between the public and private spheres, which includes the sphere of 'the social'. My contention is that not only is there no ready-made discourse for such discussion, but an awkward disjunction between the liberal and Continental thinking about this intermediate sphere. Both problems will be overcome in the course of collaborative comparative research – which Europeanization is fortunately promoting.

Acknowledgements

Thanks to Andrew Cooper and Jude Bloomfield for comments. This chapter owes much to Annette King, who was main researcher for the *Cultures of Care* project, which was ESRC funded in 1992–95 (R000233921). Frauke Ruppel, Susanne Rupp and Chris King also worked as researchers on the British part of the project which was funded by UEL 1995–97. An earlier version of this chapter was given as a paper at the ISA (International Sociological Association) Conference in Montreal, July 1998.

The researchers encountered biographical methods in the course of pilot work in Germany in 1992. The project itself then became a vehicle for learning the method and understanding the significance of its theoretical grounding in phenomenology, which has become somewhat 'foreign' to British sociology in recent decades. Particular thanks are due to Simone Kreher (Humboldt University) and Martina Schiebel (University of Bremen) for their help in this process, and particularly in running workshops for local interviewers in 1992. The *Cultures of Care* research was perhaps the first project to use biographical methods for comparative social structural analysis. The method has subsequently been used in the seven-country EC-funded SOSTRIS project (Social Strategies in Risk Societies) 1996–99, of which the author is joint coordinator with Michael Rustin.

References

Abrams, P., Abrams, S., Humphrey, R. and Snaith, R. (1989) *Neighbourhood Care and Social Policy.* London: HMSO.

Archer, M. (1996) 'Social integration and system integration: developing the distinction'. *Sociology, 30,* 679–99.

Balbo, L. (1987) 'Family, women and the state: Notes towards a typology of family roles and public intervention.' In C.S. Maier (ed) *Changing Boundaries of the Political.* Cambridge: Cambridge University Press.

Banfield, E.C. (1958) *The Moral Basis of a Backward Society.* New York: Free Press.

Barnes, M. (1997) *Care, Communities and Citizens.* London: Longman.

Beck, U. (1992) *Risk Society. Towards a New Modernity.* London: Sage.

Bell, L. and Ribbens, J. (1994) 'Isolated housewives and complex maternal worlds: The significance of social contacts between women and young children in industrial societies.' *The Sociological Review, 42,* 227–262.

Bulmer, M. (1987) 'Privacy and confidentiality as obstacles to interweaving formal and informal social care: The boundaries of the private realm.' *Journal of Voluntary Action Research, 16,* 11–25.

Chamberlayne, P. (1990a) 'The mothers' manifesto and disputes over Mütterlichkeit.' *Feminist Review, 35,* 9–23.

Chamberlayne, P. (1990b) 'Neighbourhood and tenant participation in the GDR.' In B. Deacon and J. Szalai (eds) *Social Policy in the New Eastern Europe.* Aldershot: Avebury.

Chamberlayne, P. (1995) 'Gender and the private sphere – a touchstone of misunderstanding between Eastern and Western Germany?' *Social Politics, 2,* 1, 24–36.

Chamberlayne, P. and King, A. (1996) 'Biographical approaches in comparative work: The cultures of care project.' In L. Hantrais and S. Mangen (eds) *Cross-National Research Methods in the Social Sciences.* Pinter.

Chamberlayne, P. and King, A. (1997) 'The biographical challenge of caring.' *The Sociology of Health and Illness, 5,* 601–621.

Doelling, I. (1991) 'Between hope and hopelessness: Women in the GDR after the turning point.' *Feminist Review, 39,* 3–15.

Donati, P. (1995) 'Identity and solidarity in the complex of citizenship: The relational approach.' *International Sociology, 10,* 3, 299–314.

Evers, A.S. (ed) (1988) *Shifts in the Welfare Mix.* Vienna: European Centre for Social Welfare Training and Research.

Evers, A. and Nowotny, H. (eds) (1987) *The Changing Face of Welfare.* Aldershot: Gower.

Finch, J. and Groves, D. (eds) (1983) *A Labour of Love: Women, Love and Caring.* London: Routledge.

Frankenberg, R. (1966) *Communities in Britain: Social Life in Town and Country.* Harmondsworth: Penguin.

Fraser, N. (1995) 'Politics, culture, and the public sphere: Toward a postmodern conception.' In L. Nicholson and S. Seidman (eds) *Social Postmodernism: Beyond Identity Politics.* Cambridge: Cambridge University Press.

Frazer, E. and Lacey, N. (1993) *The Politics of Community: A Feminist Critique of the Liberal-Communitarian.* Hemel Hempstead: Harvester Wheatsheaf.

Geertz, C. (1975) *The Interpretation of Cultures.* London: Hutchinson.

Giddens, A. (1990) 'Structuration theory and sociological analysis.' In J. Clark, C. Modgil and S. Modgil (eds) *Anthony Giddens: Consensus and Controversy.* London: Falmer.

Giddens, A. (1991) *Modernity and Self-Identity: Self and Society in the Late Modern Age.* Cambridge: Polity.

Gordon, D.S. and Donald, S.C. (1993) *Community Social Work, Older People and Informal Care: A Romantic Illusion?* Aldershot: Avebury.

Habermas, J. (1987) *The Theory of Communicative Action,* Volume 2. Boston: Beacon Press.

Hamel, P. (1995) 'Collective action and the paradigm of individualism.' In L. Maheu (ed) *Social Movements and Social Classes: The Future of Collective Action.* London: Sage.

Hankiss, E. (1990) *East European Alternatives.* Oxford: Oxford University Press.

Hann, C. and Dunn, E. (1996) *Civil Society: Changing Western Models.* London: Routledge.

Heinze, R. and Olk, T. (1984) 'Rueckzug des Staates: Aufwertung der Wohlfahrtsverbaende?' In R. Bauer and H. Diessenbacher (eds) *Organisierte Naechstenliebe.* Opalden: Westdentscher Verlag.

Hofmann, M. (1991) 'Bewegte Stille – Benachteiligte Menschen und Gruppen in Ostdeutschland.' In *Aufbruch im Warteland – Ostdeutsche soziale Bewegungen im Wandl.* Bamberg: Palette Verlag.

Howe, D. (1994) 'Modernity, postmodernity and social work.' *British Journal of Social Work, 24,* 513–532.

Keane, J. (ed) (1988) *Civil Society and the State.* London: Verso.

King, A. and Chamberlayne, P. (1996) 'Comparing the informal sphere: Public and private relations of welfare in East and West Germany.' *Sociology, 30,* 4, 741–761.

Kochuyt, T. (1997) 'Could objective realities tell us a story?' *Biography and Society,* Newsletter of Research Committee 38 of the ISA, December.

Kraemer, S. and Roberts, J. (eds) (1996) *The Politics of Attachment: Towards a Secure Society.* London: Free Association Books.

Lewis, J. (1992) 'Gender and the development of welfare regimes.' *European Journal of Social Policy, 2, 3.*

McCulloch, A. (1997) 'On the public and the private: A comment on Fahey.' *Sociology, 31,* 4, 793–799.

Morris, J. (1993) *Independent Lives: Community Care and Disabled People.* Basingstoke.

Morris, L. and Lyon, S. (1996) *Gender Relations in Public and Private: New Research Perspectives.*

Nolan, M., Grant, G. and Keady, J. (1996) *Understanding Family Care: A Multidimensional Model of Caring and Coping.* Buckingham: Open University Press.

Oevermann, U. with Allert, T., Konau, E. and Krambeck, J. (1987) 'Structures of meaning and objective hermeneutics.' In V. Meja, D. Misgeld and N. Stehr (eds) *Modern German Sociology.* New York: Columbia University Press.

Oliver, M. (1990) *The Politics of Disablement.* Basingstoke.

Oyen, E. (ed) (1986) *Comparing Welfare States and Their Futures.* Aldershot: Gower.

Pateman, C. (1989) *The Disorder of Women.* Cambridge: Polity.

Plaschke, J. (1984) Subsidiaritaet und 'Neue Subsidiaritaet.' In R. Bauer and H. Diessenbacher (eds) *Organisierte Naechstenliebe.* Opladen: Westdentscher Verlag.

Pollack, D. (1992) 'Zwischen alten Verhaltensdispositionen und den neuen Anforderungsprofilen: Bemerkungen zu den mentalitaetsspezifischen Voraussetzungen des Operierens von Interessenverbaenden und Organisationen in den neuen Bundeslaendern.' *Probleme der Einheit, 12,* 2, 489–508.

X Putnam, D. (1993) *Making Democracy Work: Civic Traditions in Modern Italy.* Princeton: Princeton.

Riley, D. (1988) *'Am I That Name?' Feminism and the Category of 'Women' in History.* London: MacMillan.

Rosanvallon, P. (1988) 'The decline of social visibility.' In J. Keane *Civil Society and the State.* London: Verso.

Rosenthal, G. (1993) 'Reconstruction of life stories: Principles of selection in generating stories for narrative biographical interviews.' In R. Josselson and A. Lieblich (eds) *The Narrative Study of Lives* 3 vol.1, Sage.

Rustin, M. and Rix, V. (1997) 'Anglo-Saxon individualism and its vicissitudes: Social exclusion in Britain.' *SOSTRIS Working Paper 1: Social Exclusion in Comparative Perspective.* London: BISP.

Shilling, C. (1997) 'The undersocialised conception of the embodied agent in modern sociology'. *Sociology, 31,* 4, 737–754.

Thompson, J.B. (1990) *Ideology and Modern Culture.* Cambridge: Polity.

Williams, F. (1993) 'Women and the community.' In J. Bornat, C. Pereira, D. Pilgrim, and F. Williams (eds) *Community Care: A Reader.* London: Macmillan.

Williams, F. and Pillinger, J. (1996) 'New thinking on social policy research into inequality, social exclusion and poverty.' In J. Millar and J. Bradshaw (eds) *Social Welfare Systems: Towards a Research Agenda.* Centre for the Analysis of Social Policy and the ESCR, University of Bath.

Zapf, W. (1986) 'Development, structure and prospects of the German social state.' In N. Rose *et al.* (eds) *The Welfare State East and West.* Oxford: Oxford University Press.

CHAPTER 9

The Catholic Church and Social Policy in Europe

Michael Hornsby-Smith

Introduction

The broad theme of this book is that social and welfare policies in Europe need to be reconsidered in the light of the hitherto neglected dimension of cultural differences. It has generally been recognized that a major component of culture has been the dominant religion, its institutional arrangements, relationships with the state and with the social and political élites, rituals of memory and celebration, its value and moral belief systems, and so on. There is little doubt that, historically, religion was a major organizing system in the emergence and differentiation of nation states.

However, in the main, current orthodoxies have attributed little importance to religious, and thus more broadly cultural, explanations for the differences in social and welfare policies in European nations. Earlier comparative cross-national analyses have suggested a number of explanations for the differences between European welfare systems. Geographically based categorizations of nations have been suggested by Halsey (Abrams, Gerard and Timms 1985, pp.12–13) and O'Connell (1991, p.99; quoted in Davie 1994a, pp.98–102). Esping-Andersen (1990), in a seminal work, presented a rank ordering of welfare states on the basis of measures of 'de-commodification' or the extent to which the individual had welfare rights independent of relationship to the labour market. While some have suggested that his typology was largely descriptive, his cross-national analyses drew attention to the importance of Catholic voting strength and cross-party coalitions as explanatory variables. Other researchers such as Castles and his colleagues (1993) have explored the notion of 'families of nations' and noted common experiences and policy outcomes of English-speaking, Scandinavian, German-speaking and Latin nations. Busch (1993) has attributed a number of common features to the 'greater intensity of communications' where there is a shared language. Therborn (1993a) has shown that differences of childhood rights depend largely on differences of legal traditions. Elsewhere, following Rokkan (1970), he has pointed to linkages between nations which share a similar post-Reformation ancestry (Protestant or Catholic), and to further religious differentiations resulting from the secularizing influences of the French Revolution (Therborn 1993b, pp.330–333).

In this chapter it is proposed to explore the extent to which the salience of religious differences has survived the various processes of modernization since the Enlightenment and the French (and American) Revolutions. It will focus on the impact of the chief religious divide in post-Reformation Western Europe, that between Catholicism and Protestantism, as an indicator of cultural differences, on a variety of social and welfare policies. The extent to which differences in Catholic densities are associated with variations in a wide range of social policies will be explored to ascertain the extent to which religion still makes a difference to political outcomes.

The religious variable

In order to understand and interpret contemporary social phenomena sociologists believe that it is necessary to contextualize them historically (Brown 1997; Davies 1996; Fletcher 1997; Roberts 1996). The structuring of social differences in contemporary Europe has numerous religious roots. Davies (1996), for example, has usefully identified several of these historically important cleavages, all of which have relevance for the understanding of social and cultural variations in contemporary Europe. We might note in particular the limits of expansion by the Roman Empire; its division into the Eastern Empire with its new capital at Byzantium, now Istanbul, and the Western Empire centred on Rome; the later divide between the Catholic West and the Orthodox East; the line of furthest expansion of the Ottoman Empire roughly coinciding with the limits of Islam; and the cleavage between Catholic and Protestant nations resulting from the Reformation.

What it does seem possible to conclude from a brief trawl through twenty centuries of European history is that the consequences of these various events and cleavages can still be identified in contemporary Europe. Indeed, the religious map of Europe today clearly reflects these historical legacies. As David Martin puts it: 'religion is currently providing one of the major markers of what *is* Europe' (1994, p.14; emphasis in original). On the basis of data from the 1991 World Values Surveys, there are seven Catholic members of the European Union (Spain, Portugal, Italy, the Irish Republic, Belgium, France and Austria); five other substantially Catholic countries in Central and Eastern Europe (Slovenia, Poland, Lithuania, the Czech Republic and Hungary); the Netherlands and Germany (and Northern Ireland) are religiously 'mixed' members of the European Union as are non-members Switzerland and Latvia; and three Protestant members of the EU (Denmark, Sweden and Finland) and three non-members (Norway, Iceland and Estonia). The other countries of Eastern Europe (including Byelorus, Russia, Romania and Bulgaria) are predominantly Orthodox in terms of their religious heritage (see Hornsby-Smith 1998, p.11 for details). While reliable statistics are hard to come by, it seems that there may be something of the order of one million Jews in Western Europe (Davie 1994b, p.60). There are also some seven million Muslims in Western Europe (aggregating the estimates for the individual countries in Nielsen 1992), chiefly in France, Germany and the United Kingdom, perhaps around 3 per cent overall. There are a further 7–8 million in Eastern Europe, concentrated mainly in Bosnia, Albania and Bulgaria (Szajkowski, Niblock and Nonneman 1996, p.34). Finally, Turkey is overwhelmingly a Muslim country. These data demonstrate clearly the three major religious cleavages in contemporary Europe: between Northern Protestantism and Southern Catholicism, between Western Catholicism and Eastern Orthodoxy, and between Christian Europe and Muslim Turkey.

In this section I wish to draw attention to the strong Catholic influence on the process of European integration, for example through the pursuit of 'social capitalism' by Christian Democratic parties (Hornsby-Smith 1998, pp.12–16). The strong drive for European integration and a federalist vision of Europe by mainland Christian Democrat parties in the post-war period (in spite of the Atlanticist orientation, in the sense of a concern to maintain strong political and defence links with the USA, its preference for liberal economics, and pragmatic and conservative accommodationist strategy towards coalition partners of the German CDU-CSU and its relative unconcern for the ideological roots of Christian Democracy in Europe of the early post-war years) is made abundantly clear in the recently translated history of *The Christian Democrat International* (Papini 1997, especially pp.19–158). Van Kersbergen (1995, p.184) has argued that 'the notion of solidarity as harmony is an intrinsic component of the Christian democratic tradition and is alternately paraphrased as "integration", compromise, accommodation and pluralism.' It is not surprising, therefore, that Hanley has concluded that 'within EC institutions, it is clear the CD groups are a major force behind integrationist drives such as the push for monetary and political union' (1994, p.2). More than other parties they 'have striven explicitly for some kind of supranational identity' and have 'a tangible discomfort in the face of raw nationalism ... Hence their longstanding attachment to European integration as a means of overcoming nationalism' (Hanley 1994, p.8).

One cannot but be aware that most of the key figures in the European project of social, economic and political integration have been Catholics. While I am not aware of any evidence of a Vatican conspiracy such as might reasonably fuel the concerns of those susceptible to a papal phobia (but see Chenaux 1990; Willaime 1994), it is nevertheless the case that the key initiators of the project, Adenauer, Schuman, De Gaspari and Monnet were all Catholics who seem to have been aware of Catholic social teaching as it had emerged up to the 1950s and the 'Christian Humanism' as advocated by the influential French philosopher, Jacques Maritain (1935; 1973). In more recent times, the Commission President, Jacques

Delors (1992; see also Ross 1995), with perhaps the strongest vision of the future of Europe, was also a Catholic.

In spite of continuing weaknesses in Catholic social teaching as it has developed over the past hundred years since Pope Leo XIII's (1949, first published 1891) encyclical *Rerum Novarum* (Dorr 1992, pp.369–377), there have been a number of themes which have relevance for the discussion of the European project. The dignity of the individual human being is reflected in the stress on the primacy of labour over capital and notions of the 'just wage' (Fogarty 1961), sufficient for a family. Related to this are assumptions about the 'proper' role of women and their special task of child rearing. There is a strong emphasis on parental rights in the education of their children and concerns about undue involvement of the state (Coman 1977, pp.47–59; Whyte 1981). Fears about state power are reflected in the principle of subsidiarity (Voyé 1994; see also Schumacher 1974) and the strong corporatist tradition which favours the search for consensus and collaboration rather than class conflict in industrial relations. Finally, there is a strong dimension of fraternity or solidarity in Catholic social teaching. It is this that gives it its distinctive international dimension and, by extrapolation, its potentially intergenerational concern, for example over ecological issues and the stewardship of the earth's resources and for sustainable development (see, e.g., Cleary 1989; McDonagh 1986, 1990, 1994). To the extent that such ideological resources are able to overcome sectional interests, it might be hypothesized that such beliefs will be reflected in social policies wherever Catholics are politically strong.

Apart from these tendencies, the contribution of Catholic social teaching to the new communitarianism has also been acknowledged in Boswell's (1994) influential search for an alternative to individualistic economic liberalism and collectivist state socialism (see also Grasso, Bradley and Hunt 1995). In particular he traces the contribution to 'personalist Christian democracy' of papal pronouncements after *Rerum Novarum* and the 'Christian humanism' of Jacques Maritain. Boswell's themes: democratic communitarianism, fraternity, associativeness, participation, and solidarity, are all to be found in the body of Catholic social teaching as it has evolved in the century since *Rerum Novarum*, as articulated, for example, in Pope John Paul II's encyclicals *Sollicitudo Rei Socialis* (1988) and *Centesimus Annus* (1991).

In sum, there appears to have been an 'elective affinity' (Gerth and Mills 1948, p.284) between the European project promoted by key Catholic statesmen in the post-war years, the internationalism and communitarianism found in Catholic social teaching and developed over the past hundred years since *Rerum Novarum*, and the contemporary concerns of the Vatican. The contrast with the euro-scepticism in the British Conservative Party and its articulation in Margaret Thatcher's Bruges speech in 1988 with its much greater emphasis on the interests of the individual nation state could not be more striking.

Social policies in Europe

So far I have sketched an outline of a thesis about the relationship between religion and politics in contemporary Europe. First, the deep religious cleavages which have long historical legacies in the gradual emergence of the Europe we know are likely to have continuing political salience. Second, the post-war European project was the brainchild in particular of a series of Catholic statesmen who sought to achieve a lasting settlement to the destructive squabbles between European nations by means of pragmatic projects which transcended national boundaries and interests. Third, in this project of reconciliation they were likely to have been influenced strongly by the century-long search in Catholic social teaching for a socially just 'third way' between liberal capitalism and state socialism and this teaching found its particular political expression in the post-war Christian Democrat parties in the countries of Western Europe.

In spite of national variations reflecting a variety of contingencies such as the strength of rival Social Democratic parties, there are a number of distinct elements in the social-personalist ideology of Christian Democracy, that is 'friendship between human beings who were once strangers and enemies to each other' (Dierickx 1994, p.22). Von Beyme has suggested that 'all Christian Democrats began with a belief that a middle way could be found between capitalism and socialism in the spirit of the Catholic social doctrine and the social encyclicals' (1985, p.94; quoted in Van Kersbergen 1994, p.36). Madeley (1994, p.145) has pointed to variations in Protestant political approaches and contrasts the historic weakness of the Lutheran tradition 'to generate political activism out of religious commitment' with a more active involvement of Calvinism. Van Kersbergen concludes that 'Christian Democracy is a distinctive political phenomenon and that what is distinctive about the movement concerns a religiously inspired model of social reform which is both social and capitalist' (1994, p.42).

Van Kersbergen suggests that:

> Christianity is related to welfare capitalism only so far as Protestantism involved a first step in the process of secularisation and individualisation … Protestantism qualitatively changed church-state relationships which, in turn, facilitated the construction of the welfare state … This contrast between the Protestant and the Catholic nations explains the qualitative differences between their welfare states. These differences concern the degree of 'stateness' (the level of centralisation; the level of state-church integration; the degree of state intervention in the economy) and the degree of institutional coherence (universalism versus fragmentation) (1995, pp.194–195)

Not surprisingly, he argues that the ideal type of welfare state development is found in Scandinavia 'where the distance from Rome is the greatest' (Van Kersbergen 1995, p.195).

Both Dierickx (1994) and Van Kersbergen (1994; 1995) concluded that there are distinctive differences in the approaches of Christian democracy and both social democracy and Conservative traditionalism. While both social democrats and Christian democrats differ from Conservative traditionalists in their concern to address the inequalities and sufferings resulting from uncontrolled liberal individualism, the social democrats seek to reduce inequality by radical social change while the Christian democrats pursue the 'politics of mediation, defined as the religiously inspired, ideologically condensed and politically practised conviction that conflicts of social interests can and must be reconciled politically in order to restore the natural and organic harmony of society' (Van Kersbergen 1995, p.238). Van Kersbergen argues that the 'grand' tradition of Catholic social teaching, as articulated by Vatican spokesmen, is still rooted in the moral principles of love and the duties of Christian charity. But there is also a 'little' tradition of Catholic social movements in Western Europe 'which have managed to transcend the 'bourgeois' values of love and charity by formulating a distinctive critique of capitalism' (Van Kersbergen 1995, p.193) in the search not only for the amelioration of poverty and inequality but more radically for social justice through structural change.

A number of researchers have recently carried out a series of empirical cross-national analyses of social policy outcomes by Catholic density or Christian Democrat voting strength. While there is clear evidence of changes between the 1960s and 1980s (Van Kersbergen 1995), a number of tentative generalizations can be drawn:

1. In 1980 social democracy and Christian democracy had similar levels of social spending (Van Kersbergen 1995, p.103).

2. In 1980 Christian democracy had a stronger effect on pensions spending than social democracy (Van Kersbergen 1995, p.110).

3. 'Christian democracy is positively related to the family-bias in tax-benefit regimes, whereas social democracy is not' (Van Kersbergen 1995, p.139).

4. In 1980 'Christian democratic welfare states do discourage women to enter the labour market or encourage female labour market exit' (Van Kersbergen 1995, p.144). One study has concluded that 'centre parties in Catholic countries transform the conservative stance of Catholicism in gender-related issues into public policy, such as in family policy, taxation, education, social security and care for children, the elderly and other dependents. These governments thus place priority on the maintenance of traditional patterns of gender differentiation ... That policy, of course, creates powerful disincentives and obstacles to the incorporation of female labour into the economy' (Schmidt 1993, pp.204–205; quoted in Van Kersbergen 1995, p.146).

5. Where Christian democracy is strong, the state's involvement in schemes of social security tends to be minimized and the bulk of the social security burden is carried by employers and the insured (Van Kersbergen 1995, p.150).

6. 'Social policy in Christian democratic nations can be expected to reproduce rather than overcome class and status differences. Benefits tend to be earnings-related rather than of the flat-rate type so that they preserve rather than supersede social difference' (Van Kersbergen, 1995, p.152).

7. Christian democracy is positively related to the fragmentation of social security schemes in terms of the number of special schemes for different groups (Van Kersbergen, 1995, p.153).

8. 'Christian democracy appears to enhance the negative impact on total disposable income when a married mother of two children enters the labour market' (Van Kersbergen 1995, p.173).

9. Over the period 1959–1983, Catholic party strength had a negative effect on full-employment performance. Esping-Andersen attributed this to 'Catholicism's particular brand of social policy: a willingness to subsidise family well-being, but not to guarantee employment' (1990, p.131).

10. 'Catholicism's subsidiarity principle has always insisted that private organisations (mainly the Church) be prominent in social services' (Esping-Andersen 1990, p.134).

In the following analyses we will consider briefly to what extent there is any empirical evidence that the mobilization of Catholic political interests led to the emergence of distinctive Catholic social policies in the countries of Western Europe, particularly in the areas of family policy, social welfare and unemployment.

It is, perhaps, appropriate at this point to note that there are methodological difficulties associated with cross-national research. Hantrais and Letablier, for example, have noted 'the cultural embedding of statistical concepts' (1996, p.7) in their comparative analysis of family policies in Europe. They outline some of the difficulties of making cross-national comparisons of statistical data on families and households and stress the 'need to remain alert to possible errors of interpretation that can arise if conceptual and contextual differences are ignored' (Hantrais and Letablier 1996, p.23).

Ragin (1989) distinguishes between case-oriented approaches which aim to account for significant outcomes in terms of historical legacies and context but which are weak on generalizability, while variable-oriented approaches seek to make causal generalizations about the relationships between variables (such as religion and social policies) but are weak on the holistic interpretation of historical instances (such as the secularity of Catholic France). As Ragin writes elsewhere, usually 'the choice ... is between variables and cases – between radically analytic, statistical techniques that obscure cases and qualitative-historical methods that immerse the investigator in cases' (1991, p.3). Janoski has usefully distinguished between the internal analysis of one country, for example the influence of anti-clericalism and the long tradition of conflict between Church and state in France, the extent to which Irish social policy might have been influenced by its historical relationship with Britain, etc., and the external analysis comparing countries before the internal analysis has been started (1991, p.60). In the variable-oriented, external analyses which follow, preliminary comparisons have been made between the nations of Western Europe, differentiated according to their religious composition.

The data used in the following analyses have been derived in the main from fifteen nations in Western Europe where the main religious cleavage is that between Catholicism and Protestantism. Comparisons will be made between seven Catholic countries (the Irish Republic, Italy, Austria, Spain, Portugal, Belgium and France) with an average Catholic density of 96 per cent, three religiously 'mixed' countries (Germany, the Netherlands and Switzerland) with an average Catholic density of 52 per cent, and four Protestant countries (Sweden, Norway, Denmark and Finland) with a Catholic density of under 1 per cent. The United Kingdom has been treated as a separate category because although it has an established Protestant religion, it has a much higher proportion of Catholics than the Scandinavian countries and, indeed, it will be shown to have some distinctive differences from both the 'mixed' and 'Protestant' categories. It has been suggested (e.g. by Esping-Andersen 1990) that it represents a distinctive Anglo-American type with a strong emphasis on liberal individualism. Greece has been omitted from the following analyses because it is largely Orthodox and does not reflect the cleavage between Protestantism and Catholicism.

In the secondary data analyses which follow it should be stressed that the unit of analysis is the nation and not individuals. No account has been taken here of differences in population size. Data have been extracted in the main from Eurostat's *Social Portrait of Europe* (1996) but also from a number of sources including Bailey (1992), Castles (1993), Esping-Andersen (1990), George and Taylor-Gooby (1996), Hantrais (1995), Hantrais and Letablier (1996), Kiely and Richardson (1991), Oppenheim and Harker (1996), Simpson and Walker (1993) and Therborn (1995).

Family policies

The comparison of family policies highlights some of the methodological and definitional problems that can arise in cross-national research. Bradshaw *et al.* (1993, p.266) when seeking explanations for differences in child benefit packages have recently hypothesized that: 'Countries which are broadly Catholic may tend to be more generous to families than countries which are broadly Protestant.' Nevertheless the comparison of family policies is fraught with difficulties. Barbier, in particular, warns against the use of 'misleading aggregates' and recommends taking into account 'all aspects of social policy which potentially can have an impact on the welfare and behaviour of families' (1991, p.47). This includes six categories of formal financial transfers but also public sector measures which have a potential impact on family life and welfare (Barbier 1991, p.50). The whole issue is highly complex and includes variations in tax and benefit systems and such matters as childminding provision, the effects of family allowances on fertility, and differences in the operation of labour markets for mothers.

Linda Hantrais has suggested that EU countries have pursued three main policy objectives in the post-war period: both horizontal and vertical redistribution of income; pro-natalist objectives; and the welfare of women (1993, pp.55–56). In a comprehensive overview of the variety of family policy-making styles a very wide range of arrangements emerges. It is interesting to note, however, that with the exception of Germany (and Greece), all the countries having a constitution which recognizes the family and is committed to protecting it are Catholic (including France, Ireland, Italy, Portugal and Spain) (Hantrais 1993, p.58).

Following the work of Kamerman and Kahn (1978) and Schultheis (1990), a distinction has also to be made in terms of explicit, implicit and negative family policies (Hantrais 1993, p.57). Thus Belgium and France (Catholic and developed) are categorized as having explicit and relatively coherent family policies while Denmark, Germany and the Netherlands (Mixed or Protestant) have less explicit family policies. Along with the UK (Mixed/Protestant), Ireland, Portugal and Spain (Catholic, less developed) and Italy (Catholic) are seen as having less coherent or comprehensive family policies (Hantrais 1993, p.60–61).

Other considerations include the different patterns of funding family allowances or child benefits. Notions of 'just wage' thinking (Fogarty 1961), that is that the wage earned (normally by the male earner) should be sufficient to keep his family in reasonable comfort, are reflected in the tendency in some Catholic countries for employers to be wholly or partly responsible for social security or insurance contributions (in Belgium, France, Italy, Portugal and Spain). In these countries Hantrais notes that 'family allowances were conceived as part of the wage package, and employment-related contributions were the main or sole source of funding' (1995, p.93). In the more Protestant countries (Denmark, Germany, the Netherlands and the UK) but also Catholic Ireland (strongly influenced by policy-evolution in Britain) they are funded through taxation (Hantrais 1993, p.59).

We can see the extent to which there are variations in family policies which reflect differences of national religious contexts using published data for the countries of Western Europe in Table 12.1. It can be seen that while there is a clear tendency for the proportion of married women in the labour force to increase with Protestant density as we might have anticipated, child care provision appears to follow a U-shaped distribution though the proportions are still much higher in Protestant than in Catholic societies.

Table 12.1 Family policies by religious context of country (1985–1990)

	Catholic	Mixed	UK	Protestant
Max. no. countries	7	3	1	4
Average % Catholics	95	55	16	1
Labour Force of participating women in the european community,1986	37	37	53	66
Children receiving publicly funded services as a percentage of all children in age groups:				
(a)<3 years	11	3	2	48
(b) from 3 years to compulsary school age	72	60	38	85

Source: *Simpson and Walker (1993); Kiely and Richardson (1991)*

Welfare policies

The consideration of pensions and social security policies is becoming increasingly pressing given demographic trends and the rising numbers of elderly dependants. Here it might be hypothesized that there is a significant contrast between the more communitarian and family-oriented policies in Catholic countries and more individual citizen-oriented policies in Protestant countries.

Esping-Andersen's (1990) conservative-corporatist regimes followed what Titmuss (1974, p.31) called the industrial-achievement-performance model of welfare with what Hantrais called 'systems of occupational social insurance welfare, shaped in no small measure by the influence of the Church' (1995, p.29). In what Ginn and Arber (1992, p.259) called the 'income security' model, 'social needs are met in proportion to work performance', Hantrais notes that 'women were conceptualised as wives and rewarded for having stayed at home to support their husbands and look after their children' (1995, pp.134–135). Such family-oriented arrangements were typical in the 'continental welfare states' of the mainly Catholic founding members of the EEC. Hantrais observes that the newer members, such as Catholic Spain and Portugal, 'continued to rely heavily on traditional forms of support through family and kinship networks and the Church and ... Social protection was broadly based on corporatism, as in the continental model, with employers carrying the major burden of the cost of providing benefits' (Hantrais 1995, p.34).

In the Nordic Protestant countries, on the other hand, social security systems are more individual-oriented and follow Titmuss's institutional redistributive model (1974, pp.30–32) providing universalist services to all citizens regardless of their employment status. Taylor-Gooby (1991, p.97) has pointed out that

Esping-Andersen's (1990) social democratic regimes have gone furthest in socializing care while his liberal, Anglo-Saxon regimes offer a residual (Titmuss 1974) model of targeted minimum support. Significant differences remain in the expected patterns of informal and formal care, for example of the elderly. In Protestant Denmark this is recognized as a responsibility of the state while in the Catholic countries of southern Europe and Ireland Hantrais notes that 'family care-givers performed a duty expected of them by society, and little attention was paid to their needs' (1995, p.140).

Table 12.2 De-commodification scores by religious context (1980)

	Catholic	Mixed	UK	Protestant
Max. no. countries	5	3	1	4
Average % Catholics	95	55	16	1
De-commodification scores (1980)				
in pensions	11.0	9.4	8.5	15.2
in sickness	9.6	11.3	7.7	13.5
in unemployment	7.0	9.3	7.2	7.5
Combined de-commodification score	27.7	30.0	23.4	36.2

Source: Esping-Andersen (1990)

We will begin our comparison of welfare policies by looking in Table 12.2 at Esping-Andersen's (1990, pp.50, 52) various scores for what he calls 'de-commodification'. He defines this as occurring 'when a service is rendered as a matter of right, and when a person can maintain a livelihood without reliance on the market' (Esping-Anderson 1990, pp.21–22). He shows that there is an increase in the combined de-commodification score from Catholic to Protestant societies though the component scores for pensions are U-shaped. The combined de-commodification score and component scores in pensions and sickness are lowest in the case of the United Kingdom where the Labour Party was too weak to develop the Beveridge 'universalist social citizenship' model of the early post-war years (1990, pp.53–54).

Table 12.3 shows Esping-Andersen's scores for corporatism and universalism and the results confirm that Catholic societies have higher scores on corporatism and lower scores on universalism. It is interesting to note that on all six of Esping-Andersen's scales we have considered, the United Kingdom is significantly different from both 'Mixed' and 'Protestant' societies.

Table 12.3 Corporatism and universalism by religious context (1980)

	Catholic	Mixed	UK	Protestant
Max. no. countries	5	3	1	4
Average % Catholics	95	55	16	1
Scores in 1980: corporatism × 10	70	37	20	30
Universalism	66	85	76	90

Source: Esping-Andersen (1990)

Table 12.4 Welfare policies by religious context (1991–1993)

	Catholic	Mixed	UK	Protestant
Max. no. countries	3	2	1	2
Average % Catholics	95	55	16	1
Public expenditure 1993 %	52.7	52.9	43.5	62.3
Social expenditure 1990 %	23.4	26.2	22.3	27.8
Direct taxes 1991 %	11.7	14.6	14.1	30.5
Indirect taxes 1991 %	12.6	12.9	14.3	18.1
Social security contributions 1991 %	15.1	16.9	6.4	1.6
Total taxes 1991 %	39.4	44.4	36.3	50.4

Source: George and Taylor-Gooby (1996)

Table 12.4 shows that Protestant societies have higher levels of public expenditure, social expenditure, direct, indirect and total tax levels as a percentage of GNP in 1991 than Catholic societies but lower social security contributions (George 1996, p.16). The United Kingdom is again distinctively different in having significantly lower public and social expenditures in the early 1990s.

Poverty and unemployment

The continental welfare regime which assumed that earnings from employment would be sufficient for workers and their families was relatively unproblematic as long as unemployment levels remained low during the post-war boom years. With the industrial restructuring from the 1970s, however, and the huge increase in unemployment and increasing numbers of people, especially young people, falling into poverty, policies to combat 'social exclusion' have begun to emerge in the European Union (Hantrais 1995, pp.146–147).

Responses to unemployment in the member states vary according to the different models of welfare state. Thus Hantrais notes that the corporatist welfare regimes of the founding members of the EEC, mainly Catholic, followed 'the Bismarckian employment-related social insurance model of social protection' (1995, p.161). Hantrais argues that in countries which did not originally follow the social insurance principle, two alternative paths have been taken. In the United Kingdom the emphasis has been on creating a rights-oriented scheme while in the Protestant Scandinavian countries there has been an extension of state-funded social insurance. Catholic Spain and Portugal tended to follow the continental employment-related insurance model (Hantrais 1995, p.164).

Table 12.5 Poverty and unemployment by religious context (1980–1988/1992)

	Catholic	Mixed	UK	Protestant
Max. no. of countries	6	3	1	4
Average % Catholics	95	55	16	1
Average male unemployment 1992 %	8.6	3.9	32.2	27.9
Average male long-term unemployment 1992 %	9.8	49.6	32.2	27.9
Average households in poverty 1988 %	16.6	7.6	32.2	27.9
Average Gini 1980 × 100	37.3	37.9	31.8	33.0
Average infant mortality rates mid-1980s	11.5	8.7	10.0	7.2

Source: Bailey (1992); George and Taylor-Gooby (1996)

Given the strong tradition in Catholic social teaching of stressing the primacy of labour over capital, the significant negative effect which Catholic party strength had on full-employment performance in Western European countries over the period 1959–1983, reported by Esping-Andersen, is particularly striking. Esping-Andersen argues that this 'can be said to reflect Catholicism's particular brand of social policy: a willingness to subsidise family well-being, but not to guarantee employment' (1990, pp.130–131). Table 12.5 gives five indicators of poverty, inequality and unemployment: average male unemployment rates and the proportions of long-term unemployed, the proportions of households in poverty, average Gini indices of inequality, and infant mortality rates. In every case the average figures for Catholic countries are higher than those for Protestant societ-ies, with 'mixed' societies generally in an intermediate position. As noted previously, the United Kingdom's position does not fit easily into the general pat-tern of variations between Catholic and Protestant societies. Rather, as Esping-Andersen (1990) pointed out, they have tended to pursue a liberal capitalist economic model, closer to the United States, in contrast with the stronger corporatist Catholic countries or the social democratic model pursued by the Protestant Scandinavian countries.

What conclusions can be drawn from this brief review of comparative social policies? The clear differences which have been shown to exist between Catholic and Protestant societies in Western Europe over a wide range of social policies and policy outcomes are not, by themselves, evidence of a clear causal link. The most that can be claimed here is that religion is a relevant factor. Whether the differences which have been demonstrated to exist can be explained by other factors, such as differences in GNP, or stage of modernization, or some other factor related to different historical legacies, remains to be explored in further research.

It should also be noted that the data we have considered are likely to be very time-dependent. Thus in the case of the United Kingdom, the generally universalist principles of the early post-war Beveridge welfare state came under increasing attack during the Thatcherite administrations of the 1980s and 1990s. Similarly, the structures of the Scandinavian social democratic welfare states have been strongly challenged in recent decades in response to the pressures of competition in the markets of the global capitalist economy.

The social policies which have emerged and been developed in the countries of Western Europe are the product of a whole range of different variables. In seeking to explain the differences between the social policies of different countries it has been shown that one factor which must be taken into account is the historically dominant form of religion. Further work would include the internal analysis (Janoski 1991) of individual countries in order to identify the peculiar historical configuration of circumstances and factors which together explain the emergence of particular social policies.

Conclusion

What conclusions can we draw from this study of religious roots, the promotion of the European project, and emergent social policies? The Catholic Church has developed a substantial body of social thought over the past century and has clearly influenced many European Catholics active in political and social life. The founding fathers of the post-war European project and more recent politicians such as Jacques Delors have prompted policies entirely consistent with this body of thought. Given the strongly Catholic nature of many of the mainland countries and, indeed, the frequently expressed fears of Protestant groups in the United Kingdom, it is appropriate to ask to what extent the social policies which have developed in the European Union have reflected Catholic social preoccupations.

The first thing to be said is that, perhaps unexpectedly, the direct involvement of the Vatican in the emergence and development of the European project appears to have been rather limited, probably because of its preoccupations with the survival of the Church in Central and Eastern Europe during the four decades of Soviet dominance. Rather, what Catholic influence was exerted seems to have been initiated by relatively autonomous lay Catholic politicians who may themselves have been influenced both by the string of papal social encyclicals over the past century and the writings of Jacques Maritain, an influential French philosopher of the 1930s and early post-war years, who interpreted Catholic social teaching pragmatically and imaginatively in the post-war world.

Van Kersbergen, a Dutch lecturer in Political Science at Vrije University, Amsterdam, goes so far as to distinguish between a still ambiguous 'grand' tradition of Vatican social teaching and 'the "little" tradition of social Catholicism that has provided the Christian democratic movements of Western Europe with a social concern and with a more practical theory of social policy and modern politics.' He concludes that 'Social Catholicism has managed to go beyond Medieval ideas on charity in spite of rather than thanks to the social teaching of the Church' (1995, p.228). While the different nations shared a common core view of social capitalism, the different circumstances in the various nations in Western Europe as the Christian democrat politicians attempted to concretize these views resulted in some variations between similar 'families of nations' (Van Kersbergen 1995, p.229–230; Castles 1993).

This goes some way to explaining why the evidence for a Catholic connection is somewhat mixed. There certainly do seem to be some systematic variations. Thus Catholic countries tend to follow more corporatist social policies which assume notions of the 'family just wage' and a strong obligation on the part of employers to contribute to employment-related insurance support systems. Such schemes presume a situation of full employment and a largely domestic, family-oriented role for women and, as such, have been under stress as a result of changes both in employment and in family structures over the past two decades. The Social Chapter in the Maastricht Treaty can also be seen to reflect Catholic corporatist thinking. Protestant countries, on the other hand, are more individualistic in their orientation and this has led, especially in the social democratic countries, to a greater emphasis in social policies on the universalistic rights of all citizens.

On the other hand, while the religious dimension clearly is of some importance in understanding the historical emergence of different social policy styles, it cannot be claimed that the picture is clear cut. For example, in some respects the social policies of Catholic Ireland, for obvious historical reasons, are much closer to those of Britain than they are to the corporatist policies of Catholic countries on mainland Europe. No account has been taken in this study of anti-clericalist legacies in some Catholic countries. Thus while there are some systematic variations by Catholic density, in other cases it is the religiously 'mixed' countries which have distinctive policies or policy outcomes. While it is clear that attention needs to be paid to other variables and different historical legacies in seeking to understand differences in the social policies of different European nations, what I would claim to have shown is that even in the secularized nations of Western Europe the religious dimension cannot be discounted in the search for understanding. In particular, the Catholic influence in post-war Europe has been considerable and for too long overlooked. Given the urgency paid to multiculturalism in social policy, there is also a need for research on the influence of Jewish, Muslim and Orthodox thinking and traditions within welfare. It is to be hoped that more detailed socio-historical comparative analysis of European social policies will continue to be undertaken.

Acknowledgements

I am most grateful to Grace Davie for some very helpful comments on an earlier version of this paper and to Mike Procter for tabulations from the 1990 World Values Surveys.

References

Abrams, M., Gerard, D. and Timms, N. (eds) (1985) *Values and Social Change in Britain.* Basingstoke: Macmillan.

Bailey, J. (ed) (1992) *Social Europe.* London: Longman.

Barbier, J.C. (1991) 'Comparing family policies in Europe: Some methodological problems.' In G. Kiely and V. Richardson (eds) *Family Policy: European Perspectives.* Dublin: Family Studies Centre.

✱ Boswell, J. (1994) *Community and the Economy: The Theory of Public Co-Operation.* London: Routledge.

Bradshaw, J., Ditch, J., Holmes, H. and Whiteford, P. (1993) 'A comparative study of child support in fifteen countries.' *Journal of European Social Policy, 3,* 4, 255–271.

Brown, P. (1997) *The Rise of Western Christendom: Triumph and Diversity AD200–1000.* Oxford: Blackwell.

Busch, A. (1993) 'The politics of price stability: Why the German-speaking nations are different.' In F.G. Castles (ed) *Families of Nations: Patterns of Public Policy in Western Democracies.* Aldershot: Dartmouth.

Castles, F.G. (ed) (1993) *Families of Nations: Patterns of Public Policy in Western Democracies.* Aldershot: Dartmouth.

Chenaux, P. (1990) *Une Europe Vaticane?* Brussels: Éditions Ciaco.

Cleary, S. (1989) *Renewing the Earth: Development for a Sustainable Future: An Economic Perspective.* London: CAFOD.

Coman, P. (1977) *Catholics and the Welfare State.* London: Longman.

Davie, G. (1994a) 'The religious factor in the emergence of Europe as a global region.' *Social Compass, 41,* 1, March: 95–112.

Davie, G. (1994b) 'Unity in diversity: Religion and modernity in Western Europe.' In J. Fulton and P. Gee (eds) (1994) *Religion in Contemporary Europe.* Lampeter: Edwin Mellen Press.

Davies, N. (1996) *Europe: A History.* Oxford: Oxford University Press.

Delors, J. (1992) *Our Europe: The Community and National Development.* London: Verso.

Dierickx, G. (1994) 'Christian democracy and its ideological rivals.' In D. Hanley (ed) *Christian Democracy in Europe: A Comparative Perspective.* London: Pinter.

Dorr, D. (1992) *Option for the Poor: A Hundred Years of Vatican Social Teaching.* Dublin: Gill and Macmillan.

✱ Esping-Andersen, G. (1990) *The Three Worlds of Welfare Capitalism.* Cambridge: Polity Press

Eurostat (1996) *Social Portrait of Europe.* Luxembourg: Office for Official Publications of the European Communities.

Fletcher, R. (1997) *The Conversion of Europe: From Paganism to Christianity 371–1386AD.* London: HarperCollins.

Fogarty, M. (1961) *The Just Wage.* London: Geoffrey Chapman.

George, V. (1996) 'The future of the welfare state.' In V. George and P. Taylor-Gooby (eds) *European Welfare Policy: Squaring the Welfare Circle.* Basingstoke: Macmillan.

George, V. and Taylor-Gooby, P. (eds) (1996) *European Welfare Policy: Squaring the Welfare Circle.* Basingstoke: Macmillan.

Gerth, H.H. and Mills, C.W. (eds) (1948) *From Max Weber: Essays in Sociology.* London: Routledge and Kegan Paul.

Ginn, J. and Arber, S. (1992) 'Towards women's independence: Pension systems in three contrasting welfare states.' *Journal of European Social Policy, 2,* 4, 255–277.

Grasso, K.L., Bradley, G.V. and Hunt, R.P. (eds) (1995) *Catholicism, Liberalism, and Communitarianism: The Catholic Intellectual Tradition and the Moral Foundations of Democracy.* London: Rowman and Littlefield.

Hanley, D. (ed) (1994) *Christian Democracy in Europe: A Comparative Perspective.* London: Pinter.

Hantrais, L. (1993) 'Towards a Europeanization of family policy.' In R. Simpson and R. Walker (eds) *Europe: For Richer or Poorer?* London: CPAG.

✕ Hantrais, L. (1995) *Social Policy in the European Union.* Basingstoke: Macmillan.

Hantrais, L. and Letablier, M.-T. (1996) *Families and Family Policies in Europe.* London: Longman.

Hornsby-Smith, M.P. (1998) *Roman Catholicism and the European Project.* Department of Sociology Occasional Paper No. 31, Guildford: University of Surrey.

Janoski, T. (1991) 'Synthetic strategies in comparative sociological research: Methods and problems of internal and external analysis.' In C.C. Ragin (1991) *Issues and Alternatives in Comparative Social Research.* Leiden, New York, København, Köln: E.J.Brill.

John Paul II, Pope (1988) *Sollicitudo Rei Socialis.* London: Catholic Truth Society (S400).

John Paul II, Pope (1991) *Centesimus Annus.* London: Catholic Truth Society (S423).

Kamerman, S.B. and Kahn, A.K. (eds) (1978) *Family Policy: Government and Families in Fourteen Countries.* New York: Columbia University Press.

Kiely, G. and Richardson, V. (eds) (1991) *Family Policy: European Perspectives.* Dublin: Family Studies Centre.

Leo XIII, Pope (1949; fp 1891) *The Condition of the Working Class (Rerum Novarum).* Oxford: Catholic Social Guild.

McDonagh, S. (1986) *To Care for the Earth: A Call to a New Theology.* London: Geoffrey Chapman.

McDonagh, S. (1990) *The Greening of the Church.* London: Geoffrey Chapman.

McDonagh, S. (1994) *Passion for the Earth: The Christian Vocation to Promote Justice, Peace and the Integrity of Creation.* London: Geoffrey Chapman.

Madeley, J. (1994) 'The Antimonies of Lutheran Politics: The Case of Norway's Christian People's Party'. In D. Hanley (ed) *Christian Democracy in Europe: A Comparative Perspective.* London: Pinter.

Maritain, J. (1935) *Freedom in the Modern World.* London: Sheed and Ward.

Maritain, J. (1973; fp in 1936) *Integral Humanism: Temporal and Spiritual Problems of a New Christendom.* University of Notre Dame Press.

Martin, D. (1994) 'Religion in Contemporary Europe.' In J. Fulton and P. Gee (eds) *Religion in Contemporary Europe.* Lampeter: Edwin Mellen Press.

Nielsen, J.S. (1992) *Muslims in Western Europe.* Edinburgh: Edinburgh University Press.

O'Connell, J. (1991) 'The past and future making of Europe: The role of heritage and the direction of unity.' *Peace Research Report* (26), University of Bradford: Department of Peace Studies.

Oppenheim, C. and Harker, L. (1996) *Poverty: The Facts,* 3rd. ed., London: CPAG.

Papini, R. (1997) *The Christian Democrat International.* London: Rowman and Littlefield.

Ragin, C.C. (1989) *The Comparative Method: Moving Beyond Qualitative and Quantitative Strategies.* London: University of California Press.

Ragin, C.C. (1991) 'Introduction: The problem of balancing discourse on cases and variables in comparative social science.' In C.C. Ragin (ed) *Issues and Alternatives in Comparative Social Research.* Leiden, New York: København, Köln: E.J. Brill.

Roberts, J.M. (1996) *A History of Europe.* Oxford: Helicon.

Rokkan, S. (1970) 'Nation-building, cleavage formation and the structuring of politics.' In S. Rokkan, A. Campbell, U. Torsvik and H. Valen (eds) *Citizens, Elections, Parties.* Oslo: Universitetsforlaget.

Ross, G. (1995) *Jacques Delors and European Integration.* Cambridge: Polity Press.

Schmidt, M.G. (1993) 'Gendered labour force participation.' In F.G. Castles (ed) *Families of Nations: Patterns of Public Policy in Western Democracies.* Aldershot: Dartmouth.

Schultheis, F. (1990) 'Familles d'Europe sans frontieres: Un enjeu social par dessus le marche.' Conference Proceedings, *Familles d'Europe sans frontieres,* 4–5 December 1989, Paris.

Schumacher, E.F. (1974) *Small is Beautiful: A Study of Economics as if People Mattered.* London: Abacus.

Simpson, R. and Walker, R. (eds) (1993) *Europe: For Richer or Poorer?* London: CPAG.

Szajkowski, B., Niblock, T. and Nonneman, G. (1996) 'Islam and ethnicity in Eastern Europe: Concepts, statistics, and a note on the Polish case.' In G. Nonneman, T. Niblock and B. Szajkowski (eds) *Muslim Communities in the New Europe.* Reading: Ithaca Press.

✗ Taylor-Gooby, P. (1991) 'Welfare state regimes and welfare citizenship.' *Journal of European Social Policy, 1,* 2, 93–105.

Therborn, G. (1993a) 'The politics of childhood: The rights of children in modern times.' In F.G. Castles (ed) *Families of Nations: Patterns of Public Policy in Western Democracies.* Aldershot: Dartmouth.

Therborn, G. (1993b) 'Beyond the lonely nation-state'. In F.G. Castles (ed) *Families of Nations: Patterns of Public Policy in Western Democracies.* Aldershot: Dartmouth.

Therborn, G. (1995) *European Modernity and Beyond: The Trajectory of European Societies, 1945–2000.* London: Sage.

✗ Titmuss, R.M. (1974) *Social Policy: An Introduction.* London: Allen and Unwin.

Van Kersbergen, K. (1994) 'The distinctiveness of Christian democracy.' In D. Hanley (ed) *Christian Democracy in Europe: A Comparative Perspective.* London: Pinter.

Van Kersbergen, K. (1995) *Social Capitalism: A Study of Christian Democracy and the Welfare State.* London: Routledge.

Von Beyme, K. (1985) *Political Parties in Western Europe.* Aldershot: Gower.

Voyé, L. (1994) 'The principle of subsidiarity.' In J. Fulton and P. Gee (eds) *Religion in Contemporary Europe.* Lampeter: Edwin Mellen Press.

Willaime, J.-P. (1994) 'Protestant approaches to European unification.' In J. Fulton and P. Gee (eds) *Religion in Contemporary Europe.* Lampeter: Edwin Mellen Press.

Whyte, J.H. (1981) *Catholics in Western Democracies: A Study in Political Behaviour.* Dublin: Gill and Macmillan.

Structural and Cultural Dimensions of Poverty in Italy
The Implications for Social Policies

Antonella Spanò

Introduction

This chapter aims at inquiring into the interweaving of economic, political and cultural factors (the diffusion of the informal economy, the client/patron pattern informing the welfare system, the persistence of traditional family links) which seem to give rise to a peculiar 'culture of poverty' in the South of Italy.

Although a great emphasis is laid on the connection between poverty and unemployment (since the latter is in actual fact one of the major causes of poverty in the South of Italy), the debate on poverty in Southern Italy is often distorted by stereotypes of the poor. The art of making do by doing a myriad jobs in the underground economy, the tendency – considered irresponsible – of giving birth to many children despite the scarcity of economic resources, the culture of guaranteed work, which means a passive waiting for the state to find the definitive solution to the problem of work precariousness, and, finally, the irrationality in the field of consumption behaviour which leads to the privileging of luxury goods to the detriment of the essential ones. These are just some of the rhetorical and stereotypical images which appear in the public discourse when the poor Southern population is considered.

This chapter tries to shed light upon these themes: to show how aspects that are usually defined as cultural actually stem from specific Italian characteristics, and to discuss the cultural implications of welfare policies, particularly of those related to the fight against poverty in the Southern Italian context.

For this reason, the first part of this chapter provides an outline of the structural aspects of poverty in Italy with particular reference to the differences registered between the North and the South. The second part tries to prove how and why these differences are associated with specific cultural aspects of poverty in the two areas of the country. The third part focuses on a case study: the story of a man who has been unemployed for a long time in urban Naples. The biographical approach, as will be shown, proves very useful not only for understanding the connections between structural aspects and cultural dimensions of poverty, but also for analysing concretely what the role played by social policies may be. Finally, the fourth part deals with some considerations about specific problems that social policies for the poor have to face in the North and in the South of Italy, and attempts an evaluation of the new measures recently taken by the Italian government.

Poverty in Italy: the facts

According to the Eurostat Statistical Research on Poverty in the Member States, Italy is a country of high level poverty. With the poverty line fixed at 50 per cent of average national equivalent expenditure (modified OECD scale) and based on the individual data from the Family Budget Surveys in the 12 Member States of the Community, 19 million households and 49 million people are estimated to be poor. Four distinct groups of countries emerge: those with low poverty (Denmark, the Netherlands, Belgium and Luxembourg); those with average poverty (France, Ireland, the United Kingdom and Spain); those with high poverty (Italy and Greece); those with very high poverty (Portugal).

The official national data on poverty, when measured by the International Standard Poverty Line, shows that in the last two decades poverty in Italy has increased. In real figures, the percentage of poor households was 8.3 per cent in 1980 and 10.6 per cent in 1995, while the percentage of poor persons increased from 10.3 per cent to 11.9 per cent. This means that more than 2 million households and almost 7 million people are currently living in poverty (CIPE 1996a,b). (The International Standard Poverty Line, based on expenditure data, is drawn at 50 per cent of average national expenditure.)

Of course, the causes of this increase are already well known. Not only has unemployment increased considerably, but the nature of employment has changed. As a consequence of the crisis of 'Fordism', full-time jobs for life have decreased and part-time work, self employment, temporary and casual work have also increased.

There is also a crisis in the social security system. The welfare system, shaped for full-time male workers, penalizes those who have a weak or discontinuous link with employment. Moreover, the fiscal crisis that has continued during the last decade has weakened social security protection still further.

It is clear that changes both in the labour market and in the welfare system represent general trends which are not limited to the Italian case. Saskia Sassen (1991; 1993), for example, has demonstrated that this increasing polarization of the labour market is evident in New York, London and Tokyo. Peter Townsend (1993), analysing the income data of the US Committee of Ways and Means and the Family Expenditure Survey for the United Kingdom, concludes that during the 1980s 'a process of polarisation emerged in the United States and in Europe.'

Recently, the Institute for Fiscal Studies showed that the Gini coefficient for income in Britain rose from 0.23 in 1977 to 0.34 in 1991 (*The Economist*, 5/11/94). Other authors, for example Esping-Andersen (1990), affirmed that it is not possible to explain the changes in the occupational system exclusively in terms of an increasing polarization. There are many differences among countries, so that in some countries an increasing heterogeneity, rather than a polarization, has occurred. But, as Mingione (1991) asserts, polarization and fragmentation are not totally in contrast. We are in the presence of a diffusion of different micro-typologies, which, nevertheless, tend to concentrate on two poles, very different with regard to the existing conditions, the quantity and the quality of the available resources.

Nevertheless, what is peculiar to the Italian case is the spatial dimension of polarization. Poverty has traditionally been concentrated in the South, but it is worth noting that the gap between the North and South is gradually becoming larger. While in the Northern regions the percentage of poor households in 1980 and 1995 was almost the same (4.4%), in the Southern ones it increased in a remarkable measure (16% in 1980, 21.9% in 1995). Furthermore, if in 1983 54 per cent of poor households lived in the South, in 1995 this figure had risen to 68 per cent, although the Southern population represents only 33 per cent of the total Italian population. Unemployment shows the same trend. At the beginning of the 1980s, the unemployment rate in Southern Italy was double that of the North; at the beginning of the 1990s it was triple (7.6%.in the North; 22.2% in the South in 1997). So, there is clear evidence that the 'Southern Question' is very far from being solved.

The implications for poverty of geographical dualism

The existence of a geographical dualism in Italy has had significant effects on poverty. As a consequence of the differential vitality of the labour markets, the quantity and the quality of social services, and different demographic patterns, the composition of the poor in Italy is far from homogenous. We can analyse this by comparing the main features of the Italian poor population taken as a whole, with those of the two areas of the country.

If we look at the poor in Italy, using figures from the National Committee Report (CIPE 1994), we note that poverty is more evident in both one- and two-person households and in large households (more than 5 persons). Family size and the age of the head of family are decisive factors in determining poverty. People who are more than 65 years old are over-represented in the poor population, and the poverty rate reaches the highest point (18.2%) where the head of family is aged 65 years or over. Furthermore, poverty is higher (16.1%) where a pension is the major source of maintenance for the head of the family, and lower where the major source of income is from the labour market. One of the conclusions of the report is that a clear relationship exists between age and poverty, so that it is possible to speak of the 'senilization' of poverty. Moreover, a third factor from the report is that work is the most effective antidote to poverty. The poverty rate is highest (18.1%) in those families where nobody is employed.

This is the Italian picture. But, as mentioned before, if we look at Northern and Southern Italy separately, clear differences emerge. The results of research on economic poverty in Italy conducted by Sgritta and Innocenzi (1993) show that if in Northern Italy poverty is mostly concentrated in one- and two-person households, in the South almost half of poor people live in large families (5 persons and more). In this study the official definition of poverty has been adopted, but income instead of expenditure has been chosen as a monetary indicator. According to the International Standard Poverty Line, a poor two-person family will have an income lower than, or equal to, the average per-capita income. The dataset is the same as used in the National Committee Report (Istat. Indagine sui consumi delle famiglie). Also the equivalence scale adopted is the same.

Sgritta and Innocenzi's study further shows that with regard to age only in the North are the elderly over-represented in the poor population; in the South, the main age group living in poverty is the youngest (under 30 years old). In addition, we discover that only in Northern Italy do retired people suffer a higher risk of poverty; in the South on the other hand, poverty affects people with children, and the young. Finally, it is important to underline that in the South, even the fact of employment does not always fully combat poverty. As a consequence of both the weakness of the labour market and the larger than average household size, it is usual in the South to find poverty even where the main earner of the family is employed. Sgritta and Innocenzi conclude that we are in the presence of a 'perverse effect' of familial solidarity. In other words, many people in the South are poor because of their dependence on a poor family. However, perhaps the real Catch 22 in the South is that poor people, especially the young, live in the family because of their poverty, and live in poverty because of their family.

The major differences between North and South

The picture of poverty given by the official national statistics is vague and we need a more precise idea of what being poor in the North and the South actually means. If we look at the numerous surveys on poverty that have recently been carried out in several Italian towns, we find some interesting results which show the existence of many concrete differences between the two areas.

In the North, these studies were undertaken in Ferrara (Melotti 1989), Mantova (Sarpellon 1991), Parma (Scivoletto and Zani 1989), Bologna (Guidicini and Pieretti 1988), Torino (Colabella 1991) and Milano (Mingione and Zajczyk 1992). As to the typologies of poverty, these studies have found that poverty is concentrated in one- and two-person households; that the majority of the poor population (about 80% in these studies) is elderly: that there is a remarkable level of 'feminization' of poverty – in that poverty is prevalent in broken, irregular or one-parent families; that it is often associated with other problems such as drug addiction, illness, handicap and so on. Furthermore, it is in the North that we find homelessness to be a relevant factor, even if this phenomenon is less serious than in other European countries.

However, if we look at Southern towns, like Messina (Mingione 1986) or Naples (Morlicchio and Spanò 1992), we see that poverty often afflicts quite 'normal families'; in other words, families where no traumatic event has happened and where no 'handicap' is present. There thus emerges a significant difference between North and South with respect both to the prevalence and to the main causes of poverty.

In research on poverty in Naples carried out at the Department of Sociology of the University of Naples by Ragone, Spanò and Morlicchio, three different types of poverty were found: resistant poverty, transient poverty and biographical poverty. *Transient poverty* occurs where the family life cycle is disrupted and the breadwinner's income (usually the father's) is insufficient to cope with unexpected events such as illness or redundancy. *Biographical poverty* refers to the effects of events occurring in one- and two-person families, for example illness and widowhood. *Resistant poverty* is widespread in large households, sometimes containing multiple families, where income is derived from several precarious sources (irregular and sometimes illegal jobs and social benefits) and is constantly insufficient to meet the needs of the family's members. The research showed very clearly that, while the first two types of poverty are not very remarkable, the latter – in which, in the final analysis, poverty originates from the existence of a gap between income and expenditure – is widely present.

To sum up, in the North poverty seems to be an effect both of the failure of the welfare system (as pensions are not able to raise incomes above the poverty line for those who have had an irregular or problematic working life) and of the rupture of family ties or the weakening of social relationships. In the South, on the contrary, poverty seems to be caused mainly by the failure of employment and regional development policies, or by the weakness of the labour market, whereas the weakness of family and social relationships do not appear significantly involved. In other words, we could say that Northern poverty is strongly related to more recently recognized symptoms of 'social disqualification' (Paugam 1991), or of 'affiliation loss' (Castel 1991); Southern poverty, on the other hand, can be seen as the old familiar poverty of underdevelopment.

Cultural differences

Differences in the nature of poverty (between North and South, and within the South) are in themselves sufficient to prompt reflection on the social policies required to combat poverty in the two regions. However, there is another dimension we need to highlight regarding the cultural aspects of poverty.

Mentioning 'culture' with reference to poverty could create difficulties. The debate about a 'culture of poverty', which originates with Oscar Lewis, recurs in the contemporary debate about the underclass (Auletta 1983; Murray 1984). It speaks of a social residuum with behaviours and values which are in opposition to those of the social mainstream. The major contribution of this debate has been to exhume the traditional, and erroneous, distinction between the 'deserving' and the 'undeserving' poor. This emphasis on a distinctive culture of poverty steers us away from the reality that the seemingly irrational consumption patterns of the poor are, in fact, crucially shaped by the restrictions imposed upon them by welfare benefits (Douglass and Hisherwood 1979). In other words, defining a culture of poverty as a 'syndrome', transmitted through generations by socialization, is really very different from looking at behaviour and values as reactions to, or consequences of, structural conditions (Saraceno 1976). And it is quite clear that only when we conceive of cultural differences as adaptive strategies do they appear strictly linked to territorial features.

Currently, cultural differences as adaptive strategies are shaped by three major structural factors:

1. the spatial concentration of poverty

2. the local welfare system

3. the local economy.

With regard to the first, it is important to realize that as well as differences in macro-level spatial concentration of poverty between the North and the South, there is also a micro-level spatial concentration within the South. Southern urban poverty is concentrated in particular areas of a town (whether inner city or new town) while rural poverty is concentrated in particular rural villages, especially in hinterland areas. So, for the most part, the poor spend their lives among poor people in poor neighbourhoods. As for the local welfare system, it is important to note that the pattern of patronage which characterizes the Italian welfare system (Ascoli 1984) is much more prevalent in the South. Finally, as regards to the local economy, it is worth considering the important role that both the underground economy and the illegal economy play in providing monetary resources for those who are excluded from the regular labour market, especially in the South. Typical of this is Naples with its diffusion of contraband and the 'falsification industry'.

So, if we consider these three elements, and we refer to the social characteristics of the Southern poor, we can see that they are made up of 'normal' families, living among other poor people, in a poor context where the possibility of getting public support is subject to a particularist pattern more than anywhere else, and where the opportunity for irregular or illegal jobs is far greater.

According to Ascoli (1984), the Italian welfare system has very peculiar characteristics: the excessive sectorial fragmentation of social provisions; the nearly complete delegation of care work to families, and consequently to women;

the absence of a policy meant to support the unemployed; the practice of protection through illegitimate instruments such as, for instance, disability pensions given also to people who are not entitled to them, or fictitious professional training courses: instruments that feed the patron–client relationship and the political trading system. The Italian system thus, according to Ascoli, does not fall into the typology of particularist-meritocratic systems that are typical of continental Europe, but in a model apart that he defines as 'particular-client/patron'. Like the particularist systems, the criterion governing the admission to social benefits depends on the occupational status, rather than on a right of citizenship *tout court*. But, unlike meritocratic models, social benefits are not the giving back of the contributions that have been paid, rather the result of patron–client negotiations (see also Ferrara 1984).

The spatial concentration effect

If we now consider the consequences of such a situation for culture, several assumptions can be made. In the first place, there is the risk that micro-level concentrations of poverty could produce a grouping effect. It has been suggested that where a disadvantaged person lives among other gravely disadvantaged people, the probability of their losing the hope and courage to cope with the situation becomes greater (Sen 1993; Wilson 1987). But we hypothesize that in the Southern context there are at least two factors reducing this risk. First, as the poor population is mainly composed of 'normal' people, not necessarily affected by the rupture of family and social relationships, there is less risk that their shared poverty will generate a psychology of poverty. Second, the opportunities provided by the underground economy prevent the onset of a passive or hopeless attitude. In other words, since the Southern context is very far from producing 'idle poor', the risk of spatial concentration being able to reduce the psychological resources of people is very limited.

The welfarization risk

Another question is: do social benefits generate a dependence on public aid so that the welfare system itself becomes a factor in the generation of poverty? An old question this, dating back to the eligibility principle of the New Poor Law, yet still a topical subject, for as Charles Murray (1984) discussing the American welfare system says: 'We tried to provide more for the poor and produced more poor instead' (Murray 1984, p.9).

The Italian welfare state is mainly based on monetary provision rather than service provision (Ferrera 1984). These monetary subsidies take up the greater part of public expenditure on social assistance (81% in 1991 excluding family allowances). Nevertheless, the main direct income support interventions at a national level do not show a real risk of generating a dependence on welfare. Family allowances, thought to be the most effective mechanism of monetary redistribution in favour of poor families, because they are limited to employed workers and to ex-employed pensioners cannot represent any risk to families where nobody is employed. Since even the Governmental Committee on Poverty affirms that monetary benefits provided by family allowances and other institutional monetary benefits (such as disability benefits) are very low, it is therefore difficult to think that they could be sufficient to generate a poverty trap: an institutional disincentive to take up work. With reference to this, the recent scandal of 'false invalids' in Italy teaches us something. It appears that these people posed as invalids to gain employment in public administration in order to exploit the government's policy of positive discrimination towards the disabled. Crucially, they were not using this false invalidity to claim benefit, and hence enter a relationship of dependency upon the state, but rather to gain employment within it.

As to the other kinds of monetary support, as well as non-monetary benefits provided at a local level by municipalities or county councils, two elements limit the risk of 'welfarization'. First, the temporariness of such benefits and, second, the patron–client relationship (see Judith Chubb 1982). This is much more relevant in the South, where the benefits are bestowed as favours rather than granted as rights. Furthermore, the greater scarcity of resources on the one hand and the poorer organization of social services on the other, far from creating a 'dependency on welfare', risk deterring people from welfare. As we found in our research on poverty in Naples, for example, the poor do not rely on the welfare system, the Church or on voluntary associations, but exclusively on their families. More than 60 per cent of the sample declared that in case of necessity they would appeal to their relatives; both to ask for material help and for information or advice. Only 2 per cent indicated that they would turn to the state (Morlicchio and Spanò 1992).

From the renowned study by Banfield (1958) onward, the role of the family and patron–client relationships have been regarded as the greatest obstacles to modernization in the South. And if recently the question has been whether these patterns of political culture are incompatible with the starting up of a process of economic development (the amazing development in Japan and in other Asian countries shows unequivocally that cultural contexts characterized by relationships based on ascription, particularism and affection can develop economically, without wiping out, but reinforcing, the traditional system of values (Mutti 1992)), they have never been seen as producing dependency upon the state. As it has been pointed out, patron–client behaviour is a form of political participation that fosters a pragmatic, contractual behaviour, which inclines towards compromise. As such, it discourages rigid contraposition and collective mobilization; but this consequence does not justify the conclusion that patronage causes apathy (Mutti 1992, p.25).

Perceptions of individual and collective responsibility

What has been pointed out so far is that, even though the Italian welfare system provides resources for the poor, the quantity, quality and ways through which these are provided do *not* produce dependence on welfare. This statement does not appear so clear when we consider that the Southern Italians are famous for their so-called 'fully-guaranteed job' culture, which means they are not inclined to risk either self employment or job creation, because of their tendency to wait for a 'secure' job in public administration.

But this contradiction is only superficial. As a consequence of the spatial concentration of poverty, the Southern poor are quite conscious that their condition is structural. There is widespread awareness of the weakness of the local economy and local services. Therefore, they perceive the alleviation of poverty to be a collective responsibility. That is why they ask for more security and, ultimately, for a regular job or a monetary payment offered in compensation for the precariousness to which they are condemned.

On the other hand, individual initiative in seeking opportunities in the hidden economy, or the patron–client system and the strength of the family produce a feeling of personal responsibility for the management of their existence. In other words, the causes of poverty are perceived as external, but the solutions to poverty are experienced as personal problems to be solved by individuals.

That is why the dream of a final solution to poverty (work provided by the state or a definitive monetary benefit) does not conflict with the patient work of gathering the resources to construct a patchwork of irregular or illegal jobs, benefits and non-monetary assistance whereby a 'reasonable' wage may be achieved.

Vincenzo's case-study

One of the merits of the biographical approach is undoubtedly that of giving the possibility of describing with great vividness how the characteristics of a society may shape an individual's life. In order to give evidence of what has been discussed so far, we will now present a case-study: Vincenzo's story. (The case is taken from research funded by CNR, at present in progress at the Department of Sociology of 'Federico II' University of Naples, entitled 'Social Weakness and Work: Old and New Weak Subjects in Naples', and coordinated by Antonella Spanò. It employs the Biographical-Interpretative method.)

Vincenzo is 37 and has three children; he has been unemployed for a long time and has for the last ten years survived on hand-outs from the state. In Vincenzo's case many of the above-mentioned aspects can be found: familiarization of poverty, irrationality in consumption, the simultaneous presence of the 'art of making do' and of the 'culture of a fully guaranteed job', the role played by patronage. For this reason this case may be considered as truly emblematic of the nexus between structural and cultural factors of poverty in the South.

In order to contextualize Vincenzo's story, it is necessary to give some background information about him. Vincenzo was born and has lived all his life in the city centre, which has, like other cities in the south, been much transformed by urban processes. This is crucial to the understanding of Vincenzo's history. He lives in a working class neighbourhood in the historic centre of the city, which had for many decades a thriving handicraft industry, but which has undergone remarkable changes over the years. Over the last decades, as a consequence of the boom in the shoe industry resulting from the success of 'made in Italy' products, there has been a progressive decline of the traditional artisan shops (mainly wood work), gradually replaced by a multitude of small workshops (in flats or in basements in the neighbourhood), which sprang up round an important factory situated in the area. This factory, which also started as an artisan workshop, became one of the most important exporters of leather goods in the 1970s, the Italian boom years, thus giving rise to a remarkable number of allied workshops working on commission. The number of employed workers totalled 800 in the years of the factory's greatest success.

More recently, as a consequence of the serious economic crisis which has also affected the shoe industry, a further transformation of the productive system of the area has taken place. The neighbourhood has preserved its tradition – the working of leather – yet, when the main factory collapsed, numerous workshops working illegally in the area diversified their activity, some of them specializing in the production of low-priced articles for local demand, others in counterfeiting (in both cases the products are sold illegally on the streets, which is very common in the Neapolitan area). In parallel, as a result of the progressive increase in organized crime, which has found a fertile area here (characterized by very low levels of education, a high unemployment rate and by a widespread condition of decay), the neighbourhood has become one of the areas at greatest risk in the city: it is the kingdom of the most powerful Camorra clan.

At present, therefore, the area has, so to speak, two souls. One is that of the honest workers, the offspring of the old craftsmen, mainly engaged in the underground economy (production and trade sometimes on the border-line of illegality, as in the case of contraband cigarettes or counterfeit products) or employed as unqualified workers in the municipality (for a long time the public sector has been a sort of 'sponge', employing largely unproductive workers with the objective of reducing unemployment and supporting poor families). These people often live in a condition of real poverty. The other soul is that of criminals, those who work for Camorra (often even teenagers) and, unlike the honest worker, have very high levels of income, expenditure and power.

Without doubt, Vincenzo belongs to the 'good' part of the neighbourhood. The change from traditional artisanship to the underground shoe industry, and then the spreading of the informal sector in general, is easily traceable in the history of his family. Born to a family with ten children, his father was a carpenter who had a sawmill of his own but was not able to keep up with the change in the productive system of the area: still of working age, he closed down his shop and has been unemployed since then; he has not been able to pass his skills on to any of his sons, who are nowadays mainly unemployed (some of them are employed as unqualified municipal workers as a result of a 'political' mass recruitment carried out in 1980s).

Without a paternal guide in the field of work and weighed down by his family economic necessities, Vincenzo cannot but follow the typical path of boys of his social class and generation: he dropped out of school early and had many jobs in the casual sector. By the time he was twelve, he had already been a shop boy, an errand boy, and a worker in a small shoe factory. Deprived as he was of any form of guidance or support both from his family and from the institutions (he did not finish compulsory education but nobody ever noticed or tried to intervene), he entered the informal labour market actively but without order or method, often changing his job in order to find a 'better' one, and never specializing in any trade. This is a recognized 'categorical imperative' for lower class teenagers living in large families, where children grow up on their own and are always pressed to fend for themselves.

Vincenzo had two worlds before him: that of those who, through criminal activities, had managed to escape from poverty and to reach a high standard of living; the other of people, like his father and his family, who lived in a condition of indigence. Vincenzo wanted to escape from both and aimed at work as the only means of reaching his goal: to have a normal, decorous and respectable life. In his first years of work, he paid no attention to what he did, he had no vocation and did not want to learn a skill. He just wanted to earn some money so as not to look poor. When he talks about his first job as a shoemaker's boy, he does not say anything except that: 'The boss, he clothed us all, me and my brothers working there, every Christmas and Easter, from head to foot, sweaters, socks, everything brand-new.'

Deviancy is for him a completely unfeasible option. His family did not give him any kind of capital – neither economic, social, cultural nor, as mentioned above, professional – but passed him the values of hard work and honesty, which for him represent a sort of genetic patrimony. He says: 'We are ten children. I worked with my father when I was a child, my father was a carpenter. I worked, always, I went to school and I worked, and then, little by little I grew up and I worked ... I've never fallen, partly because I was afraid. I've done many jobs but as for being a thief, never'.

His parents passed another legacy to him: a strong sense of family, resulting from his growing up in a large and close family unit ('at Christmas we were all together, we were like the twelve Apostles,' he says in the interview), a value that Vincenzo picks up. He soon opted for a stable and regular romantic life: when he was sixteen years old he started a serious and long lasting engagement and, what with work and with his relatives' help, after eight years he bought the furniture for his future house, which gave him the possibility of gaining access to social respectability: 'If you have a house you have everything. My mother-in-law bought me the kitchen fixtures, she bought it by instalments, bills. My mother, God rest her soul, bought me the sitting room furniture, and the telly too. I found that bedroom furniture. And I soon struck a bargain ... but everything new and packed, wasn't it? And little by little I got my house furnished, nothing special but a house to appreciate.'

Unlike the current situation, when young people soon become too old to get a job in the black economy (at the age of eighteen they are replaced by teenagers who are willing to work for less money), in the years of his youth Vincenzo did not have to face the competition of under-aged workforce and had no difficulties in finding opportunities of working in the informal economy. On the contrary, he managed to learn a trade by working – always as an irregular worker but with a certain continuity – as a builder. In other words, he succeeded in learning a skill and, driven by his need for a more secure job in view of his impending marriage, he tried to pull strings in order to get a regular job. Thanks to his future father-in-law, who knew a rather powerful Socialist councillor, he got a regular job in a building firm.

His securing regular, stable work marked a turning point in his life. Up to that moment, work for him represented the only way to gain access to a respectable life. Now, at last, the skills gained in so many years of precarious jobs allowed him for the first time to consider work as something more than simply a means of making money. When he talks about that job he says: 'That job, I liked it. We built a church, it's a big church, with the dome, it's got eleven beds inside too, it was nice. I earned a good monthly pay, at that time I got one million and six hundred. I lived normally, I had a car ...' In short, Vincenzo started considering work as a source of personal realization rather than a mere source of income.

The acquisition of a regular job reinforced his strategy of pursuing normality and controlling the risk of poverty. Vincenzo got married but, unlike most young couples of his social milieu, his wife did not give up working. What is more, for no less than four years – and this too is rather unusual in his milieu – the couple decided not to have children. Therefore the family strategy was that of starting a modern, nuclear family, quite different from the one where both were born.

It is clear, then, why the loss of his stable job was an extremely traumatic event for Vincenzo. He felt as though he were a Monopoly player who was about to reach the winning post but got a card saying: 'Go back to Start!' 'I worked just for six months', Vincenzo says. 'After six months the boss gave me the sack, with some money in an envelope and said: I'm sorry, work is over ... First we went on the redundancy fund and then in "mobilità", and then into the rubbish.' And although by rubbish Vincenzo means Social Utility Employment in which he has recently been involved (as a street cleaner), it is exactly that that he felt he had been thrown into when he lost his stable job: that rubbish (poor life) from which he had escaped with great difficulty. 'I've never gone forward, always backward': this is his evaluation of himself and his life.

When he was confronted with the failure of his aspirations, he wavered, and then he reacted by re-orienting himself towards the only sphere which for him represented a source of stability, that is, family. He responded to the weakening of his working identity by reinforcing his bread-winner role. Paradoxically, it was after the loss of his stable job that Vincenzo and his wife seemed to be compelled to have children. In the eleven years following the loss of the only stable job in Vincenzo's life, three daughters were born; moreover, his wife – following the normal path originating both from lower class culture and from the complete absence of services supporting working mothers – gave up her job soon after her first daughter's birth, just when a second income was really necessary.

A sort of 'perverse effect' takes shape: a vicious circle of family and work. The loss of stability in the work domain is counterbalanced by a stabilization of family sphere (the construction of a 'real' family, that in the traditional lower class culture means a large family); but the latter makes the household needs more pressing, thus strengthening the sense of precariousness which ends up by becoming a sheer sense of failure.

If these dynamics seem to account for the seeming irrationality of procreation choices, the strategy with which Vincenzo faces his condition of loser sheds light upon other irrational aspects: the distortion of consumption behaviour and the curious mixture between activism and passivity, that is between the so-called 'art of making do' and the 'culture of a fully guaranteed job' which have been mentioned above.

In his new condition as an unemployed man, Vincenzo has come to terms with the fact that he has been a 'reproducer of poverty'. He wanted to be different from his father, who has had a disastrous working path, but he finds himself just like him, doomed to unemployment. He wanted to be different from his father who has irresponsibly brought ten children into world: 'One shouldn't do it like my father, that's what I say. He has had ten children but why did he do it? How did we grow up? Just by chance?' He planned for his daughters a future different from the one he had inherited himself. But today he has three children, the youngest only five months old, and he has to face the awareness of his mistakes.

The strategy with which Vincenzo faces his responsibilities is that of explaining his biography as a chain of poverty, a chain in which he is nothing but a transmission link. On the one hand he acknowledges his failure since he has not been able to interrupt the mechanism of poverty reproduction: 'If I could put the clock back I wouldn't do it again, it's awful, I feel guilty. I told you, if I could put the clock back I wouldn't get married. Three children are too many, but I say a marriage without children, what does it mean? ... but I got married then 'cause I had a job, I couldn't know all this.' On the other hand, he feels like a victim himself: 'Dad, dad was a carpenter, he had the sawmill ... and my father's ignorance too, I mean, 'cause if dad, for example, had had a bit of brain, but I don't blame him, but we've suffered the consequences.'

A torturer and a victim at the same time, Vincenzo puts into effect a balancing strategy between his personal responsibility and public, or social, responsibility. As a victim, he feels rancorous towards the whole world: towards his father, towards his brothers born, like him, in poverty, but luckier than he is: 'When we were kids we were really brothers and sisters but then ... those brothers of mine, they have got a job, they have managed to get a job'. But above all he is resentful towards institutions. In fact, Vincenzo seems to embody perfectly the figure of 'qualunquista', he who is cross with everything and everybody, avoiding making any kind of political distinction: the mayor who neglects the outskirts; the trade unions which are seen as not reliable any longer; the Government that does not act in the interest of the lower classes; the immigrants for their competition in the itinerant trade; even the workers in 'mobilità' who are less in need than he is and therefore do not protest about getting work.

But, as a torturer, Vincenzo is not able to turn such resentment into a political rebellion. He is engaged rather in 'repairing strategies' towards his daughters: 'I've not been lucky, good, but not them, they must improve. I've had problems and suffered, but not them, they must improve.' Today, his main problem is that of providing his family with a proper standard of living. It is not by chance that, while Vincenzo often does not have the money to pay the rent and the bills, he has come to the appointment with the interviewer all dressed up, wearing stylish clothes (although they were imitations). Poverty for him means relative deprivation, that is, in the definition given by Townsend, the impossibility of sharing habits and lifestyles of the community he belongs to: a discomfort ranging from the fact he cannot go to the barber's ('I can go to the barber's once every six months, but just 'cause he's a good friend'), to the shame resulting from 'cutting a poor figure' and from his not being able to afford a respectable level of life: 'The clothes, I get them once every six months. If I think of it I'll go crazy ... you can't go to a wedding, you cut a poor figure ... you can't go on holiday. Every now and then you have to take your children out for a walk on the promenade, nothing more...'. And Vincenzo does his best to hide his poverty.

Since he was dismissed, he has never had a stable job. He has been cushioned by several social organizations: the 'Cassa Integrazione Guadagni' at first, the 'mobilità' allowance later, and finally the 'Social Utility Employment'. Remarkably, every stage is marked by the birth of another child. (The difference between the Cassa Integrazione Guadagni (CIG) or 'temporary lay-off' and 'mobilità', redundant and available for work, is as follows: in the case of CIG the contract between the firm and the worker is not broken (the assumption is that workers will be re-employed), whereas with mobilità the worker's contract with the firm is ended and s/he is dependent on the state. In the latter case the worker is liable to be placed in another firm or in the so-called 'Socially Useful Employment' (LSU). At the end of the period of 'mobilità' the worker no longer receives any form of benefits. If those who are in mobilità do not get a job, or if at the end of their mobilità period do not have the requisites for retirement, they will have no support at all. Socially Useful Employment is a workfare instrument addressed to different categories of the unemployed (often also to workers on mobilità) which implies the request for a working performance in exchange for the benefit. They are fixed term jobs in which both the work hours (20 hours a week) and the amount of the benefit (800,000 lire a month) are very low).

Therefore Vincenzo becomes very active on the black market, consenting to do anything. He works as an unloader by day, or sometimes goes to Rome to sell paper handkerchiefs to drivers waiting at the traffic lights (in Naples he is ashamed of being recognized). He is reduced to selling socks and T-shirts in the streets: "'Cause shame ends after a while. At the beginning you think of the people that look at you, then it passes, little by little, when you see the ten thousand lire in your pocket.' Sometimes, he is reduced to selling contraband cigarettes, even though he does not go further into illegality; as a matter of fact, he is ashamed of it: 'I've always had to make do, even to sell contraband cigarettes. Unfortunately I had to do it, whether I wanted or not. I was in need, 'cause I couldn't find anything else. I've been fined a lot of times by the police.'

Therefore, not only would Vincenzo's behaviour as a consumer be sufficient to charge him with irrationality, but he also seems completely overwhelmed by the present. In fact, he is more worried about clothes or holidays than about his daughters' education or his own professional training which could allow him to find a new position: he simply tries to earn some money, on a day to day basis. But behind such a lack of plans and projects there is the split between public and private responsibility, which is the strategy with which Vincenzo comes to terms with his 'guilt' (his reproducing poverty). In order to preserve his role of victim, he cannot afford to take complete responsibility for his and his daughters' problems: he is worried about their present, not about their future, about their survival not about their life. In other words, as a victim he waits for an indemnity, and entrusts the public institutions with the task of ensuring him security and stability, no matter whether in the form of social assistance: 'I don't want money, just give me food, the telephone and everything, and then a T-shirt from time to time for the kids, and nothing else'; or of work: 'I wouldn't like a lot of money, just a monthly wage to live on, to live quietly. Just a job, even toilet cleaning, as long as it is regular'.

But there is a further aspect to be taken into account, perhaps the most important one: the ambiguous role played by the institutions through social cushioning. In fact, since this only consists of monetary provisions (Vincenzo, for instance, has never been involved in a training course or in professional retraining), they neither foster a new professional identity nor do they constitute a resource allowing people to consider themselves as autonomous protagonists of their future. On the other hand, since these monetary provisions are really exiguous (they cannot satisfy even basic needs) they constitute a real 'license' to enter the black market (although, officially, the allocation of a benefit requires a condition of complete inactivity from the beneficiary), in actual fact calling for 'the art of making do' – an art that, by definition, does not foster long-term plans but, on the contrary, sentences people to be prisoner of the present, thus passing down through the generations the reproduction of poverty.

Therefore, we can conclude, the peculiar mixture of accepting responsibility for daily life and delegating responsibility for the future (a mixture with which Vincenzo, and so many like him, cope with unemployment and precariousness) seems fully in accordance with the institutions' requirements and interests rather than theirs.

The implications for social policy

So far, this analysis has shown the dualism – both cultural and structural – of the phenomenon of poverty; Vincenzo's case has also given the opportunity to point out how policies play an active role in shaping the culture of poverty and the strategies with which poverty is faced. The conclusion of this contribution is therefore dedicated to the analysis of the specific problems that social policies for the poor have to face in the North and in the South in pursuing their aim of reducing poverty and to an evaluation of the recent measures taken by our government.

The first difference which emerges concerns the different weight that must be given to *policies against poverty* and *policies for the poor.* In the North, if something is to be done against poverty, improvements in the social pension system need to be introduced. The mechanism of payment exemptions, for example for the health services, requires a radical revision and the organization of the bureaucratic machine must be changed. Nevertheless, as most of the poor comprise the elderly, the homeless, persons affected by physical or mental illness, or people who cannot rely on their own families, the most urgent problem seems to be the provision of material help like day centres, old people's homes, home helps, etc.

The order of priorities in the South appears to be very different. Since here most poverty is caused by, or at least connected with, unemployment, and as most of the poor are children and the young, policies against poverty appear much more relevant. And policies against poverty in the South necessarily mean economic and, in particular, employment policies rather than social policies. Promoting employment has the effect of reducing the number of those who are not able to provide for their own maintenance, and who later will not be able to obtain an adequate pension. Increasing employment is an effective strategy to prevent children and the young in the lowest income families becoming unemployed, and therefore poor in the future.

But it is a fact that most of the poor in the South seem to be lacking in the characteristics needed to be included in the productive system. Poor adults are usually devoid of any kind of professional qualification, while the young in poor families reach, at the most, the compulsory level of education, and truancy is still widespread. Therefore, employment policies must necessarily be accompanied, on the one hand, by professional training and educational policies. The case of Vincenzo, who has been supported for over ten years by social cushioning in terms of monetary provisions, shows clearly to what extent the latter ones are inadequate to foster the reintegration in the labour market. Even though the manifest function of the interventions devoted to the unemployed (Cassa Integrazione Guadagni, mobilità and Lavori Socialmente Utili) is that of favouring their reinsertion into the labour market, in fact the latent function they have is that of assuring social control. In the South, actually, through the combination of these three social cushions it has been possible to provide a sort of long-lasting social protection to people who, if not protected, could really become socially explosive. In other words, rather than employment policies, these measures act as mere assistance interventions.

On the other hand, employment policies must necessarily be accompanied by social assistance policies for those who are not in a position to acquire a professional qualification because of their age or their disability. So we conclude that the real challenge we have to face in fighting poverty in the South is to determine the most appropriate mix between employment, educational and social policies.

In the light of this analysis a few considerations on the new interventions in the field of social policies adopted in Italy are possible. It is very recent news that the government has decided to introduce, as a form of experimentation, a new measure: the introduction of a minimum wage, which is quite new for the Italian welfare system. Such a measure falls within a general redefinition of the Italian welfare system, which has ambitious aims, both in the field of social assistance and in every other sector (work policies, social cushioning, pension plans). The research will involve a limited number of families selected from among the poorest ones: for instance, those with disabled children, those made up of individuals who are over sixty-five and are at risk of marginality. Also the municipalities where the research will be carried out will be chosen from among those in the most depressed areas and with a high rate of unemployment.

As to the specific case of social assistance, it is a question of putting to an end the typical distortions of the Italian system which has so far given social policies a residual role – having been crushed under the economic burden of the pension system. In particular, welfare intervention has been confined to 'a series of institutes mainly concerned with monetary provisions of a passive type, that neither are able to reach appreciable redistributive results, nor do they grasp the real needs of the beneficiaries giving them actual opportunities to regain self-sufficiency' (Commission for the Macroeconomic Compatibilities of Social Expenditure, Final Report, February 1997).

The features of the reform may be summed up as follows:

1. a clean separation between social assistance and social security by means of a clear identification of the security programmes, financed through contributions, and social programmes, financed through general taxes

2. the realization of a wide and widespread net of real services which, in the framework of the general principles dictated by the State, assigns to county councils the programming task, and to municipalities the function of determining priorities, managerial choices and the promotion of extensive forms of cooperation with other local authorities, with institution in the non-profit sector and with the private enterprises

3. the rationalization of the measures of monetary redistribution through the introduction of a minimum income, that may accomplish the task of supporting lower incomes in a well constructed way, incorporating the functions so far carried out by a number of sectarian and fragmented interventions.

The introduction of a minimum income represents an important institutional innovation for many reasons: for the first time in Italy, it introduces protection addressed to all citizens; it abolishes – for new beneficiaries – the admission to already existing programmes, thus simplifying the 'jungle' of measures that have been in use up to now; finally, it is guided by a philosophy that is completely new in the Italian context.

In the first place, it is an instrument of a markedly universal kind since it is addressed to all those who have resources that are below a given threshold of income (approximately the poverty line) and, for reasons that are beyond their control, are in a condition of indigence, independent of their gender, social class or profession. Second, it is a measure less based on the organization of the family since it is not addressed to the head of the family but to individuals who are of age, even if the situation of poverty is estimated on the basis of the resources of the family unit to which the subject belongs (therefore the benefit may be shared out among all family members, according to different criteria). Third, it is a technically more appropriate instrument, both because it takes into account the family features (not only the number of its members but also its composition, considering for instance the presence of unemployed adult dependents) and because it estimates the economic resources of the household as exactly as possible, including other resources apart from the reported income (real estate, other incomes, etc.). Finally, it is an innovative instrument in terms of management, since it is handled by local communities; it is linked with local welfare policies, which provide services for people with particular needs (old age, illness, handicap), and it is combined with active policies for employment.

But the most interesting aspect is the philosophy of the intervention rather than the technical aspect. The intention of the policy makers in introducing a minimum income was to try to avoid completely the logic of dependence which, as is well known, has characterized the Italian system for a long time. It is designed to lessen the so-called poverty trap; it does not allow the beneficiary to remain passive in a situation of need, protected by public charity, since it only partially fills the gap between the individual's resources and the poverty line (AA.VV. 1997). Besides, it aims at the reintegration of beneficiaries into the labour market, since in the case of unemployed people who are not unable to work the allowance would be allocated for a limited time and only if they are willing to work by attending, for instance, a training course or taking part in 'social utility work' programmes. A significant aspect is the fact that the aid is not confined to economic support, but it includes the provision of opportunities and services meant to help people to escape from their condition of need.

It is therefore without doubt a measure that is not only innovative but also extremely perceptive in its intent. Yet, given the aim of this analysis, that is, an evaluation of this measure with respect to Italian peculiarities, this intervention asks for a closer examination. In this respect, it is worth noticing that the first, and at present the only, intervention that has been brought about in the general re-definition of the Italian welfare system is concerned, once again, with a form of monetary support; while forms of innovative services, of social and work training, coordinated with the introduction of a minimum income, are still to be put into practice.

Of course, behind the difficulties of a more radical reform of the Italian welfare system, there are reasons that account for the limits and slowness. As Paci has recently pointed out, it should be remembered that not only in social assistance but in every sector of public expenditure are intervention margins deeply influenced by tight financial restraints, and by a weak cohesion both within the coalition of government and the parliamentary majority. Nor is a consideration of a more general order to be left out: today the 'transformability' of welfare systems is far more reduced than it was in the past, when they were only relatively developed. The presence of well-established interests – not only of different social categories, but also of trade unions and of the welfare workers themselves – is indisputably a factor that slows down the reform process (Paci 1998).

But if one takes into account that this process in other sectors, and particularly in the pension sector, has gone far ahead (within a few years the new system will work at full capacity) and that these category interests are as much, if not more, relevant, it becomes easily understandable how the slowness of the reform process of social policies cannot be ascribed solely to the opposition of particularist stratified interests.

In this case too, the structural reasons, which are not necessarily wrong, for the different 'speeds' at which the welfare system reform proceeds are easily detectable. It may be easily pointed out that the priority given to the rearrangement of the pension plan has followed a logic of economic efficiency: in other words, the 'most expensive' sector of the Italian welfare system has been chosen as the starting point. Yet, the priority given to monetary intervention in social policies to combat poverty (preferring monetary support to the introduction of services that are still non-existent) leads us to believe that the slowness in the change stems from a deeper cultural resistance which prevents the overcoming of a, so to speak, 'monetarist' vision of welfare.

Therefore, if one wonders to what extent the new measures are able to oppose the distortions of the Italian welfare system, one may agree with those who state that 'at least welfare reform is before us' or, in other words, that at least the requisites for it have been set (Paci 1998). But if one wonders to what extent the new social policy interventions – particularly those addressed to poor households – meet the peculiarities of the Southern context, where poverty is mostly concentrated, the answer is less optimistic. The reason for this is not just that very little has been done to solve the problem of unemployment in the South, which is the main cause of poverty and of its reproduction in this area.

In fact, there is another aspect to be considered: the underestimation of the cultural aspects of poverty. A realistic policy must take into account the cultural aspects of poverty in the South. The feature of 'normality' that seems to characterize the experience of poverty in the South represents a particularly important issue for social policy. As suggested here, the perception of poverty as an ordinary experience acts as a stimulus which at the same time activates strategies for coping with the situation of poverty and reproduces that poverty. The people who have to overcome or avoid poverty are not 'abstract' individuals, but 'concrete' persons whose strategies are applied in the context of their material and cultural reality. This means that the habit of poverty can have an effect on the capacity to imagine a future without poverty. Whether a poor adolescent becomes an errand boy in the underground economy, a worker in a criminal organization or a drug addict, or whether, instead, he continues his studies depends on a number of factors. There are his own and his parents' expectations and the life projects he is able to imagine for himself, as well as the quality of the welfare system or the opportunities offered by the black or by the illegal economy. That is why in the South, fighting the 'culture of normality', according to which poverty, 'making do' and illegality too are perceived as ordinary dimensions of living, must be considered as important as fighting the structural causes of poverty. But it does not seem that this objective is on the policy makers' agenda at present. Their efforts have been in trying to avoid the poverty trap, and the danger of a 'dependence on welfare'; but, as we have tried to argue, in the case of the South, this is in no way the real problem.

References

AA.VV. (1997) 'La spesa per l'assistenza in italia. documento di base della commissione per le compatibilità macroeconomiche della spesa sociale.' *Prospettive Sociali e Sanitarie, 9*, 1–8.

Ascoli, U. (ed.) (1984) 'Il Sistema Italiano di Welfare.' *Welfare State all'Italiana*, Bari: Laterza.

Auletta, K. (1983) *The Underclass*. New York: Vintage Books.

Banfield E.C. (1958) *The Moral Basis of a Backward Society*. New York: The Free Press.

Castel, R. (1991) 'La Désaffiliation.' In I. Donzelot (ed) *Face à l'Exclusion: Le Modele Francais*. Paris: Editions Esprit.

Chubb, J. (1982) *Patronage, Power and Poverty in Southern Italy*. Cambridge: Cambridge University Press.

Colabella, A. (1991) 'Disoccupazione sinonimo di povertà? Una ricerca empirica sull'area metropolitana torinese.' *Economia e Lavoro, 1*, 131–146.

CIPE (1994) Commissione di indagine sulla povertà e l'emarginazione. *La Povertà in Italia nel 1993*. Roma: Istituto Poligrafico dello Stato.

CIPE (1996a) Commissione di indagine sulla povertà e l'emarginazione. *La Povertà in Italia 1980–1984*. Roma: Istituto Poligrafico dello Stato.

CIPE (1996b) Commissione di indagine sulla povertà e l'emarginazione. *La Povertà in Italia nel 1995*. Roma: Istituto Poligrafico dello Stato.

Douglass. M. and Hisherwood, B. (1979) *The World of Goods*. New York: Basic Books.

Esping-Andersen, G. (1990) *The Three Worlds of Welfare Capitalism*. Cambridge: Cambridge Polity Press.

Ferrera, M. (1984) *Il Welfare State in Italia. Sviluppo e Crisi in Prospettiva Comparata*. Bologna: Il Mulino.

Guidicini, P. and Pieretti, G. (eds) (1988) *I Volti della Povertà Urbana*. Milano: F. Angeli.

Melotti, U.(1989) 'Le Nuove Povertà nell'Area Ferrarese.' In *Up and Down, 1*, 53–70.

Mingione, E. (1986) 'La Povertà Familiare nelle Città Meridionali.' In *Inchiesta, 73*, 53–61.

Mingione, E. (1991) *Fragmented Societies. A Sociology of Economic Life Beyond the Market Paradigm*. Oxford: Blackwell.

Mingione, E. and Zajczyk, F. (1992) 'Le nuove povertà urbane in Italia: Modelli di percorsi a rischio nell'area Milanese'. In *Inchiesta*, 63–79.

Morlicchio, E. and Spanò, A. (1992) 'La Povertà a Napoli.' In *Inchiesta*, 80–88.

x Murray, C. (1984) *Losing Ground*. New York: Basic Books.

Mutti A. (1992) 'La Questione Meridionale negli Anni "90".' In F.P. Cerase (ed) *Dopo il Familismo, Cosa?* Milano: F. Angeli.

Paci, M. (1988) 'I Nodi Attuali della Riforma del Welfare in Italia.' paper presented to the Conference *Distribuzione del Reddito, Diseguaglianze, Esclusione Sociale ed Effetti delle Politiche Economiche e Sociali*. C.N.R., Roma, February.

Paugam, S. (1991) *La Disqualification Sociale, Essai sur la Nouvelle Paurverté*. Paris: Presses Universitaires de France.

Saraceno, C. (1976) 'Povertà e cultura della povertà: Il dibattito in corso in Inghilterra e negli Stati Uniti.' In *Quaderni di Sociologia, 1*, 85–101.

Sarpellon, G. (ed) (1991) *Percorsi di Povertà e Reti di Servizi*. Milano: F. Angeli.

Sassen, S. (1991) *The Global City: New York, London and Tokyo*. Princeton: Princeton University Press.

Sassen, S. (1993) 'Urban Marginality in Transnational Perspective: Comparing New York and Tokyo', paper presented to the Conference *Le Nuove Povertà Urbane*. Milano, December.

Scivoletto, A. and Zani, S. (eds) (1989) *Malessere nella Città Ricca, Milano*. F. Angeli.

Sen, A. (1993) 'Le Ragioni del Persistere della Povertà nei Paesi Ricchi.' In P. Guidicini and G. Pieretti (1993) (eds) La Residualità Come Valore. Milano: F. Angli.

Sgritta, G. and Innocenzi, G. (1994) 'La Povertà.' In M. Paci (ed) *Le Dimensioni della Disuguaglianza*. Bologna: Il Mulino.

Townsend, P. (1993) 'New York e Londra. Povertà urbana e cause internazionali.' In P. Guidicini and G. Pieretti (1993) (eds) *La Residualità come valore*. Milano: F. Angeli.

Wilson, W. (1987) *The Truly Disadvantaged. The Inner City, the Underclass and Public Policy*. Chicago: University of Chicago Press.

PART III

Theorizing Welfare as Culture

Introduction to Part III

Michael Rustin

Earlier chapters in this book have demonstrated the discovery and significance of cultural dimensions of welfare. The awareness of differences, located in both historical time and geographical space, obliges us to recognize what was previously taken for granted, namely the specific assumptions, norms and values which underpin each system of welfare provision. This recognition, in turn, raises theoretical questions. If welfare arrangements become contested, and cease to be 'common-sense', a new vocabulary is needed with which to think about alternatives and political choices. Of course, there have always been conflicts over welfare, even during the era of apparent 'post-war consensus', notably between more collectivist and more individualist positions. But these differences were for many years routinized and familiar, establishing their own limits to what could be thought of as possible. It is only recently that these boundaries to political debate have begun to dissolve, and we find ourselves having to consider, for example, not just whether families should receive more or less welfare support, but whether the conventional family form is losing its cultural dominance altogether, or not how near we can approximate to full employment, but whether we can accept the reality of a world in which long-term, secure employment has become an exception, not the norm. But where is the language to come from with which we can reflect on this new field of differences and possibilities? The final chapters of this book suggest some ways forward.

The first, by Samantha Ashenden, examines Jürgen Habermas's reflections on the development of modern welfare systems. In his view, this involves a colonization of the lifeworld by the impersonal forms and institutions of state and market, in which a loss of authenticity and responsiveness to experience offsets undoubted gains in material and other formal entitlements. Ashenden's argument is that the recognition of differences of identity and value is now essential to the development of social welfare. She describes Habermas's own attempts to incorporate such differences of value and experience within his conception of democratic political practice. Habermas recognizes that the reality of democracy is tested in the implementation of welfare policy, at the points where abstract legislation encounters the particularities of the lifeworld. Whilst she is sympathetic to Habermas's purpose, Ashenden argues that his own theoretical account of this is insufficient, and that his prescriptions fail in practice to assure adequate democratic representation. The problems of combining high-level forms of democratic representatation, with responsiveness to actual differences of experience, are shown in this chapter to be both crucial and difficult to resolve.

Caroline Knowles' chapter has as its starting-point Foucault's critical perspectives on welfare practice of different kinds. Foucault applied a critical sociological perspective to the role of social scientists in the management of modernization, exemplifying his arguments in studies of penal policy, medicine, psychiatry and sexuality. He showed the ways in which supposedly humane and emancipatory forms of intervention embodied new forms of control which were often more total and penetrating, if less physically brutal, than the pre-modern forms which preceded them. Foucault's work provided a vocabulary for investigating the new forms of surveillance, domination, and intended transformation which characterizes modern social administration – in effect its new technologies of social power. Knowles' essay adds to this perspective the specific insights into the significance of the control and management of space that she finds in the work of Henri Lefebvre. Drawing on her own empirical study of psychiatric outpatients, Knowles demonstrates the way in which their fate can be represented almost literally in spatial terms, since their loss of control of the physical spaces in which they live deprives them of a fundamental source of identity and agency. She describes a social world whose micro-texture is determined by decisions about the meaning of different spaces and places, and about the enforced relations of persons with and without authority within them. Culture is understood here as the attribution of meaning to the constituting elements of life, and physical space is deemed to be one of the most basic of these. The quality of welfare regimes can be assessed in part by reflecting on who ascribes and controls these meanings.

Michael Rustin's chapter is an argument for the relevance of modern psychoanalytic perspectives to welfare policy and practice. Welfare systems have always been society's response to the threats to well-being posed by natural and unnatural crises – poverty, disease and those misfortunes which arise from the behaviour of human beings towards one another. In pre-modern societies, these disruptions were explained, and reparative actions justified and sanctioned, chiefly within the context of religious ways of thinking. Modern welfare systems have relied on more rationalistic approaches, focusing on the minimization of pain and on the provision of incentives and sanctions – 'a just measure of pain', as Michael Ignatieff, following Bentham, has put it – as the principal means of sustaining social order. Rustin argues that the strength of psychoanalytic thinking lies in its willingness to address, in secular terms, those fundamental issues of mortality and mental pain for which there has been little space in the arid utilitarian discourses of social administration. The commitment of psychoanalysis to bringing feelings and anxieties within the domain of rational understanding attempts to mend a split between reason and the passions which he suggests has been one of the less desirable consequences of modernity. He suggests that applied psychoanalysis can provide ways of thinking about the design of social institutions and social policies which address the needs of human beings at a less superficial level than other forms of contemporary social theory.

This book argues that debates on welfare now need to take account of the latent cultural assumptions within which social policies are made. The recognition of difference, the micro-politics of space, and the recognition and containment of anxiety, are three aspects which become apparent once we look again at the question of what kinds of problem welfare systems are intended to solve, and at their individual and social subjects. Social theories which seek to draw new maps of welfare become necessary once it is shown that existing descriptions are outdated, inadequate, or too limited in their grasp of variations across space and time.

CHAPTER II

Habermas on Discursive Consensus

Rethinking the Welfare State in the Face of Cultural Pluralism

Samantha Ashenden

The legitimacy of welfare states is currently under intense scrutiny. Attention has been given to the economic sustainability of the welfare functions of the state, to the patterns of distribution and redistribution engendered by state intervention and, more recently, to the problem of the lack of recognition of diverse forms of life within welfare legislation. This latter concern has been raised most prominently by feminists disputing the normative models of family and gender relations inscribed in welfare legislation and by writers criticizing the ethnocentrism of the conceptual categories underpinning social policies.

This chapter examines the challenges to contemporary welfare states posed by struggles for recognition by previously marginalized groups. It begins by focusing on the twentieth century welfare state as an aspect of the consolidation of national cultures in which the appropriate form and content of welfare provision was *assumed* and the subsequent questioning of this by those raising demands for recognition. Having sketched the emergence of a set of dilemmas facing contemporary welfare states in relation to cultural pluralism, this chapter takes up the diagnosis of the dilemmas facing such states outlined by Jurgen Habermas. Habermas provides an account of the welfare state which draws attention to the problem of legitimation in the face of social pluralism. Furthermore, he suggests a framework for rethinking the welfare state which is explicitly formulated to accommodate diversity. The concern here is to examine how far Habermas' timely proposals can inform and provide direction to struggles for recognition within contemporary welfare states.

The first section outlines some problems posed about the welfare state by writers concerned with the recognition of cultural pluralism. The second section provides a synopsis of Habermas' account of the dynamics of the development and dilemmas of the welfare state. The third section examines Habermas' proposals for the relegitimation of the welfare state in a manner capable of recognizing and drawing upon the plurality of modern societies. The fourth section then explores the limits of this account, focusing specifically on the problems attending Habermas' attempt to ground his critical theory in a philosophy of language which privileges consensus as the goal of political dialogue and which relies on the separation of the expressive aspects of language from other types of validity claim.

Pluralism and the problem of the welfare state

Whilst the form and extent of state provision and regulation of welfare has differed according to national context, since the late nineteenth century European welfare states have been constructed around the goal of unity and their politics centred on redistribution. Welfare, provided or regulated at the level of the nation state, has supplanted previously existing plural practices of provision. (In the context of this discussion, whether welfare services are directly provided by the state or simply regulated by the state is not salient; both forms contain normative assumptions, though non-state providers of welfare may be more adept at producing culturally appropriate forms of service, see Hirst (1997).)

This can clearly be seen in Britain, particularly in the post-1945 Labour Government's legislative programme. This centred on providing universal health care, education and social security through the mechanisms of insurance and general taxation and was underpinned by Keynesian demand management, the prospect of steady economic growth and the maintenance of full employment. This programme replaced localized, market-based and charitable forms of provision with uniform standards of social policy (at least in aim) and removed the nineteenth century Poor Law, replacing this with a system of social insurance designed to ensure a basic minimum for all citizens in times of need such as unemployment. The dominant frame of this legislation was thus inclusion through redistribution. The concept of citizenship informing this legislation was elaborated most clearly by T.H. Marshall in his *Citizenship and Social Class* (1949). Marshall argued that the twentieth century welfare state was the outcome of two centuries of development of citizenship rights: the eighteenth century saw the development of civil citizenship, rights to freedom of religion, association and assembly; the nineteenth century saw the growth of political citizenship with the democratization of the franchise; the twentieth century had brought social citizenship through the social rights provided by the welfare state. As such, these developments can be considered as part of the attempt to continue the consolidation of the nation state and as an important element in the constitution of national culture (Williams 1989). In this process, the centrality of the question of the distribution and redistribution of what *is*, of assumed 'goods', concealed or at least underestimated the importance of questions concerning the definition of these goods and the appropriate forms of their provision.

Recently, attempts to incorporate or assimilate individuals through unifying conceptions of citizenship, family and so on, embodied in state social policies, have come under attack. Feminists have argued that the forms of recognition accorded to women within welfare legislation have contained a normative model of the nuclear family and the assumption of female dependence on a male breadwinner, thus entrenching dependent forms of citizenship for women (Fraser 1989, 1995; Lister 1997; Showstack-Sassoon 1987; Williams 1989; Wilson 1977, 1980; Young 1990, 1997). Feminists have thus criticized the claim to universality embodied in contemporary welfare states, demonstrating that the forms of social provision entrenched in welfare legislation have often not accorded women equal recognition as citizens. Writers concerned with the recognition and status of ethnic minority populations within Europe have raised concerns about the citizenship status of non-European immigrants and have pointed to the incipient racism of much state welfare provision, both in terms of the exclusion of immigrants from welfare services and in terms of the assimilatory effects of that which has been provided, for example through assumptions concerning normative models of the family, dress and language, which fail to recognize the diversity of forms of life of the populations to which they are addressed (Ball and Solomos 1990; Donald and Rattansi 1992; Gilroy 1987; Williams 1989). Such concerns challenge the limits of a distributive, aggregative, universalist paradigm of welfare provision and seek the acknowledgement of differences of culture within the formulation and provision of social policies.

These criticisms of state welfare provision combine concern with questions of economic distribution and redistribution and concern with the recognition of different patterns of life, either differences in life experience and chances by gender and/or by ethnic group. This set of criticisms can be restated thus: the welfare state has involved the misapplication of generic concepts to diverse individuals and groups which, in turn, has produced *dis*welfare by forcing those individuals and groups into particular ways of life or, alternatively, by effectively excluding them from the benefits of state provision. The cultural coding of welfare law and policy has failed to recognize, respect and to work with the cultural patterns of diverse groups.

In this context, neither feminists nor those concerned with ethnic minorities' struggles for recognition have been content with the turn toward the marketization of welfare witnessed during the 1980s and 1990s. Whilst state-provided welfare has often been experienced as coercive and assimilatory, giving inadequate 'voice' to those subject to welfare provisions and inscribing relations of dependency, a market-based, consumer model of welfare simply threatens to reinforce already existing inequalities by throwing individuals into markets governed by private interest or producing greater reliance on traditional resources such as families. Both of these moves depoliticize questions of social policy by foregrounding the rights of individuals to exit from particular markets and by entrenching particularist responses to social need, respectively. Such strategies undermine rather than reinforce the interconnectedness of different communities and offer little space in which alternative forms and practices of provision can be publicly debated. This raises an important question for our present: how to rework the form and content of state provision and regulation of welfare in a manner more capable of recognizing and sustaining diversity. Here, Habermas has made a significant contribution and it is to his work that we now turn.

Nancy Fraser has recently taken up this theme in relation to what she has termed the 'redistribution-recognition dilemma' (Fraser 1995, p.68), pointing to the ways in which various forms of identity politics are struggles for cultural recognition which do not sit easily with the politics of redistribution characteristic of 'socialist' and social democratic politics. Whilst Fraser attributes to such politics a diminution of attention to still important questions of redistribution, she also recognizes the importance of claims to recognition. Fraser's attempt to distinguish redistribution and recognition have been criticized by Iris Marion Young (1997) and Judith Butler (1998). I assume that demands for the distribution of resources and concern with the recognition of particular patterns of life are necessarily related, that cultures have a material existence, and thus do not follow Fraser's distinction between redistribution and recognition.

Dynamics of development and dilemmas of the welfare state

Habermas' work can be understood as an attempt to identify, explain and work through the dilemmas attending the development of modern democratic citizenship and the welfare state. In *The Theory of Communicative Action* (1984, 1987), Habermas provides a systematic account of the development and dynamics of the welfare state. This account is instructive as it focuses attention on the effects of bureaucratic state administration on the fabric of everyday life and makes some provocative suggestions as to how the ambivalent effects of the welfare state might be overcome. (Also see *Legitimation Crisis* (1976). I focus on *The Theory of Communicative Action* (1984, 1987) here as this work provides the basis for subsequent developments in Habermas' thinking about the welfare state and marks the 'linguistic turn' in his ideas. From this point onwards, Habermas characterizes the 'lifeworld' as a repository of symbolic meaning providing the cultural background to everyday life. Some of this and the next section draws on the exegesis of Habermas' ideas provided in Ashenden (1999a,b).)

Fundamental to Habermas' account of modern societies is the distinction between the lifeworld and the system. We need to outline these two concepts as it is from the differentiation of lifeworld and system through rationalization that Habermas theorizes the emergence of the welfare state and its current problems.

The lifeworld is formulated as 'a reservoir of taken for granteds, of unshaken convictions that participants in communication draw upon in cooperative processes of interpretation' (Habermas 1987, p.124). It is symbolically reproduced and structurally complex, involving processes of cultural reproduction, social integration and socialization, functions which have been differentiated through evolution (1987, p.152). The lifeworld is reproduced through communicative action, action oriented toward reaching understanding, and serves as a background source of accepted meanings. Rationalization here occurs through the pluralization of forms of life and the questioning of relations of authority. With rationalization, actors question normatively ascribed agreements and demand the independent justification of norms through the attainment of 'communicatively achieved understanding' as opposed to 'normatively ascribed agreement' (1984, p.70). Thus, rationalization within the lifeworld produces an increasing need for explicit agreement on an increasing number of contested concerns, 'a growing need for justification' (1996, p.97). In Habermas' account, the lifeworld comprises the private nuclear family and the public political sphere.

In contrast to the lifeworld, the system comprises the economy and state administration. Habermas argues that, through the process of rationalization, the system or sphere of material production and purposive rational action is progressively differentiated from the lifeworld context of symbolic reproduction. The concept of 'system', then, refers to those mechanisms in modern society that have been 'uncoupled' from the communicative context of the lifeworld and are coordinated through functional interconnections via the media of money and power (1987, p.150). System integration concerns the material reproduction of society and is organized principally through the institutionalization of purposive rational action in the modern economy and state administration. The differentiation of the system from the lifeworld reduces the complexity of action coordination and provides the 'steering capacity' (1987, p.152) that Habermas argues is necessary to the complex functioning of advanced industrial societies.

We can now look more closely at Habermas' account of the relationship between system and lifeworld and at his specification of the role of the welfare state in these developmental dynamics. In describing the rationalization processes of modernity, Habermas gives a four-stage account of the differentiation of the system and the lifeworld which results in the institutionalization of the democratic welfare state. This occurs through the process of legal codification or 'juridification', so that 'formally organized' relations are those first 'constituted in the form of modern law' (1987, p.357).

Habermas' argument accords with the account given by Marshall of the development of modern citizenship. For Habermas, the first stage of the process of juridification began with the establishment of the bourgeois state under the absolutist regimes of Europe. This regulated sovereign monopoly over coercion and instituted the contractual rights and obligations of private persons as the condition of free enterprise in a market economy. The second stage, the bourgeois constitutional state, regulated individual rights to life, liberty and property against the political authority of the monarch. The third stage, the creation of the democratic constitutional state in the wake of the French Revolution, brought political emancipation. The fourth phase of juridification, that of the twentieth century democratic welfare state, secured freedoms and social rights against the state.

Habermas describes this process as one of 'freedom guaranteeing juridification'. However, he suggests that there is an 'ambiguity in the rationalization of law' (1984, p.270); rights claims developed historically but have introduced 'ambivalences' and opened space for the possible 'colonization of the lifeworld'. In Habermas' account, the first stage of juridification is regarded as institutionalizing 'the two media [money and power] through which the economy and state were differentiated off into subsystems' (1987, p.358); that is, this stage saw the separation of the system of economy and state from the lifeworld. The latter three stages are theorized as attempts by the lifeworld to resist the autonomous working of the state and economy: 'a lifeworld that at first was placed at the disposal of the market and of absolutist rule little by little makes good its claims' (1987, p.359).

In the first two stages of juridification Habermas suggests that law's regulatory functions are internal to the regulation of the systems of money and power and are freedom-guaranteeing. (Mike Rustin has drawn to my attention that the distinction between the first two stages of juridification and the latter is difficult to maintain, and that the development of markets and of civil law also invaded and disrupted customarily regulated lifeworlds (see MacIntyre 1994; Thompson 1975).) In the third stage, ambivalence attends not the form of law but its implementation: participatory rights guarantee freedom but the bureaucratic implementation of these restricts the process of 'spontaneous opinion formation and discursive will formation' (1987, p.364). In the fourth stage, ambivalences emerge from the form of law itself. This is because, in this phase, law as a medium of state administration supplants communicative contexts of action with monetary compensation and therapeutic assistance. Thus the independent organization of the lifeworld is threatened by the tendencies of the system which 'spreads a web of client relations over the private spheres of life' (1987, p.364). This account has some similarities with Foucault's account of the development of disciplines and of biopower; see Foucault (1977, 1979).

Habermas describes the effects of the state provision of welfare on the lifeworld in terms of 'mediatization' and 'colonization'. He suggests that the lifeworld becomes 'mediatized' to the extent that 'delinguistified media of system integration' (money and power) are used to relate the system and lifeworld. This process occurs through the social roles of employee, consumer, citizen and client which crystallize around these exchange relations. In assuming these roles, actors detach themselves from the lifeworld and adapt to formally organized domains of action (1987, p.185). According to Habermas, this 'mediatization' of the lifeworld takes on the form of an 'internal colonization' when the delinguistified media of the system take over the essential symbolic reproduction functions of the lifeworld itself, thereby 'objectifying' or 'reifying' social relationships. The internal colonization of the lifeworld produces pathological effects as the lifeworld has some essentially symbolic functions, that is, it is concerned with cultural reproduction, social integration and socialization, all of which rely on communicative action and thus cannot successfully be replaced by delinguistified media (1987, p.208). Relating this to the welfare state, Habermas suggests that the situations regulated by welfare policy are 'embedded in the context of a life history and of a concrete form of life' which necessarily suffers 'violent abstraction' if it is to be dealt with within a legal and administrative, that is 'formal', framework (1987, p.363). Thus the dilemma of increasing the scope of the welfare state is that welfare guarantees destroy 'consensual mechanisms that coordinate action', transforming them into administration through the media of money and power (1987, p.361).

For Habermas, therefore, the welfare state is a central mechanism in the monetarization and bureaucratization of the lifeworld; this produces pathological effects by reducing or usurping the essential functions of communicative rationality inherent in lifeworld interaction. Examples of colonization include the bureaucratization of schools and the formalization of family relationships in law.

In schools concerns with externally determined measures of success (examination results, league tables and so on) produce the breaking up of a school's activities into 'a mosaic of legally contestable administrative acts' (Habermas 1987, p.371). This, for Habermas, endangers the social integration of educational institutions through shared values and norms and breaks down a communicatively structured area of action (the life of a school) into a depersonalized 'welfare institution that organizes and distributes schooling as a social benefit' (1987, p.372). In contrast to this, Habermas suggests the necessity of 'consensus oriented procedures for conflict resolution' (1987, p.372) whereby all those concerned with the life of a school have a role in determining and regulating its activities themselves, through participating in determining its aims and how these can best be met. This meets contemporary concerns with the impact of externally driven criteria of success in the context of the plural cultures of schools. For example, in Britain, there is great concern that national league tables of schools' performances override the capacity of schools to set goals other than those prescribed in national guidelines; attention to the particular educational needs of a school's population, a particular school's ethos and culture, is undermined rather than supported in a competitive culture in which one measure of success becomes the focus of attention and resources.

In relation to the second example of colonization, Habermas suggests that the extension of the medium of law into the family violates the previously communicatively structured relations within it. He points out that 'emancipation within the family is achieved at the cost of a new bond' (1987, p.369); that is, the individual family member, in order to constitute him- or herself as a person, is forced to make claims against and possibly become dependent upon the state. This occurs at the cost of the communicative ordering of family relationships. Whilst feminists have argued that Habermas fails to recognize relations of power within families (Fraser 1989; Honneth 1991), several writers have pointed out that social provisions which have made it easier for women to leave deleterious relationships have, in their turn, produced greater dependence for women on the state, a shift from 'private' to 'public' patriarchy (Hernes 1987; Walby 1990). Current proposals in English family law concerning compulsory mediation in divorce cases involving children may take this juridification to new lengths.

Here, one can point to forms of alienated dependency which have accompanied social security provision, where claimants are treated as instances of rules, being able to claim for the necessities of life but only by accounting for the details of their financial circumstances and personal behaviour. Feminists have criticized the normative assumptions underpinning social security provision. For example, in Britain criticisms have been levelled at cohabitation rules for treating the sexual partners of women as responsible for those women's financial support. These rules led to feminist demands for the disaggregation of welfare benefits, for the treatment of individuals *qua* individuals. Such rules, and more recently the operation of the Child Support Agency (CSA), assume women's economic dependence on men within the family. Contemporary concerns surrounding the operation of the CSA focus on the abrogation of women's privacy in relation to their sexual relationships in the face of claiming state benefits, women claiming means-tested benefits being compelled to give the names of fathers of their children or face the penalty of reduced benefits. In Habermas' terms, such regulations transform what is formally a system of entitlements securing freedom and opportunity into an apparatus of bureaucratic classification, surveillance and control. 'New Labour's' welfare reforms threaten to extend this colonization with, for example, requirements that individuals undergo compulsory counselling back into work in order to qualify for state benefits.

Habermas regards the 'pathological' effects of the welfare state as the result of 'selective' or one-sided rationalization in which law as a medium of state administration introduces 'delinguistified' media of money and power into lifeworld contexts of symbolic reproduction. The juridification associated with the welfare state undermines the bases of cultural reproduction, social integration and socialization within the lifeworld both by supplanting the communicative co-ordination of action with the media of money and power and by producing illegitimate substantive determinations of the good, overriding the ethical concerns of citizens. Thus, 'from the start, the ambivalence of guaranteeing freedom and taking it away has attached to the policies of the welfare state' (1987, p.361).

Habermas claims that what is needed is a shift in this balance; that the purposive rational orientation of the system is not inherently harmful, but that it must be brought under the control of the 'communicative rationality' of the lifeworld. Habermas sees possibilities for this in enhanced forms of democratic dialogue in the public political spheres of civil society brought into closer relation with the formulation of welfare laws and policies. He suggests that we need to 'erect a democratic dam against the colonizing encroachment of system imperatives on areas of the lifeworld' (1992b, p.444). In developing this theme, Habermas provides an account which aims to incorporate the diverse views of different groups more thoroughly into the formulation of welfare law and policy.

New legitimacy for the welfare state

In *The Theory of Communicative Action*, Habermas presented 'ambivalent effects' as intrinsic to the welfare state insofar as welfare law and policy 'juridified' previously informally organized areas of life. *Between Facts and Norms* (1996) takes up this theme but moves beyond this pessimistic diagnosis to develop a formula for the democratic justification of law which he argues is capable of recognizing and valuing cultural pluralism in the formulation of welfare legislation.

Habermas seeks to acknowledge struggles for recognition of diverse cultural conceptions of the good whilst refusing to abandon a universalist account of justice. Therefore, instead of moving toward a communitarian account of the good life or taking a postmodern path in the face of difference, Habermas proposes a proceduralist solution to the problem of the accommodation of diversity. This is grounded in reformulating the legitimacy of law, derived from proposals for enhancing forms of democratic dialogue in the public spheres of civil society. Linking this to the welfare state he stresses, for example, the importance of those subject to welfare legislation participating in its formulation. His claim is that, in this way, we can pay attention to and build upon specific communities' cultural values whilst transcending their particularism and generating an account of justice acceptable to all concerned.

How does Habermas suggest we give new legitimacy to the welfare state? In order to address this question, we need to examine his analysis of previous understandings of law, his reformulation of law's legitimacy in terms of a procedural framework and the grounding of this in an account of discursive democracy. With this, Habermas aims to specify ways in which the potential for rationality of communicative action in the lifeworld can be brought into a more dynamic relation with the formally structured systems of state administration and economy; he aims to do this in such a way that the plurality of cultures constituting the modern lifeworld are not flattened or silenced but rather provide the springboard and deliberative resources for the formulation of just laws.

In order to address Habermas' approach to the relegitimation of the welfare state it is useful to begin with his discussion of the equality-difference debate within feminism. Habermas uses this example to elucidate his argument for the need for a new paradigm of law and its justification.

Habermas points to what he calls a 'dialectic of legal and factual equality' (1996, p.420) in feminist campaigns for equal treatment. He points out that early demands for strict equality between men and women in access to educational institutions, occupations, political institutions and so on, did not produce equality in these spheres due to women's and men's substantially different life experiences and positions within the social structures of most societies. Recognition of this as a problem produced various forms of welfare state paternalism, where women were given a range of special rights and privileges such as maternity leave. He points out that such provisions have had the effect of disadvantaging women in employment, producing greater risks of job loss for women than for men, and/or confining women to secondary labour markets. That is, laws originally designed to counter discrimination against women have had the opposite effect.

Habermas locates two principal reasons for this pattern. First, he suggests that 'overgeneralized classifications [have been] used to label disadvantaging situations and disadvantaged groups of persons' (1996, p.422–423, emphasis in text), so that, for example, measures meant to promote equality have often only benefited one group of women through failure to pay attention to differences between women in relation to age, class, ethnicity and so on (for example, different groups of women will be differently affected by employers' concerns about maternity). Second, Habermas suggests that 'legislation and adjudication arrive at 'false' classifications' (1996, p.423). This, for Habermas, is due to adherence to 'an outmoded paradigmatic understanding of law (1996, p.423, emphasis in text) in which existing gender stereotypes are assumed and consolidated within legislation with resultant 'normalizing effects' (1996, p.423). In other words, legislation and adjudication, by assuming traditional definitions of gender roles, re-establish the problems they were meant to solve.

In this context, Habermas argues that any amount of preferential treatment in terms of distributive justice is misplaced so long as it 'suppresses the voices of those who could *say* what the currently relevant reasons are for equal or unequal treatment' (1996, p.420, emphasis in text). Instead, Habermas argues that, as a prerequisite to being able to create the conditions in which women and men can have genuinely equal opportunities, public discussion is necessary in order to establish which differences between men and women are relevant (1996, p.425). That is, there is a need for a 'politics of need interpretation' (Fraser 1989). Habermas puts this point forcefully:

> The pressure toward assimilation that is exerted on women by both the social welfare and the liberal politics of equality – a pressure felt precisely where these programmes succeed – ultimately stems from the fact that gender differences are not conceived as relationships involving two *equally* problematic variables *in need of interpretation*. Differences are instead seen as deviations from supposedly

unproblematic male standards ... Whereas the social-welfare paradigm makes special legal allowances for divergences and freezes them as such, the liberal market model tends to ignore and trivialize actual inequalities. (1996, p.424, emphasis in text)

In order for this to be realized, Habermas suggests a transformation in our understanding of the legitimacy of law and a more thorough grounding of this in discursively achieved consensus in public debate.

Habermas proceeds dialectically; at a political level between discourses of liberalism and republicanism, and in terms of law via an account of two competing 'paradigms' for understanding the role of law in modern society, liberal-bourgeois formal law and social welfare 'materialized' law. Locating his argument beyond liberalism and republicanism, he characterizes modern liberalism as a concern with politics in value-plural societies as a process of interest aggregation. In contrast, modern republican arguments are seen to operate through positing a vision of shared ethical community which leaves little room for diversity and autonomy in relation to different conceptions of the good. While the first position leaves individuals in their private self-interestedness, the latter presumes an orientation to the common good as prior to individuals' private autonomy. Habermas attempts to capture what is productive in both of these positions and to develop an account which goes beyond the limitations of each. To do this he develops a procedural account of law and an account of democracy centred on the principle of communicative rationality. We will look at each in turn.

Habermas argues that the history of modern law has been dominated by liberal-bourgeois formal law and social welfare 'materialized' law (1996, p.195) and their respective understandings of the realization of basic rights and constitutional principles. He suggests that the former, liberal, paradigm is centred around the idea of formal equality, individual liberty and legal protection, and fails to recognize the need for positive social supports to participation and citizenship. The limitations of this paradigm provided the spur to the development of the social welfare paradigm. However, as we have seen, this latter paradigm has produced clientelism through failing to involve recipients of welfare measures in the interpretation of their own needs (1996, pp.221, 418–419, 429).

Habermas attempts to overcome the deficits of these two paradigms by analysing their failure to develop adequate accounts of the co-original character of public and private autonomy and of the internal relation between law and democracy: 'The complementary blindspots of the social-welfare and liberal paradigms of law stem from the same error: both paradigms misunderstand the legal 'constitution' of freedom as 'distribution' and assimilate it to the model of the equal distribution of acquired or allocated goods' (1996, p.419). Against these two images of law Habermas develops an account of the 'procedural paradigm'. Here, 'the normative key is autonomy' (1996, p.418). Habermas argues that public and private autonomy are reciprocally related:

... individual self-determination manifests itself in the exercise of those rights derived from legitimately produced norms. For this reason the equal distribution of rights cannot be detached from the public autonomy that enfranchised citizens can exercise only in common, by taking part in the practice of legislation. (1996, p.397)

He suggests that a system of five rights is necessary if citizens are to 'legitimately regulate their interactions and life contexts by means of positive law': rights to 'equal individual liberties'; membership rights; rights of legal protection and due process; rights of 'political autonomy' or participation; and social welfare rights, necessary if citizens are to be able to exercise the first four rights. These rights together underpin the production of legitimacy from legality by 'secur[ing] for citizens the exercise of their political autonomy' (1996, p.83, 122). (This argument is circular; on the question of whether this circularity is virtuous or vicious, see Benhabib (1996) and Gould (1996). Gould argues for a stronger defence of human rights than is provided by Habermas' discursively achieved account of legitimacy.) This account therefore claims that there is an internal relation between the legitimacy of law and democratic processes of will formation and leads us to consideration of Habermas' account of discursive democracy.

The concept of discursive democracy underpins Habermas' account of the procedural paradigm of law. He argues that, in pluralistic societies without comprehensive or metaphysical worldviews, the only source for the legitimacy of rules is democratic procedure. Thus 'discourse theory explains the legitimacy of law by means of procedures and communicative presuppositions that, once they are legally institutionalized, ground the supposition that the processes of making and applying law lead to rational outcomes' (1996, p.414). Habermas grounds his argument for discursive democracy on a conception of communicative rationality which, he argues, can be discerned within the practices of everyday language use.

We have seen in the previous section that Habermas suggests we distinguish between purposive rational and communicative action. Communicative action takes places essentially through language and refers to the interaction of at least two subjects; it is oriented toward reaching understanding (1984, pp.85–86). Habermas regards communicative action as the original or primary form of language use (1984, p.288). A number of writers have questioned the priority that Habermas gives to the communicative use of language. Thompson (1984) and Cooke (1994) provide detailed arguments on this point. For the purposes of this chapter we will accept Habermas' arguments for the moment, drawing out (in the next section) the implications of his account for the attempt to accommodate diverse cultural forms within the framing of welfare law and policy.

Habermas argues that the processes of rationalization have decentered the worldviews of subjects, providing three validity dimensions to speech: objective, social and subjective (1992c, pp.115–148). Each of these three dimensions and the claims associated with them – respectively, claims to propositional truth, normative rightness and subjective truthfulness – have their own standards of truth, falsity and justification, and can be challenged requiring the speaker to justify their claim. That is, speech acts raise claims to intersubjective recognition on the part of the speaker. Habermas argues that, in the context of the modern lifeworld where standards of absolute authority have broken down and subjects take a reflexive relation to their claims (contexts of 'postconventional communicative action'), communicative action can lead to open-ended and critical argumentation.

In developing a theory of argumentation Habermas aims to specify the idealizing presuppositions inherent in communicative action:

> ... in rational discourse, where the speaker seeks to convince his audience through the force of the better argument, we presuppose a dialogical situation that satisfies ideal conditions in a number of respects, including ... freedom of access, equal rights to participate, truthfulness on the part of participants, absence of coercion in taking positions, and so forth. (1993, p.56)

This account of argumentation operates as a regulative ideal; its horizon is an 'unlimited communication community' in which participants enter rational discourse with one another in an attempt to reach agreement concerning a contested issue (Habermas 1992a, p.260). Habermas does not argue that these conditions are usually realized in the contexts of practical discourse but, rather, that they are logically presupposed by entering into discourse at all and provide a counterfactual against which to assess actual discourses.

Habermas then applies this account of the potential for rationality inherent in everyday communicative action to contexts of public deliberation leading to legitimate lawmaking. He specifies this in terms of a discursive account of democracy in which the 'discourse principle' 'D' is formulated thus: 'Just those action norms are valid to which all possibly affected persons could agree as participants in rational discourses' (1996, p.107). This produces an account of law as gaining legitimacy from the possibility of consensus achieved through open democratic participation.

Habermas suggests that any issue of concern to participants should be thematized in informal public discussion and that this unconstrained dialogue will involve 'struggles over needs' and bring into discussion different 'visions of the good life' (1996, p.313–314). However, legitimate regulation can only be enacted once agreement has been reached about the norm in question. 'Only after a public "struggle for recognition"' (1996, p.314) can the formal political authorities take up these concerns and work them into legislation. 'And only the *regulation* of a newly defined criminal offence or the *implementation* of a social programme intervenes in the sphere of private life and changes formal responsibilities and existing practices' (1996, p.314, emphasis in text). In this account, therefore, regulation is only legitimate once agreed upon through a process of argumentation.

With this account of the procedural justification of law through discursive democracy, Habermas produces theoretical support for the demand that those subject to welfare policies be involved in their determination; such provisions 'require *the affected parties themselves* to conduct public discourses ... this contest over the interpretation of needs cannot be delegated to judges and officials, nor even to political legislators' (Habermas 1996, p.425–426, emphasis in text). Habermas' account therefore supports feminist and minority communities' concerns over the need for those affected by legislation to participate in its formulation, while avoiding assuming fixed identities or interests; specific concerns are the *starting point* for public discourses concerning the good of all. This offers an account which suggests the necessity of articulating differences within the framing of legislation and can therefore facilitate the formulation of legislation that is more sensitive to diverse needs than that which assumes the appropriate normative content of welfare provision.

If we refer back to the examples of colonization outlined in the previous section – the ways in which the procedures governing schools are determined and implemented and the ways in which family responsibilities are established and regulated – we can see that Habermas' proposals provide important theoretical justification for rethinking how such issues are dealt with. Habermas's argument suggests the reorganization of schools as micro-level public spheres in which, given a general framework of legal regulation of liberties and powers and framework of general taxation (to be decided within a broader legislative framework), those concerned with the life of a school together discuss and formulate appropriate aims and policies for their particular institution. Publication of results could then be carried out by schools themselves, or by local education authorities, in a manner which made clear the achievements made in relation to stated aims; these may vary widely between different schools.

Turning to feminist concerns that the provision of social support to women leaving partners has produced new forms of dependence and structures of control, we can see how Habermas' formulation for arriving at just laws moves this problem on (at least as one created by law). Where feminists have criticized the normative assumptions of social security legislation, pointing to the ways in which social provision has effected a shift from dependence on individual male breadwinners (private patriarchy) to dependence on the state (public patriarchy), this concern can be rephrased in Habermas' terms as a concern with the 'normalizing' effects of social welfare law which has conceived freedom as distribution and through which the terms and conditions of women's lives are subject to alienating forms of state social provision. That is, the formulation and implementation of social policies has *assumed* models of the family and of the normative behaviour of men and women (men's financial responsibilities for children, women's emotional and practical responsibilities). For example, the operation of agencies such as the CSA is experienced by women and men alike as a

coercive and penalizing force which interacts poorly with people's understandings of their familial relationships. The answer to this, in Habermas' terms, is
not a blanket treatment of women and men as the same, nor legislation which
assumes different roles for women and men, but rather is to be found in instituting
the conditions for ongoing public political discussion in which the respective
roles of women and men are thoroughly debated and society's assumptions
concerning the welfare of children and the independence and security of its
members are subject to critical scrutiny. Such public debate could provide an
important source for more responsive forms of legal provision.

The institutional framework with which Habermas proposes to entrench this
system for the discursive justification of law combines constitutional democracy
with independent associations in civil society forming 'strong' and 'weak' publics
respectively (1996, p.307). Habermas suggests that in this way it is possible to
bridge 'the gap between enlightened self-interest and orientation to the common
good, between the roles of client and citizen' (1992b, p.449). The next section
will consider to what extent this account of the discursive justification of the
welfare state attends to the demands for recognition of the plurality of forms of
life raised by feminist and minority struggles.

Communicative consensus

The previous section specified the way in which Habermas moves from an account
of the limits of previous understandings of law and democracy to a procedural
account of legitimation as produced through public discourse. From this view-
point, it is possible to throw new light on the ambivalent effects of the welfare
state. These are seen as the result of the inadequate grounding of welfare legislation in democratic sources of legitimacy; through failing to involve recipients of
welfare measures in the interpretation of their own needs, the social welfare paradigm turns law into an instrument of administration and severs it from its sources
of legitimacy. This produces a 'dialectic of empowerment and tutelage' (1996,
p.433): at the same time as extending private and civic autonomy, the welfare state
produces the 'passive enjoyment of paternalistically dispensed rights' (1996,
p.79) and forces conformity to 'a 'normal' work relation or standard pattern of
socialization' (1996, p.415). In this way, the welfare state produces 'forms of tutelage that convert the intended *authorization* for use of freedom into a *custodial
supervision*' (1996, p.416). The task, therefore, is to reconnect the welfare state
with processes of democratic legitimation so that 'the social welfare project' can
be 'pursued at a higher level of reflection' (1996, p.410).

In support of this thesis, we have seen that Habermas' appeals to feminist
campaigning and theoretical work has focused attention on the need for those in
receipt of benefits to be involved in the interpretation of their own needs (Fraser
1989, 1995; Phillips 1995; Young 1990). This account, in highlighting the
necessity of participation among all those concerned, guards against the

misapplication of generic concepts to diverse individuals and groups. It therefore provides powerful theoretical support for a major concern of feminist and minority critics of the welfare state who have criticized the welfare states' normalizing assumptions and called for the recognition of different ways of life in the framing of legislation.

However, Habermas' account of the way in which diverse voices can be brought into the legislative process produces a number of problems in attempting to justify the welfare state in the face of cultural diversity. We will address these by examining Habermas' account of the discursive justification of law through the appeal to *consensus* achieved under ideal conditions of argumentation. The requirement of consensus for the generation of just laws helps guard against illegitimate determinations of the good in the framing of legislation; however, this requirement also places severe limits on the form and extent of diversity which can be accommodated within this model. (For a detailed discussion of Habermas' attempt to provide a procedural response to the problem of pluralism, dealing more fully with his procedural account of justice, see Ashenden (1999b).)

The mobilization of consensus works at two levels in Habermas' argument: first, at the level of the definition of problems and issues to be addressed; second, in terms of the need to reach agreements concerning what to do about such issues once identified. Problems arise at both levels.

Taking the question of the need to reach agreement concerning the principles governing social life first, we can see that Habermas' account of the discursive justification of law in terms of agreement reached through open-ended processes of argumentation has positive implications for involving diverse perspectives in the making of legislation governing social policy. His account moves beyond blanket universalism and at the same time refuses to rest with particularist accounts of different cultures. Habermas shares with communitarianism a stress on the social bases of individuality; however, unlike communitarian forms of argument he argues that in modern pluralistic societies no common account of the good which is acceptable to all can be achieved. Instead, Habermas moves to provide a procedural account of justice derived from enhanced democratic dialogue. In this way, he attempts to produce an account of legitimate lawmaking which can both recognize diversity and achieve norms of justice which all can live by.

Habermas suggests that the proceduralist understanding of law and discursive conception of democracy 'is blind neither to unequal social conditions nor to cultural differences' (1996, p.113); rather than flattening diversity this system reveals it, requiring that differences are seen in increasingly context-sensitive ways (1996, p.116). This is right, to a point. In Habermas' account, substantive value orientations are the springboard for public discussion: discourse mobilizes the ethical concerns of subjects and brings them to debates concerning justice, generating communicative power which can then have an impact on formal democratic institutions. This maintains the situated character of discourses concerning justice: 'only real argument makes moral insight possible' (1990, p.57). Moreover, in processes of argumentation concerned to justify contested norms 'each must be able to place himself in the situation of all those who would be affected by the adoption of a questionable norm' (1993, p.49). Thus, the reversal of interpretive perspectives, the recognition of others' claims and enlarged understanding are built into this account. Habermas, therefore, does not seek to privatize the substantive ethical concerns of diverse groups but suggests that these should be the starting point for debates concerning justice.

However, difficulties emerge when we examine the way in which Habermas formulates grounds for the framing of just laws. Habermas articulates this in terms of a distinction between thematization and regulation (1996, pp.313–314). He suggests that any issue of concern to participants should be thematized in open public discussion. However, regulation is only legitimate once grounded upon agreement achieved through the process of argumentation. This account therefore forces differences back into the 'weak' public of public opinion: the legitimation of welfare (or any other) provisions requires *agreement* amongst all concerned.

We have seen that Habermas pays heed to the pluralism of modern societies by producing an idealized account of communicative consensus which, he argues, is implicit in all attempts to reach understanding. His concern is to reconstruct the conditions and presuppositions of democratic deliberation which, he argues, will lead to the formulation of rationally grounded, legitimate law. Here, Habermas makes a distinction between ethics and morality. While ethical deliberations rely on substantive, contextual understandings of the good and are rooted in particular ways of life, moral discourses aim at the 'impartial resolution of conflicts' and, as such, 'require a perspective freed of all egocentrism and ethnocentrism' (1996, p.97).

Habermas recognizes that political discourse involves pragmatic, ethical, and moral concerns; therefore, bargaining and the realization of conceptions of the good have a legitimate place within political decision making. In this, the substance of discussion is left to the participants themselves, the constitution is an 'unfinished project'. However, Habermas regards bargaining and ethical discourse as insufficient to ground the legitimacy of law in modern societies; the pluralism of such societies dictates that these considerations are framed within discourses of justice in which 'the good of all' is considered (1996, p.310). Thus he suggests that 'the question that has *priority* in legislative politics is how a matter can be regulated in the equal interest of all' (1996, p.282, emphasis in text). Habermas recognizes that actually existing constitutional states are permeated by ethics, suggesting that: 'the theory of rights in no way forbids the citizens of a democratic constitutional state to assert a conception of the good in their general legal order, a conception they either already share or have come to agree on through political discussion. It does, however, forbid them to privilege one form of life at the expense of others within the nation' (1992b, p.128)

This division between the ethical (substantive conceptions of the good) and the moral (procedural criteria of justice) raises a number of problems in thinking about the legitimacy of the welfare state. Habermas suggests that, where agreement cannot be reached about a contentious validity claim, participants should abstract from the specific issue in question until they reach agreement concerning overarching principles. Alternatively, where norms that become problematic are 'inextricably interwoven with individual self-descriptions of persons and groups' (1993, p.59), that is with substantive ethical conceptions of the good, he suggests that all we may be able to expect is a 'fair compromise' in which we must search for ways in which 'the integrity and coexistence of ways of life and worldviews that generate different ethical conceptions ... can be secured under conditions of equal rights' (1993, p.60).

Habermas raises this question of the relation between ethical conceptions of the good and moral considerations with the example of abortion. However, there are many such areas of fundamental conflict of belief in contemporary societies; for example, concerning the place of religious education in schools and in terms of the rights of single parents and same-sex couples to raise children. Some form of legislation governing these issues is inevitable. Habermas' account suggests that, where fundamental disagreements exist, we try to agree overarching principles such as equal respect for all religious beliefs, the rights of individuals to live their lives according to personal choices, and so on. However, whilst it may be possible to agree on a set of minimal constitutional principles in a secular society in which individuals have 'the right to remain strangers' (1996, p.308), it is unclear that this stipulation will carry the weight of the welfare state rather than ruling out from consideration positive social supports. The latter, though, are required by Habermas' specification of the five rights necessary to the realization of public and private autonomy.

We can clarify this problem by referring to the examples of the ordering of family life and of schools set out earlier. There is likely to be more tolerance of alternative forms of family life if the families concerned do not require public support than if they do. In education, profound disagreements may occur in relation to the school curriculum. In a plural society there are likely to be religious groups as well as secular communities. Some of these groups may regard religion as intrinsic to the educational goals of a school and, on this basis, may require different curricular content for male and female children. In the face of disagreements about this, where some participants will see education as a 'merit good' and therefore demand equal provision and curriculum content for all children, others may stress that this is inappropriate and violates the rights of their culture to decide upon appropriate education for their young. It is not clear that in such a situation a 'fair compromise' can be reached. Viewing schools as purely secular institutions does not solve this problem since this is to override rather than to respect the fundamental ethical concerns of sections of the community. Furthermore, even if there is agreement amongst those *directly* concerned with a school, they may decide policies unacceptable to a broader community of tax-payers and citizens. This raises a question concerning who 'all those concerned' with a contentious issue are in any particular case. What are the boundaries of the community concerned with a school? Parents, teachers and governors certainly, but also others in the community who may have strong views about education. To give schools wide-ranging liberties in relation to such questions as curricular content potentially threatens the broader consensus among citizens concerning the public provision of education: why should I, as a taxpayer and participant in several communities, consent to fund educational provision with which I have profound disagreements stemming from my concern that the public education system should be egalitarian in its aims and policies? Habermas' account suggests that in such contexts broad public debate will be necessary; this does more to point to an already existing tension between plurality and consensus than to resolve these issues. If consensus cannot be achieved, how are we to proceed?

Further questions are raised if we examine more closely Habermas' account of discourse. Here, the question of the definition of issues to be addressed comes to the fore (my first point above). Habermas distinguishes discourses of justification and application and their respective principles of universalization and appropriateness (1996, p.162). He suggests that in discourses of justification participants abstract from their specific ethical concerns to consider the good of all. This involves a set of strong idealizing presuppositions, including 'the supposition that all participants in dialogue use the same linguistic expression with *identical meanings*' (1992c, pp.46–47, my emphasis). Habermas argues that this is often counterfactual but remains unavoidable if such discourses are to transcend merely local standards of validity and be capable of generating universalizable norms. Discourses of justification thus refer to 'standard situations' (1996, p.162, my emphasis) in which what is at issue has been agreed upon by participants before they generate a universally valid norm.

Habermas argues that discourses of justification provide only indeterminate norms, which must remain indeterminate due to the unforeseeable aspects of future situations (1996, p.217). Discourses of justification therefore require the supplement of discourses of application. Discourses of application involve a different logic of argumentation from that of justification, resting on a principle of appropriateness to the specific situation in which 'the relevant features have been described as completely as possible' (1996, p.172). 'What must be determined here is which of the norms already accepted as valid is appropriate in a given case in the light of *all the relevant features of the situation conceived as exhaustively as possible*' (1993, p.14, my emphasis). Thus they refer not to a norm's validity but to its 'appropriate reference to a situation' (1996, p.217) and require a determination of 'which descriptions of the facts are significant and *exhaustive for interpreting the situation* in a disputed case' (1996, pp.217–218, my emphasis). Habermas suggests that 'participants in an application discourse must work their *different interpretations of the same situation* into a normatively rich description of the circumstances that does not simply abstract from the existing difference in perception' (1996, p.229, my emphasis). He describes this as 'a sensitive, noncoercive coordination of different interpretive perspectives' (1996, p.229).

Difficulties for our concern with the recognition of cultural diversity arise within both moments of this process of argumentative justification and application. These difficulties concern the definition of a 'standard case', the assumption that participants give identical meanings to terms in discourses of justification, and the idea that discourses of application are centrally concerned with resolving different interpretations of the same situation which has been exhaustively described.

To specify the difficulties involved here we need to return to Habermas' account of the three validity dimensions of speech (see previous section). Habermas distinguishes claims to propositional truth, normative rightness and subjective truthfulness; he argues that, in the context of postconventional communicative action, each of these have their own standards of justification. Further, in Habermas' account questions of propositional truth and of normative rightness or morality admit universality; they raise claims which reach beyond local contexts, whereas ethical deliberations and expressive acts of subjective truthfulness are regarded as bound by local context (1996, p.97). Thus Habermas distinguishes between propositional, normative and expressive uses of language and restricts truth claims to the propositional content and normative rightness of utterances. That is, ethical, expressive claims and the world creating and disclosing functions of language do not have the weight of propositional and normative claims. Habermas splits off expressive speech acts from the domain of truth and universalizability because they are first person, disclosing inner experience which can only be validated by reference to the speakers' truthfulness, and as such they raise 'no clear-cut validity claim' (Habermas, quoted in Cooke 1994, p.75). However, this raises a problem for the recognition of cultural diversity in the framing of legislation insofar as cultures prefigure not only *what* will be struggled over but also *how* such struggles are expressed.

This limitation in Habermas' account of speech acts has been commented upon in relation to the question of aesthetic experience and in relation to the use of irony and the making of jokes (Cooke 1994; Thompson 1984). I want to suggest that the expressive use of language is inextricably tied to the question of culture and to argue that Habermas' failure to do justice to the expressive functions of language feeds back critically into the potential for his account of the discursive justification of law to deal adequately with cultural pluralism.

In splitting the expressive functions of language from claims to validity Habermas is assuming that what is said can be separated from the manner of its expression, in effect that all claims to cultural recognition can be paraphrased. We can question this presupposition by developing an insight of Wittgenstein's:

> We speak of understanding a sentence in the sense in which it can be replaced by another which says the same; but also in the sense in which it cannot be replaced by any other ... In the one case the thought in the sentence is something common to different sentences; in the other, something is expressed only by these words in these positions. (Understanding a poem; 1968, §531)

Here, Wittgenstein makes the simple but important point that there is more than one sense of understanding: I do not understand a poem unless I can give a paraphrase of it, but equally I do not understand the poem unless I recognize the difference between it and the paraphrase. In other words, the expressive functions of language, how something is said, cannot be wholly separated from what is said. While clearly all communication involves some level of translation, there are limits to the depth of understanding that this gives. My point is not the relativist one that translation between cultures is impossible, but rather that some aspects of the expressive use of language (as well as gestures and other non-linguistic forms of expression) are intrinsic to meaning. Habermas, by precluding this aspect of public speech from claiming validity, produces an unnecessarily limited model of discourse: if only propositional and normative validity claims can finally carry weight in democratic dialogue, if expressive forms of speech are ruled out from claiming such validity, this excludes a great deal of diversity a priori. (Iris Marion Young (1996) makes an argument for the importance of greeting, rhetoric and storytelling to inclusive forms of democratic dialogue, especially where previously excluded groups do not present their concerns in the form of rational argumentation. Devaluing styles of speech other than rational argument may have the effect of ensuring that those voices that already dominate discussions continue to do so.)

Habermas, in dividing the expressive role of language from its use in making propositional statements and normative claims, has the peculiar effect of reducing the weight of his claim that all those subject to a law should be able to participate in its formulation. If we can imagine a speech situation in which participants all use language in the same way and discuss a situation which has been exhaustively described, then why is it necessary that all those concerned participate? Why can these concerns not be paraphrased?

Conclusion

Claims for recognition by diverse groups have challenged the limits of a distributive, aggregative and universalist paradigm of welfare with the claim that different ways of life should be recognized within the formulation and delivery of social policies. Here, Habermas' work can help to explain why such struggles for recognition have emerged and the character of their challenge to contemporary welfare states.

Feminists and ethnic minority critics of the welfare state have focused on the normalizing character of social provision which has either forced individuals and groups into particular ways of life or excluded them from the benefits of state provision. Habermas' suggestion that we move to a procedural understanding of the legitimacy of law, derived from open and inclusive democratic dialogue, attempts to reground the welfare state through discursively achieved consensus concerning the norms governing social existence. This is a bold formulation, and the aspirations which animate it are the source of a great deal of debate in contemporary societies.

Habermas' account offers a potential way of recognizing difference whilst maintaining a focus on the importance of the inclusive character of political debate, thus moving beyond the idea of the polity as an undifferentiated whole and at the same time refusing the isolation and fragmentation that can accompany the politics of difference. However, by privileging consensus as the goal of political dialogue and by excluding the expressive aspects of language from playing a full role in such contexts, Habermas' approach is limited in its capacity to deal with rather than to transcend or marginalize diversity.

Habermas assumes that differences can be subsumed within an overarching account of justice and on this basis forwards a procedural account for the generation of just norms. Here, Habermas could be said to be trying to produce an account of argumentation without culture or with culture 'bracketed'. This offers a voice to diverse groups in the framing of legislation – any issue of concern can be thematized by participants, but severely delimits the terms in which such groups can argue for anything. Thus, this account threatens to transcend rather than to recognize diverse forms of life. For Habermas, such transcendence is not to be regarded as loss but as progression; his argument rests upon an evolutionary theory of societal rationalization in which traditional ways of life succumb to entropy in the form of the pluralization of worldviews. This requires Habermas to privilege modernity as the condition in which it becomes possible reflexively to generate universal norms, and yet it appears that this condition of modernity is one in which the question of culture cannot adequately be addressed.

Acknowledgements

I would like to thank Mike Rustin and Kelvin Knight for their helpful comments on an earlier draft of this chapter.

References

Ashenden, S. (1999) 'Questions of criticism: Habermas and Foucault on civil society and resistance.' In S. Ashenden and D. Owen (eds) *Foucault contra Habermas*. London: Sage.

Ashenden, S. (1998) 'Pluralism within the limits of reason alone? Habermas and the discursive negotiation of consensus.' *Critical Review of International Social and Political Theory*, 2.

Ball, W. and Solomos, J. (1990) (eds) *Race and Local Politics*. London: Macmillan.

Benhabib, S. (1996) 'Toward a deliberative model of democratic legitimacy.' In S. Benhabib (ed) *Democracy and Difference: Contesting the Boundaries of the Political.* New Jersey: Princeton.

Butler, J. (1998) 'Merely cultural?' *New Left Review, 227,* 33–44.

Cooke, M. (1994) *Language and Reason: A Study of Habermas's Pragmatics.* Massachusetts: Massachusetts Institute of Technology Press.

Donald, J. and Rattansi, A. (1992) (eds) *'Race', Culture and Difference.* London: Sage.

Foucault, M. (1977) *Discipline and Punish: the Birth of the Prison* (translated by A. Sheridan). London: Penguin.

Foucault, M. (1979) *The History of Sexuality: Volume 1* (translated by R. Hurley). London: Penguin.

Fraser, N. (1989) *Unruly Practices: Power, Discourse and Gender in Contemporary Social Theory.* Cambridge: Polity Press.

Fraser, N. (1995) 'From redistribution to recognition? Dilemmas of justice in a "post-socialist" age.' *New Left Review, 212,* 68–93.

Gilroy, P. (1987) *There Ain't No Black in the Union Jack.* London: Hutchinson.

Gould, C. (1996) 'Diversity and democracy: Representing differences.' In S. Benhabib (ed) *Democracy and Difference: Contesting the Boundaries of the Political.* New Jersey: Princeton.

Habermas, J. (1976) *Legitimation Crisis* (trans. T. McCarthy). London: Heinemann.

Habermas, J. (1984) *The Theory of Communicative Action Volume 1: Reason and the Rationalization of Society* (translated by T. McCarthy). London: Heinemann.

Habermas, J. (1987) *The Theory of Communicative Action Volume 2: Lifeworld and System* (translated by T. McCarthy). Cambridge: Polity Press.

Habermas, J. (1990) *Moral Consciousness and Communicative Action* (translated by C. Lenhardt and S.W. Nicholson). Cambridge: Polity Press.

Habermas, J. (1992a) *Autonomy and Solidarity,* (ed. P. Dews). London: Verso.

Habermas, J. (1992b) 'Further reflections on the public sphere.' In C. Calhoun (ed) *Habermas and the Public Sphere.* Massachusetts: Massachusetts Institute of Technology Press.

Habermas, J. (1992c) *Postmetaphysical Thinking* (translated by W.M. Hohengarten). Cambridge: Polity Press.

Habermas, J. (1993) *Justification and Application* (translated by C. Cronin). Cambridge: Polity Press.

Habermas, J. (1994) 'Struggles for recognition in the democratic constitutional state.' In A. Gutman and C. Taylor (eds) *Multiculturalism.* New Jersey: Princeton.

Habermas, J. (1996) *Between Facts and Norms: Contributions to a Discourse Theory of Law and Democracy* (trans. W. Rehg). Cambridge: Polity.

Hernes, H. (1987) 'Women and the welfare state: The transition from private to public dependence.' In A. Showstack-Sassoon (ed) *Women and the State.* London: Hutchinson.

Hirst, P.Q. (1997) *From Statism to Pluralism: Democracy, Civil Society and Global Politics.* London: University College London Press.

Honneth, A. (1991) *The Critique of Power: Reflective Stages in a Critical Social Theory* (translated by K. Baynes). Massachusetts: Massachusetts Institute of Technology Press.

Lister, R. (1997) *Citizenship: Feminist Perspectives.* London: Macmillan.

MacIntyre, A. (1994) 'The theses on Feuerbach: A road not taken.' In K. Knight (1998) (ed) *The MacIntyre Reader.* Cambridge: Polity.

Marshall, T.H. (1949) 'Citizenship and social class.' Republished in *Sociology at the Crossroads* (1963). London: Heinemann.

Phillips, A. (1995) *The Politics of Presence.* Oxford: Clarendon Press.

Showstack-Sassoon, A. (1987) (ed) *Women and the State.* London: Hutchinson.

Thompson, E.P. (1975) *Whigs and Hunters: The Origin of the Black Act.* New York: Pantheon Books.

Thompson, J.B. (1984) *Studies in the Theory of Ideology.* Cambridge: Polity Press.

Walby, S. (1990) *Theorizing Patriarchy.* Oxford: Blackwell.

Williams, F. (1989) *Social Policy: A Critical Introduction.* Cambridge: Polity Press.

Wilson, E. (1977) *Women and the Welfare State.* London: Tavistock.

Wilson, E. (1980) *Only Halfway to Paradise: Women in Post-War Britain, 1945–1968.* London: Tavistock.

Wittgenstein, L. (1968) *Philosophical Investigations* (translated by G.E.M. Anscombe). Oxford: Basil Blackwell.

Young, I.M. (1990) *Justice and the Politics of Difference.* New Jersey: Princeton.

Young, I.M. (1996) 'Communication and the other: Beyond deliberative democracy.' In S. Benhabib (ed) *Democracy and Difference: Contesting the Boundaries of the Political.* New Jersey: Princeton.

Young, I.M. (1997) 'Unruly categories: A critique of Nancy Fraser's dual systems theory.' *New Left Review, 222,* 147–60.

CHAPTER 12

Cultural Perspectives and Welfare Regimes
The Contributions of Foucault and Lefebvre

Caroline Knowles

This chapter considers the impact of cultural perspectives on the ways in which we think about welfare regimes. The *cultural turn*, as Clarke and Newman's (1998, p.5) excellent discussion of welfare under Labour's Third Way suggests, involves thinking about welfare regimes as a kind of generative culture in which those things usually considered to be contextual are instead seen as producing that which we seek to understand. The cultural turn inserts context into the centre of the analytical frame highlighting processes of social formation. It has a vast intellectual hinterland and an impressive conceptual tool box. The purpose of this chapter is to take out one or two of its tools and review their analytical value and practical utility in understanding particular aspects of welfare. Specifically, I will argue that cultural perspectives make it possible for us to understand the transactions between welfare regimes and their subjects and the generation and operation of the professional/power regimes in which these transactions are situated.

Foucault's concepts of *disciplinarity, discourse* and the *professional gaze* provide a means of understanding the matrices of professional power which make up the loosely connected regimes of welfare which operate in any given jurisdiction. These are useful concepts for understanding the mechanisms by which systems like child protection, informal caring, care of the elderly and psychiatry are produced and maintained. But, I shall argue, these concepts are limited by their ability to describe regimes only in terms of their professional practices and policy contexts. They are not able to generate an account of welfare subjects themselves and the ways in which they interface with the regimes through which their lives are organized. In terms of Foucault's framework the transactions between welfare regimes and their subjects is a one way business dominated by the constitution of the regime itself. The only effective forms of human agency and subjectivity in this cluster of concepts consists of the exercise of forms of professional agency by those whose work practices organize the regimes themselves. I shall argue that a properly transactional analysis needs to open a space in which the effectiveness of human agency and the production of subjectivities can be seen and taken into account in describing welfare systems. Lefebvre's (1996) concept of *space as a domain of social practices and social relationships* extends Foucault's analysis of regimes by opening up the other (agency and subjectivity) side of welfare transactions for analysis. Foucault and Lefebvre are philosophically connected, but contribute different things to the cultural space. They are contributors to the same conceptual tool kit in that each extends and challenges, rather than disturbs or displaces, the other. They are further connected in that both inputs are necessary in order to sustain a two-sided transactional analysis of welfare regimes and their subjects. A brief sketching-in of their intellectual genealogy will make some of the connections between Foucault's and Lefebvre's work a bit clearer.

Both Foucault and Lefebvre display in their work the markings of their particular dialogues with Marxism. Foucault's decentred conception of power is clearly a response to the centralizing tendencies of Marxist notions of state power as the political expression of capitalist interests. In offering discourse and the professional gaze as constitutive of social context, Foucault displaces the Marxist concept of ideology. Discourses are simply positioned by other discourses and their myriad relationships to the strategies of power constituting specific regimes: there is no need for an underlying system of ideas in which the dominant power relations are inscribed and articulated. Lefebvre's political analysis clearly bears the imprint of Marxism. He uses the concept of *commodification* to describe forms of subjectivity. Human alienation is the catalyst for a search for meaning and its fragile and unsatisfactory resolution in forms of consumption. Lefebvre's project in *Everyday Life in the Modern World* (1994) is the rescue of human subjectivity (not a Marxist theme) from the internalized terror of the economic arrangement of (consumer) society (very much a Marxist concept). Lefebvre firmly objects to the 'terrorist' (capitalist) society and its regimes of privilege and poverty. And he redeploys the 'dialectic' in a non-reductive account of the generation of social processes (Lefebvre 1994).

Lefebvre, and to some extent de Certeau (1988), effectively develop what is latent in Foucault's framework. The implied spatiality of Foucault's panopticon as a regime of power is evident in Lefebvre's insistence on the significance of the social relationships and practices of space. Lefebvre (1994, p.159) is evidently persuaded by Foucault's account of the controlling power of bureaucracy, although for him this takes on a more territorial form. Lefebvre's (and de Certeau's) concept of the 'quotidian', of everyday life activity and practice, broadens Marx's preoccupation with production and is rescued from an otherwise rather narrow concern with micro-systems by Foucault's broader social analysis of the ways in which regimes as a whole operate. It is the influence of Foucault and Marx which diverts Lefebvre from the logic of his own analysis which stresses the particular, the local, the individual and the parochial. Without losing sight of the bigger picture into which the smaller pieces fit, Lefebvre's analytical framework is able to see the tensions between the local and the global and the individual and the social as a mutually generative dialectic which does not collapse one into the other.

What follows is a discussion of the analytical possibilities which are opened up by Foucault's concepts of disciplinarity, discourse and the professional gaze and Lefebvre's concept of space as a domain of social relationships and social practices. I shall show that each of these concepts contributes significantly to our understanding of the transactions between welfare regimes and their subjects and how this yields specific targets for welfare reform. The theoretical arguments offered are grounded in examples drawn from the author's own research, which is primarily concerned with a particular regime in the operation of the community mental health care system in Montreal and the ways in which it deals with those who have serious and persistent mental health problems.

The displacement of Marxist formulations of state power, as centralized and forged by the social relations of capitalist society, by Foucault's concept of disciplinarity – most clearly set out in Discipline and Punish (1977), but also in The Birth of the Clinic (1973) – brought a paradigmatic shift in social analysis which is now so taken for granted that it is rarely acknowledged or discussed. Although decentred notions of power, operating through the myriad mechanisms of disciplinary society, have become a part of the implicit knowledge by which we navigate the social world, it is worth pausing to consider the impact of this shift on the ways in which we are able to think about welfare regimes. Centralized conceptions of power came with clear-cut social relationships of domination, exploitation and subordination and clear, if rather daunting, programmes of social reform which involved major realignment of the social fabric. Foucauldian concepts of disciplinarity, on the other hand, implicate any set of operations, actions or social relationships, from the organization of time and space to pedagogical methods, as having a directing effect on what people do and the social orders in which they do it. Decentred power resides in timetabling, in organization, in bureaucratic structures, in the arrangement of space, the operation of the gaze; in fact, in any set of processes with a definite outcome – this is *disciplinarity*. In the context of welfare regimes, as in other contexts, disciplinarity shapes lives by organizing the conditions in which they can be lived. The practices of kindly nurses, social workers and home carers are brought into the analytical frame as constituting micro-welfare contexts on much the same terms as 'the state' itself, and producers of academic discourse need to be mindful of the social impact of the knowledge they produce. Disciplinarity then implicates all of us, and the practical actions which make up everyday routines. The unscrupulous exploiter and the well-intentioned liberal both become targets for critical analysis and social reform. The oppressed and their advocates are all implicated in multiple regimes of social management, and this insight significantly shifts the ways in which we might think about the social relationships of welfare.

This shift to seeing welfare regimes as the product of interfacing disciplinary mechanisms means that we can think about regimes as the outcome of definite practices, and that we can think about welfare subjects as the product of particular mechanisms. We can identify which mechanisms produce specific groups of welfare subjects and the terms in which they do this. This allows us to draw distinctions which are not otherwise apparent. For example, the homeless appear to be a fairly unitary group of subjects by virtue of a common, marginal and precarious position in relation to housing and job markets. They also, at first sight, appear to be relatively unregulated in comparison with other groups of welfare subjects. However, neither of these two propositions is correct if we review the disciplinary mechanisms which produce them as a social category.

The homeless who live on the street are the product of quite different mechanisms from those who live in homeless shelters. Both groups are highly regulated but not by the same disciplinary devices. The lives of the homeless living on the street are in fact regulated by the regimes of public space and the terms on which it may be occupied. Is begging allowed? Overlooked? What are the routines by which this is successfully executed? Who is allowed to occupy which spaces and for how long before they are moved on? On what terms are the homeless allowed to use commercial space? What notions of territory, provision, danger and risk produce the restless migratory movements of the homeless? The lives of the homeless living in shelters (in Montreal where we did our research), however, are organized by other forms of discipline. Their lives are organized, not by the need to remain invisible like their counterparts on the street, but by the discipline of constant supervision even in the normally private activities of washing and sleeping. They are the product of the discipline enforced by the temporal arrangement of the day: there are times to get up, eat, go out for the day, return to reserve a bed, and go to sleep. Their conduct is regulated by rules of exclusion which require certain standards of conduct and which are enforced in shelter reception areas from behind Perspex shields with the aid of the local police when necessary. Dining occurs in a particular way. The food eaten lives in a grey area beyond shelf life and is not, under other circumstances, considered suitable for human consumption. Clothes are taken away and washed (showers are compulsory) and recirculated to other wearers. Things such as clothes are *used* and not owned. Shelter users' and shelter workers' behaviour is directed by certain assumptions about who the users are and what they must do. All of these (sometimes) gentle and well intentioned forms of discipline significantly shape the lives which can be led in shelters and the implied social value associated with them. The fact that the homeless can and do migrate between these two distinctive forms of homelessness says a great deal about the significance of individual human agency, but more about that later. The point here is that disciplinary mechanisms produce distinctive versions of lives and so provide a way of distinguishing groups of welfare subjects from each other. The mechanisms dealing with homelessness clearly sustain an edifice of moral and social assumptions about the social value of homeless people and the forms of subjectivity of which they are capable. The mechanisms dealing with child protection, for example, sustain quite different versions of subjectivity and social value.

Disciplinarity then has a number of analytic advantages. It provides a means of making broad as well as quite fine distinctions between categories of welfare subjects. It draws attention to the organization and routines of particular welfare apparatuses and provides a means of discussing those apparatuses. It grounds social analysis in the production of lives. And it makes us think about the broader frameworks within which local situations are set: people move into shelters in order to qualify for welfare payments, they comply with psychiatric diagnoses and conceptions of morbidity because they carry higher benefits and so on. Some important aspects of the transactions between welfare regimes and their subjects can be better understood by means of Foucault's concept of disciplinarity.

While it is clear from the comments above that Foucault's concept of disciplinarity has substantial analytic purchase in posing crucial and critical questions about the macro and the micro operations of specific parts of welfare regimes through their regulatory apparatuses, Foucault's framework has a limited explanatory value. It cannot explain (to pursue the example just cited) why or how the homeless are distributed between these two categories of street and shelter life. How can we explain this? The key, and this involves a significant development of Foucault's understanding of disciplinarity, is to see disciplinarity as a two-way interactive set of processes in which human agents interface with the mechanisms dealing with them. This involves a conceptual shift from systems to agent/systems interaction. The homeless enter shelters with their own bundles of hostility, expectations, fears (about danger, dirt and disease), rejections and successes with which they set about negotiating their use of these spaces with workers, volunteers and other users. They make decisions about which forms of discipline to accept or contest, and they move between shelters and between shelters and the street in order to be able to live in one way rather than another. Transactions between welfare regimes and their subjects have two (unequal) sides.

By adding *agency*, as infinitely varied and interactive, to *disciplinarity* we can think about the varieties of welfare subjects' lives and subjectivities. And we can ask some searching questions about the mechanisms which would need to be in place for other kinds of lives and subjectivities to be produced. These are, of course, judgements requiring a normative framework in which it is possible to think about 'improvement'. What, for example, would happen to the lives lived in homeless shelters if more conventional forms of privacy were instated and respected? What would happen if everyone had a private room? What would happen if timetabling became more flexible and greater participation by users was encouraged? How would we have to reform disciplinary mechanisms in order to produce forms of subjectivity which had higher levels of self determination and hence come closer to notions of social citizenship which hold for the rest of the population? Structures allowing greater self determination could narrow the gap between shelter lives and other lives. The advantage of disciplinarity – particularly a disciplinarity which is negotiated by the exercise of human agency – is that it sustains a 'tinkering approach' to welfare in which minor adjustments are seen as steps towards bigger social changes: inconceivable in the context of conceptualizations of power as a centralized property of polarized social and economic relationships.

Discourse, along with disciplinarity, is also a key element in the generation of welfare regimes which has an impact upon the ways in which regimes deal with their subjects. This too marks Foucault as a cultural theorist in quite a new way. Discourse analysis, in the sense in which Foucault conceptualized it in *The Archeology of Knowledge* (originally published in 1972), provides a grid in which certain questions can be posed about the arrangement and construction of objects of (professional) knowledge and the conditions in which some meanings gain ascendancy over others (Knowles 1992). How does this approach to discourse affect the ways in which we see welfare regimes? It allows us to conceptualize particular regimes and their target populations as composed through the various discourses which converge around them. Like disciplinarity, discourse is a constituting activity in which certain objects and meanings take priority over others. Take the case of the discourses which converge on single mothers in Britain or the United States. These feature in broad political pronouncements about the value of family life, in discourses concerning the nature of poverty, individual responsibility and social justice – such as those articulated by the Labour Party since it won the last election – and so on. Political discourses offer important parameters within which welfare regimes, and those who might be targeted for special help, can be identified as deserving/undeserving and dealt with accordingly. Specific policy departures – changes in child benefit or significant shifts in state responsibility for nursery education – have somehow to negotiate these discourses and the social priorities embedded in them. Discourses, in other words, are greatly contextualized by, and in turn contextualize, other discourses: discourses in which constituencies of subjects, objectives and so on are identified and dealt with; in which one version of social justice takes priority over others; and in which multiple possible meanings are massaged into one.

In this framework concepts like social justice and the policies into which it might conceivably be unpacked have no essential meaning of their own, but are given (contextual) meaning in the arenas in which they emerge and achieve operational effectiveness. Comparing, for example, different agency discourses (often considerations of philosophy, principles and practice) on the risk of child abuse can reveal important cleavages and convergence between agencies over the meaning of risk itself. In Canada, for example, there is a wide gap between child protection agencies' and perinatal medicine's conception of risk and family failure. Less accustomed to dealing directly with poverty, paediatric discourse often construes risk as an adjunct of poverty and single parenting, while child protection agencies are more discerning, not least because they are in the front line when it comes to finding alternatives to failed or dangerous families (Knowles 1996). Agencies operating around childhood work with different versions of what childhood (and motherhood and fatherhood for that matter) consists of. They draw upon other discourses containing psychoanalytic and psychological expertise, so all claims to expert knowledge must be carefully considered for their implied agendas.

Discourse, then, encourages us to think about welfare regimes as the product of shifting meanings, priorities and professional responsibilities. Different versions of 'reality' are not simply correct or incorrect, but more or less plausible in a given context and invoke their own moral and political values. Discourse, in the sense in which Foucault conceptualizes it, provides an important critical tool for comparing different versions of social roles and policy contexts. How is the child at risk different from the child as an object of pedagogical intervention? Asking these questions provides a way of understanding agencies themselves through their constituting discourses and the welfare regimes in which they operate. Discourse is also a means of imagining change, reconceptualizing welfare subjects and their problems, by asking what alternate versions of 'the child', 'social justice', 'the elderly' and so on are possible. And what are the policy or practice implications of these alternatives?

The problem with discourse, as Foucault failed to alert us, is precisely its relationship to practice. This is not in the least straightforward. As well as articulating the reflected-upon dimensions of practice, discourse may also act as a repository for things which cannot operate as practice, but which stand in for practice as an intention or principle. Discourse can be an inventory of the unattainable as Lefebvre (1994, p.185) reminds us. 'Thus we have a society that is obsessed with dialogue, communication, participation, integration and coherence, all the things it lacks ...' Inter-agency cooperation in community mental health care between social services and providers of psychiatric services is a case in point. The way things are presently structured in Britain, and for that matter in Canada too, mental health and social services are competing budgetary turf. Arguably cooperation is so firmly defended as a principle precisely because it cannot be enforced in practice. So statements of lofty intent coexist with the passing around of the seriously mentally ill between budgetary jurisdictions like so many hot potatoes. Discourse is a register of unimplementable intention just as much as an articulation and reflection of practice. It can also be other things, including more deliberate attempts to mislead through impression management. A good example of this is the Canadian Federal Government's generation of discourses on child abuse and protection, issues for which it has no direct administrative responsibility as these are dealt with on a provincial basis. Initially dazzled by the progressive sophistication and attention to the position of women outlined in these discourses, the fact that most provinces lacked an effective system of child protection at all had completely escaped me as a researcher. Discourse alone is of limited use. It is only of importance when contextualized by practical intervention, actions and behaviour.

The third Foucauldian concept I want to consider for its contribution to the ways in which we think about welfare regimes and their subjects is the *professional gaze*. The significance of the professional gaze in generating subjectivities has been convincingly argued by those who have developed this concept rather more than by Foucault himself. Nikolas Rose's *Governing the Soul* (1989) and Parker *et al.*'s (1995) *Deconstructing Psychopathology* have focused attention on those whose lives are produced through welfare regimes' systems of expert knowledge. Psychiatry and psychology (Rose's 'psy' industries) have been thoroughly considered as domains in which subjectivities are marked out and defined by systems of professional expertise: de-naturalized and repositioned through professional gazes and their discourses. Rose, for example, documents the constituting gaze of developmental psychology on the child and through this the governance of individual subjectivity in the private domain of the family and its emotional economy. What Rose details is a form of self-inflicted disciplinarity on the conduct of private family behaviour – the perfection of Benthams's (and Foucault's) panopticon – self, and fellow citizen, regulation. Rose's argument demonstrates most effectively how we are all implicated in the forms of disciplinarity which shape our own lives through the ways in which we see ourselves and others.

Parker *et al.* (1995) offers an excellent account of what is taken for granted in the *modus operandi* of psychiatrists in clinical settings. They develop Foucault's notion of the professional gaze in psychiatry, aired only in passing in *Madness and Civilization* where Foucault is more concerned with the separation of reason and unreason in Western culture. Foucault and, subsequently, Parker *et al.* (1995, p.67) make the point that professional practices are part of the broader cultural context in which they are situated: that professional and popular versions of the world are intimately connected. Parker *et al.*'s (1995, p.75) argument is that mad subjectivities are mostly formulated in clinical discourses and agency gazes. Clinical discourse, they contend, is so ubiquitous that it is impossible for the mad to imagine themselves in other terms: 'a place is marked out for them.' Professional gazes, in concert with discipline and discourse, hence constitute those whose lives they administer on certain terms. This insight changes the way we see welfare regimes by opening up a space in which we can speculate about what these terms and the subjectivities associated with them might be: subjectivities, of course, are contingent and contextual. We might want to ask: what is it possible to be under the professional gaze of psychiatry or under the gaze of child protection agencies? What are the imagined (or contested) human capacities allowed by these gazes? And what are the means by which those capacities are recognized, deployed and reshaped?

To conceptualize subjectivities as the product of professional gazes, discourses and specific disciplinary mechanisms only, as suggested earlier, overlooks the importance of human agency and exposes the limitations of Foucault's one-sided framing. A broader and more practical concept which incorporates elements of discourse, disciplinarity and practice and the effectiveness of human agency is *administrative action*: a concept involving a creative departure from Foucault through Lefebvre. Administrative action concerns the ways in which people are dealt with by agencies and their professionals and involves a complex interaction between agencies and those whose lives they position, along the lines suggested earlier in the example of the homeless. Posed in this way, subjectivities are interactive projects in which subjects enter into negotiations with those who deal with them about who and what they are, and what these meanings and identities sustain in terms of treatment or entitlement. Meanings attached to subjectivities worked through popular culture are obviously also a part of these processes. Agencies, like psychiatry, have to deal with what people think madness and psychiatry is, just as the mad have to negotiate popular and professional conceptions concerning the nature and meaning of madness. These are not simple processes.

Our research in Montreal collecting life-story narratives with (often homeless) users of community psychiatric services shows that the mad themselves do indeed subscribe to theories of schizophrenia which resonate with those of psychiatrists' discourses and professional gazes. But their conceptions also, unsurprisingly, resonate with those bandied about in popular culture; with their own theories about their lives and its sequences of events and relationships; with theories of good and evil; with illness as a punishment for social dysfunction; and with 'conspiracy theories of psychiatry' which are supported by an overly panoptical society and its cultures of public surveillance. Personal narratives then are as important as professional discourses/gazes in understanding user perspectives, and these are as much a part of welfare cultures as the professional gazes which seemingly dominate them. This departure from Foucault and Lefebvre (for neither encourages the collection of personal narratives, even though their frameworks do not preclude it) encourages us to look not just at welfare regimes themselves but also at the manner in which they are used. The homeless, in the example cited earlier, use shelters and other resources like soup kitchens in particular ways: ways which we cannot completely understand by examining only the services themselves. Users of welfare services – even those who are apparently powerless in that they have few options – make decisions about whether to use services, which services to use, how and in which order to use them. The mentally ill homeless decide whether to present themselves at the walk-in clinic, whether to take their medication, which shelter or drop-in or food project they will use and how they will conduct themselves when they get there. All of these things are the outcome of multiple negotiations which occur on a daily basis, and if we do not take them into consideration we will not understand the routines which make up the daily operation of welfare regimes.

Lefebvre and de Certeau, in contrast with Foucault's concern with systems of governmentality, centre on the milieu of the subject – everyday life. Their shift in focus opens an analytical space which makes it possible to see the local micro operations of welfare as culturally inscribed systems in quite a different way from Foucault. Everyday life, the quotidian, 'what is humble and solid, what is taken for granted' (Lefebvre 1994, p.24), that everyday sense of being-in-the-world, the 'homeward trudge of daily existence' (Wander 1994, pp.vii–viii) is how 'the social existence of human beings is produced' (Lefebvre 1994, p.23). While this clearly also includes forms of governmentality, it is not the whole story. The making and remaking of daily life by the ordinary living-actions of human beings clearly fulfils a generative function in producing (welfare) cultures. Lefebvre and de Certeau's contribution to the cultural turn is that they flag for analysis the significance of the habitual, the taken for granted, the unremarkable and the unexamined. In terms of understanding welfare regimes, this emphasis sustains an understanding of how welfare is used, and with it the growth of service user groups and the politicization of experience in which daily life authenticates the task of political lobbying. For researchers this has meant paying attention to lives by placing them at the centre of the research enterprise: trying to understand how people see themselves and how they use services and facilities, generate their own support networks and utilize resources inside their own families, community and so on; concerns which are very much at the centre of the Biography in Social Policy Research Unit at the University of East London.

The centrality of the everyday life of subjects conceived in biographical terms in research enterprises concerned with welfare has produced wonderfully rich results. The limitation of these projects is they are dominated by narrative. What is habitual and taken for granted is not necessarily articulated as narrative. De Certeau's (1988, p.45) distinction between discourse and procedures is useful here. Procedures or practices lack the fixity of discourse, and contain forms of knowledge which are no longer, or which are not yet, articulated as discourse. As Ricoeur (1991, p.31) says, lives can be understood through the stories which are told about them. But they can also be understood through the stories which are not told about them. Lives are lived before they are theorized as narrative. It gradually occurred to us in our research in Montreal that the lives people talked were not the lives they walked: a chasm opened between narrative and life.

Lefebvre's concept of space, which has been highly theorized although not in terms of its contribution to understanding welfare regimes, is the place where the unreflected upon, habitual parts of everyday life are inscribed. This is not so because the habitual cannot be articulated, but because it is not. Spaces are constituted by unspoken (silent) narratives which can be read for stories which are otherwise untold. Space is a domain of definite lived experiences and social relationships (Keith and Pile 1993; Cohen 1996; Massey 1993, p.156). It is a field of action transformed by the lives of its social subjects (Lefebvre 1996, pp.190–191) and which is itself constituted and transformed by the lives it sustains. Space and lives are mutually generative, and a part of the social tapestries created through the living of everyday life. These are insights which may have their origin in Foucault's (and Bentham's) panopticon, but which are much more fully developed by Lefebvre. Space, as a focus for analysis, reaches parts of the 'social' which are untouched by discourse and narrative.

In our investigation of the mentally ill in the community in Montreal we were struck by the thinness and banality of the stories people told in contrast to the stories inscribed in their daily actions and movements around the city, which spoke volumes about the kinds of lives they led, moving around the city, patching together resources and facilities. The lives people walk as opposed to talk invoke other social tapestries and they involve considerable amounts of work. What people do, their actions and movements, are embedded in their (unreflected upon) use of space. The mentally ill homeless we interviewed were able to give cogent narrative accounts of their lives. But these were significantly supplemented by the 'rich silences and wordless stories' (de Certeau 1988, p.106) they trailed around the streets of the city, their trajectories telling the story of their spatial practices and the social relationships inscribed within them.

The analysis of the spatial arrangements constituting welfare regimes offers a way of discussing specific sites in the delivery of local services and the connections between sites. It can be used to discuss city-wide distributions of particular kinds of services, as in our review of informal provision making up community mental health service in Montreal. It can be used to discuss the layout of a drop-in centre or a homeless shelter. And it can be used to discuss the local ramifications of the constitution of global space through, for example, policies concerning mobile populations like refugees and immigrants. Spatial analysis has a number of advantages when it comes to describing welfare regimes, which go well beyond Foucault's analytic framework.

First, space contains an account of *social practices* which may not be rendered in narrative, but which are significant in the constitution of welfare regimes and its relationship with its subjects. Space makes, and is made by, the things people do: it is sculpted by social action (Lefebvre 1996, p.34) in which things are done before they are conceptualized. The internal arrangement of space in one of the homeless shelters we researched in Montreal was clearly the outcome of many (unspoken) acted-out negotiations between users and staff/volunteers. The panoptical, dormitory, arrangement of sleeping space had been modified by administrative responses to client practices. The provision of separate space for seniors was a response to the pressure exerted on them by younger men because of the gap between pensions (which are relatively high) and welfare benefits (which are relatively low) in the Quebec welfare system. This spatial arrangement keeps seniors separate and stops them being hassled for money and cigarettes. Likewise the provision of side (detox) rooms is a response to the behaviour of new client groups needing intervention for drug and alcohol abuse. The provision of private rooms is a response to the city's increased production of long-term residents who are either economically vulnerable because of their long-term employment prospects, or who need long-term asylum no longer provided in psychiatric hospitals. These spatial modifications form an acknowledgment that the shelter is not a stop-gap but a long-term solution to the plight of a diverse and precariously positioned population. A tour of the shelter building and its director's account of how spaces were used, coupled with observations about what was going on in various parts of the building, helped produce a map of types of users in terms of their activities. Space contains fragments of a dialogue between discourse/ disciplinarity and professional gazes on the one hand, and the practices and actions of users on the other.

Second, the arrangement and use of space also expresses *social relationships* which may not be articulated: 'moment(s) in the intersection of configured relations' (Massey 1993, p.156). Spaces can be interrogated for clues about gender and race regimes which may only be subliminally experienced as comfort/ exclusion zones by welfare subjects. Homeless shelters again provide useful examples. These are usually gender segregated, white zones of occupation with visible minorities uncomfortably occupying the peripheries – something which is invariably denied in interviews by users and workers alike. Shelter patterns of female invisibility are repeated in the public spaces of the street and in drop-in centres where both men and women are anticipated as clients. Interviews with those who work in shelters produce highly sympathetic accounts of its users as social victims in need of support. But a review of shelter interior architecture offers quite a different perspective on social relationships between users and workers.

Shelters frequently have cell-like constructions controlled by elaborate rituals for locking users in, and out, of certain parts of the building. The Perspex-shielded entry desk is the scene of some animated conversations and even police activity in the enforcement of shelter exclusion policies. Long corridors and the immediate outside of buildings are often monitored by closed circuit television. The window from the kitchen (where staff serve meals) onto the toilet, like the other forms of surveillance, tells a story of social relations premised on a lack of trust of users by workers and supplies some significant clues answering the question: what does it mean, practically, to be a user of a homeless shelter? What forms or versions of personhood or subjectivity are invoked (and produced) by the spatial practices of homeless shelter life? The 'unfortunate' are also often the 'unpredictable', the 'potentially threatening', and the 'weak/deviant' whose unhealthy habits occupy the toilets. The stories told by space are quite different from those told by people and they provide a useful counterpoint in the task of analysis.

The third advantage of the spatial analysis of welfare regimes is that it articulates an implied moral and political order which is not otherwise evident. The spatial distribution of discharged psychiatric patients in Montreal, for example, consists of a series of privatized, deprofessionalized storage arrangements, inserted into existing local employment and housing practices. Discharged patients end up in the spare rooms of landlady/carers whose homes ring the closing psychiatric hospital, once a major source of local employment for the same women. They also end up in the cheap, inner city rooming house sector where landlord/surveillants double up as (legal and illegal) drug brokers who take direct rent payments from the benefits system. And they end up living in homeless shelters or on the streets. In spatial terms then, the community mental health care 'system' in Montreal involves various forms of cottage industry and multipurpose human warehousing which are most certainly not evident from provincial discourses on community mental health facilities. The seriously mentally distressed have effectively been removed from the provincial health budget to be either concealed in private homes, added to the burdens of private lives of women in need of additional income, or they are 'disappeared' into the ranks of what Sassen calls an urban underclass whose lack of entitlement is rarely called into question. Extracted from the domain of psychiatric care – which is occupied by more curable conditions covered by insurance policies – the seriously mentally distressed are left to their own devices.

This arrangement is far from incidental. It is part of a broader political and moral agenda in which the social worth of the mentally ill is pegged as not deserving of resources, facilities and spaces which address their specific problems, implying that they may instead be managed as part of an undifferentiated range of social problems. The seriously mentally ill live on the margins of local social compassion. They live on the margins of a social welfare budget which has off-loaded its responsibilities onto a voluntary sector which is rooted in nineteenth century philanthropy. They live on the margins of fiscal priorities which see balanced budgets, and not social justice, as a measure of political effectiveness. And (as far as shelter locations are concerned) they live on the margins of the city in what is now an extinct commercial space which belonged to the nineteenth century extraction of raw materials. Most shelters are disused warehouse-like buildings along the railway in a derelict part of the city between the old (seventeenth century, tourist attraction) and the modern (commercial and service centre occupied by shops and insurance companies) parts of Montreal.

These are not the clients of a modern welfare state and its healthcare policies composed of sophisticated psychiatric services, but the pauper clients of the religious and philanthropic networks which precede it. Space has its own power geometry (Massey 1991, 1993, p.144) and we need to ask: for whom and by whose agency is it arranged (Lefebvre 1996, p.116)?

Space also has other advantages for the analysis of welfare. It is aesthetic (Parr and Philo 1995) and the aesthetics of spaces used to deliver welfare services are matters for analysis and commentary. What is the message of scruffy or derelict buildings and interiors? Space is also a way of understanding social dynamics. We can investigate how spaces are linked by human activity. The arrangement of space by the mentally ill homeless in Montreal requires the fragmentation of lives: sleeping takes place in a different place from eating, showering, places to get groceries, hot meals and clean clothes. Those who use this system hence thread together lives in motion. The gaps in the system and the day are filled by hanging out in public spaces, in malls and cheap food joints, but these can only be occupied on certain terms. Generally, a certain invisibility is the price of using public and commercial space. Space provides a window onto the familiar, the taken for granted and the habitual. It offers another way of comprehending social morphology (Lefebvre 1996, p.89) and it has much to offer the analysis of welfare. It sustains a framework in which everything is achieved and produced (Lefebvre 1996, p.68) and in which we can pose critical questions about the arrangement of political priorities and interests.

In this chapter I have argued that the conceptual tool box associated with the cultural turn provides some significant elements of a grid which allows a detailed examination of the transactions between welfare regimes and their subjects. It provides a way of thinking about welfare regimes as being constantly generated through their discursive practices, their disciplinary mechanisms, their professional gazes, and the social relationships and practices of their spatial organization. The framework detailed in this chapter as a collection of loosely connected concepts demands that we think of welfare regimes as domains of administrative action generated in the interface between systems and the uses made of them by their clients. Welfare regimes are hence the product of decisions which its clients make about the conduct of their own lives, just as they are about the broader social and political priorities which operate around them. In this formulation agency and structure are held in tension in dialogue of constant formation and reformation and in which each slight shift produces slightly new regimes with new possibilities for human agency, client relationships and political action.

When welfare regimes are conceptualized in these terms certain things become transparent and offer themselves as targets for reform. In the preceding discussion it is evident that the framework sustained by Foucault and Lefebvre exposes the versions of human subjectivity inscribed in various transactions between regimes and subjects. Versions of subjectivity construed by the arrangements for homelessness in Montreal, for example, are radically different from those which operate around other groups of welfare subjects and the more general assumptions about personhood which hold for the population as a whole. Clearly the homeless have a special relationship to citizenship in liberal democratic orders. Mapping forms of citizenship provides a slightly different commentary on forms of social inequality from maps of entitlement and access to services. But one of the major benefits of a transactional analysis of welfare regimes is that it offers infinite possibilities for change in the directions indicated by citizenship maps and their normative frameworks. The client regimes of welfare are infinitely adjustable in minor, inexpensive and non-threatening ways which improve the lives of those who live and work within them. Homeless shelters, for example, operate around conceptions of guardianship and the reform of unacceptable ways of life bequeathed by the nineteenth century. This is equally burdensome for both its workers and its users. Many of the tensions inside shelters could be avoided if these concepts were unpicked from the operation of shelters, their discourse, gazes and the operation of space. The dismantling of warehousing arrangements to be replaced by smaller more flexible housing units in which users had a directing influence would most easily unpick some of these assumptions which are generated by means of actions and practices which are not even consciously articulated, but which happen by habit.

References

Clarke, J. and Newman, J. (1998) 'A Modern British People? New Labour and the Reconstruction of Social Welfare.' *Paper presented to the Discourse Analysis and Social Research Conference, Copenhagen Business School.*

Cohen, P. (1996) 'All white on the night? Narratives of nativism on the Isle of Dogs.' In T. Butler and M. Rustin (eds) *Rising in the East? The Regeneration of East London.* London: Lawrence and Wishart.

de Certeau, M. (1988) *The Practice of Everyday Life.* Berkeley: University of California Press.

Foucault, M. (1972) *The Archeology of Knowledge.* London: Tavistock.

Foucault, M. (1973) *The Birth of the Clinic.* London: Tavistock.

Foucault, M. (1977) *Discipline and Punish.* London: Allen Lane.

Keith, M. and Pile, S. (1993) 'Introduction Part 1. The politics of place.' In M. Keith and S. Pile (eds) *Place and the Politics of Identity.* London: Routledge.

Knowles, C. (1992) *Race, Discourse and Labourism.* London: Routledge.

Knowles, C. (1996) *Family Boundaries: The Invention of Normality and Dangerousness.* Peterborough: Broadview Press.

Lefebvre, H. (1994) *Everyday Life in the Modern World.* London: Transaction Publishers.

Lefebvre, H. (1996) *The Production of Space.* Oxford: Blackwell.

Massey, D. (1991) 'A global sense of place.' *Marxism Today*, pp.24–29.

Massey, D. (1993) 'Politics and space/time.' In M. Keith and S. Pile (eds) *Place and the Politics of Identity.* London: Routledge.

Parker, I., Georgaca, E., Harper, D., McLaughlin, T. and Stowell-Smith, M. (1995) *Deconstructing Psychopathology.* London: Sage.

Parr, H. and Philo, C. (1995) 'Mapping "mad" identities.' In S. Pile and N. Thrift (eds) *Mapping the Subject.* London: Routledge.

Rose, N. (1989) *Governing the Soul: The Shaping of the Private Self.* London: Routledge.

Ricoeur, P. (1991) 'Life in quest of narrative.' In D. Wood (ed) *On Paul Ricoeur: Narrative and Interpretation.* London: Routledge.

Wander, P. (1994) 'Introduction' Henri Lefebvre.' *Everyday Life in the Modern World.* London: Transaction Publishers.

CHAPTER 13

Missing Dimensions
in the Culture of Welfare

Michael Rustin

The two previous chapters have each presented a critique of what one might describe as the invasive rationalism of the contemporary welfare system. Samantha Ashenden has examined Habermas's attempts to find space for differences, for the lifeworld to reclaim free communicative space from the invasive bureaucratic systems of modern society. She argues that Habermas partially fails in this attempt, through neglect of the essentially expressive and cultural basis of different claims. Caroline Knowles' analysis of the micro-organization of daily life, and of its spatial dimensions in particular, as this is imposed on vulnerable subjects of welfare regimes, can be seen as a parallel critique of the effects of a rationalist order.

This chapter offers a broader critique of the implicit rationalism of the welfare system, or what one might describe as the dominant culture of welfare in Britain, and outlines an alternative way of thinking. It contrasts the pre-modern grounding of welfare provision in religious frameworks of thinking and practice with their modern secular development under the aegis of the bureaucratic state. Crucial to this contrast is the state's concern with goals of efficiency and social justice, and the displacement of earlier preoccupations with issues of meaning and moral worth, as these affected both the recipients and the providers of what religious institutions defined as obligatory charity. We go on to argue that this administrative concept of welfare has serious deficits in its capacity to acknowledge the dimensions of meaning and feeling in welfare practice. It proposes that the psychoanalytic tradition provides a secular resource for reintegrating into the welfare system affective and subjective dimensions of experience which have been excluded by rationalistic and behavioural approaches. It argues that unconscious anxieties, often deemed to be beyond the scope of reason, often shape both individual and institutional experiences in the welfare field, and need urgently to be addressed if good practice is to be achieved.

Modern welfare systems attempt by rationalistic means to respond mainly to material and practical needs, displacing ethical and emotional dimensions to the periphery of concern, or to the private sphere. This tendency has become even stronger in the recent period when ideologies reflecting the dominance of the market over all spheres of life have come to exercise greater sway in the public domain. What can't be be measured, and has no easily auditable outcome, ceases to exist within certain influential frames of policy making.

Ernest Gellner (1964, 1975, 1988) argued throughout his philosophical and sociological career that a deep change in the 'legitimation of belief' took place during the onset of modernity from the seventeenth century, substituting, in part as a result of the work of philosophers such as the English empiricists and later Kant, a scientific and technological worldview for a religious one. In the new ways of thinking, facts were held to be distinct from values, and individuals distinct from their social statuses and memberships. Nature, and human nature, became understood in 'modular' terms, according to which each aspect of the world could be analysed separately from every other, and questioned and changed according to the criteria of empirical evidence and logic alone. This liberated mankind from the constraints of traditional forms of understanding, and permitted the material transformations which have been the basis of modernity. But it also involved what Max Weber described as the 'disenchantment of the world'. Meanings cease to be given, but have to be chosen. Emotions become a personal, subjective matter, not shared and prescribed ways of relating to the world. The change in the forms of punishment described by Foucault, the replacement of public rituals of mortification and humiliation by calculated deprivations of liberty and pleasure, reflected the increasing irrelevance of shared emotions to the maintenance of social order. The public rituals described so graphically by Foucault (1975) were cultural engines for the generation and reinforcement of collective feelings of outrage and terror.

Gellner defended the transformative benefits of this modular revolution in thought and feeling, believing that it had made possible individual freedom and the material improvements on which this depended. He attacked, in the 1970s, attempts to revive what he thought of as irrational systems of belief, which sought to re-unite factual description and moral prescription – for example in the revived early Marxist concept of 'alienation', which asserted the existence and claims of an essential human potential in contrast to its non-realization in fact (Gellner 1979). Gellner's critique of psychoanalysis in *The Psychoanalytic Movement* (1985) was a key moment in his argument with what he saw as a persisting irrationalism. He developed the view that although Freud had correctly identified the problems posed for human lives by the fact that men and women were frequently governed by states of mind and feeling which were not transparent to them, he had proposed a false and illusory way of understanding these. For Gellner, to regard dreams as a source of understanding was to regress to pre-modern, irrational ways of thinking. (As was from a different perspective the Wittgensteinian reference to 'ordinary language' as a touchstone of meaning and validity, which he considered took as foundation what reason should put in question.)

The project of psychoanalysis during this century has been to bring the sphere of emotions, especially those which are unconscious, within the sphere of systematic understanding. It posited a human nature shaped by biological realities, moved by desires, emotions and identifications, and only with difficulty capable of full self-understanding. It accepted and valued this complex inheritance as the only possible material from which human lives could be made. Although in competition with religious belief-systems in its efforts to shape human understanding, it accepted that what religions had sought to explain was essential enough to need explaining in this-worldly, or as Freud said, scientific terms.

The religious origins of welfare

Whilst there are ethical and normative dimensions to all aspects and sectors of social life, these are particularly central to the sphere of welfare. Welfare systems, in all societies, are enactments of shared conceptions of human need, entitlement and obligation. 'What should society do to alleviate or prevent the actual and potential sufferings of its members?' is the core question to which welfare systems have been constructed as an answer.

Crucial issues of meaning, identity and membership are bound up with these questions. Why, after all, should anyone care about the sufferings of others at all? Are the obligations which are deemed to be owed to others due to them in their identities as family members, as fellow-believers, as co-nationals, or as human beings as such? And if, as is commonly the case, they are felt to be due according to more than one of these principles, how are the different claims which they make to be balanced and reconciled with one another?

In the pre-modern world, it was communities of religious belief which took responsibility for organizing society's response to pain and suffering. Hospitals and charitable institutions were set up under the aegis of the church, synagogue or mosque. Obligations to care, or pay for care, were placed on believers, and entitlements to care were due chiefly to fellow-members of communities of faith. One could think of membership of a community of believers as a kind of collective insurance policy in societies where religious bodies were the sole providers of aid to the destitute or diseased. Religious institutions were the principal specialists in the recognition and acknowledgement of suffering. The rich and powerful were expected to pay some dues to institutions which were dedicated to pity, and to gain moral credit for so doing. The architectural magnificence of some of the early institutions of charity symbolizes the significant role which they played in medieval and early modern Europe.

It is striking how durable this role of the churches as the locus of responsibility for social casualties has turned out to be, even in a society which had seemed to be becoming ever more secular and irreligious. As utopian hopes of post-war social democrats for a society which would make the maintenance of decent standards of life a civil right have faded, it is the churches that re-emerged as the most eloquent critics of the morality of the market place. While the Labour Party has distanced itself from the claims of the poor, the churches have stepped forward as their principal advocates. Victimized or disadvantaged ethnic communities have also turned to religions as the most dependable providers of an identity and moral order denied by the larger *gesellschaft* society. What is called rather disparagingly 'fundamentalism' by modernizers seems in some contexts to be functional in providing a voice, identity and system of support for the socially excluded, whether in Newham or Harlem (Smith 1996, Malcolm X 1965).

The role of organized religion has been to give explanatory, ethical and aesthetic meaning to the experiences of pain and evil, as well as alleviate where it could its practical consequences. The problems that produce demands for material or practical 'welfare' also usually involve challenges at the level of identity and meaning. Suffering individuals, families and communities need to find a way of understanding why terrible things are happening to them, and how to survive painful experiences with identities and hopes intact. Religions have been specialists in 'theodicies' (Kant 1791, Luckmann 1967), in the explanation of the meaning of pain and evil, not only at a level of a general explanatory system (the will of God, reparation in a later life, inevitable punishment for perpetrators and enemies) but also in providing more immediate consolation for sufferings. (A theodicy is a defence of God's goodness and omnipotence in view of the existence of evil.) Ministers of religion, and fellow-believers supported by their example, were always those most likely, apart from those with primary ties of kinship, to visit the sick, the dying and the bereaved. Ethical systems, prescribing charity, forgiveness, or in other circumstances sustaining a spirit of collective retribution, were also formerly shaped in largely religious terms. Both Christian and classical art is likewise saturated with images of suffering (so many martyrdoms, divine retributions, crucifixions, tragic deaths), its cultural function being to give the fragility and vulnerability of human lives some tolerable form within which misfortunes can be contemplated.

The secularization of welfare

In a secular age, the meanings attributed to sufferings, and the explanations and justifications given to their remedy or prevention, have been stripped of their relationship to more fundamental narratives of human existence. As medicine achieved efficacy in preventing and curing many diseases, and in alleviating pain, it substituted a detached scientific approach to illness for one which had previously only been able to provide a measure of comfort and consolation. (The larger part of this improvement (McKeown 1979) has been due to rising material standards and to public health measures rather than curative medicine, but even so, the effect is still to diminish anxiety.) The large-scale diminution in the scale of premature illness and death, and the likelihood that most individuals (in rich countries) could expect to live to something like a full natural life-span, and without frequent loss of immature children from illness, marks a major revolution in human experience, reducing the everyday disruptions of identity and meaning-structures to which religious belief attempted to provide some kind of remedy. There are now many examples, however, of biographical and autobiographical writing in which those who have suffered traumatic illnesses or bereavements seek to share the subjective meanings of these experiences (e.g. Bayley 1998).

Well before scientific medicine was able to make any significant difference to survival chances, the state began to take over responsibility for welfare from religious institutions (Jordan 1978). Where welfare systems had earlier been the specialized responsibility of the churches, offering opportunities for the recognition of virtue, and for reparation for injuries done by the privileged, they now became part of the administrative machinery of the state. Charity, conferring virtue and status on its providers, and a glimpse of God's grace on its recipients, was replaced by regulated and highly conditional measures of relief, administered by secular and increasingly bureaucratic agencies (Cooper 1995).

Their role came to be to manage disruptive social problems (for example unemployment) to impose moral discipline on the poor, and to remedy the 'market failures' which would otherwise impede the production of a workforce sufficiently healthy, educated and adequately housed to sustain a competitive economy. These became the functions of the rationalized poor laws, preventive health regulations, and reformed penal practices of urban and industrial societies. But the purpose of the emerging welfare state, from Elizabethan times onwards, was also to engender loyalty to the new nation states. Citizens for whom the state provided some measure of social protection could be expected to identify with it, and to fight and die for it.

In the post-war period, the churches, in Christian democratic welfare regimes, and socialist beliefs, in the social democracies, played a significant part in the construction of welfare states (see Hornsby-Smith, Introduction2, and Peterson, Chapter 2). But these welfare regimes have become essentially administrative systems, branches of the state apparatus. As a consequence 'social policy', or 'social administration', became one of the more desiccated of the social science disciplines. Questions of meaning, identity and value which have been at the centre of debates in sociology, cultural studies, and political theory over the past thirty years (for example, issues of recognition attached to gender, class, ethnicity, or on the distribution of power or wealth) have tended to pass social policy by.

How far does this separation of the administrative and practical functions of welfare, from its normative dimensions, matter? Are deep-level legitimations of, or debates about, welfare practices, any longer needed, so long as the practical systems seem to work? Does the welfare system need a theory or theories to explain, guide, and make sense of its own operations? And if it does, where should we look for such theories?

The 'common sense' underpinning welfare systems

The understanding proposed by this book, of welfare systems as invariably embedded in specific cultures, enables us to identify the rationalization of welfare, and its constitution as a largely administrative practice, as a cultural fact in its own right. But the Habermasian separation of welfare 'system' and 'lifeworld', by which one is constructed to manage the problems thrown up by the unruliness of the other, by no means describes the full reality of welfare practice, in which there are many feedbacks and interactions between lived experience and its legislative and bureaucratic categorization. The legislated welfare system in fact depends on underlying norms and values which continually define the limits and possibilities of what can be done. Earlier chapters in this book have explored in particular ways the role of these shared ways of thinking, what we might think of, following Gramsci, as the 'common sense' of welfare practice.

It is clear, for example, that the obligations of family membership remain the most powerful organizing principle of our welfare system, even though rising rates of cohabitation and divorce suggest that family systems are becoming more voluntaristic than they were previously. Studies of caring (Janet Finch 1989, 1993; King and Chamberlayne 1996; and others) have explored the extent to which the obligations which count most, in determining who will voluntarily sacrifice what to provide care for dependent persons, are still those of family. Within this broad sphere of obligation, personal choices are made, based on particular family histories, affection, a sense of obligation to different generations, and self-centredness or its opposite. But there is no doubting the continuing importance of family relationship as the principal source of obligation and entitlement to care. Stein Ringen (1997, 1998) has recently argued that the proportion of national wealth generated by unpaid labour within families and households more than doubles the per capita value of money income. It is not merely that norms of family relationships shape wider social practice, but that they constitute, even by material measures, a substantial part of it.

Sentiments attached to shared nationality count for a great deal too, in determining which categories of persons are eligible or ineligible for care, or indeed to seek paid work. One does not become entitled to income support, or to seek paid work, or housing benefit, unless one first gains rights of residence in the country, and these are not easily obtained. What appear to be entitlements of citizenship, everyone's claims on their fellow-citizens' help in need, turn out mainly to mean claims and obligations upon fellow-nationals. Political arguments about the rights of immigrants or refugees, about the enlargement of the European Union and what obligations it might entail, and about the possible harmonization of taxes and benefits in the EU, engage powerful sentiments attached to issues of membership and exclusion. Popular hostility can easily be mobilized when rights are claimed for, or obligations asserted towards, categories of people who are felt to be aliens or outsiders. The emergence of neo-Fascist movements in Europe, primarily mobilizing against ethnic minority communities, and the contrast between the entitlements after 1989 of citizens of the former East Germany and of those of other countries of the former Eastern Europe, are examples of how strong these boundaries of moral membership and exclusion are.

The obligations that are acknowledged to those who are not fellow-citizens, either of one's nation or of the European Union, are much weaker than those due to co-nationals. (Although the intensity of concern about international human rights, as reflected in the Pinochet judgement, indicates that change is taking place.) These obligations amount to refugees' rights of asylum, the national overseas aid budget, and the popular and governmental response to appeals to respond charitably to the needs of one material or political catastrophe or another. These moral claims sometimes touch the conscience of citizens of rich countries, but they are still very far from the recognition of universal welfare entitlements on an international scale. Rights of citizenship that might on the surface seem rather abstract matters can be seen, as Michael Walzer (1983) has shown, to form the bedrock of the welfare system, setting the limits within which it is allowed to function.

Many other shared moral sentiments underpin what is legislated and administered as the welfare system. Obligations towards children, towards the aged, the sick and the disabled are widely acknowledged. Those working in welfare daily make judgements and choices, based on assessments of need, desert, and on local affinities and affections (or their opposites), which attest to the rooting of legislated, bureaucratic or professional activities in a subtle texture of everyday assumptions. These are monitored and revised through all manner of exchanges, in writing, speech, shrugs and grimaces. An ethnography, ethnomethodology, or biographical study of care, the need for which is strongly indicated by our cultural approach to welfare, would reveal the complexity of these everyday social practices.

There are, however, signs that it is not easy to maintain consensus on welfare needs and obligations, in the absence of legitimating principles or discourses. Indicators that there remains a 'legitimation problem' are the periodic eruptions of public anxiety, usually arising from extreme offences against a 'common sense' of moral well-being. Small children commit murders, raising questions of childhood innocence and responsibility. Babies die in the care of their parents or nannies, drawing attention, if anyone cares to notice, to the intense feelings and stresses evoked by the care of small children. Institutions devoted to the residential care of children turn out to have been suborned by paedophiles, and the children abused by those professionally employed to care for them. (In Belgium recent scandals of this kind almost brought down the government.) Psychiatric patients stab to death persons with whom they come into contact, making us take note of the fact that psychosis is a sometimes intractable condition, and that the 'community' of 'community care' is often a fictitious one. Gay people demand the same rights as homosexuals, for example regarding the age of consent, or to make gay marriages, or as parents, inviting the question of whether society is entitled to discriminate in any way between one form of sexuality and another. The right or power to create or terminate life is debated, as medical technologies become more powerful, in regard to abortion, euthanasia and genetic engineering. Public opinion, orchestrated by newspapers, demands that certain convicted child murderers should live their remaining lives in prison, even though such persons are believed to be wholly unlikely to repeat their earlier crimes. Controversies like these, which attract a strong charge of emotion, focus anxieties about the presuppositions of everyday existence, about what citizens can expect of their neighbours, and indeed of themselves. The intense projections of feeling into celebrities and stars of all kinds, of which the events following the death of Princess Diana were an extreme manifestation, reveal the intensity of emotions which is left out of the normally bland and routinized exchanges of public discourse, passions which at other times have led nations enthusiastically into destructive wars. What these intrusions of intense feeling and anxiety into public discourse reveal is that the response to these 'facts of life', when they become apparent, is often no more than panic and moral denunciation.

A one-dimensional, normalized view of human behaviour is the construct of a bureaucratized society, whose institutions devote great efforts to the containment of more fundamental or 'primitive' anxieties. A significant part of the training and everyday routines of 'front line' employees who are liable to encounter the more explosive emotions of members of the public is devoted to the effective management of tension and conflict. Some social practices that were earlier attentive to affective and expressive dimensions of social life, and to the need for relationship, have become more behavioural in focus. Education is a particularly clear example, where an earlier commitment to the 'whole child', and the full range of capacities that might beneficially be developed, has been redirected towards the instilling of more utilitarian skills. The reconceptualization of social work as a set of competencies, and the disaggregation of client-needs into discrete practical segments, has a similar character. Problems disclosed in the residential care sector have recently met a similar narrowly focused government response in the introduction of new systems of regulation, licensing and inspection.

It was previously assumed that well-trained professionals, whether teachers, doctors or social workers, could be trusted by government and citizens to operate systems of care and development in a responsive and principled way. The post-war welfare state was based on a considerable delegation of responsibility to the welfare professions. Much of the professional formation and culture of the social professions was devoted to instilling norms and values consistent with this conception of self-regulation of services for the public good. It was argued by theorists of the caring professions in the 1950s that their callings embodied norms and beliefs which they reinforced through their professional practice. But this model was subject to critique, from the 1960s onwards, from both the left and right. For the left, the professions were élitist and exclusionary conspiracies against the public interest, and their high-minded beliefs and values were mainly ideological camouflage which could be better understood in terms of collective self-interest. The neo-liberal right adopted a critique that was curiously similar, in its economism and materialism, to that of the left. For the free marketeers, professions were a form of monopolistic occupational practice, a trade unionism for the middle class. The right, during the Thatcher years, was in a strong position to attack professional privileges. The competition of internal markets, the growth of audit and efficiency measures, and the insistence that managerial and enterpreneurial values had to be dominant throughout the public sector, were used to attack the autonomy of professionals, and force them to march to a different drum than their own values

Herbert Marcuse (1964) devised the concept of 'one-dimensional man' to describe the false universalism of consumer capitalism. Marcuse saw this ideology being carried primarily by the market. Since then it has found another powerful sponsor in neo-liberal governments (and New Labour's) who use the disciplinary apparatus of government to instil preferred modes of conduct and belief among both the providers and clients of public services. This process has been described in more detail in the two chapters which have preceded this one, on Habermas, and on Foucault and Lefebvre, respectively. Foucault's dystopian model of omnipresent disciplinary powers reached its apogee, not as he perhaps thought as a description alternative to the materialist critique of the Marxists, but as its complement.

However, the multidimensionality of persons will not be altered by these official redefinitions of them as compelled only by the claims of rational interest. Human beings remain creatures of feeling, responsive to ideals and values as well as to imagined pleasures. Since experiences of relative failure and suffering may if anything be increased in a more polarized, competitive and insecure society, it seems likely that these dominant utilitarian redefinitions of caring and educational tasks are merely storing up explosive trouble for the future.

Enter psychoanalysis

When psychoanalysis made its entry into social and cultural theory, it did so in explicit competition with religious modes of thought. Freud (1921, 1927, 1930, 1939), like many other great 'modernists' of his era, sought to address fundamental questions of existence and value, but from a human-centred, rather than deity-centred, point of view. Human beings, Freud said, attribute powers and intentions to Gods which are in reality projections of their own unconscious desires. The fundamental realities of existence which are addressed by the great religions – the inevitability of death, suffering and evil – must be recognized as facts of life, but responsibility for living with these must be taken by human beings, without supernatural aid. While Durkheim explained religious life as an effect of societal meanings and values, Freud explained religion as a means of coping with the psychic anxieties of human existence. Ernest Gellner, in a late essay (1995), much more sympathetic to Freud than his earlier critique of psychoanalysis had been, presents Freud as one of the first great theorists to argue that human beings must take responsibility for their own ethical beliefs. Freud was intransigent in his hostility to external forms of moral authority, whether these were religious or (in the emerging forms of mass democracy) political in nature.

Psychoanalysis has always had some of the attributes of a humanistic theodicy. It has sought to explain the origins of moral qualities in the processes of human development. In this, it has taken a view of development which is only partially environmentalist. Whilst pathological formations can often be linked to environmental deficits, psychoanalysis has always been attentive to constitutional factors in human nature, 'residues' of the irrational and antisocial which one cannot expect to be wholly removed by social improvements. In fact, the commitment of psychoanalysis to self-understanding, and the autonomy which derives from this, has made this tradition somewhat hostile to an environmentalist view of socialization. The idea of an 'unconscious' or 'inner world' postulates a barrier between the self and its external environment which precludes a simple causal dependency of the one upon the other. The formation of individuals can thus not be fully explained by an account of 'external' influences upon their development, nor has achievement of conformity to social norms been the intrinsic object of psychoanalytic intervention.

The psychoanalytic tradition has insisted on the reality principle as its main guiding-light. The reality principle implies the recognition of what Roger Money Kyrle (1968), one of the more philosophical writers in the British psychoanalytic tradition, referred to as the 'facts of life'. By this he meant the realities of gender and generation, each of them unwelcome in certain aspects to human subjects, because of the incompleteness and finality which they imply. The Oedipal narrative of development in Freud's work entails recognition that omnipotence is limited, that the opposite sex parent has to be renounced as an exclusive love-object. Loss and limitation are experienced in human lives from the very beginning, not merely as a consequence of deficient caring environments, but as facts of nature. The process of development requires learning to live with an experience of finitude, dependence and loss. One cannot be both male and female, or parent and child, nor is anyone omnipotent or immortal. Recognition of these limitations brings psychic pain, and most psychopathological states are understood as defences against pain. The theory of the life and death instincts, or more colloquially of love and hate, implies recognition of these dual proclivities of human nature, and acknowledgement that no more than a benign balance between these conflicting emotions can be hoped for. The potential for destructiveness, which can be experienced in the forms of rivalry, denigration, envy, jealousy and in countless other ways, is ever-present. One of the main problems of personal development is held to be the recognition and containment of destructiveness and its potential consequences to the self and others. Reason, in the psychoanalytic tradition, is seen as a precarious capacity, always liable to be undermined or suborned by the pressure of unconscious desires or defences, libidinal or destructive. This is not a utopian worldview. In place of an idealized view of human beings who will become rational and altruistic once material or environmental constraints are removed, is a description of a human nature in which understanding and moral responsibility are precarious achievements, requiring continuing commitment.

There are few contemporary investigations of human nature which attempt the same range and comprehensiveness as the psychoanalytic tradition. Perhaps the other most significant contemporary development is evolutionary psychology, and its dynamic attempts via ethological, neurological and game-theoretical investigations to explain the origins of language, sexual difference, cooperation and altruism, and other aspects of human nature and behaviour. The question is, do such fundamental investigations of human nature and behaviour, and the theories which ensue from them, have any place in the construction of a modern welfare system? Does anyone need to make any assumptions of such a 'foundational' kind in deciding how to treat the ill, support the poor, punish the criminal, or educate the young?

Psychoanalytic contributions to welfare theory and practice

Earlier attempts to inform social policy with psychoanalytic ideas were focused on the psychoanalytic theory of human growth and development. In the 1940s and 1950s, this synthesis was attempted in theoretical terms within the tradition of American structural functionalism. Psychoanalysis, for Talcott Parsons (1964), provided a link between the individual and the social system, explaining how individuals became socialized, at a deep and unconscious level, into the system of roles of a differentiated, democratic capitalist society. The key building block of this process was the family. The differences of gender role which Parsons believed to be normal in industrial society could be clearly mapped on to micro-processes of socialization which Freud had explained through his model of the Oedipus complex, and the identifications with paternal and maternal figures which he attributed to male and female children as aspects of their normal development. Whilst the division of roles between male breadwinner and female housewife and mother remained relatively uncontested, this explanatory link between sociology and psychoanalysis seemed a useful one. When feminists challenged this gender division, the Parsons–Freud model remained useful as an explanation even though it had been rejected as a justification of the persistence of unequal gender identities. The problem now came to be to understand how this causally effective system of reproduction of gender roles could be modified or broken.

The functionalist synthesis presupposed a normative basis for social order, and thus implicitly grounded social routines on fundamental conceptions of value. For Parsons the core beliefs were in a 'socialized individualism', in which viable individuals would be reliably 'reproduced', would find available to them clear definitions of gender and generational identity, and would be able to call on the services of professional 'specialists' to support their transition through normal and abnormal life-crises. Freud provided Parsons with a resource for explaining the depth of instinctual and emotional attachments necessary to the stability of these structures, primarily in the process of family socialization. Although this synthesis did find a way of integrating emotions into the understanding of the social order, it did so at the price of disregarding the more disruptive and conflictual aspects of the unconscious, as critics pointed out (Wrong 1961). Any renewal of psychoanalytic approaches needs not to view emotions as reinforcements of social stability, but should see the internal world also as a source of productive disturbance and innovation (Rustin 1996).

The British incorporation of psychoanalytic ideas into welfare practice was more practical and less theoretical than the American, though it tacitly drew upon functionalist approaches. Social policy came to be focused, in the early post-war period, on reconstituting the family, and on supporting and reaffirming the role of mothers in the care of children. John Bowlby's work, whose most widely-known idea was that of 'maternal deprivation', was the most significant scientific contribution, though Bowlby was always more environmentalist in his approach than the majority of his fellow-psychoanalysts. (Bowlby subsequently moved away from psychoanalysis, developing his evolutionary and ethological 'attachment theory', which though convergent in many ways with psychoanalytic approaches to development, is also much more sceptical about the existence of unconscious mental processes, especially in infants and young children (Holmes 1993).)

A more purely psychoanalytic influence on child care practice was that of Donald Winnicott. The emerging social work profession was for a period greatly influenced by psychoanalytic ideas of human development, and clinically influenced methods of 'casework' became one of its main technical resources. This intervention sought to find practically effective ways of supporting a 'socialized' society, assuming that individuals would naturally subscribe, if they could, to norms rooted in the conventional family. Casework approaches depended for their efficacy on a consensus on underlying values between professionals and clients, the idea being that individuals could be helped by professional intervention to fulfil obligations (e.g. to their children or parents) that could be taken as grounded in human nature and as morally self-evident.

The attempts of the social workers to crystallize a professional ideology as a form of applied psychodynamic casework ran into heavy criticism in the 1960s and 1970s, from several quarters. From the left, this approach was attacked for giving a pathologizing, psychological explanation of deprivations whose origin were held to be material and class-based. Most of those who became concerned with equal opportunities and antiracism in social work also had little time for psychodynamic approaches. For the new managerialists, 'professionalism' among social workers was seen as traditionalist, resistant to cost-effective approaches to resource management, and to the flexible deployment of trained personnel. Among both social workers and schoolteachers, a 'professional' identity was contested by an ideology of trade unionism, representing itself not only as a strategy for advancing the interests of employees, but also as a way of giving a political voice to their disadvantaged clients. Conflictual and bureaucratic approaches replaced the idea that problems could be solved by reflection and through the agency of relationships.

The critique of these positions from the neo-liberal right was significant in its effects. The very idea of maintaining the integrity of a social order through the managed care of dependants was deemed a mistake. The 'dependency' which had been accepted within the social democratic framework of social policy as a normal condition of the life-cycle, especially in an unequal society, was redefined as moral weakness verging on parasitism. Social policy was given the task of re-engineering individual self-reliance, through providing greater incentives for success, and larger sanctions for failure. Not only the clients of social policy were redefined in these terms, but also its practitioners. The 'professionals' – social workers, teachers, planners, etc. – were stigmatized by politicians and the press, as interfering ideologues, sometimes almost as oppressors of the people.

Thus the 'moral' and 'normative' purposes of social policy were downgraded in favour of a greater attention to practical efficacy. Social Services Departments were reorganized as agencies for the accountable delivery of specific packages of services to ostensible 'customers', and training redefined as the provision of specific practical professional 'competencies', rather than as the acquisition of capacity to exercise professional judgement. Infractions of norms, as in child abuse, were expected to be dealt with in a judicial, rather than a professional social work framework, questions of criminal responsibility taking precedence over issues of continuing relationships and needs.

In this environment, an expansion took place in many forms of physical and psychological self-cultivation provided for individual customers (health clubs, alternative medicine, counselling and psychotherapy), whilst the public services became more instrumental in approach. One might say that the search for 'meaning', hitherto included in some fashion as part of the welfare project, became privatized, and became the activity of a separate cultural marketplace.

The relevance of psychoanalysis

We have described the dependence of welfare practices on embodied social norms, and have criticized the instrumentalism of both the main tradition of social policy, and of its recent embodiments in the culture of behaviourism, audit and quasi-markets. These systems have little capacity to respond to affective needs, or to provide discourses in which the meanings of misfortune, trauma and suffering can be negotiated by subjects. Without such negotiation, we argue, these sufferings are worse, and without such discourses, social understanding and sympathies are diminished. Indeed, the generalized defence against anxiety which prevails in the absence of a capacity for understanding means that disruptions of the moral order becomes vengeful and persecutory.

We now identify a number of dimensions in which the psychoanalytic tradition should inform the rethinking of the role of welfare in modern societies. The broadest of these concerns the relation between the rational and emotional in welfare practice. Generally, there has been an opening of modern cultures over recent years to 'affective' aspects of life which were earlier liable to be dealt with mainly through codes which insisted on repression. The contemporary problem, now that repressive codes have lost their dominance, is to find ways of integrating these 'affective' dimensions of life with rational approaches – that is of finding adequate ways in which to think about feelings.

One of the main drivers of the recognition of the affective dimensions of social life has been the 'sexualization' of society during the twentieth century. The salience of sexuality in modern culture, and the recognition of sexual desires and fulfilment as of primary importance, is a key instance of the displacement of religious codes of expression, regulation and feeling, which were generally antagonistic to sexuality, from their earlier central position. Psychoanalysis, having throughout its history explored the diversity and omnipresence of sexual desire, was one of the main cultural agents of this change, from the 1920s onwards. The general 'sexualization' of the culture has given rise to many anxieties and normative dilemmas. These arise, for example, from the recognition of the diversity of the normal forms of sexuality, and from the recognition of childhood sexuality as a reality. The Freudian characterization of heterosexuality and homosexuality as normal and abnormal relative to a developmental norm, has been problematic, though the later emphasis on the role of the libidinal and destructive drives, love and hate, as dimensions distinct from their chosen objects, now provides a more adequate resource for considering the meaning and consequence of different kinds of sexual attachment. The psychoanalytic understanding of childhood sexuality, and of the consequences for development of premature sexualization, is also indispensable if child sexual abuse is to be responded to with anything more than mindless projected hatred. There seems to be no comparably rich theory or technique through which these spheres of motivation and action can be understood.

Individuals respond to life-crises in different ways, and the meaning and subjective experience of these cannot be held separate from the crises themselves. Most individuals cope with 'normal' life transitions (parents having a child, a child going to school for the first time, a first sexual experience, taking exams, adolescence for both children and their parents, children leaving home, accidents, illness and bereavement) in ways which they and their family and social networks can cope with. Professional services may cope in these normal circumstances in largely practical ways, although these services always have a relational dimension which if insensitively managed can have negative effects.

But for significant numbers of individuals, such 'normal' transitions provoke deeper and more troubled levels of response. (The incidence of depression in the first months of motherhood is a well-established example of this, Brown 1958; Murray 1997.) Capacity to engage with the subjective meanings of such difficulties is essential to their management by welfare practitioners. (We have suggested elsewhere the relevance of biographical methods of study for the formation of professionals equipped to respond to differences of individual response.) What psychoanalysis distinctively brings to this field is its recognition of the unconscious anxiety liable to be stirred up during even normal life transitions, let alone traumatic ones.

It is the field of projected anxieties and fears that psychoanalytic awareness can best equip welfare practitioners to understand, contain without 'acting out', and make helpful responses to. This form of understanding is relevant both to the construction of adequate social practices for the normal management of transitions, and to the response by professional services to situations where these transitions go wrong. Welfare workers need to sustain a capacity to recognize and engage with the anxieties of distressed people, especially where clients may feel that their distress is somehow excessive or inexplicable in relation to its apparent object. A positive example of an enlightened social practice sensitive to relational issues has been the widespread acceptance that parents should as far as possible remain with young children when they are in hospital. Our argument here is that the psychic disruptions brought about by personal transitions have dimensions of meaning, both conscious and unconscious, and that a good welfare practice has to be able to engage with these.

A second, and closely-related, dimension concerns the impact on welfare practitioners themselves of the unconscious anxieties evoked in their clients, and by traumatic situations more generally. The relevance of psychoanalytic understanding to welfare practice is in the first instance as a resource for welfare practitioners themselves, in enabling them to understand and manage the feelings evoked in them by their work or their clients. Until it becomes fully assimilated for this purpose, it is unlikely to be useful for clients. Exposure to traumatic situations (psychotic breakdown or child abuse are examples) arouses strong and often disabling responses to those who have to deal with them. Recognition of the unconscious sources of such disturbance, and the development of ways of thinking through these (both by individuals and work-groups) is a condition of rational, consistent and sensitive responses by welfare practitioners. Where such understanding is absent, or is actively negated, and where intelligent links between feeling and thought are broken, what is liable to happen is panic, over-reaction, or a cutting-off of appropriate response. The lengthy published history of failures in Social Services Departments to respond in consistent ways to situations of severe risk can best be explained in these terms. Attempts to deal with these problems by merely procedural and managerial means seem unlikely to succeed unless the anxieties which are the main source of dysfunction are recognized. Equipping welfare practitioners, both professional and other, to deal with these dimensions of their practice is in part a matter of training, and in part a question of organization and supervision. Methodologies of observational study and 'work discussion' developed within the psychoanalytic and attachment theory traditions at the Tavistock Clinic are examples of techniques whose primary object is to bring about a capacity to reflect on emotions, and to recognize unconscious anxieties, as these impinge on relationships in work settings (L. Miller *et al.* 1989; Reid 1997).

The third area of relevance of the psychoanalytic tradition to welfare is in the larger sphere of institutional design. Unconscious anxiety not only manifests itself within individuals, or in the welfare practitioners who encounter them, but has profound effects within institutions (Obholzer and Roberts 1994). Powerful projective mechanisms can transmit anxieties throughout an institution, sometimes even throughout society. Isabel Menzies Lyth's (1989a) work has shown how unconscious anxieties among nurses were defended against by dysfunctional patterns of organization whose object was to distance the staff from emotional pain which they could not tolerate. Depersonalized attitudes to patients, task-based routines which avoided continuing relationship with individuals, hierarchical structures which inhibited communication among nursing staff, were among the defences which she reported. No doubt her insights have had some effect on the understanding of nursing systems, as Bowlby and colleagues' investigations did on the understanding of the experiences of children going to hospital. Menzies Lyth (1989b) and her colleagues undertook related work in centres for the day care of very young children, discovering a comparably dysfunctional forms of organization which they called 'multiple indiscriminate care'.

Another example of such projections can be found in the prison and 'special hospital' system. Here the central issue is the hatred, fear and desire for revenge projected on offenders and psychiatric patients by an outside society which has been disturbed and outraged by extreme and perverse criminal acts. The pain experienced by the victims of crime, and the anxieties of future victims, amplified by the mass media, impose themselves on these institutions. It is difficult to sustain a humane and balanced regime against the force of these projections, which threaten to sanction any let-up in severity of treatment, especially if this leads to breaches in security. Andrew Cooper's (Chapter 5) and Rachael Hetherington's (Chapter 6) comparative work on child protection systems has revealed a similar pattern, in which identification with victims and retributive passions directed towards perpetrators has created an atmosphere in which reflection and measured judgement by professional staff become hard to sustain.

It may be useful to think of institutions within the fields of education, care and control as each liable to be beset by a particular dominant mechanism of projection. Just as institutions can be characterized in terms of their 'primary task' (E. Miller 1993) so there will often be a primary source of anxiety which is evoked by this task, with which the institution and its members have to cope in carrying this out. In institutions caring for handicapped children, the intruding emotion seems to be rejection and denigration, arising from the damage to parental narcissism and the disappointment in what is felt to have been lost in an injury or handicap. Only if the presence of these unconscious reactions is acknowledged, and their consequences understood, can their prospective effects be minimized.

In penal institutions, the dominant 'structure of feeling' may be a desire for retribution held by prison workers on behalf of, as they see it, law-abiding members of society. Another factor, where offenders are deemed to be violent, is the fear of offenders' propensity for evil or harm, which may be experienced as a boundless dread, partially projected into the inmates and perhaps acted out by them in their relations with one another. In educational institutions (even highly successful ones) the dominant projections may be an idealized but competitive need to succeed, accompanied by negative projections directed towards those who have failed, or who seem at risk of failure. So such institutions may be denigratory and exclusionary towards those outside their privileged community, or that of its favoured ,lite groups, and also harsh towards those who fail to meet its standards within. Such negative projections may be overt, or they may be transmitted unconsciously and then experienced as self-blame by pupils. The stronger the demand for schools to succeed, or to avoid failure, through published 'performance measures' of various kinds, the greater the pressure on them to exclude underperforming pupils, and to denigrate those whom they regard as worse or weaker than themselves.

Professionals may to some degree select themselves for their vocations by their propensity to share these different cultures of anxiety. The common split in the penal system between on the one hand probation officers and educationists, committed to rehabilitation and development, and prison officers allotted and embracing the tough custodial role, committed to the restraint (and covertly the punishment) of deviant impulses, is clear. Nurses are attracted to their work by the wish to care for the ill, but are also threatened by the pain to which this unavoidably gives rise. Teachers identify with the struggles for success of their pupils, but in fact the teaching profession in Britain is one which has been widely beset by its own status anxieties. One long-standing symptom of this anxiety is ambivalence between professional and trade union concepts of its collective identity. It is likely that these anxieties – the undervaluation of teaching as an occupation, its representation as a second or last-resort choice for graduates – contribute to the difficulties in maintaining a supportive educational culture. In France, by contrast, accreditation as a lycée teacher is a lengthy and competitive process.

These are some examples of the unconscious anxieties which can impose themselves on the day-to-day life practice of institutions. There is scope for a comparative psychoanalytic sociology of welfare institutions, which would map primary anxieties against primary tasks, and would investigate the characteristic defences against anxieties which such institutions generate. The contribution of the psychoanalytic tradition is in the concepts and techniques it provides to enable these unconscious dimensions of welfare practice to be recognized and reflected upon. The psychoanalytic contention, following Bion's contribution, is that only if a 'space for thinking' (about emotions in particular) can be created can the toxic effect of such anxieties and defences be understood and limited.

Unconscious projective mechanisms also function beyond the level of specific institutional cultures, at a societal level. The key process is that of projective identification, viewed as a defence against paranoid schizoid and to a lesser degree depressive anxiety. (Key papers on the psychoanalytic idea of projective identification are collected in Spillius 1988.) These processes play a major part in the reproduction of advantage and disadvantage. One crucial division across which unconscious projections take place is ethnic. Stigmatized or demeaned ethnic groups are made to carry the projected hatred, envy and denigration of the powerful, with minor physical differences serving to mark out convenient targets for these projections.

Another division is that created by material inequality, poverty and class. Richard Wilkinson's work (1996, 1997) on inequalities in health is now demonstrating the effects of steep gradients of income and wealth on those who find themselves in lowly positions. He has demonstrated that it is not poverty (above a fairly low material level) but the level of inequality in a society which gives rise to high levels of mortality and morbidity. The explanation of this connection lies in the stresses imposed on the lowly placed not only by insecurity, but also by disesteem. 'The hidden injuries of class' described in Richard Sennett and Jonathan Cobb's book of that title (1972) seem to have a very wide provenance (see also Sennett 1998).

Similarly, inequalities and differences of gender are also reinforced by projective processes, in which women are still required to carry qualities of irrationality, feeling, weakness and unintelligence, which are intolerable to men in a competitive macho world. Such projections also have a real effect on those subjected to them, when they are reinforced by power and fear, inducing their objects to enact or live out others' phantasies about them. One can thus elaborate an account of social divisions in society from the point of view of the psychic projections involved in enforcing and reproducing them. A modern debate about equality, justice and citizenship needs to take account of these toxic psychic processes, and find ways of enabling social groups to recognize what their projections impose on others. The Truth and Reconciliation Commission in South Africa is an example of an institution designed to make possible exactly this mutual recognition.

The psychoanalytic tradition can make possible the understanding of the psychic defences which inhibit equal exchange, listening and dialogue in all settings. Social relationships of all kinds are so deeply impregnated with unrecognized emotion that without a language and practice by which this can be understood, communicative dialogue becomes difficult to sustain. Few social institutions find it possible to conduct themselves in ways which fully acknowledge the subjectivity of their members. The psychoanalytic commitment to a space for thinking, especially about emotions, is thus relevant to the development of democratic practices in institutions and the wider society, as well as to the consulting room.

The key contribution of the psychoanalytic tradition to welfare lies in the possibility it offers of integrating reflection on feelings and relationships with cognitive and practical tasks. Primitive anxieties have to be processed as the boundaries of the normal and the acceptable are continually threatened. The problem is how to avoid the merely retributive or evasive, when confronting the effects of psychic pain and injury. How not to fight fire with fire, paranoia with paranoia, rejection with rejection, rage with rage, is the competence which a psychodynamic perspective can bring, in work with the clients of welfare, with the providers of welfare, and in the larger social conversation.

References

Bayley, J. (1998) *Iris Murdoch: A Memoir.* London: Duckworth.

Brown, G. (1958) *Social Origins of Depression.* London: Tavistock Publications.

Cooper, C. (1995) Philanthropic discourse, discipline and the problem of population. University of East London Ph.D. thesis.

Finch, J. (1989) *Family Obligations and Social Change.* Cambridge: Polity.

Finch, J. (1993) *Negotiating Family Responsibilities.* London: Routledge.

Foucault (1975) *Discipline and Punish: The Birth of the Prison.* Harmondsworth: Penguin (1991).

Freud, S. (1921) *Group Psychology and the Analysis of the Ego.* Volume XVIII, Standard Edition. London: Hogarth.

Freud S. (1927) *The Future of an Illusion,* Standard Edition, Volume XXI Standard Edition. London: Hogarth.

Freud, S. (1930) *Civilisation and its Discontents*, Standard Edition. Volume XX1. London: Hogarth.

Freud, (1939) *Moses and Monotheism* Volume XXIII Standard Edition. London: Hogarth.

Gellner, E. (1964) *Tradition and Change*. London: Weidenfeld & Nicolson.

Gellner, E. (1975) *The Legitimation of Belief*. Cambridge: Cambridge University Press.

Gellner, E. (1979) *Spectacles and Predicaments*. Cambridge: Cambridge University Press.

Gellner, E. (1985) *The Psychoanalytic Movement*. London: Paladin.

Gellner, E. (1988) *Plough, Sword and Book*. London: Collins Harvill.

Gellner, E. (1995) 'Freud's Social Contract.' In E.Gellner *Anthropology and Politics*. Oxford: Blackwell.

Holmes, J. (1993) *John Bowlby and Attachment Theory*. London: Routledge.

Jordan, W.K. (1978) *Philanthropy in England 1480–1660*. Westport CT: Greenwood Press.

Kant, I. (1791) 'On the miscarriage of all philosophical trials in theodicy', repr. in Kant, *Religion Within the Boundaries of Mere Reason, And Other writing*, ed. Wood and Giovanni, (1998). Cambridge: Cambridge University Press.

King, A. and Chamberlayne, P. (1996) 'Comparing the informal sphere: Public and private relations of welfare in East and West Germany'. *Sociology, 30*, 4, 741–761.

Luckmann, T. (1967) *The Invisible Religion: The Problem of Religion in Modern Society*. New York: Macmillan.

Malcolm X (1965) *The Autobiography of Malcolm X*, assisted by Alex Haley. New York: Grove Press.

Marcuse, H. (1964) *One Dimensional Man: Studies in the Ideology of Advanced Industrial Society*. London: Routledge.

McKeown, T. (1979) *The Role of Medicine: Dream, Mirage or Nemesis*. Oxford: Blackwell.

Menzies Lyth, I. (1989a) *The Dynamics of the Social*. London: Free Associations Books.

Menzies Lyth, I. (1989b) *The Containment of Anxiety in Institutions*. London: Free Associations Books.

Miller, E. (1993) *From Dependency to Autonomy*. London: Free Association Books.

Miller. L.; Rustin, M.E.; Rustin, M.J. and Shuttleworth, J. (1989) *Closely Observed Infants*. London: Duckworth.

Money Kyrle, R. (1968) 'Cognitive Development.' In *The Collected Papers of Roger Money Kyrle*, ed. Meltzer D. Perthshire: Clunie Press (1978).

Murray, L. (1997) 'The early mother–infant relationship and child development: A research perspective.' *Infant Observation, 1*, 1.

Obholzer, A. and Roberts, V. (1994) *The Unconscious at Work: Individual and Organisational Stress in the Human Services*. London: Routledge.

Parsons, T. (1964) 'The superego and the theory of social systems.' In T. Parsons *Social Structure and Personality*. New York: Collier-Macmillan.

Reid, S. (ed) (1997) *Developments in Infant Observation: The Tavistock Model*. London: Routledge.

Ringen. S. (1997) *Citizens, Families and Reform*. Oxford: Oxford University Press.

Ringen, S. (1998) *The Family in Question*. London: Demos.

Rustin, M.J. (1996) 'Attachment in Context.' In S. Kraemer and J. Roberts (eds) *The Politics of Attachment*. London: Free Association Books.

Sennett, R. (1998) *The Corrosion of Character*. New York: Norton.

Sennett, R. and Cobb, J. (1972) *The Hidden Injuries of Class*. Cambridge: Cambridge University Press.

Smith, G. (1996) 'The unsecular city: The revival of religion in East London.' In T. Butler and M.J. Rustin (eds) *Rising in the East*. London: Lawrence and Wishart.

Spillius, E. Bott (ed) (1988) *Melanie Klein Today, Volume1: Mainly Theory*. London: Routledge/ Institute of Psychoanalysis.

Ⅹ Walzer, M. (1983) *Spheres of Justice*. London: Martin Robertson.

ƴWilkinson, R. (1996) *Unhealthy Societies*. London: Routledge.

Wilkinson, R. (1997) 'What Health Tells Us About Society.' *Soundings: the Next Ten Years*. London: Lawrence and Wishart.

Wrong, D. (1961) 'The oversocialized conception of man in modern sociology.' *American Sociological Review, 26*, 183–193.

CHAPTER 14

Conclusion
A New Culture of Welfare

*Richard Freeman, Prue Chamberlayne, Andrew Cooper
and Michael Rustin*

All the papers collected here were conceived as explorations of terrain which felt very new to us as social scientists. On reading each other's material we have been constantly diverted, fascinated and provoked. Much of the time that has been enough, but one underlying question has become increasingly insistent. In so far as we have been working on culture and welfare as systems of meaning, what does this work itself mean? The relationship between welfare and culture in Europe is 'interesting', yes, but so what? What is new or distinctive about this work, and what are its implications? We can begin to answer these questions by returning to the contexts, both general and specific, within which our work was conceived.

The general context is the extended crisis of the welfare state. By this we mean the questioning of welfare arrangements, sustained over time and replicated across countries. In many respects these questions refer less to the welfare state as such, and more to the conditions in which it was made and on which it rested. They are raised by the fiscal problems of economic uncertainty and changing demography, by the passing of any enduring compact between capital and labour, by increasing diversity and instability in the structure of families and households, by a declining confidence in and of government. Grand narratives – one of the most compelling of which has been the ameliorative version of social policy – have tailed off. As we remarked in our introduction, the validity or legitimacy of doing particular things (like welfare) in particular ways has become subject to generalized doubt.

Such changes impact at the local level, as well as the national. They affect individuals and communities and the relations between them as well as whole countries and, in turn (in a way which seems particularly germane to the international and cross-national work collected here), the relations between them. For culture appears to be one of the more testing aspects of European integration: its functionalist logic comes unstuck on the problem of legitimacy. The symbolic value of national currencies seems to matter at least as much as their exchange value. Building a European state is made more difficult in the absence of a common European culture while, at the same time, the integrating Europe is in some respects, in particular in its ethnicities, a Europe of increasing cultural diversity. Both globally and locally, welfare arrangements are subject to an intensified pluralism, of both values and interests. This diversity seems to have been arrived at by fragmentation as much as by innovation and creativity, and is being managed more by competition than cooperation. It invokes two kinds of response: one pessimistic, marked by a retreat into fundamentalism, and one more optimistic, marked by faith in dialogue.

There are parallels with the specific, intellectual context in which this seminar met. As we explained in our preface, we came together because of the concerns raised by the cross-national, comparative research on welfare in which we had been involved. Much of what we were doing was motivated by a reaction against what is (in our view still rightly) regarded as the classic school of comparative welfare research. This tended to deal in whole states or systems, albeit sometimes disaggregated into programmes (but then often because individual programmes, and usually readily quantifiable cash transfers, were being taken to be indicative of states). It tended to be positivistic; it was often evaluative, interested in function and performance, for which it tended to rely on quantifiable indicators. Its fixation with administrative institutions seemed to deny the significance or even possibility of an autonomous sphere of social action and culture, in much the same way that states themselves did. Modernist social policy was framed intellectually by a modernist social research.

Some of us had become interested in a different kind of work. This sought to be as cross-national and comparative, and as theoretically informed, as what had gone before. But it was a qualitative, micro-level sociology. It set out to study differences between welfare regimes 'from the bottom up'. Essentially, it was about studying people – workers and clients and the welfare contexts in which they meet – in more than one country. It felt (and still feels) new, but we don't pretend that it is unique. If our concerns really are rooted in the kind of general problematic to which our introduction points, it is more than likely that they will be expressed elsewhere by others. Recent work in anthropology in particular seems to parallel what we have been trying to do here. The defining characteristics of a new 'anthropology of welfare', for example, include comparativism, which means relating the world 'out there' to the world 'at home'; a concern with representation and reflexivity, as with biographical and subjective experience, each of which implies a qualitative research methodology; a concern with social organization, especially at the micro level; the attention to culture, taken as the construction of meaning, and a commitment to practice and change (Russell and Edgar 1998).

Inevitably, ours was not a descriptive endeavour, but an inherently critical one: all sociological work is critical in so far as it reveals previously hidden possibilities of social organization by exposing as traditional and historically contingent what may once have been experienced as inevitable and timeless. Much of what is learned as being natural may be unlearned through critical analysis, and revealed as cultural. The risk, which we have tried to acknowledge, is that by exposing cultures of welfare in all their embedded richness and complexity we might provoke a renewed defence of the traditional (the welfare equivalent of the retreat into fundamentalism) as much as any more vigorous engagement with the new and the different. We are concerned that culture be taken not as an indication of failure, but as a potential resource.

Uncertainty and change surround both established modes of organizing and delivering welfare and established methodologies of comparative social research. We think there is some connection to be drawn between the two. In the introduction to this book, we referred to a number of fields of social science research in which new methods, more sensitive to the experience of social actors, had changed theoretical and policy perspectives. Similar potentials emerge in the field of welfare once cultural difference, and the subjective experience of those who experience welfare systems in different societies, become serious topics of study. Once a new field of inquiry emerges, so it becomes possible to see the relevance to it of theories and perspectives (like those discussed in our final section) which previously had little purchase on the subject. Theoretical developments often arise from seeing familiar subjects in new ways, or from the generative power of metaphor, where an explanatory model already powerful in one field is seen to have application to another previously distant from it. The idea that there are cultures of welfare itself involves a shift of perspective of this kind.

A substantive common theme emerges from the innovations of method which are reported in this book. This centres on the significance of subjects and their interactions. One of the key principles behind the empirical work collected here is the need to communicate ideas of each other (not of 'the other'). This is a central feature of the practitioner and client-based research reported by Cooper and Hetherington, as of the biographical method deployed by Chamberlayne, Tejero and Torrabadella, and Spanò. For Cooper and Hetherington, the research process must be constructed as not merely reflexive but reciprocal. Doing research like this implies a different kind of relationship between researcher and subject, and even between subjects; it does not merely rediscover but begins to reconstitute culture. Of course, it seems less 'new' in any given national context. In social work research in Britain, Mayer and Timms's (1970) study was seminal work of its kind. In cross-national, comparative research, though, it remains remarkable (if understandable) how little the client – or anybody else – actually 'speaks'.

Communicative interaction is a dominant theme of the more theoretical chapters (Part III), too. It is central to Habermas's work, as explored by Samantha

Ashenden. The issue is that of finding genuinely neutral (or shared) terms of communication on which a new welfare consensus might be based. But talk is also fundamental to psychotherapeutic intervention, on which Michael Rustin's argument draws. It resonates, too, with a certain conception of culture (one rooted in ethnomethodology) as iterative or dialogic, a system of meaning. It is not by accident that we have written much more about people than about institutions: culture is, where people are. At their best we think culture, research and normative proposition become fused: the dialogue constituted in and by research is in itself both cultural process and policy goal.

This emerging perspective derives from the specific context within which we met; from our research and our own subsequent discussions. The more general context to which we referred was one of change, uncertainty and considerable anxiety. Almost inevitably, dialogue is most needed in conditions where it is most difficult. Lest we be misunderstood, we have no doubt of the need for material, existential security – for those things that we might conventionally take to be the object of welfare. A new discursive space for welfare must be constructed and protected by material means. Simple social security matters, of course, but what we might describe as a 'security of significance' matters, too. These different studies of welfare and culture in Europe suggest that meaning is a key resource in the management of need and risk. In so far as it is separable at all, the distribution and allocation of meaning matters as well as that of material goods; one of the reasons material or welfare resources matter is because they have meaning.

We also believe that our approach to welfare is synchronous with, and can contribute to, new ways of making policy and practice. The traditional empiricist ways of doing social research in this field supported a somewhat bureaucratised model of welfare. Although major problems – for example of inequality, poverty, or housing need – were identified, solutions tended to be generalized, administrative, rather than deriving from the actual experience and claims of the supposed beneficiaries of welfare systems.

We might say that the welfare state of the post-war period represented an only partial democratization and conferment of social claims and entitlements. Whilst citizens, in Marshall's terms, acquired new rights, they did not acquire much voice or say. 'One size fits all' tended to be the assumption of welfare providers. It was reaction to this uniform, and often somewhat authoritarian, system of provision (this was even more marked, of course, in Eastern Europe) that gave legitimacy to the individualist, market-based critique of the 1980s. Individual choice was counterposed to the insensitivity and drabness of collective provision.

The new welfare paradigm which we are seeking to develop takes as its starting point that subjects and citizens must have a voice. Not doing good to people, but the enabling of people, is what the new welfare practice needs to be about. And by this we mean not only the enabling of individuals, by the demand that those receiving benefits accept training or work in return, but also the enabling of groups of people, in networks or organizations, to develop their own new social scripts. Our research methodologies, which require us to learn from our subjects and to report their experience of the world, are an initial way into this practice of 'active welfare', as we have earlier called it. Without particularizing culturally-sensitive methods of investigation and reporting, no-one will even know what problems a modern welfare practice needs to address. Legislators may be reluctant to recognize such specific and variegated descriptions as culturally-sensitive research provides as being relevant to policy at all. But part of the problem is that 'policy' in its received senses has been as much about controlling citizens as enfranchising or empowering them. Social policy falls squarely in the camp of what Zigmunt Bauman refers to as the legislators, those who would lay down blueprints for improving and transforming the world (Bauman 1987). Our cultural approach to welfare implies a large move towards the other pole, that of the interpreters, whose role is to facilitate voice and dialogue, not impose a programme.

The idea of a 'social policy' being made all around us, as many different institutions are enabled to evolve and elaborate their own goals and methods, may create a sense of vertigo, confusion and fear. Its prospective variety threatens to transcend the political and administrative framework which we depend on to manage the public domain. Nor is this like the variety of the consumer market, where in the end common measures of value, money and profit, tend to impose their own underlying uniformity of ends. Our political and administrative system is deeply intolerant of difference, so that even where it purports to encourage devolution and local autonomy, as in the schools, it has at the same time sought to impose a standardized curriculum and assessment system on everyone.

The problem is to recognize that a genuinely democratic society would generate and sustain a variety of social goals and patterns of life, and to accept this as one of its prospective benefits. The containment of diversity is a difficult task, whether in a family, a small social organization, or a society, and a new welfare paradigm needs to give attention to the forms of governance, management and shared decision making that can make this possible. The problem and the goal can be formulated in a number of idioms, which include theories of extended democracy (Held 1996; Hirst 1994), the philosophical conception of a continuing democratic conversation about ends and values (Rorty 1989), and the psychoanalytic idea, influenced by Bion (1962), of a 'space for thinking', where emphasis is given to the need to reflect on affective dimensions of social life. Different idioms will be found to be appropriate in different settings.

There is an analogy here with the dilemmas now understood to be facing the management of organizations, whether in the public, private or independent sectors. Traditional structures and forms of hierarchical, 'top-down' authority and leadership no longer suffice to meet the challenges of 'post-modern' economic and social environments; the pace of socio-economic change, rapidity of information flow, the reliance on specialized staff working in fluid combinations, unpredictability in the global market-place – all the factors now associated with the concept of risk – lead to the idea that organizations must be led not from above or below but somewhere 'in the centre'. In welfare, openness to cross-national as well as internal diversity, allied with sensitivity to experience at the point of contact between the 'system' and the 'lifeworld' suggests a similar conclusion. In some ways, the development of 'focus group culture' in policy making is a response to this recognition. The perceptions, moods, attitudes and evolving preferences of 'active citizens' cannot be taken for granted. But clearly such methods of testing public responses to policy proposals are insufficient, for they offer nothing directly in return for the data gathered. We have in mind something closer to the work undertaken by Helen Morgan and her colleagues, discussed in the *Active Welfare* special issue of *Soundings* journal (1998), in which users of mental health services were engaged to design and run their own conferences to debate services and needs; professionals and policy-makers attended, but were obliged to listen, learn and reorganize their thinking in unfamiliar and disruptive ways. There is a sense of creative turbulence, of *cultural* resistances being challenged and renegotiated in this endeavour, so that something new can emerge. 'Dialogue' is too comfortable a word to denote or connote this process, and it is no accident that both social scientists and management theorists are turning to the insights of the 'new science of complexity' for models capable of theorizing the process of evolutionary conflict which we would argue is implied by the work discussed in *Welfare and Culture in Europe*.

This 'new welfare paradigm' is one way of giving tangible meaning to the New Labour idea of the 'Third Way', though we do not share its apparent view that the development of a pluralist and democratic welfare practice can be accomplished without conflict, or without facing painful decisions about priorities. But we think our 'cultural' perspective on welfare requires a shift of attention from the spheres of the market, and of the administrative state, to the networks and social relations of society itself. A culturally informed approach to welfare has implications for research, for the political context in which policies are made, and for the implementation of welfare practice. It is only possible at this stage to begin to sketch out what the various implications of this new paradigm are, but we hope that this book is a beginning.

Note

For an effective complementary account of the anthropology of policy, see Shore and Wright (1997).

References

Bauman, Z. (1987) *Legislators and Interpreters.* Cambridge: Polity.
Bion, W.R. (1962) *Learning from Experience.* London: Heinemann, reprinted 1984. London: Karnac.
Held, D. (1996) *Models of Democracy.* Cambridge: Polity.

Hirst, P.Q. (1994) *Associative Democracy*. Cambridge: Polity.

Mayer, J.E. and Timms, N. (1970) *The Client Speaks: Working Class Impressions of Casework*. London: Routledge and Kegan Paul.

Morgan H. (1998) 'Looking for the Crevices'. *Soundings*, 8, 171–83.

Rorty, R. (1989) *Contingency, Irony and Solidarity*. Cambridge: Cambridge University Press.

Russell, A and Edgar, I.R. (1998) 'Research and practice in the anthropology of welfare.' In I.R. Edgar and A. Russell (eds) *The Anthropology of Welfare*. London: Routledge.

Shore, C. and Wright, S. (1997) 'Policy. A new field of anthropology.' In C. Shore and S. Wright (eds) *The Anthropology of Policy. Critical Perspectives on Governance and Power*. London: Routledge.

The Contributors

Samantha Ashenden is lecturer in Sociology in the Department of Politics and Sociology at Birkbeck College, University of London. Her main research interests are feminist political theory, governance and theories of the State, legal theory and the sociology of the law. She is currently writing a book on the governance of child sexual abuse for Routledge.

John Baldock is Reader in Social Policy at the University of Kent at Canterbury. His main research interests are the ageing of the populations in industrial societies and the provision of care services for older people. He has also published widely on the personal social services. His new book, *Consumption, Markets and Community Care* written with Clare Ungerson, which addresses all these issues, will be published by Cambridge University Press in 2000.

Prue Chamberlayne is Director of the Centre for Biography in Social Policy at the University of East London, where she is also Principle Lecturer in European Social Policy. She first became interested in biographical methods in the course of study of caring in East and West Germany and as a means of extending comparative social policy to the informal sphere. Having studied German, she taught in Africa and East London before changing direction to social science.

Richard Freeman is lecturer in European Policy and Politics in the Department of Politics at the University of Edinburgh. His main research interests are health policy and politics in Europe, and his studies include the role of prevention in health policy, the politics of HIV and AIDS, and health care reform. He is co-editor of *Social Policy in Germany* (1994) and author of *The Politics of Health in Europe*, Manchester University Press (forthcoming). He was previously a Jean Monnet Fellow and participated in the European University Institute's *European Forum: Recasting the European Welfare State 1998–99*. He is currently working on health policy transfer between countries and on cultural accounts of health policy regimes.

Caroline Knowles is lecturer in the Department of Sociology and Social Policy at the University of Southampton and was formerly an Associate Professor at Concordia University in Montreal. She is joint editor of *Resituating Identities* (1996), author of *Family Boundaries: The Invention of Normality and Dangerousness*, Broadview Press (1996) and *Race Discourse and Labourism*, Routledge (1992). She is currently working on a number of articles on race and ethnicity, and on her forthcoming book *Bedlam on the Streets*, Routledge (2000) which is an account of mental illness and homelessness in Montreal.

Walter Lorenz holds a Jean Monnet Chair in Social Europe at the National University of Ireland, University College, Cork where he teaches European perspectives in social work and social policy. He is co-editor of *The European Journal of Social Work* and his main research interests are cultural diversity and racism in Europe, and responses in the social professions.

Martin Peterson is Professor of History at the University of Göteborg and holds a part-time chair in Cultural Studies at the University of Bergen in Norway. He is also a member of the Board of the Interdisciplinary Centre for Comparative Research in the Social Sciences. His key research interests are interdisciplinary research and cultural change in contemporary global society.

Michael Rustin is Professor of Sociology at the University of East London, and a Visiting Professor at the Tavistock Clinic. He is co-editor of *Soundings* and is author of *The Good Society and the Inner Word* (1991) and many articles in the fields of psychoanalysis and social theory. He is currently working on a book on drama, psychoanalysis and society.

Steve Trevillion is Reader in Social Work and Social Policy at Brunel University. His main research interests are in the field of community care and he is closely associated with the development of networking theory and practice. In recent years he has begun to explore the relationship between practice cultures and patterns of interaction both in the UK and in Europe. He was originally trained as a social anthropologist and subsequently as a social worker. He has practised social work in Devon and London and was inspired by the neighbourhood ideal to develop patch social work. He is currently involved in social work education.

Subject Index

Author Index